Necessity, Proportionality and

There has been considerable deba
as to the legality of the forceful ac
in 2002 and Iraq in 2003 under th
been consensus, however, that the use of force in all these situations had to be both necessary and proportional. Against the background of these recent armed conflicts, this book offers the first comprehensive assessment of the twin requirements of necessity and proportionality as legal restraints on the forceful actions of States. It also provides a much-needed examination of the relationship between proportionality in the law on the use of force and international humanitarian law.

Judith Gardam teaches public international law at Adelaide Law School in South Australia. She is an acknowledged international expert in the field of the protection of civilians in times of armed conflict, and in particular on the issue of women and international humanitarian law. She has published widely on international humanitarian law and the United Nations Charter regime on the use of force.

CAMBRIDGE STUDIES IN INTERNATIONAL AND COMPARATIVE LAW

Established in 1946, this series produces high quality scholarship in the fields of public and private international law and comparative law. Although these are distinct legal subdisciplines, developments since 1946 confirm their interrelation.

Comparative law is increasingly used as a tool in the making of law at national, regional and international levels. Private international law is now often affected by international conventions, and the issues faced by classical conflicts rules are frequently dealt with by substantive harmonisation of law under international auspices. Mixed international arbitrations, especially those involving state economic activity, raise mixed questions of public and private international law, while in many fields (such as the protection of human rights and democratic standards, investment guarantees and international criminal law) international and national systems interact. National constitutional arrangements relating to 'foreign affairs', and to the implementation of international norms, are a focus of attention.

Professor Sir Robert Jennings edited the series from 1981. Following his retirement as General Editor, an editorial board has been created and Cambridge University Press has recommitted itself to the series, affirming its broad scope.

The Board welcomes works of a theoretical or interdisciplinary character, and those focusing on new approaches to international or comparative law or conflicts of law. Studies of particular institutions or problems are equally welcome, as are translations of the best work published in other languages.

A list of books in the series can be found at the end of this volume.

Necessity, Proportionality and the Use of Force by States

Judith Gardam
University of Adelaide School of Law

CAMBRIDGE UNIVERSITY PRESS
Cambridge, New York, Melbourne, Madrid, Cape Town, Singapore,
São Paulo, Delhi, Dubai, Tokyo, Mexico City

Cambridge University Press
The Edinburgh Building, Cambridge CB2 8RU, UK

Published in the United States of America by Cambridge University Press, New York

www.cambridge.org
Information on this title: www.cambridge.org/9780521173490

First published 2004
Third printing 2006

A catalogue record for this publication is available from the British Library

Library of Congress Cataloguing in Publication Data

Gardam, Judith Gail.
Necessity, proportionality and the use of force by States / by Judith Gardam.
p. cm. – (Cambridge studies in international and comparative law ; 35)
Includes bibliographical references and index.
ISBN 0 521 83752 9
1. War (International law) 2. Necessity (International law) 3. Proportionality in law.
I. Title. II. Cambridge studies in international and comparative law (Cambridge,
England : 1996) ; 35.
KZ6385.G368 2004
341.6 – dc22 2004045671

ISBN 978-0-521-83752-1 Hardback
ISBN 978-0-521-17349-0 Paperback

For Adrian

Contents

Foreword

Those who regard the present as a period when the rules of international law concerning the use of force by States are specially contested are probably new to the field, or have short memories. They have always been contested. This has been so ever since the end of World War I when attempts began to be made to institute, or re-institute, constraints on resort to war. Whether they concerned Korea, Suez, Hungary, Cuba, the Congo, Czechoslovakia, Vietnam, Panama, Grenada, Nicaragua, Iraq or Yugoslavia (to cite some cases since 1945) debates over intervention, pre-emption and anticipatory self-defence have raged. Indeed, they have often seemed little more than a dialogue of the deaf.

Dr Gardam's aim is more restricted and may be correspondingly more determinate. In this well-informed study, she seeks to analyse the specific requirement of proportionality (and the related concept of necessity) as it relates both to the rules relating to the use of force and the rules of international humanitarian law restricting how force should be used in international and increasingly also in internal armed conflict. There is a considerable point to this inquiry. Even when the occasion for the use of force is controversial, as it so often is, the protagonists will assert that their action is limited to what is necessary and is proportionate, and this assertion will often be able to be tested against the facts in a way which does not depend on the underlying controversy about whether force should have been used at all. Moreover, arguments based on necessity and proportionality have a useful strategic value even after the decision to use force has been taken and acted on and is effectively irrevocable. Have the intervening forces withdrawn promptly? Have they caused wanton damage, unrelated to the needs of the mission? More fundamentally, perhaps, have they left the people of the target State freer or less free in terms of their capacity to manage their own affairs?

Most international lawyers are (with the late Oscar Schachter) reluctant to regard denial of self-determination or violation of human rights as a justification for unilateral military action, at least in circumstances falling short of extreme emergency. But these considerations, among others, remain relevant in assessing the issue of quantum, so to speak.

At the same time, and almost in counterpoint with the fluctuating fortunes of the *jus ad bellum*, international humanitarian law has been developing its own rules of proportionality in the attempt to limit the scope for so-called military necessity. Again, this has sometimes been an effective basis for criticism of the conduct of actions already undertaken on other grounds, and the issues are even becoming the subject of a certain volume of jurisprudence, not limited to the work of the *ad hoc* international criminal tribunals. Hersch Lauterpacht once remarked that the laws of war were at the vanishing point of international law. We would not say that today, whereas we might be tempted to think so of the *jus ad bellum*, subject as it has been to distortion and arguably abusive interpretations.

For this and other reasons we maintain the functional separation of international humanitarian law from the rules relating to the use of force by States. But that separation prompts one to ask whether the notions of proportionality at play in the two fields have much in common. In the area of international humanitarian law proportionality concerns the relation of means to ends, the latter being assumed to be licit for this purpose. In the context of the rules concerning the use of force the matter is more difficult. For example, in a case of so-called preemptive self-defence considerations of proportionality may be difficult if not impossible to apply, and that impossibility may reflect back on the very issue of the lawfulness of the conduct taken. In the absence of a clearly defined and reasonably proximate or imminent attack, to what must the conduct be proportionate? And how can necessity be judged in such cases?

Dr Gardam does not ignore these difficulties. At the same time, she provides a balanced and careful review of the practice and doctrine in this difficult area, and thereby makes a distinct contribution to the literature.

James Crawford
Lauterpacht Research Centre for International Law
University of Cambridge
April 2004

Preface

Proportionality is a familiar idea and is designed to ensure that the ends justify the means. Its requirements are reflected today in several diverse areas of international law. The focus of this work is the operation of proportionality as a restraint on the forceful actions of States. The concept is incorporated in the norms that govern the use of force in international relations (*ius ad bellum*) and those that regulate the conduct of hostilities (*ius in bello* or international humanitarian law (IHL)). Necessity is also a familiar idea and in common with proportionality finds various expressions in international law. It is considered here for its role in determining whether a forceful response is warranted in any particular situation.

The general structure of the work is as follows. First, I assess the development and current content of proportionality in the twin international law regimes of *ius in bello* and *ius ad bellum*. Secondly, I undertake the same task in relation to necessity but only as a component of *ius ad bellum*. In my view necessity has no detailed form in *ius in bello* and is not covered in any depth in this work. The title of the work, therefore, may initially be somewhat misleading in that a great deal more of the work is devoted to a consideration of proportionality than to necessity.

The somewhat disjointed development of the legal framework in which proportionality has operated over the years has significantly dictated the structure of this work. Prior to the emergence of a separate *ius in bello* in the nineteenth century, restraints on the resort to force and its subsequent conduct were all part of the one regime. This is no longer the case. Currently there are two separate systems of rules relevant to the forceful actions of States that incorporate the requirement of proportionality.

Chapter 1, therefore, is primarily designed to clarify the relationship between these two systems, *ius ad bellum* and *ius in bello*, and the part played by the requirement of necessity and proportionality in these two legal regimes over the years. The discussion also assesses the shortcomings and significance of these two requirements and the extent to which they can be seen as making a contribution to ameliorating the impact of armed conflict in today's world.

Chapter 2 considers the historical development of necessity and proportionality as restraints on the forceful actions of States up to the adoption of the United Nations Charter in 1945. Although originally a single set of norms governed these events, during the nineteenth century *ius in bello* emerged as an independent set of legal rules. Indeed at the turn of the twentieth century *ius ad bellum* had been through a period of decline as the idea had gained ascendancy that war was a sovereign right of States. In contrast *ius in bello* was firmly established as a separate regime.

This situation was short-lived, however, and the twentieth century witnessed the attempts to establish a comprehensive prohibition on war that culminated in the ban on the use of force in Article 2(4) of the United Nations Charter adopted by States in 1945. Henceforth, the work takes what are now two separate areas of international law and studies in detail, first, the requirement of proportionality in *ius in bello* and, secondly, the requirements of necessity and proportionality in *ius ad bellum*.

Chapter 3 analyses the modern requirements of proportionality in IHL as it affects combatants. Proportionality in this context is represented by the fundamental principle outlawing the use of weapons causing superfluous injury or unnecessary suffering. Chapter 4 undertakes the same task in the context of civilians and civilian objects. The complex conventional provisions in Additional Protocol I to the four 1949 Geneva Conventions of 1977 that address indiscriminate attacks and the place of proportionality therein are analysed in detail. The extent to which the conventional norms are reflected in the practice of States is then assessed. The significance of non-international armed conflicts in the world today cannot be overlooked and I consider whether proportionality has any role in that context.

IHL has a distinctive regime of enforcement that includes individual criminal responsibility. In both Chapters 3 and 4 I assess the significance of this scheme for ensuring compliance with the requirements of proportionality.

Chapter 5 returns to *ius ad bellum* and examines the content of necessity and proportionality in the modern law on the use of force in relation to unilateral State action. Chapter 6 deals with collective as opposed to unilateral actions involving the use of force. There is a significant threshold question in this latter context, namely, the extent to which the legal requirements of necessity and proportionality in *ius ad bellum* and proportionality in *ius in bello* apply in such circumstances. Only when this issue has been resolved can one turn to consider the detail of their operation. Consequently, the emphasis of Chapter 6 differs somewhat from that of the earlier chapters dealing with unilateral State action. It considers whether these requirements are applicable in the first place and, if they are, what they comprise.

The general system of State responsibility is applicable to any failure by States to abide by the constraints imposed by these norms of international law but is not discussed in any detail, as it is outside the scope of this work. The same is the case with the vexed question of the relationship between the International Court of Justice and the Security Council and the role of the former in ensuring compliance with any restraints on the Council's powers.

Chapters 5 and 6 do not consider in any comprehensive manner the situations in which States can lawfully resort to force under the United Nations Charter regime. No topic appears to receive more attention from scholars than the assessment of what State practice indicates as to *lex lata* or *lex ferenda* in this area. There is endless debate about such questions as the scope of self-defence (both individual and collective) under the Charter regime, the compatibility of humanitarian intervention with Charter principles and how, or indeed whether, the Charter can adapt itself to the phenomenon of global terrorism. Scholars even question whether there is any law on this topic at all. Moreover, the relationship between unilateral and collective forceful actions under the Charter remains controversial. I do not intend to add anything new to this debate.

What I do provide is an in-depth analysis of a hitherto neglected question. That is, once it has been determined that there are legal grounds for the resort to force, how does the extra requirement that force be necessary operate in the practice of States? Additionally, how does proportionality act as a constraint on the nature and degree of force that States may utilise in their response? Throughout the work I consider the basic framework of the situations in which States assert the right to use force, but only in order to provide a context for the discussion of necessity and proportionality. Indeed, it is impossible to apply proportionality without identifying the aim of the forceful action against which the response is to be measured.

Overall, the work seeks to clarify an area of international law that is of considerable importance and frequently misunderstood. References to necessity and proportionality abound in the public utterances of States and in the work of commentators. There is, however, no comprehensive assessment of the detailed operation of these restraints in the context of the forceful actions of States. Neither is there such a study of the relationship between proportionality in *ius ad bellum* and IHL. This work remedies that omission.

Acknowledgments

There are a number of people who have assisted me in the preparation of this work. In particular, I thank my colleague, John Gava, who commented on parts of the manuscript, and Hans Peter Gasser, formerly of the ICRC, who kindly read drafts of the chapters on international humanitarian law.

I received expert research assistance at various stages of the work from Letitia Anderson, Carly de Jonge, Natalie Klein and Carolyn Nash.

Table of cases

Abbreviations

AJIL	*American Journal of International Law*
AYIL	*African Yearbook of International Law*
BYIL	*British Yearbook of International Law*
Columbia JTL	*Columbia Journal of Transnational Law*
CWC	Conventional Weapons Convention
ECtHR	European Court of Human Rights
EJIL	*European Journal of International Law*
GAOR	*General Assembly Official Records*
ICC	International Criminal Court
ICJ	International Court of Justice
ICLQ	*International and Comparative Law Quarterly*
ICRC	International Committee of the Red Cross
ICTR	International Criminal Tribunal for Rwanda
ICTY	International Criminal Tribunal for the Former Yugoslavia
IHL	international humanitarian law
ILJ	International Law Journal
ILM	*International Legal Materials*
IRRC	*International Review of the Red Cross*
JIL	Journal of International Law
LJ	Law Journal
LR	Law Review
MLR	*Modern Law Review*
MULR	*Melbourne University Law Review*
NYIL	*Netherlands Yearbook of International Law*
OTP	Office of the Prosecutor
Proc. ASIL	*Proceedings of the American Society of International Law*
RIAA	*Reports of International Arbitral Awards*

Riv. DI	*Rivista di Diritto Internazionale*
SC	Security Council
SCOR	*Security Council Official Records*
TIAS	*Treaties and Other International Acts Series*
UCLA PBLJ	*UCLA Pacific Basin Law Journal*
UNGA	United Nations General Assembly
UNTS	*United Nations Treaty Series*
WVLR	*West Virginia Law Review*
YBILC	*Yearbook of the International Law Commission*
YIL	Yearbook of International Law

1 The place of necessity and proportionality in restraints on the forceful actions of States

Introduction

This work addresses the development and current content of necessity and proportionality in the law on the use of force (*ius ad bellum*) and the law of armed conflict (*ius in bello*) or international humanitarian law (IHL).[1] Before turning to a detailed consideration of the history and the modern content of necessity and proportionality in these two regimes, this first chapter provides an overview of the evolution of these twin concepts as part of the attempt by States through the development of legal norms to restrict the circumstances in which States can resort to force and, where these restraints fail, to place limits on the manner in which ensuing hostilities are conducted.

Necessity and proportionality are concepts that over the years have had differing applications in international law in the context of both pacific and non-pacific actions of States. Today, for example, a state of necessity may be invoked by a State as a defence to a breach of an obligation imposed by international law.[2] Currently, the practical relevance

[1] The terms *ius in bello* and *ius ad bellum* are of recent coinage, although used to describe developments that occurred over many centuries. See R. Kolb, 'Origin of the Twin Terms *Jus ad Bellum* and *Jus in Bello*' (1997) 320 *IRRC* 553. The term IHL is increasingly used to refer to the body of law that was previously known as the law of armed conflict. Moreover, within the regime of IHL, a distinction is sometimes drawn between those rules that govern the conduct of hostilities, the 'Law of The Hague', and those that protect the victims of armed conflict, the 'Law of Geneva'. See J. Gardam (ed.), *Humanitarian Law* (Dartmouth Publishing Co. Ltd, Aldershot (UK), 1999), p. xi (for an explanation of the various terms used to describe this area of the law). Today, the choice of terminology is a matter of preference without legal significance.

[2] See Art. 25 of the Draft Articles on the Responsibility of States for Internationally Wrongful Acts, Report of the International Law Commission 53rd Sess. (23 April–1 June and 2 July–10 August 2001), GAOR 56th Sess. Supp. No. 10 (A/56/10) (hereafter Draft

of the doctrine of necessity in the context of the forceful actions of States is largely limited to its operation in *ius ad bellum*. In that regime, necessity determines whether the situation warrants the use of armed force. As for IHL, the idea of necessity is traditionally regarded as a fundamental concept within that system. IHL is commonly described as a balance between the demands of military necessity and considerations of humanity. However, necessity has never assumed a clearly identifiable role in IHL, despite its seeming centrality to the regime.[3]

Proportionality is familiar to international lawyers as a requirement of legitimate counter-measures.[4] The doctrine is also represented in the law of treaties,[5] human rights law[6] and maritime delimitation.[7] The fundamental nature and operation of proportionality in international law

Articles); see also B. Cheng, *General Principles of Law as Applied by International Courts and Tribunals* (Stevens and Sons, London, 1953), pp. 69–77; and B. Rodick, *The Doctrine of Necessity in International Law* (Columbia University Press, New York, 1928) (tracing the development of the doctrine of necessity from the time of Grotius until the early period of the League of Nations).

[3] But see E. Rauch, 'Le Concept de Nécessité Militaire dans le Droit de la Guerre', Rapport présenté au Comité pour la protection de la vie humaine dans les conflits armés, VIIIe Congrès de la Société internationale de droit pénal militaire et de droit de la guerre, Ankara, October 1979 (Brussels, Societé international de droit pénal militaire et de droit de la guerre, 1981) (arguing that military necessity is the most misunderstood of all the principles of the law of war, and outlining the four fundamental concepts (of which proportionality is one) that together constitute the doctrine of military necessity in IHL). See the further discussion of this doctrine in IHL, note 26 below and the accompanying text.

[4] See Art. 51 of the Draft Articles; and G. Arangio-Ruiz, 'Third Report on State Responsibility' (1991) II *YBILC*, paras. 63–8. See also *Case Concerning the Gabcikovo-Nagymaros Project (Hungary* v. *Slovakia)*, ICJ Reports 1997, 3 at 56, where the test of proportionality is articulated to require that 'the effects of a countermeasure must be commensurate with the injury suffered, taking account of the rights in question'.

[5] See D. Greig, 'Reciprocity, Proportionality and the Law of Treaties' (1994) 34 *Virginia JIL* 295.

[6] See e.g. General Comment No. 29, States of Emergency (Article 4), CCPR/C/21/Rev.1/Add. 11, 31 August 2001, para. 4 (stressing the need for derogation from human rights norms to be demonstrably proportionate); and the Individual Opinion of Elizabeth Evatt and David Kretzmer Co-signed by Eckart Klein (Concurring) in *Faurisson* v. *France*, Communication No. 550/1993, Human Rights Committee, Views of Committee, 8 November 1996, UN Doc. A/52/40 (1999), vol. II, p. 84 (considering proportionality as an element of determining whether restrictions on freedom of speech met the test of being necessary for the respect of the rights or reputations of others in terms of Art. 19(3)(a) of the International Covenant on Civil and Political Rights). See also the reference to proportionality in the work of other human rights agencies and tribunals; for example, Report of the Director of the United Nations Mission for the Verification of Human Rights and of Compliance with the Commitments of the Comprehensive Agreement on Human Rights in Guatemala, UN Doc. A/49/856, paras. 133–7 (1995); and *Ergi* v. *Turkey*, 1998-IV ECtHR, paras. 79, 80 and 86.

[7] See *North Sea Continental Shelf Cases (Federal Republic of Germany* v. *Denmark*; *Federal Republic of Germany* v. *The Netherlands)*, ICJ Reports 1969, 3 at 52–4; *Tunisia* v. *Libya*, ICJ Reports

is by no means settled and awaits further development.[8] In the context of IHL, proportionality is widely acknowledged as a general principle of law in the sense that it underlies and guides the application of the whole regime.[9] Nowadays, the principle also functions within IHL as a concrete legal norm that requires a balance to be struck between the achievement of a particular military goal and the cost in terms of civilian lives.[10] Moreover, several of the other specific rules of IHL owe their derivation to its influence. For example, the emerging protections for the environment in IHL are based on considerations of proportionality.[11] Also proportionality (along with necessity) not only is one of the requirements of legitimate self-defence under the United Nations system but has a part to play in the collective security system.[12] The claim of

1982, 1 at 75; *Gulf of Maine Case*, ICJ Reports 1982, 246 at 334–7; and *Libya* v. *Malta*, ICJ Reports 1995, 29 at 43.

[8] See R. Higgins, *Problems and Process: International Law and How We Use It* (Oxford University Press, Oxford, 1994), pp. 228–37 (for an analysis of the operation of proportionality in international law). Proportionality in municipal legal systems is also still in the formative stage: see J. Delbruck, 'Proportionality' in R. Bernhardt (ed.), *The Encyclopedia of Public International Law* (New Holland Publishing, New York, 1981–91), vol. 3, p. 1144.

[9] As one commentator observes, proportionality in *ius in bello* contributes to the 'equitable balance between the necessities of war and humanitarian requirements': C. Pilloud *et al.* (eds.), *Commentary on the Additional Protocols of 8 June 1977 to the Geneva Conventions of 12 August 1949* (ICRC, Geneva, 1987), p. 683; and see M. Bothe, K. Partsch and W. Solf, *New Rules for Victims of Armed Conflicts* (Martinus Nijhoff, The Hague, 1982), pp. 192–8, 297–320 and 348–69. See also the judgment of the Trial Chamber of the ICTY in the *Kupreskic Case*, Case No. IT-95-16-T-14, Judgment, January 2000, para. 524 (observing that proportionality in *ius in bello* is a general principle of law); and Higgins, *Problems and Process*, pp. 232–4.

[10] See Art. 51(5) of Protocol Additional to the Geneva Conventions of 12 August 1949, and Relating to the Protection of Victims of International Armed Conflicts, adopted in 1977, 12 December 1977, (1979) 1125 UNTS 3 (hereafter Additional Protocol I); and J. Gardam, 'Proportionality and Force in International Law' (1993) 87 *AJIL* 391 at 407–10.

[11] E.g. Art. 35(3) of Additional Protocol I prohibits the employment of 'methods or means of warfare which are intended, or may be expected, to cause widespread, long-term and severe damage to the natural environment'; and see Art. 8 (2) (b)(iv) of the Rome Statute of the International Criminal Court, UN Doc. A/Conf.183/9 (17 July 1998) (hereafter Statute of the ICC), criminalising the launching of an attack in the knowledge that it will cause excessive, widespread, long-term and severe damage to the natural environment.

[12] See J. Barboza, 'Necessity (Revisited) in International Law' in J. Makarczyk (ed.), *Essays in International Law in Honour of Judge Manfred Lachs* (Martinus Nijhoff, The Hague, 1984), p. 27 at p. 34: 'the outer limits of self-defence are established by necessity . . . It is the rule of proportionality which expresses just that meaning. In the last analysis, proportionality means that the defensive action must not go beyond what is necessary in order to defeat the purpose of attack.' See also J. Quigley, 'The United States and the United Nations in the Persian Gulf War: New Order or Disorder' (1992) 25 *Cornell JIL* 1 at 17. In the context of collective security action, see B. Simma (ed.), *The Charter of*

proportionality to have progressed further, however, so as to have a wider role as a principle that infuses international law generally, derives support from its origins and prevalence in the municipal system of States,[13] but remains a matter of debate.[14]

Necessity

Necessity and ius ad bellum

The modern idea that force is only necessary when peaceful means have been to no avail is evident throughout analyses of the just war by commentators such as Vattel.[15] Over the years, however, necessity has had a number of meanings in different contexts in the relations between

the United Nations: A Commentary (Oxford University Press, Oxford, 1994), p. 631: 'The principle of proportionality, as recognised in international law, must be taken into consideration especially with regard to measures under Article 42. This principle finds expression in the Charter in the fact that these measures must be necessary ("as may be necessary").'

[13] For examples of the varying role of proportionality in municipal legal systems, see T. Hartley, *The Foundations of European Community Law* (4th edn, Clarendon Press, Oxford, 1998), pp. 148–9 (discussing the derivation from German constitutional law of proportionality in European Community law, as embodied in the Maastricht Agreement (Treaty on European Union)); and see J. Kirk, 'Constitutional Guarantees, Characterisation and the Concept of Proportionality' (1997) 21 *MULR* 1 (detailing the role of proportionality in Australian constitutional law). Proportionality is a well-established component of the criminal law of many municipal systems in the context of provocation, self-defence and sentencing: see e.g. S. Yeo, 'Proportionality in Criminal Defences' (1988) 12 *Criminal LJ* 211; and R. G. Fox, 'The Meaning of Proportionality in Sentencing' (1994) 19 *MULR* 489. The doctrine has encountered a mixed reception in administrative law in the context of delegated legislation: see S. Boyron, 'Proportionality in English Administrative Law: A Faulty Translation?' (1992) *Oxford Journal of Legal Studies* 237; and cf. the position in Australia, in P. Bayne, 'Reasonableness, Proportionality and Delegated Legislation' (1993) 67 *Australian LJ* 448.

[14] See e.g. Higgins, *Problems and Process*, pp. 228–36, who doubts whether proportionality has attained the status of a general principle of law but concludes that it nevertheless operates to 'ease' the 'appropriate application' of other norms of international law. Even this function, Higgins suggests, is in reality limited to the context of *ius ad bellum*. Cf. the approach of Delbruck, 'Proportionality', p. 1144; F. Krüger-Sprengel, 'Le Concept de Proportionnalité dans le Droit de la Guerre', Rapport présenté au Comité pour la protection de la vie humaine dans les conflits armés, VIIIe Congrès de la Société internationale de droit pénal militaire et de droit de la guerre, Ankara, October 1979 (Brussels, Société international de droit pénal militaire et de droit de la guerre, 1981), p. 194; and M. Bothe, 'Les Limites des Pouvoirs du Conseil de Sécurité' in R. Dupuy (ed.), *The Development of the Role of the Security Council Peace-Keeping and Peace-Building: Workshop, The Hague, 21–23 July 1992* (Martinus Nijhoff, Dordrecht, 1993), p. 67 at pp. 78–9, all of whom regard proportionality as a general principle of law.

[15] See e.g. E. de Vattel, 'Le Droit de Gens, ou Principes de la Loi Naturelle, Appliqués à la Conduite et aux Affaires des Nations et des Souverains', vol. III, trans. by C. Fenwick,

States. It is perhaps best known as the plea that States began to rely on during the nineteenth century to justify actions, including the use of force, that were in breach of the State's international obligations or were otherwise perceived as unfriendly.[16] A component of this developing practice, however, was what is now known as necessity in the modern law of self-defence, in the sense that the action must be by way of a last resort after all peaceful means have failed.[17]

In the context of the use of force, at this time, the resort to war was regarded as a sovereign right of States. There were no legal rules limiting its use. The situation was described by Hall in his *Treatise on International Law* as follows:

> However able law might be to declare one or two combatants to have committed a wrong, it would be idle for it to affect to impart the character of a penalty to war, when it is unable to enforce its decisions . . . International law has consequently no alternative but to accept war, independently of the justice of its origin, as a relation which the parties to it may set up if they choose, and to busy itself only in regulating the effects of the relation.[18]

There were, however, legal rules regulating what were known as hostile measures short of war. As Brierly observes, this distinction was never very satisfactory, as States were at liberty to legalise any measures of dubious legality by declaring a state of war to exist.[19] Although the right to resort to war was unregulated, nevertheless the practice of States was generally to provide reasons for their resort to war. That is, States argued that their actions were necessary to avoid being perceived as engaging in untrammelled aggression.[20] This behaviour, however, was dictated by political not legal considerations. In the context of hostile measures short of war and other non-forceful measures, similar practices were adopted. Various broad categories were developed by commentators to encompass these differing practices.[21] For many years, the right of self-preservation explained much State practice of the period. Other so-called

in J. Scott (ed.), *The Classics of International Law* (Carnegie Institute, Washington DC, 1916), p. 305, para. 190.

[16] See Cheng, *General Principles of Law*, pp. 70–7.

[17] See *ibid.*, pp. 71 and 74 (citing *The Neptune*, 4 *International Adjudication Manuscripts* 372 (1797)).

[18] W. E. Hall, *A Treatise on International Law* (ed. by P. Higgins, 8th edn, Clarendon Press, Oxford, 1924), p. 82.

[19] J. Brierly, *The Law of Nations* (6th edn, Clarendon Press, Oxford, 1963), p. 398.

[20] See I. Brownlie, *International Law and the Use of Force by States* (Clarendon Press, Oxford, 1963), pp. 40–4.

[21] *Ibid.*, pp. 46–9.

rights arguably available to States were those of self-help and necessity of defence, all with varying contents.[22] The borders between these situations were not clearly defined and the practice of States did not at this time coalesce into clearly established principles of international law. Slowly, however, these practices developed into firm legal doctrines. Self-defence henceforth became a distinct legal category and has come to take its place as the situation in which there is universal consensus that States can legitimately resort to force as a matter of both conventional and customary law. Necessity was one of the components of this emerging doctrine.

The broader concept of necessity also survived this transition period and became conceptually distinct from its role in self-defence. Unlike self-defence, which is only legitimate in response to an armed attack, the modern plea of necessity outside this context does not presuppose any wrongful action by the State against which the act of necessity is taken.[23] The discussion of necessity in this work, however, is restricted to this requirement in the context of force, except to the extent that its development requires an appreciation of its broader origins. Its operation in other contexts is well described by other commentators.[24]

Necessity is nowadays firmly established as a component of legitimate self-defence. Moreover, it is assumed that any forceful action must be by way of last resort in other situations where States assert the right to use force unilaterally. The relevance of necessity in the context of force under the United Nations Charter scheme does not finish there. The requirement of necessity plays a part in the collective security system. The text of Article 42 of the Charter requires the Security Council to consider whether non-forceful measures under Article 41 would be or have proved to be inadequate before adopting forceful measures. The Charter, moreover, sets up an elaborate system that is designed to ensure that the use of force is indeed the last resort available to the Council.[25] It

[22] *Ibid.*

[23] See commentary on Art. 25, in Commentaries to the Draft Articles on the Responsibility of States for Internationally Wrongful Acts, adopted by the International Law Commission at its 53rd Sess., Report of the International Law Commission, 53rd Sess. (23 April–1 June and 2 July–10 August 2001), GAOR 56th Sess. Supp. No. 10 (A/56/10).

[24] See e.g. Cheng, *General Principles of Law*; and R. Ago, 'Addendum to the Eighth Report on State Responsibility' (1980-II) *YBILC* 15 (where the distinction between the modern doctrines of necessity and self-defence is explained).

[25] See generally Simma, *The Charter of the United Nations* (for a discussion of the Charter system for the peaceful settlement of disputes).

is debatable, however, to what extent necessity in the context of Article 42 has a legal dimension in the sense of being a justiciable issue.

Necessity and ius in bello

In relation to *ius in bello*, necessity has a somewhat chequered history. The idea of necessity is reflected in the doctrine of military necessity and as such is consistently referred to as one of the general principles on which IHL is based.[26] Indeed, military necessity is sometimes characterised as the source of the requirement that warfare be proportionate.[27] One of its earliest formulations is contained in Article 13 of the Lieber Code, drawn up in 1863 during the American Civil War: 'Military necessity . . . consists of the necessity of those measures which are indispensable for securing the ends of the war, and which are lawful according to the modern law and usages of war.'[28] Its restraining role is apparent, but in this formulation it added nothing concrete to the existing rules of armed conflict. There was, however, some suggestion that military necessity was an additional limitation on the positive rules regulating armed conflict and operated as an additional restraint on State action.[29]

Irrespective of the exact operation of the concept of military necessity, its original conception was not seen as in opposition to humanitarian values, in fact quite the reverse. Military necessity, however, was to acquire a somewhat disreputable air, particularly in the guise of the doctrine of *kraegraeson*, advanced by belligerents to justify their failure to comply with the applicable rules of armed conflict in situations of pressing military necessity.[30] Its articulation thenceforth underwent a

[26] See e.g. Pilloud, *Commentary on the Additional Protocols*, pp. 392–6 (in relation to military necessity and means and methods of combat).

[27] See e.g. Bothe, Partsch and Solf, *New Rules for Victims*, pp. 194–5; M. McDougal and F. Feliciano, *Law and Minimum World Public Order: The Legal Regulation of International Coercion* (New Haven, Yale University Press, 1961), p. 528; and Rauch, 'Le Concept de Nécessité Militaire', p. 213.

[28] *Instructions for the Government of the Armies of the United States in the Field*, prepared by F. Lieber, promulgated as General Orders No. 100, 24 April 1863, reprinted in D. Schindler and J. Toman (eds.), *The Laws of Armed Conflicts: A Collection of Conventions, Resolutions and Other Documents* (3rd edn, Martinus Nijhoff, Dordrecht, 1988), p. 3.

[29] See H. Meyrowitz, 'The Principle of Superfluous Injury or Unnecessary Suffering' (1994) 299 *IRRC* 98 at 106–8.

[30] This idea of military necessity is nowadays reflected in some of the provisions of IHL. See e.g. Art. 34(5) of Additional Protocol I (allowing for derogation from the provisions relating to objects indispensable to the survival of the civilian population by a party to the conflict 'where required by imperative military necessity'). For a discussion of the attitude of war crimes tribunals to pleas of military necessity, see N. Dunbar, 'Military Necessity in War Crimes Trials' (1952) 29 *BYIL* 442.

subtle change. Nowadays, military necessity is often characterised as in conflict with humanitarian values rather than as a general limitation on the resort to violence in armed conflict. Consequently, it has never really developed its potential, and arguably has no substantive content, other than where it is incorporated specifically in the provisions of IHL. In the words of one commentator, although 'military necessity is formally acknowledged as one of the primary foundations of the modern law of war' (similarly to the Martens Clause),[31] its limiting role has been largely forgotten.[32]

One area, however, in which necessity in a more general sense operates as a real restraint in IHL is in relation to belligerent reprisals. Belligerent reprisals are generally understood as measures taken by a party to the conflict that are otherwise unlawful but are justified as an enforcement measure in response to violations of international law by the adversary.[33] The resort to such means of ensuring compliance with the provisions of IHL is accepted as only legitimate by way of last resort.

Given for the most part this formal role of military necessity in IHL, in the remainder of this work it is considered only to the extent of its relevance to the particular rules that protect civilians and combatants against disproportionate attacks and means and methods of warfare that inflict superfluous injury or unnecessary suffering.

Proportionality

Proportionality prior to the United Nations Charter

The modern form of proportionality as a legal restraint on the use of force finds its derivation in just war theory.[34] A just war, *ipso facto*, was

[31] The Martens Clause, first reflected in the Preamble to the 1907 Hague Convention on the Laws and Customs of War on Land, refers to cases not covered specifically by the existing conventional rules and places all those affected by armed conflict 'under the protection and the rule of the principles of the law of nations, as they result from the usage established among civilised peoples, from the laws of humanity and the dictates of the public conscience'.

[32] B. Carnahan, 'Lincoln, Lieber and the Laws of War: The Origins and Limits of the Principle of Military Necessity' (1998) 92 *AJIL* 213 at 230.

[33] See e.g. Department of the Army Field Manual No. 27-10, *The Law of Land Warfare* (Department of the Army, Washington DC, 1956), para. 497(a); War Office, WO Code No. 12333, 'The Law of War on Land', Part III of the *Manual of Military Law* (War Office, London, 1958), para. 642; and see the further discussion of belligerent reprisals, in chapter 3, note 85 and the accompanying text, below.

[34] There are many just war theories, as most civilisations have had highly developed rules relating to the justness of the resort to war. See e.g. M. Sornarajah, 'An Overview

a proportional one. Proportionality in that tradition, however, had a broader operation than is the case today. In just war theory, the means and ends equation of proportionality primarily involved an assessment of whether the overall evil of resorting to war was balanced by the overall good that would ensue. Moreover, just war theory was inextricably intertwined with Christian moral values, and mercy and charity were an integral part of the proportionality equation in those times. There remains a lively debate in modern times as to what constitutes a just war in this sense.[35] This aspect of proportionality, however, never became part of the legal regime on the unilateral resort to force by States. States are under no legal obligation to assess the overall relative merits of a forceful response in self-defence against its likely consequences. Indeed, it is this very failure of the legal regime to incorporate such judgments and to allow States to act in what they perceive as 'just' and moral causes that has placed the existing framework under considerable pressure. Neither is such an assessment explicitly part of the collective security system, although it is inherent in the Security Council's mandate of maintaining or restoring peace that it would consider whether the perceived advantages of coercive actions outweigh their possible negative impact.

of the Asian Approaches to International Humanitarian Law' (1985) 9 *AYIL* 238. However, the Christian theory of the just war formed the basis of the secular just war writings of early commentators on the developing discipline of international law, such as Grotius and de Vattel. See H. Grotius, 'De Jure Belli ac Pacis Libri Tres', trans. by F. Kelsey, in J. Scott (ed.), *The Classics of International Law*, vol. II, book III (Carnegie Endowment for International Peace, Washington DC, 1925); and de Vattel, 'Le Droit de Gens'. There are a number of excellent works on the historical development and modern form of the Christian theory of the just war: see e.g. J. Johnson, *Ideology, Reason and the Limitation of War* (Princeton University Press, Princeton, 1975); J. Johnson, *Just War Tradition and Restraint of War* (Princeton University Press, Princeton, 1981); F. Russell, *The Just War in the Middle Ages* (Cambridge University Press, Cambridge, 1975); and M. Walzer, *Just and Unjust Wars: A Moral Argument with Historical Illustrations* (2nd edn, Basic Books, New York, 1992). The just war has also received attention from legal scholars: see e.g. W. O'Brien, *The Conduct of Just and Limited War* (Praeger, New York, 1981).

[35] For a discussion of the role of proportionality in modern just war theory, see P. Ramsey, *The Just War: Force and Political Responsibility* (University of America Press, Lanham MD, 1983), pp. 189–210; and Johnson, *Just War Tradition*, pp. 196–204. See also generally P. Ramsey, *War and the Christian Conscience: How Shall Modern War Be Conducted Justly?* (Duke University Press, Durham, NC, 1961); J. Ryan, *Modern War and Basic Ethics* (Bruce Publishing Company, Milwaukee WI, 1941); J. Ford, 'The Morality of Obliteration Bombing' (1955) 5 *Theological Studies* 261; T. Taylor, *Nuremberg and Vietnam: An American Tragedy* (Quadrangle, Chicago, 1970); Walzer, *Just and Unjust Wars*; and W. O'Brien, *The Conduct of Just and Limited War* (Praeger, New York, 1981).

The assessment of proportionality in just war doctrine, however, also took into account the means by which war was conducted and in theory operated as a restraint on the amount of damage that could be inflicted on the enemy to achieve the legitimate ends of war. It appears that it also imposed some restraints on the means of warfare. It is this latter aspect of proportionality in just war theory that found its way into the modern legal regime of proportionality and is now represented in the separate regimes of *ius ad bellum* and IHL.

During the period when war was a sovereign right of States and the resort to force was unregulated, a separate body of rules that was to become modern IHL began to emerge. Today, proportionality in IHL consists of highly developed rules prohibiting disproportionate attacks and means and methods of warfare causing superfluous injury or unnecessary suffering. How attacks and the choice of means and methods of warfare relate in general to the aims of force is an issue for *ius ad bellum*. Proportionality in this latter sense of limiting a State's overall forceful response, however, did not fall entirely into disuse despite the lack of regulation of the resort to war. States perceived some mutual benefit in limiting the impact of war even if at the time they saw no advantage to restricting the right to wage war. Thus, the limitations flowing from considerations of proportionality at this time were sometimes expressed in broad terms so as to take account not only of the use of weapons against combatants (limits on civilian casualties were as yet in the future) but also overall disproportionate warfare.

During this developmental period of IHL, proportionality therefore performed to some extent the role of the modern proportionality equations in both IHL and *ius ad bellum*. Once again the actual influence of ideas of proportionality in limiting the use of force in these times must not be over-emphasised. It was a considerable period of time before the concrete manifestations of its requirements in IHL (and indeed *ius ad bellum*) were to materialise.

Proportionality and the Charter regime on the use of force

When States once again turned their attention to limiting the right of States to resort to force, the division between IHL and the emerging *ius ad bellum* remained. Henceforth, there were two proportionality equations with distinct contents that States had to satisfy in their actions involving the use of force. Consequently, under the Charter scheme, a State must not only ensure that any forceful action it takes satisfies the requirements of IHL relating to disproportionate attacks and legitimate means and methods of warfare, but also that the forceful response is a proportionate measure in relation to the legitimate ends of force. Failure to satisfy either test in theory renders the action unlawful in international law. Thus, meticulous compliance with the proportionality requirements of IHL will not prevent an action being disproportionate under *ius ad bellum*.[36] Conversely, a disproportionate action under IHL will be illegitimate even if it satisfies the requirements of proportionality under *ius ad bellum*.

What appears clear as an abstract proposition, however, comes under considerable strain when subjected to the rigours of application. In practice, the existence of the two proportionality requirements from quite separate regimes purporting to simultaneously govern the same activity has led to some seemingly intractable problems about the relationship between its two aspects, a phenomenon illustrated by the Advisory Opinion of the International Court of Justice (ICJ) in the *Legality of the Threat or Use of Nuclear Weapons*.[37]

Proportionality and the Charter *ius ad bellum*

Despite wide differences expressed by commentators and as evidenced in the practice of States as to when the resort to force is legitimate in international law, there has been consistent agreement ever since the adoption of the United Nations Charter on the need for any forceful action, irrespective of its legal basis, to be proportionate.[38] For example, Higgins, in the context of preventative action against State-supported border raids by irregulars, observes that force may legitimately be used

[36] See generally F. Kalshoven, 'State Responsibility for Warlike Acts of the Armed Forces' (1991) 40 *ICLQ* 827.

[37] *Legality of the Threat or Use of Nuclear Weapons*, Advisory Opinion, ICJ Reports 1996, 226 (General Assembly Opinion) (hereafter *Nuclear Weapons* Advisory Opinion). The Court was confronted in that case with determining the legality of a weapon that seemingly was totally incompatible with the requirements of IHL but was nevertheless an integral component of the defensive strategies of a significant number of States. The demands of *ius ad bellum* prevailed. See J. Gardam, 'Necessity and Proportionality in *Jus ad Bellum* and *Jus in Bello*'; and C. Greenwood, '*Jus ad Bellum* and *Jus in Bello* in the *Nuclear Weapons Advisory Opinion*' in L. Boisson de Chazournes and P. Sands (eds.), *International Law, the International Court of Justice and Nuclear Weapons* (Cambridge University Press, Cambridge, 1999), p. 275 at p. 247.

[38] See e.g. H. Waldock, 'The Regulation of the Use of Force by Individual States in International Law' (1952) 81 *Recueil des Cours* 455 at 463–4; and D. P. O'Connell, *The International Law of the Sea* vol. I. (ed. by Shearer, Clarendon Press, Oxford, 1984), p. 1096 (observing that all naval operations since the Second World War have been conducted on the basis that proportionality is a limiting factor).

in such a situation 'but always with the proviso that the action in self-defence is proportionate, in nature and degree, to the prior illegality or the imminent attack'.[39] The same view is articulated in the contexts of humanitarian intervention both unilateral and collective[40] and in relation to responses to terrorist activities.[41] The concrete application of proportionality, and particularly the question of 'proportionate to what?', however, are far from uniform. In the context of self-defence, for example, Bowett measures the proportionality of the response against the danger,[42] Higgins, against the injury being inflicted,[43] and Waldock writes in terms of what is 'required for achieving the object'.[44]

The question of the overall 'good' of the use of force in contexts other than in the restricted circumstances where the unilateral resort to force is legitimate is left to the Security Council. The mandate of the Security Council is to take whatever action it determines appropriate (including the use of force) in order to restore international peace and security in the face of a threat to the peace, breach of the peace or act of aggression.[45] As with the unilateral resort to force, it is generally assumed that any forceful action, either by United Nations forces under the control and command of the United Nations[46] or State forces acting in pursuance of Security Council authorisation, should be proportionate.[47]

[39] R. Higgins, *The Development of International Law Through the Political Organs of the United Nations* (Oxford University Press, Oxford, 1963), p. 201.

[40] See e.g. V. Nanda, 'The Validity of United States Intervention in Panama under International Law' (1990) 84 *AJIL* 494 at 496; C. Chinkin, 'Kosovo: A Good or Bad War?' (1999) 93 *AJIL* 84 at 84–5; J. Charney, 'Anticipatory Humanitarian Intervention in Kosovo' (1999) 93 *AJIL* 834 at 839; A. Cassese, '*Ex Iniuria Ius Oritur*: Are We Moving Towards International Legitimation of Forcible Humanitarian Countermeasures in the World Community?' (1999) 10 *EJIL* 23 at 27.

[41] See F. L. Kirgis, 'Terrorist Attacks on the World Trade Center and the Pentagon', *ASIL Insight*, September 2001.

[42] D. Bowett, *Self-Defence in International Law* (Manchester University Press, Manchester, 1958), p. 269.

[43] Higgins, *Problems and Process*, p. 231, citing J. Hargrove, 'The Nicaragua Judgement and the Future of the Law of Force and Self-Defence' (1987) 81 *AJIL* 135 at 136.

[44] See Waldock, 'Regulation of the Use of Force', pp. 463–4.

[45] See Arts. 39, 40, 41 and 42 of the United Nations Charter.

[46] Peacekeepers, generally speaking, use minimum amounts of force in self-defence. Nevertheless, the requirement of proportionality equally applies to the use of force in self-defence by peacekeepers. See e.g. Aide-Mémoire of the Secretary-General Relating to the Function and Operation of the United Nations Peacekeeping Force in Cyprus, UN Doc. S/5653, 11 April 1964, paras. 16–18. See also G.-J. F. van Hegelson, 'The Law of Armed Conflict and UN Peacekeeping and Peace-Enforcing Operations' (1993) 6 *Hague YIL* 44 at 54 (for a discussion of the application of proportionality in the case of self-defence by peacekeepers).

[47] See e.g. Simma, *The Charter of the United Nations*, p. 631.

Little attention is accorded, however, to the juridical analysis underlying such views.

The question of the relevance of the requirements of necessity and proportionality to the Charter system of collective security theoretically has always been present in light of the existence of Article 43 of the Charter providing for the establishment of a permanent military force. The issue never had to be confronted, as this force never eventuated. However, since the end of the Cold War era, the practice has been adopted from time to time of conferring the Chapter VII powers of the Council on willing States.[48] This development has given rise to many complex and interrelated legal problems. There were initially doubts as to the ability of the Council to legitimately confer Chapter VII powers on States. Although it is now accepted that this practice of the Council is lawful, the analysis that supports this development is as yet unresolved.[49] Moreover, the precise relationship between the Council, the States that act in pursuance of its authority and the position of third States who may be injured by such activities, awaits further clarification. In this work the focus of the discussion is the general question of whether there are any limits derived from necessity and proportionality that restrain the exercise of the enforcement powers of the Council. This in turn determines the position of States acting under its authority. All the vexed queries as to the respective responsibility of the various actors (including issues of control and command of the forces involved) and where judicial scrutiny fits within this picture are largely outside the scope of this work.[50]

[48] See D. Sarooshi, *The United Nations and the Development of Collective Security* (Clarendon Press, Oxford, 1999), pp. 174–246 (for details of these initiatives of the Security Council).

[49] For a discussion of the legal basis of this practice, see e.g. Higgins, *Problems and Process*, pp. 263–6; Sarooshi, *Development of Collective Security*; and N. Blokker, 'Is the Authorization Authorized? Powers and Practice of the UN Security Council to Authorize the Use of Force by "Coalitions of the Able and Willing"' (2000) 11 *EJIL* 541. The latter two writers explicitly base their conclusions as to the legality of the practice of authorisation on an implied power of delegation.

[50] There is an increasing body of literature addressing these issues: see e.g. Sarooshi, *Development of Collective Security*, pp. 163–6 (discussing the issue of responsibility for forces acting under the authority of the Security Council). Sarooshi distinguishes between 'operational' control on a day-to-day basis which rests with the States supplying forces to the 'authorised' operation and overall authority and control of these forces which he argues remains with the Security Council. This overall retention of authority by the Security Council incurs the responsibility of the UN: see Blokker, 'Is the Authorization Authorized?', pp. 551–2 and 555–67 (discussing the issue of control and command); and T. D. Gill, 'Legal and Some Political Limitations on the

Proportionality and IHL under the United Nations Charter

With the adoption of the United Nations Charter outlawing the resort to force except in self-defence or by way of collective security, the continued relevance of IHL may have seemed threatened. After all, it appears somewhat incongruous to meticulously regulate the conduct of an unlawful activity. There were some initial theoretical difficulties in harmonising the Charter proscription on the aggressive use of force and a system of rules that was intended to mitigate the horrors of warfare for all participants. Once, however, the idea was established that, irrespective of the legal position of the adversaries under *ius ad bellum*, IHL was of equal application to both parties, IHL has gone from strength to strength, particularly in the post-Cold War era.

Modern IHL limits the effects of warfare for both combatants and civilians. The concept of proportionality, along with restraints derived from humanity and chivalry, plays a pivotal role in this process. It is part of the 'Law of The Hague' that deals with the conduct of warfare.[51] The rules derived from the principle that armed conflict should not be conducted in a disproportionate manner take different forms in relation to combatants and civilians under IHL, a distinction that is not reflected in *ius ad bellum*. Combatants are legitimate targets in armed conflict, whereas civilians are not. For this reason, the level of combatant casualties never became an issue in IHL and remains a matter for the proportionality equation in *ius ad bellum*. In IHL, it is the prohibition of means and methods of warfare that are of a nature to cause superfluous injury or unnecessary suffering that today purports to limit the impact of armed conflict on combatants[52] and for many years has enjoyed customary and conventional status.[53] In the context of civilians, the development of proportionality is linked with the growth over the centuries of the idea that civilians should be protected from the effects of warfare.

Power of the UN Security Council to Exercise Its Enforcement Powers Under Chapter VII of the Charter' (1995) 26 *NYIL* 33.

51 See note 1 above.

52 See S. Oeter, 'Methods and Means of Combat' in D. Fleck (ed.), *Handbook of Humanitarian Law in Armed Conflict* (Oxford University Press, Oxford, 1995), pp. 105–53 (for a discussion of this prohibition).

53 See F. Hampson, 'Means and Methods of Warfare in the Conflict in the Gulf' in P. Rowe (ed.), *The Gulf War 1990–91 in International and English Law* (Routledge, London, 1993), p. 89 at p. 101 (the extent to which this principle in itself has achieved anything in advancing the protection of combatants is controversial, see the further discussion in chapter 3 below).

By the beginning of the twentieth century, it was accepted in a general sense that civilians were not legitimate objects of attack.[54] However, this limitation was inadequate to deal with the growing impact of armed conflict on civilians, particularly in the light of the development of means and methods of warfare that inevitably resulted in civilian casualties. In current international law, the concept of proportionality, along with measures to minimise civilian casualties, including the prohibition of indiscriminate attacks, plays a pivotal role in determining the extent to which civilians and civilian objects are entitled to be protected from the collateral effects of armed conflict. Since the adoption in 1977 of Additional Protocol I to the four 1945 Geneva Conventions, the requirement that attacks shall not result in disproportionate collateral civilian damage is both a conventional and a customary rule of IHL.[55]

The use of the term 'proportionality' in relation to the rules that regulate the means and methods of warfare for the protection of combatants has been criticised.[56] Technically, it is more accurate today to talk in terms of superfluous injury or unnecessary suffering in the context of combatants, rather than proportionality.[57] The principle that prohibits the infliction of superfluous injury or unnecessary suffering on combatants and the modern rule of proportionality in relation to civilians, however, have a common origin and goal – to minimise the torment caused by war – to ensure that the suffering and loss of life of both combatant and civilian are not disproportionate to the legitimate ends. They find a common source in the foundation principle of IHL that belligerents do not have unlimited choice in the means chosen to inflict damage on the enemy. Although strictly speaking this latter principle was developed with combatants in mind, it provided the basis for the movement that coalesced after the Second World War (1939–45) to place real limits on the impact of warfare on civilians.

54 See J. Gardam, *Non-Combatant Immunity as a Norm of International Humanitarian Law* (Martinus Nijhoff, Dordrecht, 1993), pp. 16–20; and G. Best, *War and Law Since 1945* (Oxford University Press, Oxford, 1994), pp. 26–44.

55 See Arts. 51(5)(b) and 57(2)(a)(iii) of Additional Protocol I, that encapsulate the concept of proportionality. The exact content of the customary rule, however, is controversial. See the further discussion in chapter 4 below.

56 See Meyrowitz, 'The Principle of Superfluous Injury', pp. 109–10 (observing that the particular application of the rule in relation to civilians is not reflected in the regime protecting combatants).

57 Nevertheless, commentators constantly use the word 'proportionate' in relation to the regulation of weapons to protect combatants. See e.g. S. Oeter, 'Methods and Means', p. 114; and A. Cassese, 'Weapons Causing Unnecessary Suffering: Are They Prohibited?' (1975) 58 *Rivista di Diritto Internazionale* 12 at 27–9.

Proportionality, therefore, is not only the specific rule expressed in Additional Protocol I in relation to civilians, it is the basis of the rules protecting combatants.[58]

The relationship between IHL (including the rule of proportionality) and the military enforcement powers of the Security Council is part of the wider debate as to the applicability of IHL to United Nations forces.[59] These forces, depending on their mandate, may be established by the General Assembly or by the Security Council under either Chapter VI or VII of the Charter. Although there remain certain outstanding juridical issues, it is accepted in principle that these forces operate within the constraints of IHL.[60]

Underlying basis of proportionality in the modern era

The rationale behind proportionality in *ius ad bellum* and IHL differs. The limitations imposed by proportionality in the former relate to the minimisation of the disruption of international peace and security.[61] Proportionality in self-defence, for example, is designed to ensure that States are allowed the minimum that is required to defend themselves against an aggressor. To go any further and allow excessive destruction of another State is seen as destabilising a system that is founded on the peaceful settlement of disputes and a collective security system.[62] Thus, the conduct of self-defence in a disproportionate manner is likely to embitter relations between the adversaries and their respective protagonists, with inevitable consequences for the harmony of the international community. Consequently, the major considerations in the application of proportionality in modern *ius ad bellum* (whether it be in the context

[58] See e.g. Bothe, Partsch and Solf, *New Rules for Victims*, p. 195 (confirming that the prohibition on weapons causing superfluous injury or unnecessary suffering is 'another way of stating the rule of proportionality defined in the context of the civilian population').

[59] For a discussion of this issue, see e.g. C. Greenwood, 'International Humanitarian Law and United Nations Military Operations' (1998) 1 *Yearbook of International Humanitarian Law* 3, and the sources cited in note 1 above.

[60] See generally Greenwood, 'International Humanitarian Law'.

[61] See C. Greenwood, 'Self-Defence and the Conduct of International Armed Conflict' in Y. Dinstein (ed.), *International Law at a Time of Perplexity: Essays in Honour of Shabtai Rosenne* (Martinus Nijhoff, Dordrecht, 1989), p. 273 at p. 278.

[62] O'Connell, *Law of the Sea*, vol. II, p. 1096, in the context of the exercise of sea power, observes that 'world opinion . . . has been supposed . . . to be tolerant towards localized conflict but apt to be dangerously alarmed by eruptions of violence in the sea lanes of international commerce'.

of self-defence or any other ground on which the use of force is argued to be legitimate) are the level of destruction of enemy territory and the infrastructure of the State; overall collateral civilian damage and combatant casualties; and the impact of the use of force on third States (with a developing emphasis in the latter context on damage to the environment). The balance between these factors varies considerably depending on the particular circumstances and the justification for the resort to force. For example, civilian casualties and damage to civilian objects of any magnitude sit uneasily with forceful action that has a humanitarian objective.[63] There is, moreover, growing recognition of the potential of proportionality in *ius ad bellum* to incorporate overtly humanitarian considerations.[64] To date, however, commentators rely on IHL rather than *ius ad bellum* to achieve this result.

The general view is that provisions of IHL derived from proportionality that limit the level of damage to civilians and combatants, are based on humanitarian considerations.[65] The emphasis on humanity is a relatively late development. Its influence generally in *ius in bello* is controversial and it would be simplistic to see the foundations of the system as purely humanitarian. The notion that the needless suffering of combatants and high levels of civilian casualties are unacceptable in warfare was largely unknown until the growth of humanism in the eighteenth century. During the period of the just war, it is debatable as to the extent to which humanity played any significant role in the regulation of warfare. The proportionality equation in that era was intimately connected with Christian ideas of good and evil, intermingled with secular influences. Today, the issue is no less complex. At a superficial level, IHL is widely acknowledged as being based on humanitarian considerations. This explains the changing nomenclature of this area of the law.[66] To some commentators, however, the term IHL disguises the reality, particularly in the context of those rules of IHL that regulate the conduct of hostilities, such as proportionality.

[63] See M. Bothe, 'The Protection of the Civilian Population and NATO Bombing on Yugoslavia: Comments on a Report to the Prosecutor of the ICTY' (2001) 12 *EJIL* 531 at 535.

[64] See T. Meron, 'The Humanization of Humanitarian Law' (2000) 94 *AJIL* 239 at 242 (referring to the potential of proportionality in *ius ad bellum* to impose limits on the territorial and temporal dimensions of war so as to reduce the suffering of civilians and combatants).

[65] See e.g. Krüger-Sprengel, 'Le Concept de Proportionnalité', p. 181.

[66] See note 1 above.

A study of IHL reveals that developments in the protections offered to all victims of armed conflict, both combatants and non-combatants, have been in spite of the military rather than at its instigation. Some restrictions on weapons to protect combatants have been tolerated and there are the extremely detailed provisions protecting prisoners of war.[67] These rules may appear humanitarian in nature but they are also compatible with military imperatives.[68] Generally speaking, however, there is broad-based support for the view that humanitarian considerations have led to little real progress in improving the protection for combatants against means and methods of warfare causing superfluous injury or unnecessary suffering.[69]

In the case of civilians (apart from arguments as to efficiency) there is frequently no particular military advantage to be gained from measures for their protection. Indeed, the targeting of civilians can sometimes serve a military purpose, as for example in undermining the morale of the enemy. Strategies to protect civilians can also increase the risk for combatants. Consequently, despite the appalling suffering of civilians in armed conflict from the development in the twentieth century of weapons of mass destruction, it was not until the influence of human rights began to make its impact on IHL, that steps were taken to improve the protection offered to civilians during times of armed conflict.[70] These advances were hard-won in the face of much opposition from the military establishment of States, and the actual application of these rules in subsequent conflicts has been disappointing. Nevertheless, the view that IHL is primarily humanitarian in nature is gaining ground.[71]

[67] The Third Geneva Convention in relation to prisoners of war, has some 143 Articles and five Annexes and goes to the lengths of stipulating what should be available in the prison canteen. For a study of the long and complex history of the rules protecting prisoners of war, see generally A. Rosas, *The Legal Status of Prisoners of War* (Suomalainen tiedeakatemia, Helsinki, 1976).

[68] See C. Jochnick and R. Normand, 'The Legitimation of Violence: A Critical History of the Laws of War' (1994) 35 *Harvard ILJ* 49 at 53–4, 68. Cf. a traditional description of the humanitarian ideal underlying IHL and its relationship with military necessity by G. Draper, 'The Development of International Humanitarian Law' (1998) 67 *International Dimensions of Humanitarian Law* 179.

[69] See L. Doswald-Beck, 'Obstacles to Regulating New Weaponry: Battlefield Laser Weapons' in H. Fox and M. Meyer (eds.), *Effecting Compliance, Armed Conflict and the New Law* (British Institute of International and Comparative Law, London, 1993), p. 107; and Jochnick and Normand, 'The Legitimation of Violence'.

[70] See G. Draper, 'Human Rights and the Law of War' (1972) 12 *Virginia JIL* 326 at 336.

[71] See e.g. J. Gardam, 'The Contribution of the International Court of Justice to the Development of International Humanitarian Law' (2001) 14 *Leiden JIL* 349.

Irrespective of the motivation behind IHL, unlike *ius ad bellum*, its rules (including proportionality) primarily take individuals as their focus.[72] In contrast, proportionality in *ius ad bellum* has always focused on damage to the enemy State as an abstract entity apart from its individual inhabitants. As a result, in current times, the dual proportionality equations incorporate a consideration of the same general factors but with a different emphasis. For example, the issue of weapons is relevant for proportionality in both IHL and *ius ad bellum*. However, in the former regime, it is the effect of a weapon on civilians and combatants as individuals that requires assessment. In the latter system, the relevant factors when considering whether a particular weapon or its use is a proportionate action in self-defence, relate to damage to the civilian population as a whole, the level of destruction of the enemy forces and damage to enemy territory, infrastructure and the environment generally.

The practical significance of necessity and proportionality in modern times

To what extent are the principles of necessity and proportionality (in both *ius ad bellum* and IHL) of real significance in practice? Schachter, writing in the context of *ius ad bellum*, regards this question as 'one of the most sensitive subjects of contemporary international law . . . In virtually all wars, questions of necessity and proportionality have given rise to controversy that is troubling and divisive.'[73] He concludes that the existence of these legal principles, although incapable of providing a straightforward answer to concrete situations, nevertheless acts as a general restraint on decision-makers, and that is their value. It is difficult, however, to see that this is uniformly the case. For example, in the case of one major international conflict since the adoption of the Charter, the Iran/Iraq war (1981–8), necessity and proportionality played no part in the conduct of the hostilities between the belligerents.[74]

[72] Note, however, the rules in relation to cultural property. See e.g. Protocol for the Protection of Cultural Property in the Event of Armed Conflict, The Hague, 14 May 1954, 249 UNTS 358; and Second Protocol to the Hague Convention of 1954 for the Protection of Cultural Property in the Event of Armed Conflict, The Hague, 26 March 1999.

[73] O. Schachter, 'Implementing Limitations on the Use of Force: The Doctrine of Proportionality and Necessity' (1992) 85 *Proc ASIL* 39.

[74] See generally I. F. Dekker and H. H. G. Post (eds.), *The Gulf War of 1980–1988: The Iran–Iraq War in International Legal Perspective* (Martinus Nijhoff, Dordrecht, 1992).

Despite the considerable potential of proportionality in *ius ad bellum* to limit the destructive impact of armed conflict, it has never been subjected to rigorous legal analysis. Brownlie, in his 1963 authoritative work on the use of force, expressed surprise that in light of the ambiguity of the statement of the test of proportionality in the 1837 *Caroline Incident* (nowadays accepted as the genesis of the modern rule in *ius ad bellum*)[75] so little attention has been paid by jurists to its requirements.[76] Very little has changed in more recent times,[77] although proportionality was considered by the International Court of Justice in the *Nicaragua Case*[78] and the *Nuclear Weapons Advisory Opinion*.

There is no doubt as to the theoretical relevance of proportionality in *ius ad bellum*. However, its practical expression is a different matter. In the practice of States it is rarely accorded more than lip service. Commentators mirror this approach where proportionality primarily serves as a rhetorical tool to support whatever view is taken as to the morality of a particular use of force.[79] Any detailed examination of its requirements is conspicuously absent. Proportionality in *ius ad bellum*, moreover, is often misunderstood and misapplied. For example, from time to time, particularly in the context of reprisals, the concept is used as a mechanism to support arguments that the use of force is illegitimate under the Charter.[80] However, proportionality does not operate as a determinant of the situation in which States can legitimately resort to force but rather is intended to monitor the use of force itself irrespective of its legitimacy in the first place.

Undoubtedly, part of the explanation of this reluctance to engage with proportionality in any meaningful way is the fact that it operates in

[75] For a full description of the *Caroline Incident*, see R. Jennings, 'The Caroline and McLeod Cases' (1938) 32 *AJIL* 82 at 91.

[76] See Brownlie, *International Law*, p. 261.

[77] A notable exception, however, is the study of proportionality in the context of sea power by D. P. O'Connell, *The Influence of Law on Sea Power* (Manchester University Press, Manchester, 1975).

[78] *Case Concerning Military and Paramilitary Activities in and against Nicaragua (Nicaragua v. United States)*, Merits, ICJ Reports 1986, 14.

[79] E.g. cf. the differing conclusions reached as to the legality of the forceful actions of NATO in Kosovo by Chinkin, 'Kosova', pp. 844–5; and M. Reisman, 'Kosovo's Antinomies' (1999) 93 *AJIL* 860 at 861–2. Both authors refer to proportionality to support their views. Professor Chinkin, however, transcends rhetoric and provides an analysis of the factors that she regards as part of the proportionality equation that were not satisfied by NATO's response in Kosovo.

[80] See the discussion of reprisals and proportionality in chapter 5 below, note 206 and the accompanying text.

two separate regimes, *ius ad bellum* and IHL, and the exact nature of the relationship between its two components is far from readily apparent. The connection between the regimes of *ius ad bellum* and IHL generally is complex. It is rarely clearly articulated despite the fact that an appreciation of the distinction is fundamental to the understanding of the manner in which proportionality operates in the context of the hostile actions of States.[81]

An illustration of how proportionality operates in these separate regimes can be drawn from the air campaign plan of the United States in the 1990–1 Persian Gulf conflict. The United States 1992 Department of Defense Report to Congress on *The Conduct of the Persian Gulf War* details the overall strategic objectives of the air campaign (one of the four phases of Operation Desert Storm) and the sets of targets involved in achieving these objectives.[82] For example, one objective was to isolate and incapacitate the Iraqi regime. To achieve this aim it was deemed necessary to attack aspects of the Iraqi electricity production facilities and the telecommunications system. The legitimacy of this objective of incapacitating the regime and the targets selected to achieve it is a matter for the proportionality equation in *ius ad bellum*. The detailed conduct of the attacks on these targets is a matter for the proportionality equation in IHL, and in the case of the Persian Gulf conflict was worked out frequently on a daily basis.[83] The timing and level of command at which the decisions are made in *ius ad bellum* and IHL respectively, therefore, will differ. Strategic decisions involve a high level of command and occur primarily (although by no means exclusively) at the planning stages of the forceful response. In contrast, the majority of the decision-making in relation to IHL occurs at a lower level of command on a continuous basis.

A further explanation for the relative dearth of analysis of the requirements of proportionality in *ius ad bellum* is the difficulties in its application and the fact that whether actions are proportionate (and indeed necessary) will always depend on the particular facts.[84] There is no doubt that the assessment of proportionality in *ius ad bellum* is a far from

[81] See, however, the careful analysis by C. Greenwood, 'The Relationship Between *Ius ad Bellum* and *Ius in Bello*' (1983) 9 *Review of International Studies* 221.

[82] See Department of Defense, *Final Report to Congress: Conduct of the Persian Gulf War* (USGPO, Washington DC, 1992), p. 95.

[83] *Ibid.*

[84] See e.g. C. Gray, *International Law and the Use of Force* (Oxford University Press, Oxford, 2000), p. 106; and R. R. Baxter, 'The Legal Consequences of the Unlawful Use of Force under the Charter' (1968) *Proc ASIL* 68 at 73–4.

straightforward task. As O'Connell observes, '[i]t is a matter of judgement in concrete instances what level and mode of response are proportionate to the assault, and all attempts to standardize the guidelines have proved unsuccessful, because, as in the case of any other general principle of legal conduct, so much resides in the contingencies of a situation'.[85]

The conduct of the Falkland Islands conflict (1982) is an example of the challenges of applying proportionality in self-defence. In that conflict the United Kingdom was faced with particularly difficult strategic decisions relating to the geographical extent of the hostile actions at sea and the appropriateness of attacking targets on the Argentine mainland. Many of these decisions were in the political arena. However, from a legal perspective, the United Kingdom had to consider the impact of its maritime hostilities on other States and also whether it was proportionate to attack targets on the Argentine mainland in order to expel the Argentine forces from the Islands. A similar process was required of the coalition allies in the 1990–1 Persian Gulf conflict in terms of the extent to which the campaign could legitimately extend into Iraqi territory.

Difficulty in application, however, is also a characteristic of proportionality in IHL. Proportionality in IHL is universally regarded as a troublesome concept to apply in practice, although no one doubts the need to abide by its restraints.[86] Moreover, theoretically the consequences of a faulty application of the proportionality test can lead to individual criminal liability.[87] Nevertheless, despite its defects, proportionality plays a much more central part in that legal regime. For example, in the 1990–1 Persian Gulf conflict and the 1999 NATO action in Kosovo, proportionality in IHL has been relied on in many contexts where there have been differences as to the legality of actions of the attacking forces.[88]

A further factor that contributes to the resistance to proportionality in *ius ad bellum* is that its constraints are equally applicable to all

[85] O'Connell, *The Influence of Law*, p. 34.

[86] See e.g. W. J, Fenrick, 'Attacking the Enemy Civilian as a Punishable Offence' (1997) 7 *Duke JIL* 539 at 545–9 (describing the issues that remain unresolved in the application of proportionality in IHL).

[87] See Art. 85(3) of Additional Protocol I (in relation to civilians) and Art. 8 of the Statute of the ICC (in relation to civilians and combatants); and see the further discussion of enforcement of proportionality in chapters 3 and 4 below.

[88] See e.g. Human Rights Watch, *Civilian Deaths in the NATO Air Campaign* (2000), available at www.hrw.org/reports/2000/nato/ (discussing the proportionality of the attacks on the Serb radio and television headquarters in Belgrade and on urban bridges in daylight hours).

parties irrespective of the legality or perceived 'justness' of a party's resort to force. This requirement of equality of application is also a characteristic of IHL and has been problematic in that regime over the years. The International Committee of the Red Cross (ICRC), however, has been particularly successful in ensuring that this fundamental aspect of IHL is acknowledged and respected.[89] It has not always been an easy task. It has, however, proved possible to mount a convincing argument for the equal application of IHL on humanitarian grounds, on the basis that the State is a separate entity from its peoples. This approach is reflected in the statement of General Wesley Clark, Supreme Allied Commander of NATO in Europe, in the context of the NATO action in Kosovo:

> As the campaign progressed, it grew in intensity. However, it was not a campaign against the Serbian people. It focused specifically on the forces of repression from top to bottom to coerce a change in their behaviour or, failing that, to degrade and ultimately destroy their means of repression. Allied planners, targeters and pilots worked diligently to prevent injuries and loss of life among the civilian population and to prevent collateral damage.[90]

Moreover, in practice it is a more straightforward task to determine what are the relevant rules of IHL and when they apply. The requirements of IHL apply on the objective fact of the existence of a certain level of armed conflict. The legality of the respective parties' resort to force, although it may subtly affect the implementation of IHL, is not a relevant consideration for the regime to come into operation.

In contrast, the existence of an objective state of affairs that brings into operation the equal application of the rules is not a feature of modern *ius ad bellum*. For example, in the context of self-defence, one party will be exercising the right under Article 51 of the United Nations Charter, whereas the other party will be an unlawful aggressor. The party resorting to force in self-defence theoretically will be bound by the

[89] See e.g. the Preamble to Additional Protocol I, which reads '[r]eaffirming further that the provisions of the Geneva Conventions of 12 August 1949 and of this Protocol must be fully applied in all circumstances to all persons who are protected by those instruments, without any adverse distinction based on the nature or origin of the armed conflict or on the causes espoused by or attributed to the Parties to the conflict'.

[90] General W. K. Clark, 'When Force is Necessary: NATO's Military Response to the Kosovo Crisis' (1999) 47(2) *NATO Review* 14; see also Human Rights Watch, *Civilian Deaths* (citing remarks of General Shelton and Lt General Esmond in relation to the emphasis on avoiding 'collateral damage').

requirements of necessity and proportionality but the question arises as to the obligations of the other party.[91] There is, thus, a potential imbalance of obligations. It is, therefore, not so readily apparent that proportionality, in its *ius ad bellum* sense as a limitation on the level of destruction of a State and its territory, should be respected against a State that is in breach of the United Nations Charter ban on the use of force, or is engaged in widespread breaches of basic human rights. Consequently, there is the view that, once the requirement of necessity is met, the conduct of the conflict is governed solely by IHL and to expect any more restraints on the use of force is unrealistic and, moreover, not required as a matter of law. This tendency to rely totally on IHL to regulate the conduct of a conflict is apparent in a range of fora as, for example, in the work of NGOs, amongst the military, and elsewhere in bodies dealing with the use of force.[92]

One specific illustration of this phenomenon of reliance solely on IHL to regulate the conduct of a conflict can be found in the practice of selecting certain methods of warfare, such as high-altitude aerial bombardment, in order to minimise combatant casualties. This tactic can be seen in operation in the 1990–1 Persian Gulf and Kosovo conflicts.[93] Human rights bodies have been critical of the impact of such strategies on the level of civilian casualties, and have queried whether such methods are compatible with the prohibition on indiscriminate attacks in IHL.[94] However, it is by no means clear how far the minimisation of combatant casualties is a factor in the proportionality equation

[91] See *Final Report to the Prosecutor by the Committee Established to Review the NATO Bombing Campaign Against the Federal Republic of Yugoslavia* (2000), paras. 30–4 (for a discussion of this issue).

[92] See e.g. the reports of Human Rights Watch, *Civilian Deaths* and Amnesty International, *NATO/Federal Republic of Yugoslavia 'Collateral Damage' or Unlawful Killing? Violations of the Laws of War by NATO During Operation Allied Force* (2000), www.amnesty.org/ailib/intcam/Kosovo/docs/nato_summ.pdf, discussing indiscriminate attacks and criticising the reliance on campaigns involving high-altitude aerial bombardment to minimise combatant casualties. These reports are arguably unrealistic in their expectations of what can be achieved by IHL and demonstrate a tendency to overstate its requirements. It is the constraints of *ius ad bellum* that could in theory achieve the restraints sought.

[93] See e.g. in the context of Kosovo, A. P. V. Rogers, 'Zero-Casualty Warfare' (2000) 837 *IRRC* 165.

[94] Note that Additional Protocol I includes disproportionate attacks within the definition of indiscriminate attacks: see the discussion in chapter 4, note 32 and the accompanying text below.

in IHL.[95] Such a policy, however, clearly weighs in the proportionality equation in *ius ad bellum*. In the case of Kosovo, for example, the legitimate aim of the forceful action by NATO was to bring an end to the human rights abuses against the Kosovars.[96] Were the means employed, however, proportionate to achieve this end? It is debatable as to whether a campaign of high-altitude aerial bombardment dictated by the policy of zero casualties for the attacking force was in fact more likely to exacerbate the humanitarian problem (as indeed appears in hindsight to be the case) than to achieve the ends.[97] There were many who regarded the involvement of ground forces as indispensable to achieving a rapid end to the atrocities. Despite this seeming relevance of proportionality in *ius ad bellum*, scrutiny of the conduct of both the 1990–1 Persian Gulf and Kosovo conflicts has been almost exclusively focused on the requirements of IHL.[98]

Although it is true to say that there will be a theoretical divide between States involved in an armed conflict in terms of their respective legal position under the Charter ban on the use of force, its practical impact is negligible. With some notable exceptions, States invariably conduct themselves on the basis that, whatever the legal status of their forceful actions, be it self-defence or what may be perceived by others as unlawful aggression, proportionality and necessity govern their actions. Even States that claim expansive rights to resort to force do not regard themselves as having the right to use unlimited force.

At the end of the day it is probably as much the mere existence of two differing rules of proportionality that operate simultaneously and in relation to the same activity that is responsible for the marginal attention accorded to the requirements in *ius ad bellum*. The dominant position of the rule in IHL, moreover, owes much to the fact that the

[95] See the further discussion of this issue in chapter 4, note 120 and the accompanying text below.

[96] For the aims of the NATO action in Kosovo, see the statement by the Secretary-General of NATO, Lord Robertson of Port Ellen, 'Kosovo One Year On: Achievement and Challenge', available at www.nato.int/kosovo/repo2000/.

[97] See e.g. Draft Special Report by V. Kröning, 'Kosovo and International Humanitarian Law' (15 October 1999), paras. 26–7, Civilian Affairs Committee, NATO Parliamentary Assembly (copy on file with author); and L. Boisson de Chazournes and L. Condorelli, 'Common Article 1 of the Geneva Conventions Revisited: Protecting Collective Interests' (2000) 837 *IRRC* 67.

[98] See e.g. *Final Report to the Prosecutor by the Committee Established to Review the NATO Bombing Campaign Against the Federal Republic of Yugoslavia*.

tangible human cost of a disproportionate action under IHL is readily demonstrable. Consequently, a considerable range of actors such as the military, the ICRC and legal experts devote their time and expertise to developing, interpreting and disseminating the rule of proportionality in IHL. There is no comparable commitment to the more abstract requirements of proportionality in *ius ad bellum*.

On reflection, proportionality in IHL can be seen as somewhat of a success story. Despite the limitations in that regime and the controversy that it always appears to generate, it has been possible to incorporate the restraints of proportionality into concrete norms that have proved capable of broad application to particular situations. Whether or not its requirements are sufficiently precise to withstand the rigours of criminal prosecutions, however, is another matter that needs careful consideration. Indeed, the difficulties encountered in reaching consensus as to the form of the rule in the Statute of the International Criminal Court and the accompanying Elements of Crimes consolidates the reputation of the norm as one of the most politically contentious of the rules of IHL.[99]

The same conclusion cannot be reached in relation to proportionality in *ius ad bellum*. As yet, an explicit and detailed set of norms for the operation of the principle is lacking. Nevertheless, a general framework for the further refinement of the concept can be discerned from the practice of States.

The application of the requirement of necessity is more straightforward than proportionality. There are not so many variables that can contribute to the decision-making process in determining the necessity to resort to forceful measures in any given situation. What is involved, in the final analysis, is an assessment of when it is reasonable to conclude that all peaceful means have been exhausted or would be to no avail. In that general sense, necessity plays a significant role as a restraint in the use of force under current international law. This is not to suggest, however, that there is not scope for considerable disagreement as to when this situation has in fact been reached, as was evidenced in the response by States to the Iraq disarmament crisis of 2002–3. Nevertheless, the mere fact of the intense debates in this and other situations where forceful action is considered indicates the constraining role of necessity.

[99] See the further discussion of this issue in chapter 4, note 201 and the accompanying text below.

The need for further refinement of these norms has been highlighted by the revival of the global terrorist threat and the 2001 National Security Strategy of the United States in relation to the use of pre-emptive force.[100] With the constraints of the Charter norms on the use of force subjected to considerable strain, necessity and proportionality arguably are all that is left uncontested in the legal regime.

[100] The National Security Strategy of the United States of America, 17 September 2002 available at www.whitehouse.gov/nsc/print/nssall.html.

2 Necessity, proportionality and the forceful actions of States prior to the adoption of the United Nations Charter in 1945

Introduction

This chapter considers the role of necessity and proportionality in the delimitation of the use of force by States up to the adoption of the United Nations Charter in 1945. In relation to unilateral State action, the requirements of necessity and proportionality in *ius ad bellum* find their only current expression in the context of self-defence against an armed attack.[1] These principles, however, have a long history associated with the history of the regulation of the resort to force over the years. Proportionality in particular has played an integral role in the development over many centuries of theories restraining violence. Although the content of the equation has differed widely over the years, the idea that there should be some equivalence between means and ends is a consistent theme of debates over licit and illicit force. During the Middle Ages, proportionality operated both as a limit on the resort to arms and to some extent as a general restraint on the conduct of warfare, albeit without a great deal of definite content in the latter context. Such limitations were derived from the view that disproportionate violence was both unnecessary and undesirable and combined aspects of what is found today in *ius ad bellum* and international humanitarian law (IHL).

Necessity, in the sense that war is by way of last resort when other means have failed to achieve the object, is inherent in much of just war theory.[2] After all, a major impetus for the development of such theories

[1] There is some support for the unilateral right of States to intervene in cases of gross violations of human rights norms: see the discussion in Chapter 5 below.

[2] For example, the canonist St Raymond of Pennaforte (c. 1185–1275) defined the basic position of his fellow canonists as to what was a just cause of war. Included in its

was to limit outbreaks of violence, and if other peaceful means were available for achieving the desired aim then force was not warranted.

In the latter part of the eighteenth century and in the nineteenth century, the resort to force became unregulated and a sovereign right of States. The declining interest in just war theories, combined with the growth in humanism, allowed for a growing focus on the conduct of warfare, and what is today known as IHL emerged as a set of independent rules.[3] The division between the law on the use of force and IHL that occurred during this period was to be permanent. Even with the modern efforts to regulate the resort to force by States, IHL remains theoretically a separate system.[4]

The development of a system of laws regulating the conduct of warfare was slow but accelerated in the latter part of the nineteenth century. Its first focus was the protection of combatants.[5] The genesis of the modern reflection of proportionality in the treatment of combatants, the rules protecting combatants against means and methods of warfare causing unnecessary suffering, occurred during this period. In contrast, proportionality as an identifiable principle in limiting the impact of armed conflict on civilians did not become established until the United Nations Charter era. For some time prior to this, it had been accepted that there should be a distinction between civilians and combatants in armed conflict. This concept, however, was of a very general nature and its philosophical basis and operation varied widely over the years.[6] Even this basic idea that non-combatants should be protected as much as possible from the impact of warfare, an aspiration that was incorporated into the emerging principles of international law,[7] came under

elements was the requirement that the cause be necessary in the sense that there was no other way of achieving the object other than recourse to arms: see M. Keen, *The Laws of War in the Late Middle Ages* (Routledge, London, 1965), pp. 66–7.

3 See P. Haggenmacher, *Grotius et la Doctrine de la Guerre Juste* (Presses universitaires de France, Paris, 1983), p. 599; and G. Best, *War and Law Since 1945* (Oxford University Press, Oxford, 1994), p. 20.

4 See e.g. Opinion and Judgment of the United States Military Tribunal at Nuremberg in *United States* v. *List et al.*, 11 USMT 1948, 757: 'Whatever may be the cause of a war that has broken out, and whether or no the cause be a so-called just cause, the same rules of international law are valid as to what must not be done, and must be done by the belligerents themselves in making war against each other and as between the belligerents and neutral states. This is so, even if the declaration of war is *ipso facto* a violation of international law.'

5 G. Best, 'Restraints on War by Land Before 1945' in M. Howard (ed.), *Restraints on War: Studies in the Limitation of Armed Conflict* (Oxford University Press, Oxford, 1979), p. 17 at p. 27.

6 *Ibid.*, pp. 49–52. 7 *Ibid.*, pp. 27–8.

intense pressure with the development in the first half of the twentieth century of methods of warfare such as aerial bombardment and weapons of mass destruction.[8] Civilians thenceforth became increasingly affected by warfare. IHL responded to these developments and increasingly focused on achieving a legal regime that would provide non-combatants with real protections against modern warfare. The first achievement in this process was the prohibition on the direct targeting of civilians. An additional limit on collateral casualties was a much later development.

Despite the lack of a legal framework for the resort to force following the decline of the just war and until the attempts in the early part of the twentieth century to regulate the resort to force, necessity and proportionality in the *ius ad bellum* sense did not fall entirely into disuse. As for necessity, States did not in reality resort to force with impunity. It seems to have been accepted that force was only warranted as a last resort. Moreover, in most cases, States attempted to justify their forceful actions on a number of grounds.

Proportionality, in the sense of taking account of the broad question as to whether the end justifies the means, found its place to a limited extent during this period in the developing principles of *ius in bello*. States may not have felt constrained to consider whether the resort to force in any given situation would do more harm than good in an overall sense. Nevertheless, proportionality can also moderate the conduct of warfare and limit the overall level of destruction to life and property. It was not surprising, therefore, that States, although asserting that their right to resort to force was unlimited, would still perceive that some limits on its conduct were in their best interests. This broader role for proportionality in assessing whether the means adopted to achieve the ends of war are justified became part of the crystallising new regime restraining the resort to force in the twentieth century. Proportionality in *ius in bello* from then on assumed a narrower focus (albeit more detailed) of protecting civilians and combatants as individuals from the effects of armed conflict. The old just war idea of proportionality as an assessment of whether force was warranted at all when measured against its likely consequences never found its way into this new legal regime regulating the use of force and remains in the realm of politics.

[8] *Ibid.*, pp. 40–53; and R. S. Hartigan, *The Forgotten Victim: A History of the Civilian* (Precedent, Chicago, 1982), pp. 119–20.

This is not to suggest that necessity and proportionality as a restraint on the use of force were established legal concepts in these earlier times. It was inevitable that, with the demise of the just war and the growth of the modern system of nation States, with sovereignty as its basic ordering principle, there would be a gap for a time until States saw it as being in their interests to develop a new system to regulate the resort to force. During this period, the pre-occupation of European States (which to a large extent made up the international community at the time) was on the expansion and consolidation of territorial boundaries. The threat or use of force was integral to the accomplishment of this aim.

The practices that gradually emerged encompassed a broader range of situations in which the use of force was regarded as acceptable than is the case under the United Nations Charter. It appears that considerations as to whether force was necessary and, if so, to what extent, found their place in all these developments. In fact, it was during this era that the 1837 *Caroline Incident*[9] occurred. The ensuing correspondence in relation to the events surrounding this episode is accepted as expressing the modern requirements of legitimate self-defence (and indeed all forceful actions irrespective of their legal basis), namely, necessity and proportionality.

During the latter part of the nineteenth century and the early twentieth century, at the same time as States were moving towards a system based on the peaceful settlement of disputes, the practice developed of States resorting to hostile measures not amounting to war.[10] These took the form of reprisals, pacific blockade and intervention. It appears that one of the requirements of legitimate reprisals was that they be necessary in light of the failure of other methods to achieve satisfaction. Whether or not legitimate reprisals also had to be proportionate was a matter on which views differed.[11]

[9] See note 62 below and the accompanying text for a discussion of the *Caroline Incident*.

[10] For the history of private and public reprisals, see S. Maccoby, 'Reprisals as a Measure of Redress Short of War' (1924) 2 *Cambridge LJ* 60; and E. S. Colbert, *Retaliation in International Law* (King's Crown, New York, 1948), pp. 9–99.

[11] Cf. L. Oppenheim, *International Law: A Treatise*, vol. II, *War and Neutrality* (1st edn, Longmans, Green & Co. Ltd, London, 1906), p. 36; Colbert, *Retaliation in International Law*, p. 76 (writing that proportionality was not evident in the practice of States); and I. Brownlie, *International Law and the Use of Force by States* (Clarendon Press, Oxford, 1963), p. 28 (writing that all forms of intervention had to be proportionate).

The origins of necessity and proportionality in hostile actions between States

Necessity

For centuries, the resort to force was governed by doctrines of the just war that prevailed from early Christian times up to the late seventeenth century.[12] With the collapse of the Holy Roman Empire and the development of the modern system of nation States during the seventeenth and eighteenth centuries, just war theory gradually became secular in nature and then obsolete.[13] However, the medieval Christian theory of the just war, along with secular influences primarily derived from the institution of Chivalry,[14] formed the basis of the secular just war theories of such early international law commentators as Grotius (1583–1645) and Vattel (1714–67). In Grotian theory, war was just for defence, recovery of property and punishment.[15] Although counselling against the hasty resort to force, it is nowhere explicit in his work that a just cause for waging war is dependent on the prior resort to peaceful means to achieve the legitimate ends. Instead, Grotius concentrates on the expectation that a wise ruler will forsake his rights in order to avoid war, especially in the case of punishment.[16] In cases where the justness of the cause was doubtful, however, Grotius identified three methods by which war could be prevented, namely, by means of a conference, through arbitration and by lot.[17]

For Vattel, a just cause of war was for defence and the 'maintenance of rights'.[18] A nation also had the right to use force to prevent such an

[12] Just war theory is the term used to describe the Western tradition that justifies and limits war. See J. Johnson, *Just War Tradition and the Restraint of War* (Princeton University Press, Princeton, 1981), p. xxi. There is considerable debate amongst scholars as to the development and content of just war theory. See e.g. R. Bainton, *Christian Attitudes Toward War and Peace* (Abingdon, Nashville, 1960); J. Johnson, *Ideology, Reason and the Limitation of War* (Princeton University Press, Princeton, 1975); F. H. Russell, *The Just War in the Middle Ages* (Cambridge University Press, Cambridge, 1975).

[13] Just war theory continues to be represented in modern debates over the use of force. See the sources cited in Chapter 1, note 35 and the accompanying text above.

[14] For a discussion of the law of arms based on the institution of chivalry, see M. Keen, *The Laws of War in the Late Middle Ages* (Routledge, London, 1965).

[15] H. Grotius, 'De Jure Belli ac Pacis', trans. by F. Kelsey, in J. Scott (ed.), *The Classics of International Law*, vol. II, book II, Chapter I (Carnegie Endowment for International Peace, Washington DC, 1925), p. 171.

[16] *Ibid.*, Chapter XXIV, pp. 567–77.

[17] *Ibid.*, vol. II, book II, Chapter XXIII, Parts VII, VIII and IX at pp. 560–3.

[18] E. de Vattel, 'Le Droit des Gens, ou Principes de la Loi Naturelle' (1758) trans. by C. Fenwick, in J. Scott (ed.), *The Classics of International Law* (Carnegie Endowment for International Peace, Washington DC, 1916), vol. 3, p. 243, para. 26.

injury and to punish an aggressor. It was an element of a just resort to an offensive war that 'we are unable to obtain it [the just right asserted] otherwise than by force of arms. Necessity alone warrants the use of force. Nature . . . allows of it only in cases of the last extremity, and when all other means fail.'[19] In the context of offensive war undertaken to punish an aggressor nation (the forerunner of reprisals in international law), Vattel wrote: 'A war of this kind must have necessity to justify it: that is to say, that, to be lawful it must be the only remaining mode to obtain a just satisfaction.'[20]

Proportionality

The concept of proportionality was an integral component of just war theory. It is beyond the scope of this work to assess in any detail the influence and operation of proportionality in that tradition. In summary, proportionality in just war theory required an assessment as to whether the overall evil a war would cause was balanced by the good that would be achieved.[21] Once that judgment was made, the conduct of war was of secondary concern.[22] There was, moreover, no independent doctrine of *ius in bello* as exists in international law today. Although just war theory did not entirely dispense with just means, the justness of the resort to war determined to a large extent the limits on the conduct of war, that is, *ius ad bellum* and *ius in bello* were interdependent.[23] As a result, once the cause was just, any means to achieve the end was permissible. This characteristic marked in particular the early Christian just war theory of St Augustine. St Augustine is regarded as having first developed the Christian theory of the just war. There is no suggestion in St Augustine's theory of any significant limitations on the methods of warfare. Once the cause was just, the means used for its implementation were irrelevant.[24]

Despite the concentration on the justness of the resort to force that prevailed during the long reign of the just war, the idea of proportionality in the conduct of war can be discerned in the work of the later canonists and the secular law of arms of the Middle Ages.[25] For example,

[19] *Ibid.*, p. 246, para. 37. [20] *Ibid.*, p. 247, para. 41.

[21] For an assessment of proportionality in the just war theory of St Thomas Aquinas, see P. Ramsey, *War and the Christian Conscience: How Shall Modern War Be Conducted Justly?* (Duke University Press, Durham, NC, 1961), pp. 34–6; and Johnson, *Just War Tradition*, p. xxii.

[22] Russell, *The Just War*, pp. 307–8. [23] *Ibid.*

[24] See *ibid.*, pp. 16–39; and Ramsey, *War and the Christian Conscience*, pp. 15–33.

[25] See Johnson, *Ideology, Reason and the Limitation of War*, pp. 26–80 (for a description of the development and content of the so-called classic doctrine of the just war that had

over the centuries there were attempts to regulate the means of warfare. The use of crossbows, bows and arrows and siege machines was banned in wars between Christians by the Second Lateran Council of 1139.[26] The extent to which, however, the medieval prohibitions were based on considerations of proportionality is not clear. Johnson argues that the question of the unnecessary suffering caused by the use of these weapons was not the issue as this limitation on weapons was restricted to wars amongst Christians. Rather, the ban on such weapons, more likely to be used by soldiers and mercenaries, was an attempt to limit warfare to the knightly classes.[27]

In the case of civilians, the modern idea that they should be immune to some extent from the effects of warfare is by no means a new development. The idea of distinguishing between those who participate in hostilities and those who do not has a long history and evolved over the many centuries in which just war theory prevailed.[28] The origins and theoretical basis of the rules protecting non-combatants were not, however, as is the case today, concerned with protecting individuals. Non-combatant immunity, as it became known, functioned as a means of containing or limiting violence in the interests of society generally. During the era of the just war, Canon law, through such means as the 'Peace of God', developed categories of persons who were immune from the effects of warfare.[29] The distinction between combatants and non-combatants was drawn in the Canonical doctrine on the basis of occupation. Clerics, monks and friars, for example, were entitled to 'full security against the ravages of war'.[30] The basis of this immunity in the Canon tradition was self-interest, to protect the institution of Christianity. Humanitarian considerations were not involved. Over the years, the categories of persons who were immune from warfare expanded

emerged at the end of the Middle Ages). In Johnson's view, the limits on warfare in classic just war doctrine were primarily derived from the influence of the Chivalric code (*ibid.*, p. 80).

[26] See Johnson, *Just War Tradition*, p. 128; and Russell, *The Just War*, pp. 156–7.

[27] See Johnson, *Just War Tradition*, pp. xxiii and 128–39.

[28] For an account of the evolution of non-combatant immunity, from its earliest foundations in primitive and ancient warfare to modern times, see Hartigan, *The Forgotten Victim*.

[29] The Peace of God was drawn up during the reign of Pope Gregory IX in the eleventh century and listed eight classes of persons who were entitled to full protection from the direct effects of warfare. For a description of the Peace of God, see F. H. Russell, *A History of Medieval Christianity: Prophecy and Order* (T. Y. Crowell, New York, 1968), p. 25; and Hartigan, *The Forgotten Victim*, pp. 65–75.

[30] Johnson, *Just War Tradition*, p. 127.

in the interests of keeping society stable. Once again, the motivation for such initiatives was not humanitarian. It is doubtful, moreover, whether these protections were effective in practice for the ordinary peasant.[31]

The secular Chivalric tradition similarly provided protection for other groups.[32] In Chivalric tradition, the distinction between non-combatants and combatants was drawn between the 'enemy' and the 'innocents'. The enemy were those who carried arms; the innocents did not. This differentiation created a class of inferior individuals requiring protection and thus ratified the superior position of knightly men.

As the just war theories of the Middle Ages merged into the purely secular theories of such commentators as Grotius and Vattel, proportionality was a component of their analyses, but in the *ius ad bellum* sense of the word. After defining the just and unjust causes of war, Grotius counsels against the rash resort to war even in a just cause.[33] A ruler should balance the evil and the good that may result from the just war. The effectiveness of the means to contribute to the good must be part of this balancing process and resort should be had to war only if the likely result will contribute more to good than to evil.[34] This is a classic proportionality argument, and Grotius provides by way of example a dilemma between the forceful pursuit of freedom that may result in the slaughter of one's own people and the alternative of peace without freedom. The evil of the former, in his view, outweighs the good of the latter and thus does not warrant a resort to war.[35]

Consequently, proportionality in the time of the just war and in both the Christian and secular doctrines had a considerably broader focus than the current test of proportionality under the United Nations Charter regime on the use of force. Unlike today, in these earlier theories proportionality was part of the rules that determined whether a resort to force was initially warranted and took account of what are nowadays a combination of political, legal, moral and philosophical factors. The

[31] Keen, *The Laws of War*, p. 190.

[32] See Johnson, *Just War Tradition*, pp. 131ff, where the author traces the impact of the complex rules and practices of the law of arms based on Chivalric notions on the developing *ius in bello*. See also R. S. Hartigan, 'Noncombatant Immunity: Reflections on Its Origins and Present Status' (1966) 29 *Review of Politics* 204 at 214. For an excellent study of the law of arms, see Keen, *The Laws of War*, who describes this body of law as 'some sort of prototype of the Geneva Convention, a branch of international law governing the conduct of war' (*ibid.*, p. 2).

[33] Grotius, 'De Jure Belli ac Pacis', Chapter XXIV, Part I, p. 567.

[34] *Ibid.*, Part V, pp. 571–2.

[35] *Ibid.*, Parts V–VI, pp. 573–4.

decision to use force in just war theory was a two-stage process. Was the cause just? Was it proportionate to pursue this cause given the costs involved? Proportionality in those times was theoretically a restraint on the resort to force, not just its conduct, and it is this wider role of proportionality that modern just war scholars would like to see as part of the current legal proportionality equation. To some extent, their criticism is unwarranted, as the situations in which States nowadays can legitimately resort to the unilateral use of force have been drastically curtailed. That is, under the United Nations Charter system the costs of forceful actions always outweigh the benefits except in cases of a defensive response to an armed attack and arguably in cases of widespread human rights violations.

In so far as the conduct of war was concerned, the theme of restraints on weapons is reflected during the secular just war era in the continuation of the age-old debate over poisoned weapons. Gentili (1550–1608), drawing on historical practices, observes, '[w]hat the law permits to be done you may not therefore do in any way you choose', and condemned the use of poisoned weapons in war.[36] Grotius and Vattel concurred.[37] The basis of this denouncement varies. A common theme is the incompatibility of these weapons with Chivalric principles of what is honourable and princely in warfare.[38] Moreover, they are 'utterly destructive in nature'[39] and although '[y]ou must of course strike your enemy in order to get the better of his efforts: but if he is once disabled, is it necessary that he should inevitably die of his wounds?'[40] Here can be seen the forerunner of the modern prohibition on weapons causing superfluous injury or unnecessary suffering. It is nowadays well established that the only purpose of war is to disable the enemy, not to render their death inevitable or needlessly painful. According to Grotius, such a law was to

[36] A. Gentili, 'De Jure Belli Libri Tres' (1612), trans. by J. Rolfe, in J. Scott (ed.), *The Classics of International Law*, vol. II, book II, Chapter I (Carnegie Endowment for International Peace, Washington DC, 1933), para. 250 at para. 255.

[37] Grotius, 'De Jure Belli ac Pacis', book III, Chapter IV, Parts XV and XVI, pp. 651–3; de Vattel, 'Le Droit des Gens', Chapter VIII, para. 156 at para. 289. Cf. C. van Bynkershoek, 'Quaestionum Juris Publici Libri Duo' (1737), trans. by T. Frank, in J. Scott (ed.), *The Classics of International Law* (Carnegie Endowment for International Peace, Washington DC, 1930), book I, p. 16; and C. Wolff, 'Jus Gentium Methodo Scientifica Pertractatum' (1764), trans. by J. Drake, in J. Scott (ed.), *The Classics of International Law* (Carnegie Endowment for International Peace, Washington DC, 1934), p. 450.

[38] Gentili, 'De Jure Belli Libri Tres', paras. 250–6.

[39] *Ibid.*, para. 250.

[40] De Vattel, 'Le Droit des Gens', para. 156.

the 'common advantage, in order that the dangers of war, which had begun to be frequent, might not be too widely extended'.[41]

As for non-combatants, according to Grotius the law of nations confers an unlimited right to injure persons and property in a just cause.[42] This right 'extends not only to those who actually bear arms, or are subjects of him that stirs up the war, but in addition to all persons who are in the enemy's territory', including women and children.[43] What is permissible under the law of nations, however, is not without moral limitations.[44] For example, Grotius cautions '[n]ot even in a lawful war ought we to admit that which is said in the line, He, who refuses what is just, yields all'.[45] On the issue of innocent persons, Grotius writes: 'It is the bidding of mercy, if not of justice, that except for reasons that are weighty and will affect the safety of many, no action should be attempted whereby innocent persons may be threatened with destruction.'[46] This classification of the enemy and the innocent is based primarily, although not exclusively, on those who carry arms and those who do not and is derived from the earlier Chivalric tradition.[47]

Vattel, writing a century later, was somewhat more specific. He was the last of the writers of comprehensive treatises of international law to deal with just war theory.[48] In his view, moderation was an essential component of the just war. Vattel further developed the idea discernible in the writings of Grotius that it was possible to have a war that was just on both sides.[49] This allowed for the greater focus in Vattel's work

[41] Grotius, 'De Jure Belli ac Pacis', book III, Part XV, pp. 651–2.

[42] *Ibid.*, book III, Chapter IV, Parts III–XV, pp. 643–51.

[43] *Ibid.*, Chapter IV, Part VI, p. 646 and Part IX, p. 648. F. Kalshoven, 'Grotius' *Jus in Bello* with Special Reference to Ruses of War and Perfidy' in A. Dufour, P. Haggenmacher and J. Toman (eds.), *Grotius et l'Ordre Juridique International* (Payot, Lausanne, 1985), p. 101 at p. 105 (confirming that Grotius cannot be interpreted as suggesting any limitations on the conduct of warfare comparable to the requirements of the modern rule of proportionality). See also G. Best, 'The Place of Grotius in the Development of International Humanitarian Law' in *Grotius et l'Ordre Juridique International*, p. 101 at pp. 105–6.

[44] Grotius, 'De Jure Belli ac Pacis', Chapter IV, Part II, pp. 641–3 (distinguishing between that which is 'permissible' (lawful) and that which is without moral wrong).

[45] *Ibid.*, Chapter XI, Part I, p. 722.

[46] *Ibid.*, Part VIII, pp. 733–4. Grotius then sets out several categories of persons who should be spared: see Chapter XI, Parts IX–XVIII, pp. 734–43.

[47] Grotius, 'De Jure Belli ac Pacis', Part VIII, pp. 733–4.

[48] See H. Bull, B. Kingsbury and A. Roberts (eds.), *Hugo Grotius and International Relations* (Clarendon Press, Oxford, 1990), p. 22.

[49] Vattel, 'Le Droit de Gens', Chapter III, p. 247, para. 40.

on what we know as *ius in bello*. For him, the emphasis of the law of nations with respect to war was on its conduct. Consequently, in Vattel's view: 'Apart from the case in which there is no question of punishing the enemy, the whole may be summed up in this general rule: All acts of hostility which injure the enemy without necessity or which do not tend to procure victory . . . are unjustifiable, and as such are condemned by the natural law.'[50] Here the emergence of the shift from *ius ad bellum* to *ius in bello* can be clearly seen. The distinction between the enemy as those who carry arms and the innocents, who do not, is also reflected in the work of Vattel.[51]

With the advent of the system of nation States, the philosophy underlying the distinction between combatants and civilians underwent a change. The writings of commentators such as Rousseau (1712–78) contributed significantly to the modern view that the individual is entitled to be protected from the effects of warfare to the extent consistent with the demands of military necessity, and allowed for rapid progress in the development of *ius in bello*. Rousseau based his views of the position of civilians during times of armed conflict on the theory that war was a contest between States and not individuals:

> War is constituted by a relation between things, not between persons . . . War then is a relation not between man and man, but between State and State, in war individuals are enemies only accidentally, not as men, not even as citizens, but only as soldiers, not as members of their country, but as its defenders.[52]

War as a sovereign right of States: the demise of *ius ad bellum*

The demise of the just war and the emergence of the system of nation States saw the growth of the concept of war as an instrument of national policy.[53] Clausewitz's famous aphorism sums up this development: 'War

[50] *Ibid.*, Chapter IX, pp. 294–5, para. 172. See also G. Best, *Humanity in Warfare: The Modern History of the International Law of Armed Conflict* (Weidenfeld & Nicolson, London, 1980), pp. 54–5.

[51] Vattel, 'Le Droit des Gens', Chapter V, paras. 71–2, 259 and Chapter VIII, paras. 136ff and 279ff and paras. 147 and 283.

[52] J. Rousseau, *The Social Contract and Discourses* (trans. by G. Cole, Dent, London, 1973), pp. 170–1. Rousseau based these principles not on the writings of Grotius but on 'the nature of reality and reason'.

[53] See Brownlie, *International Law and the Use of Force by States in International Law*, pp. 10–50 (for a discussion of developments during this period).

is a mere continuation of policy by other means.'[54] The age-old debate as to the distinction between just and unjust causes of war, that had been the focus of all studies of war since Christian times, was abandoned during this period. There were several factors that led to the demise of the notion of the just war. First, a final arbiter of the justness of the resort to force was intrinsic to the Christian doctrine of the just war.[55] During the era of the just war, theoretically it was the Pope who was the final arbiter in the determination of a just resort to force. It was not purely a matter for individual princes to assess the justness of their cause. With the decline in the overall authority of the Church, how was the justness of the resort to force to be determined? The question had to be left to each individual State. War, thus, could be subjectively just on both sides, logically leading to the legality of every resort to force.[56] Secondly, the nineteenth century was the era of the growth of positivism. Just war theory was based on divine law and the law of nature and had no part to play in the scientific discipline of international law. The emphasis was on determining not what law should be but what it was.[57] The attitude of international law to war was described by Hall in the following terms: 'International law has no alternative but to accept war, independently of the justice of its origin, as a relation which the parties to it may set up if they choose, and to busy itself only in regulating the effects.'[58]

Although at this time it would have been inaccurate to talk in terms of rules regulating the resort to force, Brownlie, in the context of the nineteenth century, observes that '[t]he customary law shows greater complexity than is commonly assumed'.[59] Although theoretically the resort to war was a sovereign right of States, there was a complex body of customary rules emerging from the practice of States of providing

[54] C. Clausewitz, *On War* (trans. by Colonel J. J. Graham, Penguin, Baltimore, 1968), p. 119.

[55] See A. Nussbaum, *A Concise History of the Law of Nations* (Macmillan, New York, 1947), p. 23; and Myres S. McDougal and Florentino P. Feliciano, *Law and Minimum World Public Order: The Legal Regulation of International Coercion* (Yale University Press, New Haven, 1961), p. 113.

[56] J. Kunz, 'Bellum Justum and Bellum Legale' (1951) 45 *AJIL* 528 at 531.

[57] See e.g. H. Wheaton, 'Elements of International Law' (1866) in J. Scott (ed.), *Classics of International Law* (Oxford University Press, Oxford, 1936), p. 309, para. 290.

[58] W. Hall, *A Treatise on International Law* (ed. by P. Higgins, 8th edn, Clarendon Press, Oxford, 1924), p. 82.

[59] Brownlie, *International Law and the Use of Force by States*, p. 40, and see the summary of the state of the customary law by 1920, *ibid.*, pp. 46–7.

justifications for such uses of force.[60] Included in these emerging practices was also the idea that war should be a matter of last resort.[61]

The *Caroline Incident* occurred during this time and its formulation of necessity and proportionality has come to represent the position under the United Nations Charter system. The *Caroline Incident* was set against the background of the 1837 Canadian rebellion against the British.[62] The rebels, many of them American citizens, had established bases both within Canada and in the adjacent territory of the United States from which various aggressive actions against British forces were taken. Although requested to do so, the American authorities had been unable to enforce the laws of neutrality in relation to these activities taking place on its territory.[63] At the time of the incident, the steamer *Caroline* had been ferrying supplies and reinforcements from the United States to a group of rebels established on Navy Island in Upper Canada. To bring an end to these activities, a British force from Canada entered United States territory, boarded the *Caroline* and sent her over the Niagara Falls. Two United States nationals were killed in the incident.

It is the ensuing correspondence between Webster, the American Secretary of State, and Lord Ashburton, acting on behalf of the British Government, that is of significance to international lawyers.[64] After an exchange of notes, Webster, in the now famous elaboration of necessity of self-defence, required the British Government to show a 'necessity of

[60] See *ibid.*, p. 41. See also R. Age, *Addendum to the Eighth Report on State Responsibility*, Agenda Item 2, A/CN.4/Ser.A/1980/Add.1 (Part 1), Doc. A/CN.4/318/Add.5–7 (1980-II) (1) *YBILC* 69 (observing that these practices of States of providing justifications for their aggressive actions 'could not be regarded as reflecting any realisation of the need for a "legal justification" of their comportment'). There was a lack of unanimity amongst commentators as to these developments, and a confusing range of terminology characterised the debate. According to Brownlie, *International Law and the Use of Force by States*, p. 43, the terms 'self-defence' and 'self-preservation' were used interchangeably, along with 'necessity' and 'necessity of defence', and, for Bowett, 'self-preservation' was a generic term for 'self-defence', 'self-help' and 'necessity' (D. Bowett, *Self-Defence in International Law* (Manchester University Press, Manchester, 1958), pp. 9–10). See also G. Schwarzenberger, 'The Fundamental Principles of International Law' (1955–I) 87 *Recueil des Cours* 195 at 343–6; and J. L. Brierly, *The Law of Nations: An Introduction to the International Law of Peace* (Clarendon Press, Oxford, 1928), pp. 158–9.

[61] See Brownlie, *International Law and the Use of Force by States*, pp. 21–2 and 49.

[62] For a full description of the *Caroline Incident*, see R. Jennings, 'The Caroline and McLeod Cases' (1938) 32 *AJIL* 82 at 91; and Brownlie, *International Law and the Use of Force by States*, p. 43.

[63] See B. Cheng, *General Principles of Law as Applied by International Courts and Tribunals* (Stevens and Sons, London, 1953), p. 85.

[64] The relevant correspondence can be found in Parliamentary Papers (1842), vol. LXI in *British and Foreign State Papers* vol. 30, p. 195 at p. 201.

self-defence, instant, overwhelming, leaving no choice of means, and no moment for deliberation'.[65] Lord Ashburton replied: 'we are perfectly agreed as to the general principles of international law applicable to this unfortunate case.'[66] The only question, therefore, was whether the facts of the case fitted within the description of necessity of self-defence, and Lord Ashburton set out at some length reasons why this was the case. Although not conceding the point, the United States allowed the matter to rest there.

As to proportionality, Webster wrote: 'It will be for it to be shown, also, that the local authorities of Canada, even supposing the necessity of the moment . . . did nothing unreasonable or excessive; since the act justified by that necessity of self-defence, must be limited by that necessity, and kept clearly within it.'[67] None of the contemporary commentaries on the incident deals with this aspect of the proposed test, despite the fact that Webster expressed the view (in relation to the setting on fire of the *Caroline* and sending her over the falls) that '[a] necessity for all this, the Government of the United States cannot believe existed'.[68] Lord Ashburton responded to this allegation of disproportionate conduct as follows:

> I have only further to notice the highly coloured picture drawn in your note, of the facts attending the execution of this service. Some importance is attached to the attack having been made in the night, and the vessel having been set on fire and floated down the falls of the river, and it is insinuated, rather than asserted, that there was carelessness as to the lives of the persons on board . . . The time of night was purposely selected as most likely to ensure the execution with the least loss of life . . . that the strength of the current not permitting the vessel to be carried off, and it being necessary to destroy her by fire, she was drawn into the stream for the express purpose of preventing injury to persons or property of the inhabitants of Schlosser.[69]

Commentators differ as to the legal basis of the British response, although in the correspondence of the Law Officers the only reference was to self-preservation. In Bowett's view, as there was no pre-existing delictual act by the United States Government, it was a case of self-preservation, not self-defence: 'strictly speaking, therefore, vis-à-vis the United States the action taken by Great Britain was taken by virtue of its

[65] *Ibid*., p. 201. [66] *Ibid*., p. 195. [67] *Ibid*., p. 202.

[68] This is from the enclosure in the note to Ashburton dated 17 July 1842 and is reproduced earlier in the *British and Foreign State Papers*.

[69] Parliamentary Papers (1842), vol. LXI, in *British and Foreign State Papers*, vol. 30, p. 195 at p. 199.

right of necessity, though the principles governing the actual exercise of the right, as stated by Webster, were applicable both to necessity and self-defence.'[70] As Jennings observes, however, the term self-defence 'whether inadvertently or by design, crept into the correspondence. In using that phrase the diplomatists were almost certainly not consciously attempting to introduce a new concept into the law. But once the phrase had been introduced, it was possible for lawyers of a later day to give it a legal content.'[71] In the opinion of other commentators, however, the British justification for its action was self-defence.[72] For Jennings, 'it was in the Caroline case that self-defence was changed from a political excuse to a legal doctrine'.[73] Moreover, it now had a distinctive formulation that was to make the transition to the Charter system on the use of force.

Irrespective of the correct categorisation of the *Caroline Incident*, the idea that the use of force must be both necessary and proportionate was by no means from then on established in the practice of States. As to necessity, up to the First World War (1914–18) and the attempts thereafter to restrict the right to resort to force, the idea that States should seek pacific means of settling disputes before resorting to force co-existed uneasily with the use of force as a sovereign right of States.[74] There were as yet no developed customary rules that limited the situations in which States could resort to force. It would, therefore, be premature to suggest that there was at this time an accepted doctrine of necessity in the context of the use of force as we see it today. Brownlie concludes that the right of States to resort to force and the idea of war as the last resort in asserting rights after peaceful means had failed existed together in 'the somewhat contradictory practice of States'.[75]

To what extent was proportionality relevant during this period in the context of the use of force? As we have seen, it was a component of the *Caroline* formulation. Although the correspondence in this incident is referred to in various contexts, commentators infrequently address

[70] Bowett, *Self-Defence*, pp. 59–60; see also Commentary on the Draft Articles on Responsibility of States for Internationally Wrongful Acts, Report of the International Law Commission on the Work of Its Fifty-Sixth session, GAOR, 56th Sess., Supp. No. 10, UN Doc. A/56/10 (2001), pp. 196–7.

[71] Jennings, 'The Caroline and McLeod Cases', p. 92.

[72] See Brownlie, *International Law and the Use of Force by States*, p. 261.

[73] See Jennings, 'The Caroline and McLeod Cases', p. 82.

[74] See Brownlie, *International Law and the Use of Force by States*, pp. 49–50.

[75] *Ibid.*, p. 50.

its proportionality aspect until the time of the League of Nations.[76] Wheaton, for example, writing in 1866, does not even categorise the *Caroline Incident* as illustrative of any limitation on the right of self-preservation (which he regards as an absolute right of States)[77] but as an example of the rights of war as to neutrals.[78] Hall, in contrast, some thirty years later in 1895, reaffirms the requirement of the *Caroline Incident* (which he regards as an example of the right of self-preservation) 'that the acts done by way of self-protection shall be limited to those which are barely necessary for the purpose'.[79] Oppenheim, early last century, deals with the necessity aspect of the *Caroline Incident* but does not mention proportionality.[80]

One explanation for this lack of focus on proportionality may have been that, during the period when war was a sovereign right of States, the developing rules of *ius in bello* performed to some extent the function of proportionality that was encompassed in the *Caroline* formulation and is nowadays reflected in the law on self-defence. Today, proportionality in *ius in bello* no longer regulates the broad question of how attacks relate to the aims of the use of force. This function is part of *ius ad bellum*. However, when the resort to force was a sovereign right of States, proportionality in that latter broad sense did not fall entirely into disuse. This is clear from the writings of commentators during this period. Wheaton writes:

> In general it may be stated, that the rights of war, in respect of the enemy, are to be measured by the object of the war. Until that object is attained, the belligerent has, strictly speaking, a right to use every means to accomplish the end for which he has taken up arms . . . No use of force is lawful, except so far as it is necessary. A belligerent has, therefore, no right to take away the lives of those subjects of the enemy whom he can subdue by any other means.[81]

Hall continues this process of combining to some extent the modern *ius ad bellum* and *ius in bello* notions of proportionality. He includes in his discussion of limitations on the kinds of violence available to a belligerent 'that acts not only cease to be permitted so soon as it is shown that they are wanton, but when they are grossly disproportioned to the

[76] *Ibid.*, p. 261.
[77] Wheaton, 'Elements of International Law', p. 441. [78] *Ibid.*, pp. 75ff.
[79] See W. E. Hall, *A Treatise on International Law* (4th edn, Clarendon Press, Oxford, 1895), p. 282.
[80] See L. Oppenheim, *International Law: A Treatise*, vol. I, *Peace* (1st edn, Longmans, Green & Co. Ltd, London, 1906), pp. 177–81.
[81] Wheaton, 'Elements of International Law', pp. 358–9, para. 342.

object to be attained'.[82] Although Hall is here discussing the law of war, the limitations he refers to would today be regarded as incorporating considerations belonging to *ius ad bellum*.[83]

In conclusion, at the end of the nineteenth century, although the idea was expressed from time to time that the use of force should not be out of proportion to the situation that had provoked it, this limitation had not received the support of States necessary for it to acquire the status of customary international law.

The revival of *ius ad bellum* in the twentieth century

The Covenant of the League of Nations adopted in 1919 imposed restraints on the liberty of States to resort to war.[84] A system of peaceful settlement of disputes was set up under the Covenant and the resort to force was forbidden without the dispute being first submitted to arbitration, judicial settlement or the League Council.[85] Necessity, therefore, was an integral component of the system established by the Covenant and, as Waldock observes, the legitimacy of war was dependent on prior efforts to achieve settlement of the dispute and not, as is the case today, on the grounds for resorting to war.[86] The General Treaty for the Renunciation of War (the Kellogg–Briand Pact) was signed at Paris in 1928 and ratified or adhered to by sixty-three States.[87] By Article 1, State Parties condemned recourse to war 'for the solution of international controversies and renounce[d] it as an instrument of national policy in their relations with one another'. By Article 2 it was agreed by the parties that 'the settlement or solution of all disputes or conflicts, of whatever nature or whatever origin they may be, which may arise among

[82] Hall, *International Law* (4th edn), p. 551.

[83] *Ibid.*, pp. 551ff (one such limitation relates to the 'conditions under which a country may be devastated' (*ibid.*, pp. 553–7)).

[84] For the effect of the Covenant of the League of Nations on the right of States to resort to force, see J. Brierly, *The Law of Nations* (Clarendon Press, Oxford, 1928), pp. 310–11. See also Brownlie, *International Law and the Use of Force by States*, pp. 239–40.

[85] See *ibid.*, pp. 55–6.

[86] See C. H. M. Waldock, 'The Regulation of the Use of Force by Individual States in International Law' (1952-II) 81 *Recueil des Cours* 455 at 469.

[87] For details of the Pact, see Q. Wright, 'The Meaning of the Pact of Paris' (1933) 27 *AJIL* 39; and *Oppenheim's International Law: A Treatise*, vol. II, *Disputes, War and Neutrality* (ed. by H. Lauterpacht, 7th edn, Longmans, Green & Co. Ltd, London, 1952), pp. 181ff.

them, shall never be sought except by pacific means'.[88] The adoption of the Pact, however, was on the basis that the right of self-defence was expressly reserved to States and a very wide interpretation was placed on what that right entailed.[89]

The resort to force, however, was not otherwise unregulated.[90] Waldock writes that the customary law at the time strictly limited self-defence to 'cases where there [was] an instant need to take defensive action against an imminent invasion of legal rights'.[91] The proportionality equation, moreover, was articulated by several commentators during the period of the League. The focus tended to be on the gravity of the attack: '[q]ue les moyens employés pour la défense soient proportionnés à l'attaque'.[92] It will be recalled that self-defence at this time was a much broader right than a response to an armed attack: 'A state, like an individual, may protect itself against an attack, actual or threatened. Moreover, the security of a state may be threatened by another, either of set policy, or by the latter's impotence or misgovernment.'[93] The assessment of proportionality, therefore, reflected this wider scope as, for example, in the response to an anticipated attack: 'la riposte ne dépasse pas ce qui est nécessaire pour le péril qui menace l'attaque.'[94] Brierly, however, stressed the illegitimacy of the continued use of force to achieve ulterior goals after the danger had passed.[95] In the broader, ill-defined right of self-preservation, still maintained by some writers, proportionality based on the *Caroline* formulation was a component. Consequently, the 1924 edition of Hall's *International Law* reiterates 'that the acts done by way of self-protection shall be limited to those which are barely necessary for the purpose'.[96]

[88] For a discussion of the meaning of the treaty, see D. Miller, *The Peace Pact of Paris* (Putnam, 1928), pp. 121–8; and cf. Brownlie, *International Law and the Use of Force by States*, p. 90.

[89] See *ibid.*, pp. 235–46.

[90] On the right of self-defence generally during the time of the League of Nations, see E. Giraud, 'La Théorie de la Légitime Défence' (1934-III) 49 *Recueil des Cours* 691.

[91] Waldock, 'The Regulation of the Use of Force by Individual States in International Law', p. 77.

[92] L. de Brouckère, 'La Prévention de la Guerre' (1934-IV) 50 *Recueil des Cours* 1 at 33. See also H. Accioly, *Traité de Droit International Public* (Recueil Sirey, Paris, 1940), p. 461.

[93] See Brierly, *The Law of Nations*, p. 157.

[94] L. de Brouckère, 'La Prévention de la Guerre', p. 33.

[95] J. L. Brierly, 'Règles Générales du Droit de la Paix' (1936-IV) 58 *Recueil des Cours* 5 at 139.

[96] W. E. Hall, *A Treatise on International Law* (ed. by P. Higgins, 8th edn, Clarendon Press, Oxford, 1924), p. 323.

Measures short of war

Reprisals emerged in the practice of States in the latter half of the nineteenth century and were of considerable significance.[97] States resorted to these measures in attempts to settle their differences without recourse to war. Oppenheim defined reprisals as 'such injurious and otherwise internationally illegal acts of one State against another as are exceptionally permitted for the purpose of compelling the latter to consent to a satisfactory settlement of a difference created by its own international delinquency'.[98] The coercive nature of reprisals is confirmed by Colbert in her thorough study of State practice in relation to public reprisals during the nineteenth and twentieth centuries.[99]

Most commentators regard the *Naulilaa Arbitration* as authoritatively establishing the conditions for legitimate reprisals.[100] The arbitration arose out of an incident in 1915 in which three German nationals were killed by members of the Portuguese frontier post at Naulilaa in Portuguese South West Africa (now Angola). By way of reprisal, the Governor of German South West Africa (now Namibia) ordered the attack and destruction of a number of forts in the frontier region of Portuguese territory. After forcing the surrender of the garrison at Naulilaa who retreated into Portuguese territory, the German forces withdrew, whereupon the indigenous population looted the evacuated areas. Portugal claimed that the reprisal was excessive and that Germany was responsible for the damage caused.

The Arbitral Commission to which the dispute was referred decided that for a reprisal to be lawful the State against which the reprisal was directed must have committed a breach of international law. An action by way of legitimate reprisal, moreover, must be preceded by a request that the injury be redressed. In the view of the Commission, even if Portugal had committed a breach of international law, the reprisal action was unlawful for two reasons. First, there had been no previous request

[97] For a discussion of reprisals in international law prior to the adoption of the United Nations Charter, see E. S. Colbert, *Retaliation in International Law*; and M. S. Séfériadès, 'La Question des Represailles Armées en Temps de Paix, en l'Etat actuel du Droit des Gens' (1934) 17 *Révue de Droit International et de Legislation Comparée* 138.

[98] *Oppenheim's International Law: A Treatise*, vol. II, *Disputes, War and Neutrality* (ed. by H. Lauterpacht, 7th edn, Longmans, Green and Co. Ltd, London, 1952), p. 136.

[99] See Colbert, *Retaliation in International Law*, pp. 60–103.

[100] *Naulilaa Arbitration (Portugal* v. *Germany)*, 2 RIAA 1928, 1012. See Waldock, 'The Regulation of the Use of Force by Individual States in International Law', p. 460 (for a discussion of the *Naulilaa* case). As to the effect of the League of Nations on reprisals, see *ibid.*, pp. 475–6 and 458–9.

for redress: 'Employment of force is not justified . . . except by the character of necessity. There was . . . recourse to force without previous attempt to obtain satisfaction by legal means.'[101] Secondly, the reprisal was disproportionate. On the issue of proportionality and reprisals, the Arbitral Commission noted:

> The most recent doctrine [of reprisals], notably the German doctrine . . . does not require that the reprisal be proportioned to the offence. On this point, authors, unanimous for some years, are now divided in opinion. The majority considers a certain proportion between offence and reprisal a necessary condition of the legitimacy of the latter. International law in process of formation as a result of the experience of the last war tends certainly to restrain the notion of legitimate reprisals and to prohibit their abuse.[102]

The Arbitral Commission concluded: 'Even if one admits that international law does not require that reprisals be measured approximately by the offence, one must certainly consider as excessive, and consequently illicit, reprisals out of all proportion to the act that has motivated them.'[103] In the present case, 'there was an evident disproportion between the incident of *Naulilaa* and the six acts of reprisals which have followed it'.[104]

Although the Arbitral Commission was of the view that forcible reprisals were only legitimate if dictated by necessity, other means of obtaining satisfaction having failed, the extent to which this requirement reflected the practice of States at the time is not clear.[105] The matter became moot, however, with the decline in resort to reprisals in the period leading up to the Second World War.[106]

In relation to proportionality, as the Arbitral Commission in the *Naulilaa Arbitration* observed, there were writers who regarded it as a necessary element of reprisal action.[107] According to a leading authority of the time 'reprisals must be in proportion to the wrong done, and to the amount of compulsion necessary to get reparation'.[108] State practice, however, was not consistent in this regard.[109] There were numerous

[101] *Naulilaa Arbitration*, para. 1027.
[102] *Ibid.*, para. 1026. [103] *Ibid.*, para. 1028. [104] *Ibid.*
[105] See e.g. Brownlie, *International Law and the Use of Force by States*, pp. 220–2.
[106] See *ibid.*, p. 222.
[107] See e.g. Hall, *International Law* (ed. by P. Higgins, 8th edn, Clarendon Press, Oxford, 1924), p. 434; and Waldock, 'The Regulation of the Use of Force by Individual States in International Law', pp. 458–9.
[108] See *Oppenheim's International Law: A Treatise*, vol. II, *Disputes, War and Neutrality* (ed. by H. Lauterpacht, 7th edn), p. 141 (citing in note 2 authors who disagreed with this view).
[109] See Brownlie, *International Law and the Use of Force by States*, p. 220.

examples of reprisals where proportionality was clearly not a restraining factor. Amongst the outstanding examples is the forceful occupation by the United States of Vera Cruz in 1914 in response to the unlawful arrest by the Mexican authorities of three United States seamen. President Wilson articulated the resort to armed force as necessary to obtain the 'fullest recognition of the rights and dignity of the United States'.[110] The 1923 bombardment and occupation of the island of Corfu by Italian forces also involved an excessive response to an alleged wrong on the part of Greece, but was uncondemned by the Conference of Ambassadors convened by the Council of the League of Nations to consider the issue.[111]

In the view of one commentator, the statement of the *Naulilaa* Arbitral Commission on proportionality 'although reflecting the opinions of international lawyers, has little or no support in the practice of states'.[112] Moreover, amongst those who accepted that proportionality was a requirement of legitimate reprisals, there was no unanimity as to its application.[113] Many of the difficulties experienced in articulating the test of proportionality in relation to reprisals stemmed from the failure to agree as to their goal. An established referent against which to measure the reprisal action was missing.[114] Consequently, if retribution were the aim, the gravity of the offence could be a relevant factor in the assessment of proportionality. If what was sought was reparations, then the damage or injury suffered would be a primary factor to take into account in the assessment of what was a proportionate response. In the *Naulilaa Arbitration*, the important factor that led to a finding by

[110] See C. C. Hyde, *International Law Chiefly as Interpreted and Applied by the United States* (3 vols., 2nd edn, Little, Brown & Co., Boston, 1951), vol. II, p. 1665.

[111] For the detail of the Italian demands for reparations, the response thereto of the Greek Government, and the forceful action against the island of Corfu, see 'Dispute Between Italy and Greece: Appeal from the Greek Government under Articles 12 and 15 of the Covenant' (1923) *Official Journal of the League of Nations* 1412–25, Annex 554. See also J. H. Wigmore, 'The Case of Italy v. Greece under International Law and the Pact of Nations' (1923) 18 *Illinois LR* 131.

[112] See Colbert, *Retaliation in International Law*, p. 76; and see the examples she provides of excessive reprisals, *ibid.*, pp. 76–7.

[113] Nor has its determination been any more straightforward in the context of non-forcible countermeasures. See generally Commentary to the Draft Articles on the Responsibility of States for Internationally Wrongful Acts, note 70 above, pp. 324–50.

[114] See Colbert, *Retaliation in International Law*, pp. 4 and 77–9 (concluding after a review of State practice that the aim of reprisals was to force the offender to do justice rather than to provide reparation). See also M. McDougal and F. Feliciano, *Law and Minimum World Public Order: The Legal Regulation of International Coercion* (Yale University Press, New Haven, 1961), pp. 682–3.

the Arbitral Commission that the reprisal action was disproportionate, was the lack of equivalence between the act and the reprisal.[115]

Overall, it is difficult to assert with confidence in light of State practice prior to the adoption of the United Nations Charter that proportionality was ever clearly established as a requirement of legitimate reprisals. The conditions of legitimate reprisal action should have become of historical interest only. Opinions differed as to the effect of the League of Nations Covenant and the Kellogg–Briand Pact on the legality of reprisals.[116] Nevertheless, the practice declined during the two World Wars, and the requirement that States settle their disputes by peaceful means in Article 2(3) of the United Nations Charter and the ban on the use of force (otherwise than in self-defence) in Article 2(4) led to the almost unanimous view that armed reprisals were unlawful under its terms.[117] Despite this apparent consensus, there have been situations in which the question of reprisals has arisen in the Charter era. It has always been assumed, however, in the post-Charter era that necessity and proportionality are an integral component of any theory justifying the resort to force, including reprisals.[118]

Proportionality and the emerging independent *ius in bello*

One of the effects of the demise of the just war and the emergence during the nineteenth century of the view that the resort to war was a sovereign right of States was that the process that had begun as early as in the writings of Grotius became a reality. That is, *ius in bello* and *ius ad bellum* became separate bodies of rules. Perhaps more correctly, one should talk at this stage of the demise of *ius ad bellum*, although as we have seen, this was to be a short-lived phenomenon. With the resort to force largely unregulated *ius in bello* became an independent body of rules severing its historical dependence on *ius ad bellum*. Indeed, this period could be regarded as the golden age of *ius in bello* with much of

[115] See *Case Concerning the Gabcikovo-Nagymaros Project (Hungary* v. *Slovakia)* ICJ Reports 1997, 52 at 56 (for a similar articulation of proportionality in the context of countermeasures).

[116] See Brownlie, *International Law and the Use of Force by States*, pp. 220–2; and Waldock, 'The Regulation of the Use of Force by Individual States in International Law', pp. 475–6.

[117] See e.g. Brownlie, *International Law and the Use of Force by States*, p. 281 (particularly at note 4 setting out the views of commentators).

[118] See the further discussion of reprisals under the United Nations Charter regime, in Chapter 5 below.

the law on the means and methods of warfare codified in the second half of the nineteenth century, a process that culminated in the Hague Conferences of 1899 and 1907. The influence of the idea that suffering in warfare had some limits dictated by what was proportionate was reflected in this developmental movement.

When attention became focused on the conduct of warfare rather than its causes, the emphasis on the developing rules was on providing protections for combatants. As new means of warfare developed the idea of the Middle Ages that weapons should not cause superfluous injury or unnecessary suffering remained. In 1866, Wheaton wrote: 'perhaps the only test [of what is a legitimate weapon] . . . is that material shall not owe its efficacy, or the fear it may inspire, to a distinct quality of producing pain, or of causing or increasing the chance of death to individuals'.[119] These limitations were derived from 'the general limitation forbidding wanton or disproportionate violence'.[120]

The restriction on the choices available to belligerents to inflict damage on the enemy found expression in the 1868 St Petersburg Declaration.[121] The Declaration was the first major international agreement to regulate the use of weapons and prohibited the use of explosive bullets under 400 grams in time of war. The significance of the Declaration does not lie in its actual provisions which are no longer of any practical import (if they ever were) but in its preambular paragraphs, which read as follows:

> That the progress of civilisation should have the effect of alleviating as much as possible the calamities of war;
>
> That the only legitimate object which States should endeavour to accomplish during war is to weaken the military forces of the enemy;
>
> That for this purpose it is sufficient to disable the greatest possible number of men;

[119] Wheaton, 'Elements of International Law', Part IV, Chapter II, para. 343, note 166.

[120] W. E. Hall, *A Treatise on International Law* (8th edn), p. 635.

[121] See St Petersburg Declaration Renouncing the Use, in Time of War, of Explosive Projectiles Under 400 Grammes Weight, 11 December 1868, reprinted in A. Roberts and R. Guelff (eds.), *Documents on the Laws of War* (2nd edn, Oxford University Press, Oxford, 1989), pp. 30–1. See also C. Pilloud *et al.* (eds.), *Commentary on the Additional Protocols of 8 June 1977 to the Geneva Conventions of 12 August 1949* (ICRC, Geneva, 1987), p. 477: 'The deliberate and pointless extermination of the defending enemy constitutes disproportionate damage as compared with the concrete and direct advantage that the attacker has the right to achieve.'

That this object would be exceeded by the employment of arms which uselessly aggravate the sufferings of disabled men, or render their death inevitable;

That the employment of such arms would, therefore, be contrary to the laws of humanity.

The St Petersburg Declaration commenced the practice that continues today in conventional documents of stating the general prohibition against the use of weapons causing superfluous injury or unnecessary suffering and at the same time specifically banning certain weapons.[122] The extent to which the general principle itself prohibits the use of certain weapons is debatable and is considered in more detail in Chapter 3 below.

The general limitation on the means of injuring the enemy, the specific prohibition on the denial of quarter, and the prohibition on the use of poison or poisoned weapons and 'arms, projectiles or material calculated to cause unnecessary suffering', were incorporated in the Brussels Declaration, a draft international agreement on the laws and customs of war, adopted by the Brussels Conference of 1874.[123] The Brussels Declaration was never ratified, as not all the parties were willing to accept it as a binding agreement. This practice of prohibiting specific means of warfare continued. For example, in 1899, twenty-three States signed a Declaration agreeing to forego the use in wars between them of so-called 'dum-dum' bullets that expand and flatten in the body causing superfluous injury.[124]

Article 23 of the Regulations annexed to the 1899 and 1907 Hague Convention IV Respecting the Laws and Customs of War on Land adopted

[122] The prohibition on weapons causing unnecessary suffering was either customary international law at the time of the adoption of the Declaration or attained that status very shortly thereafter: see e.g. Roberts and Guelff, *Documents on the Laws of War*, p. 29 (stating the prohibition as customary at the time of its adoption in the St Petersburg Declaration). See further Chapter 3 below; but cf. Additional Protocol I which limits itself to a statement of the general principle and does not impose a specific prohibition on any weapon: see Chapter 3, note 19 and the accompanying text below.

[123] The Conference was summoned by Tsar Alexander II of Russia and attended by delegates of fifteen European States at Brussels. The Brussels Project of an International Declaration Concerning the Laws and Customs of War, 27 August 1874, is reprinted in D. Schindler and J. Toman (eds.), *The Laws of Armed Conflicts: A Collection of Conventions, Resolutions and other Documents* (3rd edn, Martinus Nijhoff, Dordrecht, 1988), p. 25.

[124] 1899 Hague Declaration III Concerning Expanding Bullets, 29 July 1899, reprinted in Roberts and Guelff, *Documents on the Laws of* War, p. 39.

at the Hague Peace Conference reiterated the prohibitions contained in the unratified Brussels Declaration.[125] However, differences between the French and English texts of Article 23 caused difficulties. The authentic French text of the Regulations annexed to the 1899 Hague Convention prohibited arms, projectiles or materials 'propres à causer des maux superflus'. The English translation of these words was 'of a nature to cause superfluous injury'. The identical phrase in French appeared again in Article 23(e) of the Regulations annexed to the 1907 Hague Convention IV but the English translation this time was 'calculated to cause unnecessary suffering'.

This difference caused a great deal of debate and confusion as to what exactly was encompassed by these phrases. Was unnecessary suffering distinct from superfluous injury, and what was the difference between 'calculated' and 'of a nature'?[126] This somewhat sterile debate was not resolved until the adoption of Additional Protocol I[127] where the matter is resolved by Article 35(2) thereof, which includes both the terms superfluous injury and unnecessary suffering.[128]

The Hague Peace Conference of 1899 also adopted two Declarations relating to weapons: Declaration II Concerning Asphyxiating Gases and Declaration III Concerning Expanding Bullets. The general limitation of the Brussels Declaration on the means of injuring the enemy was also reiterated in Articles 22 of both the 1899 and 1907 Regulations.

As the nineteenth century progressed, it was accepted in a general sense that warfare was the province of the combatant. Theories such as those of Rousseau of the distinction between the State and its citizens[129]

[125] Regulations annexed to the Hague Convention Respecting the Laws and Customs of War on Land, 29 July 1899, and Regulations annexed to the Hague Convention IV Respecting the Laws and Customs of War on Land, 18 October 1907, reprinted in Roberts and Guelff, *Documents on the Laws of War*, pp. 35 and 43 respectively.

[126] See H. Meyrowitz, 'The Principle of Superfluous Injury or Unnecessary Suffering' (1994) 299 *IRRC* 98 at 104–5; and see ICRC, Conference of Government Experts on the Use of Certain Conventional Weapons, Lucerne, 24 September–18 October 1974 (Geneva, ICRC, 1975), pp. 7–13.

[127] See the discussion of this point in Chapter 3, note 20 and the accompanying text below.

[128] There is still little agreement on what these terms encompass. The Report of Committee III to the Diplomatic Conference states that the 'phrase "superfluous injury or unnecessary suffering" was chosen by the Working Group as the preferred translation of the French, "maux superflus", which includes both physical and moral injury', *Official Records of the Diplomatic Conference on the Reaffirmation and Development of International Humanitarian Law Applicable in Armed Conflicts* (Geneva, 1974–7) (17 vols., Federal Political Department, Bern, 1978), CDDH/III/293.

[129] See note 52 and the accompanying text above.

were paving the way for acceptance that warfare must be restricted to combatants. Nowadays, it is taken for granted in some quarters that the fundamental principle of the 1868 St Petersburg Declaration, 'that the laws of war do not allow belligerents an unlimited power as to the choice of injuring the enemy', is the genesis of the modern legal regime protecting civilians.[130] Taking the declaration in its historical context, however, it had little to do with non-combatants.[131] Whatever the reality, there was as yet no suggestion of any legal requirements to protect civilians from the impact of armed conflict, although contemporary commentators talked in general terms of the illegitimacy of wanton and disproportionate warfare.[132]

Proportionality and IHL between the two World Wars

Apart from the adoption of the Gas Protocol in 1925, for many years no progress was made in further restraints on weapons.[133] Attempts were made, however, to address the situation of civilians in times of armed conflict. The impetus for the modern rule of proportionality in IHL can be directly traced to the effect of aerial bombardment on the civilian population. The First World War (1914–18) and the Spanish Civil War (1936–9) saw the emergence of this new method of warfare that led to an unprecedented focus on the relationship between military necessity and civilian casualties.[134] With aerial warfare, civilians became extremely vulnerable and were inevitably collateral targets, potentially on a much larger scale than previously.[135]

The response of the international community to this new phenomenon was to attempt to develop legal norms aimed at providing protection for the civilian population and civilian objects from the effects

[130] See e.g. H. Blix, 'Area Bombardment: Rules and Reasons' (1978) 49 *BYIL* 31 at 32.

[131] See Best, *War and Law Since 1945*, p. 43.

[132] See Hall, *International Law* (4th edn), p. 551; and see J. Gardam, *Non-Combatant Immunity as a Norm of International Humanitarian Law* (Martinus Nijhoff, Dordrecht, 1993), pp. 12–21.

[133] In 1925, the Protocol for the Prohibition of the Use in War of Asphyxiating, Poisonous or Other Gases, and of Bacteriological Methods of Warfare, 17 June 1925, reprinted in Roberts and Guelff, *Documents on the Laws of War*, was adopted, which expanded the prohibition in the 1899 Hague Declaration II Concerning Asphyxiating Gases to bacteriological weapons on the basis that these were 'justly condemned by the general opinion of the civilized world'.

[134] For a description of aerial bombardment during the First World War, see M. Cooper, *The Birth of Independent Air Power* (Allen & Unwin, London, 1986).

[135] See H. Blix, 'Area Bombardment', p. 31.

of these new forms of warfare. The modern regime of IHL designed to achieve this aim is based on the fundamental underlying premise of the distinction between civilian and military targets. Consequently, the starting point in the process was to impose limits on aerial bombardment by restricting attacks to military targets and most importantly to define such targets narrowly.[136] A widely accepted definition of military targets that imposed real limits on aerial attacks was to remain elusive for many years and continues to be a controversial issue.[137]

In conjunction with the focus on restricting attacks to defined military targets were the attempts to regulate indiscriminate bombardment. The designation 'indiscriminate' encompasses attacks in which, although the civilian population is not directly targeted, no attempt is made to select means and methods of combat that would facilitate a distinction being drawn between military and civilian targets, or the attack is conducted negligently so that targets are hit without distinction.[138]

Spaight, after surveying State practice in the First World War, confirms that the rule of attacking only military targets was adopted in principle; however, in many cases bombardments were indiscriminate.[139] On balance, it appears that, although the direct targeting of civilians was contrary to international law at this time, the practice of States was not to take collateral casualties into account in attacks on military targets. The idea that there should be some balance between the level of civilian losses and the achievement of the military objective was not even identified as a relevant issue in the law regulating civilian losses.

Despite the obstacles to regulating this new type of warfare, the international community attempted to formulate a code of rules for the regulation of aircraft and radio in time of war. In 1922–3, an international conference of six States at The Hague established a Commission of Jurists to consider whether the existing rules were adequate to cover the emergence of new methods of warfare since the Hague Conventions and, if not, to consider what changes should be adopted. The

[136] See H. Lauterpacht, 'The Problem of the Revision of the Law of War' (1952) 29 *BYIL* 360 at 365.

[137] The issue of the definition of military targets remains controversial in IHL, as illustrated by the events of the Persian Gulf conflict (1990–1) and the Kosovo action by NATO forces in 1999.

[138] This complex area of the law is not assisted by the lack of uniformity by commentators in their use of the term 'indiscriminate'. See Blix, 'Area Bombardment', p. 47.

[139] J. M. Spaight, *Air Power and War Rights* (3rd edn, Longmans, Green & Co. Ltd, London, 1947), pp. 227–8 and 230–40.

result was the 1923 Hague Rules of Air Warfare and, although never ratified by States, they were a significant step in the development of the protection of civilians against aerial bombardment.[140] They represented the first attempt to devise specific rules to overcome the problem of indiscriminate bombardment.[141] The emphasis moved from the distinction between defended and undefended targets contained in the Hague Regulations – a distinction made obsolete by the developing methods of warfare – to the development of a definition of military objectives, the consideration of the concept of indiscriminate attacks and the introduction of proportionality. Article 24 required aerial bombardment to be directed exclusively at defined military objectives 'that is to say, an object of which the destruction or injury would constitute a distinct military advantage to the belligerent'.[142] Military objectives were unlawful targets if their attack would involve indiscriminate bombardment of the civilian population.[143] Military objectives in civilian areas were legitimate targets if they were in the immediate area of the operations of land forces and there was 'a reasonable presumption that the military concentration is sufficiently important to justify such bombardment, having regard to the danger thus caused to the civilian population'.[144]

The fact that the rules were never ratified does not mean that aerial bombardment of civilian targets was unregulated by customary norms.[145] In the period preceding the outbreak of the Second World War, there were indications that it was a requirement of international law that care be taken in attacks on military targets, although as one commentator observes 'the actual military practice of the period pointed . . . to an increasing lack of restraint in the use of aircraft in armed conflicts'.[146] In 1938, the British Prime Minister stated in the House of

[140] Rules of Air Warfare Drafted by a Commission of Jurists at the Hague, December 1922–February 1923, reproduced in Spaight, *Air Power and War Rights*, pp. 498–508. For a detailed discussion of the conference, see 'Rules of Warfare: Aircraft and Radio' in J. Bassett Moore (ed.), *International Law and Some Current Illusions and Other Essays* (Macmillan, New York, 1924), p. 182. See also L. Oppenheim, *International Law: A Treatise*, vol. II, *Disputes, War and Neutrality* (ed. by H. Lauterpacht, 7th edn), pp. 518–27ff. For the reasons for this failure by States to ratify the Rules, see W. Hays Parks, 'Air War and the Law of War' (1990) 32 *Air Force Law Review* 1 at 35.

[141] See generally H. DeSaussure, 'The Laws of Air Warfare: Are There Any?' (1971) 5 *International Lawyer* 527.

[142] See also Art. 24(2). [143] See Art. 24(3). [144] See Art. 24(4).

[145] *Oppenheim's International Law: A Treatise*, vol. II, *Disputes, War and Neutrality* (ed. by H. Lauterpacht, 7th edn), p. 524.

[146] Blix, 'Area Bombardment', p. 35.

Commons that the law required that 'reasonable care must be taken in attacking military objectives so that by carelessness a civilian population in the neighbourhood is not bombed'.[147] This statement of the legal position was adopted in the League of Nations in the following year.[148]

Whatever may have been the theoretical position at that time, it was not reflected in practice in the Second World War – indeed, quite the contrary. Although the events of the First World War had caused disquiet as to the protection of civilians in future armed conflicts, it was the Second World War that led to intense pessimism on the part of many commentators and to a claim that the remains of the distinction between combatants and non-combatants had disappeared.[149] More sophisticated methods of warfare and the practice of target area bombardment posed great difficulties in distinguishing between military and non-military targets and consequently between combatants and non-combatants.[150] Moreover, there was the ongoing problem of defining the civilian population in modern warfare.[151] It is estimated that aerial bombardment alone was responsible for the death of twelve million civilians and the practice of saturation bombing of civilian targets was widespread.[152]

It appears that States initially were concerned to avoid the direct targeting of civilians and, moreover, to exercise care to avoid widespread civilian casualties.[153] To a large extent this was a stance taken for pragmatic reasons. It was militarily efficient to direct attacks against objects contributing to the military capability of the enemy. As the conflict developed, however, the perceived demands of military necessity eroded these standards. The direct targeting of civilians for the purpose of terrorising the population to bring an early end to the conflict was

[147] House of Commons Debates, vol. 382, col. 1360 (1938).

[148] League of Nations Paper A 69, 1938 IX (28 September 1938).

[149] See e.g. C. Fenwick, *International Law* (4th edn, Appleton Century Crofts, New York, 1965), pp. 656–7; L. Nurick, 'The Distinction Between Combatant and NonCombatant in the Law of War' (1945) 39 *AJIL* 680; and H. Lauterpacht, 'The Problem of the Revision of the Law of War' (1952) 29 *BYIL* 360 at 364–5.

[150] See G. Draper, 'The Modern Pattern of War Criminality', p. 141.

[151] See Lauterpacht, 'The Problem of the Revision of the Law of War', p. 364.

[152] See H. Levie, *When Battle Rages How Can Law Protect?* (Oceana, Dobbs Ferry, NY, 1971), pp. 24 and 70.

[153] See Lauterpacht, 'The Problem of the Revision of the Law of War', p. 365; and Blix, 'Area Bombardment', pp. 36–7.

resorted to.[154] Indeed, by 1941 the British Chiefs of Staff had included the morale of the enemy population as a target of aerial bombardment.[155] This practice, however, was very controversial and appears to have been unlawful.[156]

A survey of scholarly opinion reveals agreement on only one point: that at the end of the Second World War the practice of States revealed the 'prohibition . . . of intentional terrorization – or destruction – of the civilian population as an avowed or obvious object of attack'.[157] There was some support for the view that indiscriminate attacks were illegitimate, although it was a difficult position to sustain in light of the prevailing State practice.[158] Any suggestion that a belligerent was bound to refrain from attacking a military object because it may lead to large civilian losses was 'controversial, [or] at least practice had made it controversial'.[159]

Conclusion

The events of the First and Second World Wars led to concerted efforts to regulate the resort of States to force to settle their disputes. It was during the period between these two conflicts that the right of self-defence

[154] See D. Johnson, *Rights in Air Space* (Manchester University Press, Manchester, 1965), p. 48.
[155] *Ibid.*, p. 48, and see the discussion of the terror bombing of the civilian population during the remainder of the conflict, pp. 48–53.
[156] See Blix, 'Area Bombardment', p. 32; and K. Raby, *The Bombardment of Land Targets – Necessity and Proportionality Interpellated* (publisher and place of publication not stated 1968), p. 33, note 3.
[157] See Lauterpacht, 'The Problem of the Revision of the Law of War', p. 369; Johnson, *Rights in Air Space*, p. 57; Spaight, *Air Power and War Rights*, p. 277; and the summary of opinion in Blix, 'Area Bombardment', pp. 37–8.
[158] The issue of the indiscriminate bombardment of civilians was not addressed by the war crimes trials that took place after the Second World War at the Nuremberg and Tokyo Tribunals. See Agreement for the Prosecution and Punishment of the Major War Criminals of the European Axis, London, 8 August 1945, 5 UNTS 251; and Special Proclamation by the Supreme Commander for the Allied Powers at Tokyo, 19 January 1946, TIAS No. 1589, 4 Bevans 20. Cf. *Shimoda* v. *State* (1963) 32 ILR 626 (District Court of Tokyo) (considering the lawfulness of the nuclear attacks on Hiroshima and Nagasaki in 1945).
[159] Lauterpacht, 'The Problem of the Revision of the Law of War', p. 365; and see E. Rauch, 'Le Concept de Nécessité Militaire dans le Droit de la Guerre' Rapport présenté au Comité pour la protection de la vie humaine dans les conflits armés, VIIIe Congrès de la Société internationale de droit pénal militaire et de droit de la guerre, Ankara, October 1979, p. 13.

developed and finally took the form that we see today in Article 51 of the United Nations Charter.[160] State practice indicates that necessity and proportionality, although infrequently addressed by commentators, were part of the developing law of self-defence.

Moreover, a vigorous and independent *ius in bello* was firmly established by that time. An integral component of this regime, the notion that certain types of weapons were unacceptable because their effects on combatants were excessive in light of the legitimate aims of warfare, became part of international law. So far this concept was only manifested in the prohibition of certain designated weapons. As the century progressed, approaches to weapons control became much more sophisticated and varied. This phenomenon was dictated by the immense developments in weaponry that rapidly occurred along with the resistance by States to controls limiting the means and methods by which warfare was conducted.

In contrast, although the groundwork had been laid for the idea that there should be some relationship between the achievement of a military objective and the cost in terms of civilian lives and damage to civilian objects, its reflection in the practice of States was as yet unrealised.

[160] Art. 51 of the United Nations Charter is also regarded as representing customary international law: see e.g. *Oppenheim's International Law*, vol. I, *Peace* (ed. by R. Jennings and A. Watts, 9th edn, Longman, Harlow, 1992).

3 Proportionality and combatants in modern international humanitarian law

Introduction

The previous discussion considered the early development of proportionality as a restraint on the treatment of combatants in armed conflict. It will be recalled that its limiting influence in that context came to be represented in the prohibition on the use of means and methods of warfare of a nature to cause superfluous injury or unnecessary suffering. This chapter continues the process of tracing the development of this prohibition and details its content in current international humanitarian law (IHL) and includes the system for the suppression of breaches of IHL.

The question of weapons control languished after the initial successes with the regulation of weapons in the early part of the twentieth century. The issue is at the borders of IHL and disarmament, a situation that has not facilitated developments.[1] Moreover, it has proved difficult to persuade States that there should be rules protecting combatants from the means and methods of combat, although the idea that civilians should be protected was accepted at least in theory.[2]

When the movement to improve the protection available to the victims of armed conflict gained momentum, largely as a consequence of the growing emphasis through the work of the United Nations on the protection of human rights, the question of further regulation of weapons arose again. The International Committee of the Red Cross (ICRC), which

[1] See ICRC, Report of the ICRC for the Review Conference of the 1980 United Nations Convention on Prohibitions or Restrictions on the Use of Certain Conventional Weapons Which May Be Deemed to Be Excessively Injurious or to Have Indiscriminate Effects (ICRC, Geneva, 1994), pp. 130–1.

[2] See *ibid.*

for many years had been instrumental in achieving advances in the protection for victims of armed conflict, was somewhat ambivalent in its approach to weapons controls. Its traditional mandate had been for the protection of victims of armed conflict in the narrow sense (the 'Law of Geneva')[3] rather than the means and methods of combat (the 'Law of The Hague').[4] Even when the ICRC expanded its role to incorporate the means and methods of warfare, the primary focus of the efforts in this area remained on the need to protect civilians against their indiscriminate use. This attitude was dictated to some extent by the fact that States have been prepared to accept the idea that IHL has a legitimate involvement with the protection of civilians against the indiscriminate effects of warfare. The issue of banning specific weapons, however, directly raises strategic considerations that are considered more appropriate to disarmament fora. Overall, States are traditionally far more sensitive about the regulation of means and methods of conflict than they are about rules dealing with the victims of armed conflict. Consequently, obtaining restrictions on specific weapons has been a difficult task, although the adoption of general principles in relation to the use of weapons has been relatively easily achieved, as their impact on the liberty of States has been minimal.[5]

The discussion that follows focuses primarily on international armed conflicts. It is apparent, however, that the legal regime of IHL that regulates the means and methods of warfare, including the prohibition on weapons causing superfluous injury and unnecessary suffering, is exerting its influence in the context of non-international armed conflicts. These developments are also considered in this chapter.

Developments in weapons control

In 1971 and 1972, the ICRC convened two meetings of government experts preparatory to the calling of a diplomatic conference for 'the

[3] See Chapter 1, note 1, above for an explanation of this term.

[4] See Chapter 1, note 1, above for an explanation of this term. For an analysis of the ICRC's approach and its contribution to the issue of the regulation of weapons in armed conflict, see F. Kalshoven, 'Arms, Armaments and International Law' (1985-II) 191 *Receuil des Cours* 183 at 225–50.

[5] See *ibid.*, p. 227; L. Doswald-Beck, 'Obstacles to Regulating New Weaponry: Battlefield Laser Weapons' in H. Fox and M. Meyer (eds.), *Effecting Compliance* (British Institute of International and Comparative Law, London, 1993), p. 107; and R. J. Mathews and T. L. H. McCormack, 'The Influence of Humanitarian Principles in the Negotiation of Arms Control Treaties' (1999) 834 *IRRC* 331.

reaffirmation and development of international humanitarian law' (the 'Diplomatic Conference').[6] Amongst the topics considered in these meetings was the question of the further regulation of specific weapons and in what forum this should take place. The ICRC's stated position was that, although it 'was fully conscious of the importance of the question of arms for the protection of human beings in the event of armed conflict', it had limited its draft articles presented to the Conference to general principles in relation to weapons.[7] It had done so, first, because the question of arms and their prohibition was dealt with by other organisations. Secondly, 'the prohibition of specific weapons had always been the subject of legal instruments separate from the Geneva Conventions', the latter imposing rules of an absolute nature whereas the weapons prohibitions were subject to reciprocity and reprisals.[8]

At these deliberations considerable differences emerged amongst States as to the most appropriate way to deal with questions of weapons regulation. There was consensus that weapons of mass destruction such as nuclear, chemical and bacteriological weapons were more appropriately left in the domain of the United Nations and the Committee on Disarmament.[9] Agreement was reached, however, in relation to conventional weapons to request the ICRC to summon a further meeting

[6] Conference of Government Experts on the Reaffirmation and Development of International Humanitarian Law Applicable in Armed Conflicts, Geneva, 24 May–12 June 1971; and Conference of Government Experts on the Reaffirmation and Development of International Humanitarian Law Applicable in Armed Conflicts, Geneva, 3 May–3 June 1972.

[7] ICRC, Report of the Conference of Government Experts on the Reaffirmation and Development of International Humanitarian Law Applicable in Armed Conflicts (ICRC, Geneva, 1972), p. 127, para. 314.

[8] Frits Kalshoven, the principal rapporteur at the Conference of Government Experts on Conventional Weapons preparatory to the Diplomatic Conference at Lucerne in 1974, suggests other explanations for the official position of the ICRC on weapons. See F. Kalshoven, 'The Conference of Government Experts on the Use of Certain Conventional Weapons, Lucerne, 24 September–18 October 1974' (1975) 6 *NYIL* 77 at 81.

[9] As a result, the ICRC Draft Additional Protocols presented to the 1974–7 Diplomatic Conference stated in the Introduction that it was not the intention of the ICRC to address the problems of atomic, chemical and bacteriological warfare. See Introduction, Draft Protocol Additional to the Geneva Conventions of August 12, 1949, and Relating to the Protection of Victims of International Armed Conflicts (ICRC, Geneva, 1973) (hereafter Draft Protocol I); and Draft Protocol Additional to the Geneva Conventions of August 12, 1949, and Relating to the Protection of Victims of Non-International Armed Conflicts (ICRC, Geneva, 1973) (hereafter Draft Protocol II). Reprinted in *Official Records of the Diplomatic Conference on the Reaffirmation and Development of International Humanitarian Law Applicable in Armed Conflicts* (Geneva, 1974–7) (17 vols., Federal Political Department, Bern, 1978), vol. I, Part 3, 2, 33 (hereafter *Official Records*).

of experts to consider specifically the issue of weapons.[10] There were two meetings of experts in 1973, and these were followed up by the Conference of Government Experts on the Use of Certain Conventional Weapons, at Lucerne in 1974 and Lugano in 1976.[11]

In the meantime, the Diplomatic Conference that adopted Additional Protocols I and II had been convened.[12] The main motivation for the adoption of new rules of armed conflict was to increase the protection available to civilians in both international and non-international armed conflict. The draft Additional Protocols prepared by the ICRC contained no restrictions on specific weapons, although they did contain the general principles that restricted the means and methods of warfare to those that did not 'uselessly aggravate the suffering of disabled adversaries or render their death inevitable in all circumstances'.[13] At the Conference, exception was taken to this omission by some delegations and as a result an Ad Hoc Committee was established to consider the problem of particular conventional weapons.[14] Its function was to lay the groundwork for the planned special conferences on weapons.[15] Nevertheless, a resolution entitled 'Follow-up Regarding Prohibition or Restriction of Use of Certain Conventional Weapons' was adopted by the Diplomatic Conference.[16] This resolution recommended to States and the Secretary-General of the United Nations that a conference of governments should be convened to consider 'prohibitions or restrictions on the use of specific conventional weapons including those which may be deemed to be excessively injurious or to have indiscriminate effects, taking into account humanitarian and military considerations'.

[10] See Kalshoven, 'Arms, Armaments', pp. 227–9.

[11] See ICRC, *Report of the Conference of Government Experts on the Use of Certain Conventional Weapons* (Lucerne, 24 September–18 October, 1974) (ICRC, Geneva, 1975); and *ibid.*, 2nd Sess., Lugano, 28 January–26 February, 1976 (ICRC, Geneva, 1976).

[12] For a comprehensive analysis of the proceedings of the Diplomatic Conference and the provisions of Additional Protocols I and II, see M. Bothe, K. Partsch and W. Solf, *New Rules for Victims of Armed Conflict* (Martinus Nijhoff, The Hague, 1982); and C. Pilloud *et al.*, *Commentary on the Additional Protocols of 8 June 1977 to the Geneva Conventions of 12 August 1949* (ICRC, Geneva, 1987). For a description of the work of the Conference, see R. Baxter, 'Humanitarian Law or Humanitarian Politics? The 1974 Diplomatic Conference on Humanitarian Law' (1975) 16 *Harvard ILJ* 1.

[13] Art. 33(2) of Draft Protocol I.

[14] *Official Records* CDDH/SR 9, vol. 5, p. 14 paras. 12–54.

[15] See Kalshoven, 'Arms, Armaments', pp. 247–9, who refers to the deliberations of the Ad Hoc Committee as a 'side-show' to 'the real work on conventional weapons going on elsewhere'.

[16] *Official Records*, vol. 1, Part 1, p. 215.

Means and methods of warfare are not completely excluded from Additional Protocol I. Article 35 was adopted by consensus. Paragraph 1 of this Article repeats the basic rule of Hague Convention IV that the right of parties to choose means and methods of warfare is not unlimited. The word 'warfare' is substituted for 'combat' on the basis that the latter may be of narrower import.[17] Paragraph 2 prohibits the employment of 'weapons of warfare, projectiles and material and methods of a nature to cause superfluous injury or unnecessary suffering'. Thus the concept of superfluous injury is added to the 1907 Hague Regulations and the true import of the French phrase 'maux superflus' is achieved.[18] The phrase 'methods of warfare' is added to 'means', but it is not clear whether this adds anything to the substance of the rule.[19]

Article 36 backs up the prohibition against the use of weapons of a nature to cause superfluous injury or unnecessary suffering in Article 35 and requires that '[i]n the study, development, acquisition or adoption of a new weapon, means or method of warfare, a High Contracting Party is under an obligation to determine whether its employment would, in some or all circumstances, be prohibited by this Protocol or by any other rule of international law applicable to the High Contracting Party'.[20]

As a result of the recommendation adopted by the Diplomatic Conference for a follow-up conference specifically on weapons, the United Nations Conference on Prohibitions or Restrictions of Use of Certain Conventional Weapons Which May Be Deemed to Be Excessively Injurious or to Have Indiscriminate Effects, was convened in 1980. The Conference adopted the framework Convention on Prohibitions or Restrictions on the Use of Certain Conventional Weapons Which May Be Deemed to Be Excessively Injurious or to Have Indiscriminate Effects, 1981 (CWC) and three Annexed Protocols, Protocol I, Non-Detectable Fragments, Protocol II, Prohibitions or Restrictions on the Use of Mines, Booby-Traps and

[17] See Report of Committee III, *ibid.*, vol. 15, CDDH/215 Rev.1, p. 267, para. 20.

[18] See G. Best, *Law and Armed Conflict Since 1945* (Oxford University Press, Oxford, 1994), p. 294, note 37. There is still, however, little agreement on what these terms encompass.

[19] See Kalshoven, 'Arms, Armaments', p. 243; and see C. Pilloud *et al.*, *Commentary on the Additional Protocols*, p. 398.

[20] See Depleted Uranium Munitions, Comments of the International Committee of the Red Cross, Geneva, 26 March 2001 (urging States to ensure that they comply with the requirements of Art. 36 of Protocol I if they develop, acquire or adopt munitions containing depleted uranium).

Other Devices, and Protocol III, Prohibitions or Restrictions on the Use of Incendiary Weapons.[21]

Protocol I to the CWC deals with weapons that do not exist or for which there does not appear to be any use for them if they did. Consequently, it was not difficult for States to reach consensus on their prohibition.[22] Protocols II and III are primarily designed to protect the civilian population against means and methods of warfare of an indiscriminate nature. However, by Article 6 of Protocol II, '[i]t is prohibited in all circumstances to use any booby-trap which is designed to cause superfluous injury or unnecessary suffering'.

In 1995, the first Review Conference of the 1980 CWC in its first session adopted a new Protocol IV, on Blinding Laser Weapons.[23] By Article 1 of the Protocol, '[it] is prohibited to employ laser weapons specifically designed, as their sole combat function or as one of their combat functions, to cause permanent blindness to unenhanced vision, that is to the naked eye or to the eye with corrective eyesight'.

The Review Conference also had before it the question of anti-personnel mines. For some years, the goal of outlawing these weapons had been vigorously pursued by a number of non-government organisations and the ICRC. The major cause of concern was the indiscriminate effect of such devices on the civilian population, particularly in non-international armed conflicts. However, there was also the question of whether these weapons inflicted superfluous injury or unnecessary suffering to combatants out of proportion to their military effectiveness. Although there was some evidence that this was in fact the case, as their military effectiveness was very questionable given the injuries inflicted,[24] it was their effect on civilians that was instrumental in

[21] Convention on Prohibitions or Restrictions on the Use of Certain Conventional Weapons Which May Be Deemed to Be Excessively Injurious or to Have Indiscriminate Effects, Protocol I on Non-Detectable Fragments (Protocol I), Protocol on Prohibitions or Restrictions on the Use of Mines, Booby-Traps and Other Devices (Protocol II) and Protocol on Prohibitions or Restrictions on the Use of Incendiary Weapons (Protocol III), 10 April 1981, (1980) 19 ILM 1523.

[22] See W. Fenrick, 'New Developments in the Law Concerning the Use of Conventional Weapons in Armed Conflict' (1981) 19 *Canadian YIL* 229 at 242; and Kalshoven, 'Arms, Armaments', p. 252.

[23] Protocol on Blinding Laser Weapons (Protocol IV), 13 October 1995, available at www.icrc.org/ihl.nsf/WebPRES?OpenView/. See 'Blinding Weapons', Reports of the Meetings of Experts Convened by the International Committee of the Red Cross on Battlefield Laser Weapons (1989–91) (ICRC, Geneva, 1993), pp. 71 and 330ff.

[24] See ICRC, *Anti-Personnel Landmines: Friend or Foe?* (ICRC, Geneva, 1996), pp. 40–51 (military effectiveness) and pp. 67–8 (effect of weapons).

the adoption of an amended Protocol improving the existing regulatory scheme.[25] The pressure for a total ban on the use of land mines continued, and, as a result of the so-called 'Ottawa process' launched by the Canadian Government, in 1997 States adopted the Convention on the Prohibition of the Use, Stockpiling, Production and Transfer of Anti-Personnel Mines and on Their Destruction.[26] This instrument represents the first conventional prohibition of a weapon in widespread use.

In the context of non-conventional weapons, the 1972 UN Convention on Biological Weapons not only bans the development and production of these weapons but requires States to destroy their stockpiles thereof.[27] The same is the case with the 1993 UN Convention on Chemical Weapons.[28] This latter Convention supplements the ban on the use of chemical and biological weapons imposed by the 1925 Geneva Protocol, by banning the development, production and stockpiling of such weapons, and requiring the destruction of existing stockpiles.

Traditionally, IHL has drawn a rigid distinction between the applicable norms depending on the characterisation of the conflict as international or non-international. This structure is in the process of being undermined and it is now apparent that the general prohibition of weapons causing superfluous injury or unnecessary suffering is of relevance to the conduct of non-international armed conflicts. The precise scope of its operation in that latter context is in the process of development.[29] For example, Article 3 of the Statute of the International Criminal Tribunal for the Former Yugoslavia criminalises violations of the laws or customs of war committed in the territory of the former Yugoslavia, including the 'employment of poisonous weapons or other weapons calculated

[25] Protocol on Prohibitions or Restrictions on the Use of Mines, Booby-Traps and Other Devices, as amended on 3 May 1996 (Protocol II to the 1980 Convention, as amended on 3 May 1996), available at www.icrc.org/ihl.nsf/WebPRES?OpenView/.

[26] Convention on the Prohibition of the Use, Stockpiling, Production, and Transfer of Anti-Personnel Mines and on Their Destruction, 18 September 1997, available at www.icrc.org/ihl.nsf/WebPRES?OpenView/. See generally ICRC, *Banning Anti-Personnel Mines: The Ottawa Treaty Explained* (ICRC, Geneva, 1998).

[27] Convention on the Prohibition of the Development, Production and Stockpiling of Bacteriological (Biological) Weapons, 10 April 1972, (1976) 1015 UNTS 164. For a discussion of the history of the ban on biological weapons, see Mathews and McCormack, 'Influence of Humanitarian Principles', p. 339.

[28] Convention on the Prohibition of the Development, Production, Stockpiling and Use of Chemical Weapons and on Their Destruction, 13 January 1993, (1993) 31 ILM 800. For a discussion of the history of the ban on chemical weapons, see Mathews and McCormack, 'Influence of Humanitarian Principles', p. 335.

[29] E.g. the Appeal Chamber in *Prosecutor* v. *Dusko Tadic*, Case No. IT-94-I-AR72, Decision on the Defence Motion for Interlocutory Appeal on Jurisdiction, 2 October 1995, para. 126.

to cause unnecessary suffering'.[30] In the *Tadic* case, the Appeals Chamber of the International Criminal Tribunal for the Former Yugoslavia (ICTY) considered in detail the question of whether customary norms governed the conduct of non-international armed conflicts.[31] In answering this query in the affirmative and using as an example the prohibition on chemical weapons in the 1925 Geneva Gas Protocol, the Tribunal referred to:

> elementary considerations of humanity and common sense [that] make it preposterous that the use by States of weapons prohibited in armed conflicts between themselves be allowed when States try to put down rebellion by their own nationals on their own territory. What is inhumane, and consequently proscribed, in international wars, cannot but be inhumane and inadmissible in civil strife.[32]

The Court, however, cautioned against the 'full and mechanical transport' of the rules of international armed conflicts into the regime for non-international armed conflicts. What in their view was applicable in such conflicts was the 'general essence' of the rules applicable to international armed conflicts.[33]

This movement towards diluting the distinction between international and non-international armed conflicts is not only a customary development. In 2001, the Second Review Conference of the CWC amended the scope of the Convention and its annexed Protocols to cover non-international armed conflicts.[34]

[30] The ICTY was established in 1993 by the UN Security Council: see SC Res. 808, 22 February 1993; and SC Res. 827, 25 May 1993. Moreover, the Rome Statute of the International Criminal Court, UN Doc. A/Conf.183/9, 17 July 1998, in force 1 July 2002 (hereafter Statute of the ICC), available at www.icrc.org/ihl.nsf/WebPRES?OpenView/, criminalises some actions against combatants in non-international armed conflicts: see Art. 8(2)(e)(ix) (killing or wounding treacherously a combatant adversary) and (x) (declaring that no quarter will be given).

[31] *Prosecutor* v. *Dusko Tadic*, note 29 above, paras. 96–127. See also Promotion and Protection of Human Rights, Fundamental Standards of Humanity, 'Report of the Secretary-General Submitted Pursuant to Commission Resolution 2000/69', Commission on Human Rights 57th Sess., E/CN.4/2001/91, 12 January 2001 (referring to the contribution of the ICTY and the ICTR to the development of a common core of general rules and principles designed to regulate, *inter alia*, the means of combat in non-international armed conflicts).

[32] *Prosecutor* v. *Dusko Tadic*, note 29 above, para. 119.

[33] *Ibid*., para. 126.

[34] See amended Art. I of Second Review Conference of the State Parties to the Convention on Prohibitions or Restrictions on the Use of Certain Conventional Weapons Which May Be Deemed to Be Excessively Injurious or to Have Indiscriminate Effects, Final Document, Doc. CWC/Conf II/2 (2001), pp. 34–5.

The ambit of the prohibition on superfluous injury and unnecessary suffering

It has not been an easy task to expand the range of weapons covered by specific treaty provisions. Nevertheless, it is the general concept of superfluous injury and unnecessary suffering that has occupied a great deal of time, not the least of which as we have seen has been devoted to the difference between the French and English texts of the Hague Regulations.[35] This confusion did not assist in clarifying the concept of superfluous injury or unnecessary suffering. As Cassese observes: 'Article 23(e) of the Hague Regulations is one of the most unclear and controversial rules of warfare.'[36]

What is clear, however, is that the prohibition encompasses both weapons that inherently cause superfluous injury or unnecessary suffering and those that may do so if used in a certain manner.[37] This does not, however, mean that such weapons are automatically prohibited from use, either *per se* or in certain circumstances. It is debatable whether the maxim in Article 23(e) of the Hague Conventions (which is accepted as reflected in customary law) of itself renders a weapon prohibited without any further action by States. The practice of States in this context has been to specifically outlaw a number of weapons on the basis that they infringe the prohibition against superfluous injury or unnecessary suffering.[38] The argument that other weapons are nevertheless outlawed by the general prohibition has not been accepted in practice.[39] As one commentator observes:

[35] See the discussion of this issue in Chapter 2, note 127 and the accompanying text above.

[36] A. Cassese, 'Weapons Causing Unnecessary Suffering: Are They Prohibited?' (1975) 58 *Riv. DI* 12 at 15.

[37] See S. Oeter, 'Methods and Means of Combat' in D. Fleck (ed.), *The Handbook of Humanitarian Law in Armed Conflicts* (Oxford University Press, Oxford, 1995), p. 114; and C. Pilloud *et al.*, *Commentary on the Additional Protocols*, p. 398. This dichotomy is also reflected in the proportionality test in relation to civilians. Some weapons arguably are of a nature to impact disproportionately on the civilian population; others will do so depending on the circumstances in which they are used.

[38] See Cassese, 'Unnecessary Suffering', pp. 13–15.

[39] See C. Pilloud *et al.*, *Commentary on the Additional Protocols*, pp. 393–4. For the practice of States in relation to invoking the general prohibition, see Cassese, 'Unnecessary Suffering', pp. 23–7; and see K. Dörmann, *Elements of War Crimes under the Rome Statute of the International Criminal Court* (Cambridge University Press, Cambridge, 2003), pp. 298–300 (for details of the interpretation of the prohibition on means and methods of warfare of a nature to cause superfluous injury or unnecessary suffering in the military manuals of States).

> [T]he prohibition of *maux superflus* is characterised by a particularly complex mixture of very definite prohibitions of certain specific categories of arms on the one hand, and a rather abstract prohibition of means of warfare which cause unnecessary sufferings on the other; the relationship between these two sets of rules is far from clear. How far the definite prohibitions are only specific expressions or materializations of the general prohibitory provision, and to what extent they are, to the contrary, constitutive developments of a merely political programme envisaged in Art. 23(e) Hague Regulations, is a question which still needs careful consideration.[40]

Irrespective of whether the prohibition against weapons of a nature to cause superfluous injury or unnecessary suffering on its own outlaws weapons or their use in particular circumstances, what is the meaning of the terms 'superfluous injury' and 'unnecessary suffering' and how is it determined whether a weapon falls within these terms? There are a variety of approaches as to whether a particular weapon has the prohibited effects.[41] Some stress the humanitarian aim of the prohibition; others focus on the more pragmatic military efficiency aspect.[42] The ICRC has consistently supported a humanitarian or health-based approach to determining the legitimacy of weapons under IHL.[43]

It is to be expected that there will be considerable differences between commentators depending upon their perspective. But whether a weapon falls within the prohibition is clearly a question of balance or proportionality: 'unnecessary' 'involved some sort of equation between, on the one hand, the degree of injury or suffering inflicted (the humanitarian aspect) and, on the other, the degree of necessity underlying the choice of a particular weapon (the military aspect)'.[44] Proportionality

[40] Oeter, 'Methods and Means', p. 114; and see L. Doswald-Beck, 'International Humanitarian Law and the Advisory Opinion of the International Court of Justice on the Legality of the Threat or Use of Nuclear Weapons' (1997) 316 *IRRC* 35 at 45.

[41] See e.g. Cassese, 'Unnecessary Suffering', pp. 23–30; F. Kalshoven, 'The Soldier and His Golf Clubs' in C. Swinarski (ed.), *Studies and Essays on International Humanitarian Law and Red Cross Principles* (Martinus Nijhoff, Geneva, 1984), p. 369.

[42] See e.g. 'Memorandum of Law: The Use of Lasers as Antipersonnel Weapons', Judge Advocate General, September 1988, in 'Blinding Weapons', Reports of the Meetings of Experts Convened by the International Committee of the Red Cross on Battlefield Laser Weapons (1989–91) (ICRC, Geneva, 1993), p. 71 at p. 367.

[43] See the discussion of Jean Pictet's 'humanitarian' approach as evidenced in the work of the ICRC, *Les Principes du Droit International Humanitaire* (1966), cited in Kalshoven, 'Golf Clubs', p. 378; and see generally H. Meyrowitz, 'The Principle of Superfluous Injury or Unnecessary Suffering' (1994) 299 *IRRC* 98. See also the SirUS project of the ICRC discussed at note 52 and the accompanying text below.

[44] See ICRC, *Certain Conventional Weapons*, p. 8. See also Bothe, Partsch and Solf, *New Rules*, p. 196.

is not used here in the sense of balancing the suffering if the weapon were used against the direct military advantage that might be anticipated (the rule in relation to civilians). It is relied on in this context as a general principle that can support a variety of different applications that, in the case of weapons, results in the outright prohibition on the weapon or a particular use thereof.[45] The relevance of proportionality to the assessment of weapons is borne out by the fact that many articulations of the test of superfluous injury or unnecessary suffering use this term.[46] Thus, for example, the ICRC in its study of the military use and effectiveness of anti-personnel mines refers to the following 'basic rule' of IHL, that '[i]t is prohibited to use weapons which cause unnecessary suffering. Therefore, the use of weapons whose damaging effects are disproportionate to their military purpose is prohibited.'[47]

How then is the proportionality equation formulated in the context of weapons and their effects on combatants? According to Greenwood, 'the crucial question is whether other weapons or methods of warfare available at the time would have achieved the same military goal as effectively while causing less suffering or injury'.[48] A comparison of weapons is thus required between their effects in terms of suffering and injury on the one hand and their military effectiveness on the other. The factors that fall to be considered in the equation in terms of suffering or injury encompass both the physical and psychological effects of weapons, the long-term nature of the injuries, the painfulness or severity of the wounds, mortality rates and the treatment available in conflict situations.[49] In the treaty negotiations regarding blinding weapons, the long-term impact on society of blind veterans was an additional influencing factor that led to the prohibition of these weapons.[50]

[45] See Doswald-Beck, 'Nuclear Weapons', p. 45.

[46] See e.g. Oeter, 'Methods and Means', p. 114; and Cassese, 'Unnecessary Suffering', pp. 27–9 (citing, *inter alia*, the Military Manual of the Federal Republic of Germany and the Austrian Military Manual).

[47] ICRC, *Anti-Personnel Landmines*, p. 24.

[48] C. Greenwood, 'Command and the Laws of Armed Conflict' (1993) 4 *The Occasional* 24; Bothe, Partsch and Solf, *New Rules*, p. 196; and Oeter, 'Methods and Means', p. 114, para. 402. See also the test proposed by the ICRC in its SirUS (superfluous injury and unnecessary suffering) project. The SirUS Project and Reviewing the Legality of New Weapons, ICRC, June 1999 (detailing the equation that should be applied in order to determine the legality of a weapon).

[49] ICRC, *Certain Conventional Weapons*, p. 8; and see Greenwood, 'Laws of Armed Conflict', p. 37; and Bothe, Partsch and Solf, *New Rules*, p. 196.

[50] See B. Carnahan and M. Robertson, 'The Protocol on "Blinding Laser Weapons": A New Direction for International Humanitarian Law' (1996) 90 *AJIL* 484.

The notion of 'suffering' has caused difficulties in terms of its definition given its highly subjective nature. The informal group of medical experts at the 1976 Lugano Conference explained in relation to the term unnecessary suffering, 'that it seems impossible at the present stage of medical knowledge to objectively define "suffering" or to give absolute values permitting comparison between human individuals'. Therefore, in their view, 'instead of "suffering" the wound or injury caused by a weapon offered a better but still very complex way of defining the effect of that particular weapon . . . it seemed preferable to use injury instead of suffering'.[51]

The ICRC SirUS project, an attempt to quantify more fully the health side of the proportionality equation, mirrors this approach.[52] This project commenced in 1996 and is designed to provide information on the objective effects of weapons on health in order to allow States to review the legality of particular weapons in order to meet their obligations under Articles 35 and 36 of Additional Protocol I. The proposals arising from the project to determine what constitutes superfluous injury or unnecessary suffering specify a number of effects of weapons on humans that have not been commonly seen as a result of armed conflict over the last five decades.[53] The legality of a weapon or its use should then be judged in light of these effects.

It has been very difficult to achieve consensus over the years as to the military effectiveness or necessity part of the equation. Necessary is a relative term and requires a determination of 'necessary for what'. According to the 1868 St Petersburg Declaration, what is necessary in armed conflict is to disable the greatest possible number of men and no more in order to weaken the enemy forces. Superfluous injury results when means are used that inflict disablement or render death inevitable to an extent that offers no real advantage in achieving this objective.[54] Using

[51] See ICRC, Report of the Conference of Government Experts on the Use of Certain Conventional Weapons, Lucerne, 24 September–18 October 1974, p. 140.

[52] The SirUS project originated from an ICRC symposium held in Montreux in 1996 entitled 'The Medical Profession and the Effects of Weapons'. See generally R. Coupland (ed.), *The SirUS Project: Towards a Determination of Which Weapons Cause Superfluous Injury or Unnecessary Suffering* (ICRC, Geneva, 1997).

[53] See R. M. Coupland and P. Herby, 'Review of the Legality of Weapons: A New Approach – The SirUS Project' (1999) 835 *IRRC* 538.

[54] See Cassese, 'Unnecessary Suffering', p. 17; and see the Report of Committee III on Conventional Weapons of the Diplomatic Conference that adopted Protocol I, *Official Records*, CDDH/215/Rev.1, vol. 15, p. 267, para. 21.

this approach, military effectiveness is defined in terms of rendering the enemy *hors de combat*.[55] However, this approach is only valid when anti-personnel weapons are being considered.[56] Weapons are used for a range of other objectives than to render the enemy *hors de combat* and their effectiveness in such cases must be determined by other criteria. Thus to determine the military effectiveness of a weapon you look at the primary purpose for which it was designed.[57]

A number of experts at the 1974 Lucerne Conference were of the view that military necessity in the context of weapons 'included, besides their capacity to disable enemy combatants, such other requirements as the destruction or neutralisation of enemy material, restriction of movement, interdiction of lines of communication, weakening of resources and, last but not least, enhancement of the security of friendly forces'.[58] Kalshoven agrees, and points out that, when a weapon that can be used for a range of purposes is being evaluated, the requirement of military necessity must be assessed in light of the practical circumstances in which it is to be used.[59] Ammunition containing depleted uranium is a case in point. Depleted uranium has many military uses.[60] It is 1.7 times as dense as lead and is particularly effective in penetrating armour, and has considerable advantages over other materials used for the same purpose. Weapons containing this substance were used in the 1990–1 and 2003 Persian Gulf conflicts, in Bosnia-Herzegovina (1995) and in Kosovo (1999).[61] Ammunition containing depleted uranium is only mildly radioactive but on impact with a solid object the uranium burns off in a spray of very fine dust.[62] The use of this substance can have detrimental health effects on combatants and also civilians through contamination of the environment.[63] The general view appears to be that any

[55] See C. Pilloud *et al.*, *Commentary on the Additional Protocols*, p. 403.
[56] See Bothe, Partsch and Solf, *New Rules*, p. 196.
[57] Fenrick, 'New Developments', p. 234. [58] ICRC, *Certain Conventional Weapons*, p. 9.
[59] Kalshoven, 'Arms, Armaments', p. 235.
[60] See UNEP, Depleted Uranium in Kosovo – Post-Conflict Environmental Assessment (2001), Appendix IV (Military Uses of Depleted Uranium).
[61] See e.g. Press Release Hab/163 Unep/67, 'NATO Confirms to United Nations Use of Depleted Uranium During Kosovo Conflict', 22 March 2000.
[62] *Ibid.*
[63] See S. A. Egerov, 'The Kosovo Crisis and the Law of Armed Conflicts' (2000) 837 *IRRC* 183; and UNEP, *Depleted Uranium in Kosovo*, Appendices I (Risk Assessment), IV.2 (Potential Health and Environmental Effects) and V (Possible Effects of DU on Groundwater). See also *Legality of Use of Force (Yugoslavia* v. *United Kingdom)*, available at

hazards that do exist are far outweighed by the military usefulness of the substance, particularly against tanks.

Protocol IV to CWC banning those 'laser weapons, specifically designed, as their sole combat function, to cause permanent blindness', is an example of an approach to the regulation of weapons which can regulate their anti-personnel use but leave their operation in other circumstances covered by the general principle banning superfluous injury or unnecessary suffering.

The question of superfluous injury or unnecessary suffering and weapons was directly raised before the International Court of Justice (ICJ) in the *Nuclear Weapons Advisory Opinion*.[64] Nuclear weapons are not specifically outlawed as causing superfluous injury or unnecessary suffering. Therefore, the issue fell to be determined under the general provisions of IHL. The Court had no difficulty in applying this body of law to the use of nuclear weapons. The argument had been put to the Court that these weapons were in a class of their own, that they had developed subsequently to the majority of the rules of IHL and, moreover, were not dealt with specifically by the Geneva Conventions and Additional Protocols.[65] This proposition was rejected summarily by the Court.[66] There was unanimity that the provisions of IHL apply to nuclear weapons, despite their being developed after the fundamental structure of the regime was in place and regardless of the fact that the existing principles had never envisaged a weapon of such destructive power.[67] The difficulty, however, with the argument that nuclear weapons are unlawful due to the level of suffering and injury that they inflict on combatants is that it is doubtful, as we have seen, if the general principle in the Hague Regulations prohibiting superfluous injury or unnecessary suffering *per se* outlaws any particular weapon.[68] However, the Court described as a 'cardinal principle' the rule prohibiting unnecessary suffering to combatants and was of the view that this principle outlawed certain weapons (although not nuclear weapons) irrespective of whether they were specifically prohibited by treaty or not:

www.icj-cij.org/icjwww/idocket/iyuk/iyukframe.htm, in which the applicant State argues that ammunition containing depleted uranium (and also cluster bombs) are prohibited under IHL.

64 *Legality of the Threat or Use of Nuclear Weapons*, Advisory Opinion (hereafter *Nuclear Weapons* Advisory Opinion), ICJ Reports 1996, 26.

65 For the background to the Protocols and the issue of nuclear weapons, see Kalshoven, 'Arms, Armaments', pp. 278–82.

66 *Nuclear Weapons* Advisory Opinion, pp. 259–60. 67 *Ibid.*

68 See the discussion in note 38 above and the accompanying text.

it is accordingly prohibited to use weapons causing them [combatants] such harm or uselessly aggravating their suffering . . . that is to say a harm greater than that unavoidable to achieve legitimate military objectives . . . In conformity with the aforementioned principles, humanitarian law, at a very early stage, prohibited certain types of weapons either because of their indiscriminate effect on combatants and civilians or because of the unnecessary suffering caused to combatants, that is to say, a harm greater than that unavoidable to achieve legitimate military objectives. If an envisaged use of weapons would not meet the requirements of humanitarian law, a threat to engage in such use would also be contrary to that law.[69]

Other than this general statement little is added to the jurisprudence on the question of weapons by the majority opinion, other than the implication that, if nuclear weapons are legitimate under *ius ad bellum* in extreme cases of self-defence, then the superfluous injury or unnecessary suffering test is either satisfied or irrelevant in such cases. Some of the other opinions, however, make more of a contribution to this question. Judge Higgins, although not deciding the issue, stresses that the notion of unnecessary suffering in relation to combatants, is not an assessment that is made in a void. Although, as she says, it is perhaps difficult to comprehend the use of nuclear weapons as not involving unnecessary suffering, the assessment of their legitimacy involves a comparison between this suffering and what is necessary to achieve military success in the particular circumstances.[70] It is on this basis that certain weapons have been successfully outlawed as involving unnecessary suffering. In these instances there was consensus amongst States that military objectives could be achieved using other means and methods of warfare that did not inflict such levels of suffering on combatants.[71]

Judge Weeramantry, on the other hand, to support his view that nuclear weapons are unlawful, compares the cruelty of their effects with that of a single expanding bullet outlawed in 1899.[72] A comparison of weapons and their relative cruelty, however, without at the same time an assessment of their military effectiveness is not the approach that has received majority support to date.

Several other members of the Court find the use of nuclear weapons illegitimate in relation to combatants.[73] Judge Shahabuddeen considers that the Court had before it sufficient material 'to reasonably find that the public conscience considers that the use of nuclear weapons

[69] *Nuclear Weapons* Advisory Opinion, p. 257.
[70] *Ibid.*, p. 586. [71] *Ibid.* [72] *Ibid.*, p. 485.
[73] *Ibid.*, Dissenting Opinion of Judge Koroma, p. 580.

causes suffering which is unacceptable whatever might be the military advantage derivable from such use'.[74] He takes a novel approach and argues that the prohibition against weapons causing superfluous injury or unnecessary suffering should extend to civilians and so prohibit the use of nuclear weapons even if it were the case that the discrimination and proportionality requirements were regarded as satisfied.[75]

The proportionality equation in relation to weapons deals with whether the suffering or injury to individual combatants is justified by the military advantage provided by the weapon. The rule of proportionality that protects civilians, however, delimits the number of casualties that are legitimate. They must not be excessive in light of the military advantage anticipated from the particular attack. Does the prohibition on superfluous injury and unnecessary suffering perform the same function in relation to combatant casualties or is its only function in that context to outlaw disproportionate suffering or injury inflicted by weapons? One approach is that any constraint on the number of combatant casualties is a matter for the proportionality requirement of the *ius ad bellum*.[76] This is consistent with the fundamental principle of IHL that the only legitimate aim of warfare is to weaken the military forces of the enemy. The extent to which you can weaken these forces depends on the lawful purpose of the use of force. This was a relevant issue in the Persian Gulf conflict (1990–1): how many Iraqi combatant casualties were dictated by the demands of self-defence? The difference between the rules protecting civilians and combatants in this context is based on the fact that combatants are legitimate targets in armed conflict whereas civilians are not. It therefore became accepted that there should be some restraints on the number of civilian casualties in warfare. Such an approach in relation to combatants has its proponents. For example, Bothe, Partsch and Solf are of the view that the prohibition on the infliction of superfluous injury or unnecessary suffering is 'another way of stating the rule of proportionality defined in the context of the protection of the civilian population', and regard all forceful measures as needing to be proportionate to 'the achievement of a definite military advantage'.[77]

[74] *Ibid.*, p. 403. [75] *Ibid.*, pp. 403–5.

[76] See F. Hampson, 'Means and Methods of Warfare in the Conflict in the Gulf' in Peter Rowe (ed.), *The Gulf War (1990–91) in International and English Law* (Routledge, London, 1993), p. 89.

[77] Bothe, Partsch and Solf, *New Rules*, p. 195.

The discussion of superfluous injury or unnecessary suffering highlights the pragmatic nature of this area of the law. It is a mistake to regard it as predominantly humanitarian in nature. To do so obscures the real position of States.[78] It is only when a weapon is militarily ineffective that it will be outlawed. In the words of one commentator: 'a weapon will be restricted in inverse proportion, more or less, to its effectiveness; that the more efficient a weapon or method of warfare the less likelihood there is of its being restricted in action by the rules of war'.[79] The example is provided of the explosive bullet outlawed by the 1868 St Petersburg Declaration which, having demonstrated its efficiency in aerial warfare, was legitimised by Article 18 of The Hague Rules on Aerial Warfare. This trend has continued. In the context of the CWC negotiations, Kalshoven describes the resistance to increased protections for combatants, using the example of incendiary weapons.[80] The success with weapons designed to blind, moreover, could be attributed to the fact that they serve no real military purpose, and States were not in the process of developing them for military purposes.[81]

The suppression of breaches of the requirements of proportionality with respect to combatants[82]

The foregoing discussion established that a failure to comply with the prohibition on weapons causing superfluous injury or unnecessary suffering is a breach of both customary and conventional provisions of IHL. It remains to consider the consequences for States and individuals responsible for such violations of IHL.

Before considering, however, the special regime that has developed over the years to enforce the provisions of IHL, it must be kept in mind

[78] On the influence of humanity generally over the years in relation to the regulation of the conduct of armed conflict, see Best, *Law and Armed Conflict*.

[79] M. Royse, *Aerial Bombardment and the International Regulation of Warfare* (H. Vinal Ltd, New York, 1928), p. 132. A similar theme is expanded in C. Jochnick and R. Normand, 'The Legitimation of Violence: A Critical History of the Law of War' (1994) 35 *Harvard ILJ* 49, who focus on the development of the Law of The Hague and attack the underlying assumption that these rules are based on humanitarian considerations.

[80] Kalshoven, 'Arms, Armament', pp. 256ff, although Kalshoven's pessimism (p. 264) as to the likelihood of review and amendment as provided for in the CWC has not come to pass.

[81] Carnahan and Robertson, 'Blinding Laser Weapons', p. 487.

[82] For a discussion of issues of responsibility and enforcement in the context of IHL and peacekeeping forces, see Chapter 6 below.

that the general principles of State responsibility for internationally wrongful acts are applicable to the conduct of the armed forces of a State.[83] An illustration of the operation of these principles in practice is the United Nations Compensation Commission established by the Security Council in Resolution 687 to deal with claims against Iraq arising from the 1990–1 Persian Gulf conflict.[84] These principles are theoretically brought into operation by the use of weapons prohibited under IHL. Indeed, the use of unlawful weapons, namely, depleted uranium and cluster bombs, has been alleged by the former Yugoslavia in proceedings before the ICJ against various member States of NATO for their actions in Kosovo in 1999.[85]

The modern system of suppression of breaches of IHL is quite distinctive in international law. First, the institution of belligerent reprisals has traditionally performed an important role as a mechanism to ensure compliance with the requirements of IHL. Reprisals in *ius in bello* are known as belligerent reprisals.[86] They are distinct from reprisals involving the use of force that were legitimate prior to the United Nations Charter.[87] Belligerent reprisals are defined in the United States Army Field Manual as 'acts of retaliation in the form of conduct which would otherwise be unlawful, resorted to by one belligerent against enemy personnel or property for acts of warfare committed by the other belligerent in violation of the law of war for the purpose of enforcing future compliance with the recognised rules of civilized warfare'.[88] The taking of reprisal action is very controversial in international law. It is based on the concept of collective responsibility of members of the offending

[83] See Art. 91 of Additional Protocol I: 'A Party to the conflict which violates the provisions of the Conventions or of this Protocol shall, if the case demands, be liable to pay compensation. It shall be responsible for all acts committed by persons forming part of its armed forces.' See also F. Kalshoven, 'State Responsibility for Warlike Acts of the Armed Forces: From Article 3 of Hague Convention IV of 1907 to Article 91 of Additional Protocol I of 1977 and Beyond' (1991) 40 *ICLQ* 827 (for a discussion of the relationship between the principles of State responsibility and IHL).

[84] See SC Res. 687 (3 April 1991).

[85] See e.g. *Legality of Use of Force* (*Yugoslavia* v. *United Kingdom*) available at www.icj-cij.org/icjwww/idocket/iyuk/iyukframe.htm.

[86] See generally F. Kalshoven, *Belligerent Reprisals* (Sijthoff, Leiden, 1971).

[87] See the discussion of the system of reprisals in *ius ad bellum*, in Chapter 2, note 97 and the accompanying text above.

[88] See Department of the Army Field Manual, The Law of Land Warfare No. 27-10 (Washington DC, 1956), para. 497. See also The War Office, WO Code No. 12333, The Law of War on Land, Part III of the Manual of Military Law (London, 1958), paras. 642–8, to the same effect.

State, and in most cases the victims of the reprisal have nothing to do with the illegal act that provoked the retaliatory action.[89]

A number of attempts have been made to codify the law of reprisals.[90] These were not attended by any success until the period between the two World Wars when Article 2 of the Geneva Prisoners of War Convention of 1929 prohibited reprisals against prisoners of war. This process continued with all four Geneva Conventions of 1949 containing provisions prohibiting reprisals in certain circumstances.[91] Despite considerable difficulties experienced during the negotiations, Additional Protocol I considerably expands the scope of persons or objects against which reprisal action is prohibited.[92] Article 51(6) prohibits reprisals against the civilian population. It represents a significant advance in humanitarian law. Article 20 broadens the definition of the groups that were already protected from reprisals in the First and Second Geneva Conventions of 1949. Other prohibited targets are civilian objects (Article 52(1)); objects indispensable to the survival of the civilian population (Article 54(4)); the natural environment (Article 55(2)); and works and installations containing dangerous forces such as dams, dykes and nuclear electrical generating stations (Article 56(4)). Many of these provisions are an advance on the customary position and only bind State parties to the Protocol.[93]

There are, however, well-developed customary rules governing the use of reprisals. The resort to reprisals in armed conflict has a long history

[89] See e.g. S. Nahlik, 'Belligerent Reprisals as Seen in the Light of the Diplomatic Conference on Humanitarian Law, Geneva, 1974–1977' (1978) 42 *Law and Contemporary Problems* 36 at 37; F. Hampson, 'Belligerent Reprisals and the 1977 Protocols to the Geneva Conventions' (1988) 37 *ICLQ* 818.

[90] See Kalshoven, *Belligerent Reprisals*, pp. 69–114.

[91] Art. 46 of the Geneva Convention for the Amelioration of the Condition of the Wounded and Sick in Armed Forces in the Field, 12 August 1949, (1950) 75 UNTS 31 (hereafter the First Geneva Convention); Art. 47 of the Geneva Convention for the Amelioration of the Condition of the Wounded, Sick and Shipwrecked Members of Armed Forces at Sea, 12 August 1949, (1950) 75 UNTS 85 (hereafter the Second Geneva Convention); Art. 134(3) of the Geneva Convention Relative to the Protection of Prisoners of War, 12 August 1949, (1950) 75 UNTS 135 (hereafter the Third Geneva Convention); and Art. 33(3) of the Geneva Convention Relative to the Protection of Civilian Persons in Time of War, 12 August 1949, (1950) 75 UNTS 287 (hereafter the Fourth Geneva Convention).

[92] For an account of the negotiations in relation to reprisals at the Diplomatic Conference, see C. Pilloud *et al.*, *Commentary on the Additional Protocols*, pp. 982ff.

[93] On the customary status of the conventional norms of IHL, see generally L. Doswald-Beck and J. Henckaerts (eds.), *Customary International Humanitarian Law* (Cambridge University Press, Cambridge, 2003).

and, although accepted by most commentators as legitimate, they were nevertheless regarded as subject, amongst other things, to the requirement of proportionality. For example, the 1880 Oxford Manual stipulated that reprisals must 'never exceed the measure of the infraction of the laws of war committed by the enemy'.[94] Commentators were of the same view. For example, Holland wrote that reprisals 'must not be disproportionate to the offence, and must in no case be of a barbarous character'.[95] Modern military manuals confirm that acts of reprisals should not be excessive and should bear a reasonable relation to the violations by the enemy.[96]

The same approach was taken by the Trial Chamber of the ICTY in the *Kupreskic* case where the Tribunal included proportionality as one of the limiting factors in reprisal action, describing it as entailing 'not only that the reprisals must not be excessive compared to the precedent unlawful act of warfare, but also that they must stop as soon as that unlawful act has been discontinued'.[97]

The requirement of proportionality in relation to reprisals is not, therefore, in dispute. Its application, however, is complicated for a number of reasons. It is regarded as requiring some form of equivalence between the illegal act provoking the reprisal and the response. This requirement was established in the *Naulilaa Arbitration*.[98] Although strictly speaking that incident raised the issue of proportionality in *ius ad bellum*, it is regarded as also establishing the test of proportionality for reprisal action in *ius in bello*.[99]

The difficulty, however, with the requirement of equivalence is that many targets can no longer be the object of reprisal action. For parties to Additional Protocol I, the only legitimate object of reprisal action

[94] See Art. 85, *The Laws of War on Land, Manual Published by the Institute of International Law 1880*, reprinted in D. Schindler and J. Toman (eds.), *The Laws of Armed Conflicts: A Collection of Conventions, Resolutions and Other Documents* (3rd edn, Martinus Nijhoff, Dordrecht, 1988), pp. 35 and 48.

[95] See T. Holland, *The Laws of War on Land (Written and Unwritten)* (Clarendon Press, Oxford, 1928), p. 61. See also W. Hall, *A Treatise on International Law* (4th edn, Clarendon Press, Oxford, 1895), p. 432.

[96] The Law of War on Land, Part III of the Manual of Military Law (UK), para. 648; and Field Manual No. 27-10, The Law of Land Warfare (US), para. 497.

[97] *Prosecutor* v. *Kupreskic*, Case No. IT-95-16-T-14, Judgment, January 2000, para. 535.

[98] *Naulilaa Arbitration (Portugal* v. *Germany)*, 2 RIAA 1928, 1012.

[99] At the time of the *Naulilaa Arbitration* there was no need, as is the case under the Charter system, to distinguish between reprisals in *ius in bello* and *ius ad bellum*.

is the armed forces of the other State.[100] Even for States not party to the Protocol, the customary rules considerably restrict the targets that can be legitimately the object of reprisal action. Given these difficulties, doubts have been expressed as to whether the requirement of equivalence prohibits a reprisal except against the same target, as was the subject of the illegal act provoking it.[101] It appears, however, that exact equivalence between the target of the attack and the response has never been a requirement of belligerent reprisals. It is, however, possible that a finding of a disproportionate response will more easily be reached in such circumstances.

One of the other requirements of legitimate reprisals in IHL is that they are necessary, that is, they must be by way of last resort.[102] The ICTY has confirmed that reprisals are restricted by 'the principle whereby they must be a last resort in attempts to impose compliance by the adversary with legal standards'.[103]

Secondly, the system of suppression of breaches of IHL also includes the concept of individual criminal liability. The four Geneva Conventions of 1949 and Additional Protocol I, which regulate international armed conflicts, employ a system of 'grave breaches' to identify those breaches of IHL considered most serious.[104] It is clear that 'grave breaches' of the four Geneva Conventions entail individual criminal responsibility, although the term 'war crime' is not generally used.[105] In some cases, disproportionate attacks involving the civilian population or civilian

[100] For a discussion of whether the Protocol system operates on reciprocity in this context, see Hampson, 'Belligerent Reprisals', pp. 829–32.

[101] For example, if one State illegally targets the civilian population of the opposing State, that State if bound by the Protocol will be unable to respond in kind. The question then may arise as to whether it would be legitimate for the aggrieved State to target the adversaries' armed forces with, for example, an illegal weapon: see *ibid.*, p. 824. Cf. Hall, *Treatise* (4th edn), p. 556.

[102] See e.g. Field Manual No. 27-10, The Law of Land Warfare (US), para. 497(a); The Law of War on Land, Part III of the Manual of Military Law (UK), para. 646.

[103] *Prosecutor* v. *Kupreskic*, Case No. IT-95-16-T-14, Judgment.

[104] See Arts. 49 and 50 of the First Geneva Convention; Arts. 50 and 51 of the Second Geneva Convention; Arts. 129 and 130 of the Third Geneva Convention; Arts. 146 and 147 of the Fourth Geneva Convention; and Arts. 85 and 86 of Additional Protocol I.

[105] As G. Draper, 'The Modern Pattern of War Criminality' in Y. Dinstein and M. Tabory (eds.), *War Crimes in International Law* (Martinus Nijhoff, Boston, 1996), p. 157, observes, the term 'war crime' appears only once in the 417 articles that comprise the four Geneva Conventions of 1949. However, by Art. 85(5) of Additional Protocol I, grave breaches of the Conventions and Protocols are designated as war crimes.

objects amount to a grave breach of Additional Protocol I.[106] The use of prohibited weapons, however, is not specifically included in the grave breach provisions. Nevertheless, breaches of the Geneva Conventions and Additional Protocol I that are not listed as grave breaches, but that nonetheless reach an accepted level of 'seriousness', may still constitute war crimes.[107]

State parties have a duty to enact legislation to provide effective penal sanctions for persons committing grave breaches of the conventional provisions, as well as for persons who have ordered the commission of grave breaches.[108] State parties also have a duty to actively search for those who are alleged to have committed grave breaches and if found within their territory to bring them before their courts or, alternatively, to extradite them for prosecution.[109] The Geneva Conventions impose a positive obligation on States to exercise jurisdiction over persons committing grave breaches[110] and no State is permitted to absolve itself, or any other State, of liability incurred with respect to grave breaches.[111] In respect of non-grave breaches, the Geneva Conventions impose upon States the less rigorous duty to take measures necessary to 'suppress' those breaches.[112]

[106] See Art. 85(3) of Additional Protocol I; and see the further discussion in Chapter 4, note 174, and the accompanying text below.

[107] See e.g. Y. Dinstein, 'The Distinctions Between War Crimes and Crimes Against Peace' in Y. Dinstein and M. Tabory (eds.), *War Crimes in International Law* (Martinus Nijhoff, Boston, 1996), pp. 1 and 4. The Statute of the ICTY provides an example of the practical application of this principle: see note 118 and the accompanying text below.

[108] See Art. 49 of the First Geneva Convention; Art. 50 of the Second Geneva Convention; Art. 129 of the Third Geneva Convention; and Art. 146 of the Fourth Geneva Convention. By Art. 85(1) of Additional Protocol I, State parties are under the same obligations regarding the repression of grave breaches in Additional Protocol I as those arising under the four Geneva Conventions.

[109] See Art. 49 of the First Geneva Convention; Art. 50 of the Second Geneva Convention; Art. 129 of the Third Geneva Convention; and Art. 146 of the Fourth Geneva Convention. See also O. Uhler, *Geneva Convention Relative to the Protection of Civilian Persons in Time of War* (ICRC, Geneva, 1958), pp. 590–6.

[110] See T. Meron, 'International Criminalization of Internal Atrocities' (1995) 89 *AJIL* 554 at 569.

[111] See Art. 51 of the First Geneva Convention; Art. 52 of the Second Geneva Convention; Art. 131 of the Third Geneva Convention; and Art. 148 of the Fourth Geneva Convention.

[112] See Art. 49 of the First Geneva Convention; Art. 50 of the Second Geneva Convention; Art. 129 of the Third Geneva Convention; and Art. 146 of the Fourth Geneva Convention. See also Meron, 'International Criminalization', p. 566 (arguing that universal jurisdiction may also arise in respect of non-grave breaches. The difference is that grave breaches entail an *obligation* to prosecute, whereas other violations may simply give rise to a *right* to prosecute).

Little has been achieved, however, in practical terms from the treaty system of universal jurisdiction for the punishment of war crimes. More significant for the enforcement of individual criminal responsibility has been the establishment on occasion of *ad hoc* tribunals to punish persons alleged to have committed serious breaches of IHL. The first of these initiatives, the Nuremberg War Crimes Tribunal established by treaty after the Second World War to try offences committed by the Axis powers, included no indictments for the use of prohibited weapons.

There have been, however, considerable developments in the context of *ad hoc* international criminal tribunals since Nuremberg. The Security Council in the post-Cold War era has played an important role in the enforcement of IHL and not just in the context of the establishment of *ad hoc* international criminal tribunals.[113] The United Nations contribution to IHL in standard-setting and humanitarian diplomacy is of growing significance. An ICRC commentator describes the role of the various organs of the United Nations in relation to IHL as, first, the 'reaffirmation and progressive codification of IHL (standard-setting)'; secondly, 'ensuring prosecution and punishment of persons who have committed serious violations of that law'; and, thirdly, 'increasing respect on the part of parties to specific conflicts for their obligations under IHL (humanitarian diplomacy)'.

Article 89 of Additional Protocol I specifically refers to the role of the United Nations in relation to serious violations of the Conventions or Protocol. However, prior to the reactivation of the Security Council in the 1990s, IHL was addressed infrequently in Security Council resolutions. One example was Resolution 540, adopted during the Iran/Iraq conflict (1980–8), condemning the parties for the use of poisonous gases under the Gas Protocol of 1925. At the end of the Cold War era, this lack of involvement underwent a fundamental change, with the Security Council taking an active role in the maintenance of international peace and security. Commentators began to observe the potential of the Security Council to take a role in the implementation and enforcement of IHL.[114]

[113] See H. P. Gasser, 'The United Nations and International IHL: The International Committee of the Red Cross and the United Nations' Involvement in the Implementation of International IHL', paper presented to the International Symposium on the occasion of the fiftieth anniversary of the United Nations, Geneva (1995), pp. 19–21.

[114] See e.g. L. Boisson de Chazournes, 'The Collective Responsibility of States to Ensure Respect for Humanitarian Principles' in A. Bloed *et al.* (eds.), *Monitoring Human Rights in Europe: Comparing International Procedures and Mechanisms* (Martinus Nijhoff, Dordrecht, 1993), pp. 247 and 251–6.

Indeed, in the period 1990–6 the Security Council adopted over ninety resolutions dealing with some aspect of IHL.[115] The majority of these resolutions, however, have been concerned either with civil conflicts or international armed conflicts involving guerrilla-style warfare and their emphasis has been on the mistreatment of the civilian population. They have not referred to such issues as indiscriminate attacks or the use of prohibited weapons.

A particularly important development in the enforcement of IHL is the frequently expressed view of the Security Council that it regards breaches of IHL as having the potential to constitute a 'threat to the peace' within the meaning of Article 39, thereby conferring jurisdiction on the Security Council under Chapter VII of the Charter. As a consequence, in the 1990s, the Security Council, using its Chapter VII powers, established two *ad hoc* international war crimes tribunals (the ICTY and the International Criminal Tribunal for Rwanda (ICTR))[116] as measures to restore international peace and security. Additionally, in 2000, the Security Council entered into an agreement with Sierra Leone to establish a Special Court to prosecute persons responsible for, *inter alia*, war crimes and other serious violations of IHL.[117]

The ICTY has jurisdiction over grave breaches of the Geneva Conventions of 1949 (Article 2) and violations of the laws or customs of war (Article 3). The resort to weapons causing superfluous injury or unnecessary suffering is not a grave breach of the 1949 Geneva Conventions. However, the 'employment of poisonous weapons or other weapons calculated to cause unnecessary suffering' is specifically included in Article 3 as a violation of the laws or customs of war.[118] Neither the ICTR nor the Special Court for Sierra Leone has jurisdiction over the use of unlawful weapons.

[115] See e.g. SC Res. 666, 13 September 1990 (applicability of the Fourth Geneva Convention); SC Res. 950, 21 October 1994 (Liberia); SC Res. 935, 1 July 1994 (Rwanda); SC Res. 794, 3 December 1992 (Somalia); and SC Res. 771, 13 August 1992 (former Yugoslavia).

[116] The International Criminal Tribunal for Rwanda was established by the UN Security Council pursuant to SC Res. 955, 8 November 1994.

[117] See Report of the Secretary-General on the Establishment of a Special Court for Sierra Leone, S/2000/915, 4 October 2000, Annex.

[118] This definition adopts the terminology of Art. 23(e) of the Regulations annexed to Hague Convention II Respecting the Laws and Customs of War on Land, 29 July 1899, and Regulations annexed to Hague Convention IV Respecting the Laws and Customs of War on Land, 18 October 1907 (hereafter the Hague Regulations). Cf. the Statute of the ICC, which adopts the language of Art. 35(2) of Additional Protocol II; see note 119 below.

Finally, in the context of war crimes tribunals, the Statute of the ICC confers jurisdiction on the ICC for, *inter alia*, war crimes.[119] War crimes are defined in Article 2(b) to include:

[o]ther serious violations of the laws and customs applicable in international armed conflict, within the established framework of international law, namely, any of the following acts:

. . .

(xvii) Employing poison or poisoned weapons;[120]

(xviii) Employing asphyxiating, poisonous or other gases, and all analogous liquids, materials or devices;[121]

. . .

(xix) Employing bullets which expand or flatten easily in the human body, such as bullets with a hard envelope which does not entirely cover the core or is pierced with incisions;[122]

. . .

(xx) Employing weapons, projectiles and material and methods of warfare which are of a nature to cause superfluous injury or unnecessary suffering or which are inherently indiscriminate in violation of the international law of armed conflict, provided that such weapons, projectiles and material and methods of warfare are the subject of a comprehensive prohibition and are included in an annex to this Statute, by an amendment in accordance with the relevant provisions set forth in articles 121 and 123;

. . .

The issue of prohibited weapons, apart from the traditional established categories in paragraphs (xvii), (xviii) and (xix), was very contentious during the negotiations of the Statute.[123] The traditional lack of consensus as to whether the general prohibition on weapons with a certain effect actually outlaws any weapon continued to manifest itself. Debate

119 See Art. 8 of the Statute of the ICC.

120 This prohibition is derived from Art. 23(a) of the Hague Regulations.

121 This prohibition is derived from the 1925 Protocol for the Prohibition of the Use in War of Asphyxiating, Poisonous or Other Gases, and of Bacteriological Methods of Warfare: see Dörmann, *Elements of War Crimes*, pp. 285–91 (for a discussion of the Elements of Crimes of the Statute of the ICC for this offence).

122 This prohibition is derived from Art. 23(a) of the 1899 Hague Declaration Concerning Expanding Bullets (Declaration No. 3 annexed to Hague Convention IV). See Dörmann, *Elements of War Crimes* (for a discussion of the Elements of Crimes of the Statute of the ICC for this offence).

123 See H. von Hebel and D. Robinson, 'Crimes Within the Jurisdiction of the Court' in R. S. Lee (ed.), *The International Criminal Court – Issues, Negotiations, Results* (Kluwer Law International, The Hague, 1999), pp. 79 and 114–16 (for a discussion of the negotiating history of the crimes relating to weapons in the Statute of the ICC).

revolved around the option of either identifying a list of prohibited weapons or including a general prohibitory clause in the Statute. The difficulty with the first option is that there is little consensus as to candidates for inclusion in such a list. A general prohibitory clause was also perceived as unsatisfactory as it provided no certainty for decision-makers as to the weapons that fall under such a clause.[124] The final text is a compromise that in effect leaves the definition of this crime to be decided at a later date.

Conclusion

The current challenge for IHL in the area of the control of weapons that inflict superfluous injury or unnecessary suffering is to give some concrete definition to these concepts. That is, to develop legal criteria so that States developing new weapons will be obliged to measure the anticipated effects of such weapons in order to ensure that their use does not infringe this norm of international law. Significantly, for the first time, a State has been prepared to declare that blinding laser weapons which can cause permanent blindness are contrary to the customary principle prohibiting means and methods of warfare which cause unnecessary suffering.[125] In relation to conventional developments, the blinding weapons Protocol may indicate a new direction, as it 'represents the first time since 1868, when the use of exploding bullets was banned, that a weapon of military interest has been banned before its use on the battlefield and before a stream of victims gave visible proof of its tragic effects'.[126] Moreover, there are indications that the division between disarmament and IHL is to some extent being eroded and humanitarian law instruments dealing with conventional weapons are now incorporating arms-control provisions. This development has, however, been dictated by the movement to protect civilians against the indiscriminate use of weapons and not by arguments based on the fact that these weapons inflict superfluous injury or unnecessary suffering on combatants.

[124] See *ibid.*, pp. 113–16 (for the negotiating history of this clause).

[125] See Declaration by Sweden on the ratification of Protocol IV to the CWC, 9 January 1997.

[126] ICRC News Release, 'Vienna Diplomatic Conference Achieves New Prohibition on Blinding Laser Weapons and Deadlock on Landmines', 13 October 1995, p. 3.

4 Proportionality and civilians in modern international humanitarian law

Introduction

This chapter details the content of the modern rule of proportionality in international humanitarian law (IHL) that is designed to limit the impact of armed conflict on the civilian population and civilian objects. The main focus of the analysis is the conventional and customary norm of proportionality in the context of international armed conflicts.[1] There are increasing indications, however, that proportionality has a role to play as part of the emergent customary law regime regulating the conduct of non-international armed conflicts. Consequently, these developments are also assessed. The discussion that follows is limited to unilateral State action. The question of the application of proportionality in the context of collective enforcement actions, including peacekeeping operations, is considered in Chapter 6.

It will be recalled that, with the advent of such means of warfare as aerial bombardment, attempts had been made to develop legal protections for civilians against the impact of such practices.[2] However, the requirement to balance the achievement of a military objective against the likely civilian losses was not established in the practice of States

[1] See Arts. 51(5)(b) and 57(2)(a)(iii) and (b) of Protocol Additional to the Geneva Conventions of 12 August 1949, and Relating to the Protection of Victims of International Armed Conflicts, adopted in 1977 (Protocol I), 12 December 1977, (1979) 1125 UNTS 3 (hereafter Additional Protocol I). See also Art. 3(8) of the United Nations Convention on Prohibitions or Restrictions on the Use of Certain Conventional Weapons Which May Be Deemed to Be Excessively Injurious or to Have Indiscriminate Effects, 10 April 1981, (1980) 19 ILM 1523, Protocol on Prohibitions or Restrictions on the Use of Mines, Booby-Traps and Other Devices, as amended on 3 May 1996 (hereafter Protocol I to the CWC), discussed further in note 172 and the accompanying text below.

[2] See the discussion in Chapter 2, note 136 and the accompanying text above.

in the period preceding the adoption of the United Nations Charter in 1945. It was not until developments in human rights after the adoption of the Charter began to influence the law of armed conflict (as it was then known) that the movement to provide expanded protections for civilians culminated in the acceptance of the idea that even attacks on military targets must not lead to excessive collateral casualties. This process came to fruition in 1977 with the adoption of the treaty rule of proportionality in Additional Protocol I to the four 1949 Geneva Conventions.

The advances in the legal regime protecting civilians from the collateral effects of armed conflict have been hard won. In the period since the end of the Cold War new challenges have confronted IHL in its efforts to protect civilians from the effects of armed conflict. This era has witnessed the development of armed interventions against so-called 'rogue' States or regimes, as illustrated by the 1990–1 and 2003 Persian Gulf, the 1999 Kosovo and the 2002 Afghanistan conflicts. Two potentially conflicting imperatives have characterised these undertakings. First, the minimisation of combatant casualties has assumed unprecedented significance. In both Persian Gulf conflicts, considerable reliance was placed on high-altitude aerial bombardment. This tactic was even more marked in the 1999 Kosovo action by NATO.[3] Arguably, such methods increase the likelihood of civilian casualties. Secondly, public tolerance of collateral casualties has been decreasing, with human rights agencies and other critics subjecting these forceful actions to considerable scrutiny.[4] A great deal is now expected of the legal regime in terms of providing adequate protection for civilians in such situations. Against this background, the

[3] See e.g. A. Roberts, 'NATO's "Humanitarian" War over Kosovo' (1999) 41(3) *Survival* 102 at 110 (referring to the reliance on air power by Western States in 'humanitarian' interventions in the 1990s in order to avoid the risk of combatant casualties). See also the careful analysis from a military perspective of this phenomenon by A. P. V. Rogers, 'Zero-Casualty Warfare' (2000) 837 *IRRC* 165.

[4] See e.g. Amnesty International, NATO/Federal Republic of Yugoslavia, *'Collateral Damage' or Unlawful Killing? Violations of the Laws of War by NATO During Operation Allied Force* (2000), available at http://web.amnesty.org/library/index/ENGEUR700182000/; Human Rights Watch, *Civilian Deaths in the NATO Air Campaign, 2000* (No. 1 (D) 2000), vol. 12, available at www.hrw.org/hrw/reports/2000/nato/; and see also *Final Report to the Prosecutor by the Committee Established to Review the NATO Bombing Campaign Against the Federal Republic of Yugoslavia*, available at www.un.org/icty/pressreal/nato061300.htm; and the critical response to the report by M. Bothe, 'The Protection of the Civilian Population and NATO Bombing on Yugoslavia: Comments on a Report to the Prosecutor of the ICTY' (2001) 12 *EJIL* 531.

rules of IHL protecting civilians and civilian objects from the impact of armed conflict, including proportionality, have assumed more significance. However, at the same time, their shortcomings have become increasingly apparent.

The discussion commences with an analysis of the conventional rule of proportionality in Additional Protocol I dealing with international armed conflicts in order to clarify how the rule was envisaged to operate at the time of its adoption. There were considerable uncertainties in the detail of the rule at that time. Therefore, subsequent State practice in the application of proportionality assumes considerable importance and is considered in detail as it not only indicates what treaty parties regard as their conventional obligations but also supplies evidence of the customary position for non-State parties.[5] The relevance of proportionality in the case of non-international armed conflicts is then assessed. Additional Protocol I is not the only conventional IHL instrument that includes the concept of proportionality. Protocol II to the Conventional Weapons Convention includes a test of proportionality that is considered in this chapter.

Finally, the system by which the requirements of proportionality in IHL are enforced is examined. The criminalisation of launching a disproportionate attack in Additional Protocol I[6] and the Statutes of the International Criminal Tribunal for the Former Yugoslavia (ICTY)[7] and the International Criminal Court (ICC)[8] has exacerbated the unease that the norm has always generated amongst States. The equation applies to everyday battlefield decisions and its requirements are regarded as uncertain and vague by those responsible for its implementation. The fact that these judgments can now result in criminal liability has intensified the debate over the rule.

[5] As at 20 January 2003, there were 161 State parties to Additional Protocol I.

[6] See the further discussion of this issue in note 177 and the accompanying text below.

[7] The International Criminal Tribunal for the former Yugoslavia (ICTY) was established by the UN Security Council pursuant to SC Res. 808, 22 February 1993, and SC Res. 827, 25 May 1993; and see the further discussion of this issue in note 186 and the accompanying text below.

[8] Rome Statute of the International Criminal Court, UN Doc. A/Conf.183/9 (17 July 1998) (hereafter Statute of the ICC). The Statute was adopted by the United Nations Diplomatic Conference of Plenipotentiaries on the Establishment of an International Criminal Court on 17 July 1998 and came into force on 1 July 2002; and see the further discussion of this issue in note 198 and the accompanying text below.

Proportionality in the United Nations era

Background to the adoption of the rule of proportionality in Additional Protocol I to the Geneva Conventions

As early as 1956, the nineteenth International Conference of the Red Cross (ICRC) adopted the Draft Rules for the Limitation of the Dangers Incurred by the Civilian Population in Time of War.[9] The Draft Rules dealt with the issue of civilian casualties:

Article 8 The person responsible for ordering or launching an attack shall, first of all:

(a) make sure that the objectives, or objectives, to be attacked are military objectives within the meaning of the present rules, and are duly identified.

When the military advantage to be gained leaves the choice open between several objectives, he is required to select the one, an attack on which involves least danger for the civilian population;

(b) take into account the loss and destruction which the attack, even if carried out with the precautions prescribed under Article 9, is liable to inflict upon the civilian population.

He is required to refrain from the attack if, after due consideration, it is apparent that the loss and destruction would be disproportionate to the military advantage anticipated.

. . .

Article 9 All possible precautions shall be taken, both in the choice of the weapons and methods to be used, and in the context of carrying out of an attack, to ensure that no losses or damage are caused to the civilian population in the vicinity of the objective, or to its dwelling, or that such losses or damage are at least reduced to a minimum.

In particular, in towns and other places with a large civilian population, which are not in the vicinity of military or naval operations, the attack shall be conducted with the greatest degree of precision. It must not cause losses or destruction beyond the immediate surroundings of the objective attacked.

The person responsible for carrying out the attack must abandon or break off the operation if he perceives that the conditions set forth above cannot be respected.

[9] See Draft Rules for the Limitation of the Dangers Incurred by the Civilian Population in Time of War (ICRC, Geneva, 1956), reprinted in D. Schindler and J. Toman (eds.), *The Laws of Armed Conflicts: A Collection of Conventions, Resolutions and Other Documents* (3rd edn, Martinus Nijhoff, Dordrecht, 1988), p. 251.

These Draft Rules were a considerable advance on the legal position established by the practice of States in the Second World War (1939–45).[10] No action was taken, however, on the Draft Rules, and the question of the further revision of the law of armed conflict was shelved by the international community until the work undertaken by the United Nations Commission on Human Rights and the General Assembly on human rights in times of peace began to expand logically into concern for human rights in armed conflicts. The International Conference on Human Rights held in Teheran in 1968 adopted a resolution requesting the General Assembly to invite the Secretary-General to consider the need for new or revised humanitarian instruments.[11] The General Assembly adopted a series of resolutions over the next few years continuing this process of focusing attention on improving the protection of civilians in armed conflict.[12]

As a result of the requests from the General Assembly, the Secretary-General submitted three substantial reports in 1969,[13] 1970[14] and 1971,[15] setting out the areas of the law of armed conflict that needed attention. The protection of the civilian population from indiscriminate warfare was one of the major foci of these initiatives and was described in terms that a 'distinction must be made at all times between persons taking part in the hostilities and members of the civilian population to the effect that the latter be spared as much as possible'.[16] The idea that attacks should not result in casualties disproportionate to the anticipated military advantage was as yet not specifically articulated.

By this time it was probably correct to say that indiscriminate attacks, in the sense of those that failed to draw a distinction between civilian and military targets, were rapidly becoming unacceptable in international law. This view is confirmed by the practices in relation to aerial

[10] For details of the legal position prior to the Second World War, see Chapter 2 above.

[11] Res. XXIII, 12 May 1968. See Final Act of the International Conference on Human Rights, UN Doc. A/Conf.32/41 (1968), p. 18.

[12] See GA Res. 2444 (XXIII) 19 December 1968; GA Res. 2597 (XXIV) 16 December 1969; GA Res. 2675 (XXV) 9 December 1970.

[13] Respect for Human Rights in Armed Conflicts, (First) Report of the Secretary-General, UN Doc. A/7720 (1969).

[14] Respect for Human Rights in Armed Conflicts, (Second) Report of the Secretary-General, UN Doc. A/8052 (1970).

[15] Respect for Human Rights in Armed Conflicts, (Third) Report of the Secretary-General, UN Doc. A/8370 (1971).

[16] See GA Res. 2444 (XXIII) 19 December 1968.

bombardment in the Vietnam War (1961–75). In particular, the reaction to the so-called 'Christmas bombings' of Hanoi in December 1972 gave some indication of the emerging legal rules protecting civilians from the effects of armed conflict and provided further impetus for the development of treaty rules to that effect.[17] The legal status of that conflict and the applicable law were controversial.[18] Irrespective of this lack of clarity, the legitimacy of excessive civilian casualties was an issue of concern amongst commentators. However, the main focus in the context of civilian losses remained as it had been between the two World Wars, on defining what were military targets and what constituted indiscriminate attacks.[19] The need for a balance between the military achievement and collateral civilian damage was rarely part of the debate.[20] Nevertheless, in 1972, against the background of this conflict, the United States indicated the following view of the law relating to the protection of civilians in armed conflict:

> it is recognised by all States that they may not lawfully use their weapons against the civilian population or civilians as such, but there is no rule of international law that restricts them against using weapons against enemy armed forces or military targets. The correct rule which has applied in the past and continues to apply to the conduct of our military operations in Southeast Asia is that 'the loss of life and property must not be out of proportion to the military advantage to be gained'.[21]

The time had now come to consolidate in conventional form this changing perception as to the protections that must be accorded to civilians and civilian objects during times of armed conflict. In 1970 and 1971, the ICRC convened two Conferences of Government Experts and on the basis of these deliberations the ICRC produced the text of two draft Additional Protocols to the 1949 Geneva Conventions, Additional Protocol I,

[17] See e.g. H. DeSaussure and R. Glasser, *Law and Responsibility in Warfare: The Vietnam Experience* (ed. by P. Trooboff, University of North Carolina Press, Chapel Hill, NC, 1975), p. 119 (for a description of the bombing campaign in North Vietnam).

[18] See e.g. Q. Wright, 'Legal Aspects of the Viet-Nam Situation' (1966) 60 *AJIL* 750.

[19] See e.g. DeSaussure and Glasser, *Law and Responsibility in Warfare*; and see the discussion in Chapter 2, note 136, and the accompanying text above.

[20] See, however, W. Hays Parks, 'Linebacker and the Law of War' (1983) 34 *Air University Review* 2; and W. Hays Parks, 'Rolling Thunder and the Law of War' (1982) 33 *Air University Review* 2 (discussing in some detail the application of the principle of proportionality in the Vietnam War).

[21] Letter from the General Counsel of the Department of Defense to Senator Edward Kennedy, Chairman of the Subcommittee on Refugees of the Committee of the Judiciary, 22 September 1972, reprinted in (1973) 67 *AJIL* 122.

relating to international conflicts, and Additional Protocol II, relating to non-international conflicts.[22] These draft texts were submitted to the Diplomatic Conference summoned by the Swiss Federal Council in 1974. The Conference met every year, on each occasion for a period of several months, until 8 June 1977 when the two Additional Protocols were adopted by consensus.[23]

The final text of Additional Protocol I not only contains a prohibition on disproportionate attacks but also identifies those responsible for ensuring that precautions are taken to avoid the carrying out of or for suspending such attacks. The clarification of where the onus lies for complying with the requirements of proportionality paves the way for the criminal liability of the individuals concerned for any such failure.[24]

The initial draft of what was to become Additional Protocol I did not reflect this end result. A provision in relation to proportionality was first submitted in a draft Protocol to the Conference of Government Experts by the ICRC in 1972. It was included in Chapter III dealing with 'Precautionary Measures' and was part of the Article entitled 'Principle of Proportionality'. The rule was expressed as follows: 'Those who order or launch an attack shall refrain from doing so when the probable losses and destruction are disproportionate to the concrete military advantage sought by them.'[25] However, the draft Protocol did not include a general

[22] Additional Protocol I and Protocol Additional to the Geneva Conventions of 12 August 1949, and Relating to the Protection of Victims of Non-International Armed Conflicts, adopted in 1977, 12 December 1977, (1979) 1125 UNTS 609 (hereafter Additional Protocol II). For details of the two Conferences of Government Experts, see Conference of Government Experts on the Reaffirmation and Development of International Humanitarian Law Applicable in Armed Conflicts, Geneva, 24 May–12 June 1971, *Report on the Work of the Conference* (ICRC, Geneva, 1971); and Conference of Government Experts on the Reaffirmation and Development of International Humanitarian Law Applicable in Armed Conflicts, Geneva, 3 May–3 June 1972, second session, *Report on the Work of the Conference* (ICRC, Geneva, 1972), vols. I and II, Annexes.

[23] The Protocols are documents supplementing the four Geneva Conventions of 1949 and have to be read in conjunction with the latter's provisions. For a comprehensive analysis of the proceedings of the Diplomatic Conference and the provisions of Additional Protocols I and II, see M. Bothe, K. Partsch and W. Solf, *New Rules for Victims of Armed Conflicts* (Martinus Nijhoff, The Hague, 1982); Y. Sandoz, C. Swinarski and B. Zimmerman (eds.), *Commentary on the Additional Protocols of 8 June 1977 to the Geneva Conventions of 12 August 1949* (Martinus Nijhoff, Geneva, 1987).

[24] The failure to suspend a potentially disproportionate attack does not constitute a grave breach of the Protocol: see the further discussion of enforcement in note 176 and the accompanying text below.

[25] See Art. 45 of Draft Additional Protocol to the Four Geneva Conventions of August 12 1949, Basic Texts Documentary Material Submitted by the International Committee of the Red Cross, Conference of Government Experts on the Reaffirmation and

prohibition of disproportionate attacks or an obligation to suspend or cancel an attack if it became apparent that it was likely to be disproportionate.[26]

In contrast to the 1972 draft, the draft text of proportionality submitted by the ICRC to the Diplomatic Conference in 1974 included two references to the proportionality rule. The first was included under the prohibition on indiscriminate attacks as one of the general principles protecting the civilian population against dangers resulting from hostilities, and read as follows:

> The employment of means of combat, and any methods which strike or affect indiscriminately the civilian population and combatants, or civilian objects and military objects, are prohibited. In particular it is forbidden:
> to launch attacks which may be expected to entail incidental losses among the civilian population and cause the destruction of civilian objects to an extent disproportionate to the direct and substantial military advantage anticipated.[27]

The requirement of proportionality appeared for the second time in the context of 'precautions in attack':

> Those who plan or decide upon an attack shall ensure [shall take all reasonable steps to ensure][28] that the objectives to be attacked are duly identified as military objectives within the meaning of paragraph 1 of Article 47 and may be attacked without incidental losses in civilian lives and damage to civilian objects in their vicinity being caused or that at all events those losses or damage are not disproportionate to the direct and substantial military advantage anticipated.[29]

The draft Article on precautions in attack, moreover, required the suspension or cancellation of an attack (if possible) if it appeared that the requirements of proportionality would not be met.[30]

Development of International Humanitarian Law Applicable in Armed Conflicts, Geneva, 3 May–3 June 1972 (ICRC, Geneva, 1972), p. 8.

[26] Although indiscriminate attacks were prohibited, there was no inclusion of disproportionate attacks within the scope of this prohibition: see Art. 45 of Draft Additional Protocol to the Four Geneva Conventions of August 12 1949, in *ibid.*, pp. 16–17.

[27] Art. 46 of the Draft Protocol Additional to the Geneva Conventions of August 12 1949, and Relating to the Protection of Victims of International Armed Conflicts, *Official Records of the Diplomatic Conference on the Reaffirmation and Development of International Humanitarian Law Applicable in Armed Conflicts* (Geneva, 1974–7) (17 vols., Federal Political Department, Bern, 1978) (hereafter *Official Records*), vol. I, p. 3 at p. 16.

[28] Proposal II of Art. 50, 'Precautions in Attack', of the Draft Protocol Additional to the Geneva Conventions of August 12 1949, and Relating to the Protection of Victims of International Armed Conflicts, *ibid.*, p. 17.

[29] See Proposal I of Art. 50(1)(a), *ibid.* [30] See Art. 50(1)(b), *ibid.*

Additional Protocol I and proportionality

The rule of proportionality that was finally adopted by the Diplomatic Conference in 1977 is contained in Part IV of Additional Protocol I. Part IV provides a detailed set of rules for the protection of civilians against the effects of hostilities, including aerial attacks.[31] Article 48 of Additional Protocol I codifies the customary rule as to the distinction that must always be drawn in military operations between the civilian population and combatants and between civilian and military objects. Military objectives by Article 52 'are limited to those objectives which by their nature, location, purpose or use make an effective contribution to military action and whose total or partial destruction, capture or neutralization, in the circumstances ruling at the time, offers a definite military advantage'. The basic rule in Article 48 is supplemented by specific rules in Article 51 designed to spell out how the distinction between civilian and military objects is to be facilitated and how the level of damage to the civilian population and civilian objects is to be contained. Central to this scheme is the prohibition of indiscriminate attacks the definition of which includes disproportionate attacks.

Indiscriminate and disproportionate attacks

Indiscriminate attacks are defined in Article 51(4) as:

(a) those which are not directed at a specific military objective;
(b) those which employ a method or means of combat which cannot be directed at a specific military objective; or
(c) those which employ a method or means of combat the effects of which cannot be limited as required by this Protocol;
and consequently, in each case, are of a nature to strike military objectives or civilian objects without distinction.[32]

The rule of proportionality appears as a species of indiscriminate attack. Article 51(5) states:

[31] See Arts. 48–58 of Additional Protocol I.

[32] It is not clear what is encompassed within the phrase 'the effects of which cannot be limited as required by this Protocol'. For some commentators, disproportionate attacks in Art. 51(5)(b) are one of the category of attacks that fall within this phrase. See Bothe, Partsch and Solf, *New Rules*, p. 306. Others take a different view: see the interpretation given to this phrase by L. Doswald-Beck, 'International Humanitarian Law and the Advisory Opinion of the International Court of Justice on the Legality of the Threat or Use of Nuclear Weapons' (1997) 316 *IRRC* 35 at 40–1; and see A. P. V. Rogers, *Law on the Battlefield* (Manchester University Press, Manchester, 1996), p. 22.

Among others, the following types of attacks are to be considered as indiscriminate:

. . .

(b) an attack which may be expected to cause incidental loss of civilian life, injury to civilians, damage to civilian objects, or a combination thereof, which would be excessive[33] in relation to the concrete and direct military advantage anticipated.

The definition of indiscriminate attacks in Article 51 is complicated and reflects the difficulties encountered at the Diplomatic Conference in reaching agreement on the controversial issue as to how to reconcile the demands of military necessity with the growing movement to protect the civilian population and civilian objects from the collateral effects of armed conflict. Moreover, the activity that is being addressed by these provisions, the conduct of armed conflict, is constantly evolving and is characterised by seemingly endless variables.

The imprecision of the Article 51 rule on indiscriminate attacks is exacerbated by the fact that it combines what are generally understood as separate concepts, that is, indiscriminate and disproportionate attacks. The designation of proportionality as a species of indiscriminate attack confuses the idea of proportionality with the requirement to distinguish between civilian and military targets.[34] Although the requirement of proportionality and the prohibition of indiscriminate attacks have the same aim – the protection of the civilian population and civilian objects – they are conceptually different. According to the Protocol, the other categories of indiscriminate attacks in Article 51(4)[35] and (5)[36] are prohibited regardless of whether casualties occur or not. In other

[33] The use of the term 'excessive' rather than 'proportional' in relation to collateral injury to civilians is in response to objections from several States that the principle of proportionality was contrary to humanitarian principles and international law. See *Official Records*, CDDH/III/SR.31, vol. 14, p. 305, para. 42. Irrespective of the terminology used, Art. 51(5)(b) is a specific articulation of the principle of proportionality.

[34] See Rogers, *Law on the Battlefield*, p. 23; and see also Doswald-Beck, 'International Humanitarian Law and the Advisory Opinion of the International Court of Justice', p. 36.

[35] See S. Oeter, 'Methods and Means of Combat' in D. Fleck (ed.), *The Handbook of Humanitarian Law in Armed Conflicts* (Oxford University Press, Oxford, 1995), pp. 174–6 (detailing the attacks covered by the prohibition in Art. 51(4)(a) and (b)).

[36] See Art. 51(5)(a) prohibiting 'target area bombardment'. In light of the experience from the Second World War, it was determined that this type of attack always leads to unacceptable levels of collateral injury to civilians. See H. Blix, 'Area Bombardment: Rules and Reasons' (1978) 49 *BYIL* 31 at 52–6.

words, it is not the likely effects of the attack that are the determinant of their legality. Indiscriminate attacks, therefore, strictly speaking delineate the situations in which the international community has decided on the basis of prior experience that the level of civilian casualties and damage to civilian objects is more than likely to be unacceptable. Proportionality, by contrast, allows for an assessment to be made in the particular circumstances, taking into account the factors referred to in the rule, before a particular attack becomes illegitimate. Consequently, the tests of discrimination and proportionality operate cumulatively with the result that, if the attack is indiscriminate under the Protocol, it is irrelevant whether in fact it meets the proportionality requirement or not. The reverse is also the case, namely, that, even if the attack is discriminate, it will be prohibited if it fails to meet the proportionality requirement.[37] As the Trial Chamber of the ICTY observed in the *Kupreskic* case, the rule of proportionality is to be applied in conjunction with the prohibition of negligent and indiscriminate attacks.[38]

However, not all commentators agree that the approach outlined above is the correct one to apply to the relationship between the provisions of Article 51(4) prohibiting indiscriminate attacks on the one hand and Article 51(5) containing the rule of proportionality on the other. There is the view that it is the likely effects of the attack that prevail and that if an attack complies with the proportionality rule it will not be rendered unlawful by the fact that it does not satisfy the requirements of discrimination.[39]

The distinction between the requirements of discrimination and proportionality can be illustrated by the debate on whether any weapon is

[37] Consequently, on this interpretation Art. 51 prohibits an attack as indiscriminate even if it results in no civilian casualties. Rogers, *Law on the Battlefield*, p. 21, regards this as an 'absurd and unintended result of the drafting' and as untenable in light of the fact that launching an indiscriminate attack constitutes a grave breach of the Protocol.

[38] See *Prosecutor* v. *Kupreskic et al.*, Judgment, Case No. IT-95-16-T-14 (January 2000).

[39] For a discussion of the possible approaches to these provisions of the Protocol, see F. Krüger-Sprengel, 'Le Concept de Proportionnalité dans le Droit de la Guerre', Rapport présenté au Comité pour la protection de la vie humaine dans les conflits armés, VIIIe Congrès de la Société internationale de droit pénal militaire et de droit de la guerre, Ankara, October 1979 (Société International de Droit Pénal Militaire et de Droit de la Guerre, Brussels, 1981), pp. 191–2; and E. Rauch, 'Le Concept de Nécessité Militaire dans le Droit de la Guerre', Rapport présenté au Comité pour la protection de la vie humaine dans les conflits armés, VIIIe Congrès de la Société internationale de droit pénal Militaire et de droit de la guerre, Ankara, October 1979 (Société International de Droit Pénal Militaire et de Droit de la Guerre, Brussels, 1981), pp. 209 and 223–9.

inherently indiscriminate in nature or whether the legality of its use falls to be determined under the proportionality equation.[40] It is only if a weapon is inherently capable of distinguishing between civilian and military objects that the question of proportionality becomes relevant. Thus, in the *Nuclear Weapons* Advisory Opinion, the issue that the Court had to first address in relation to nuclear weapons and civilians was not one of proportionality but of the capability of these weapons of meeting the threshold test of discrimination.[41] If nuclear weapons are incapable of distinguishing between civilian and military targets, then their use is illegitimate. If, however, some of these weapons could meet the test of discrimination their use in any particular situation must then meet the requirements of proportionality.

It is of course possible to argue that a weapon is inherently disproportionate, and consequently unlawful, on the ground that in any circumstances in which it might be used it will inevitably result in excessive civilian casualties no matter how great the military advantage.[42] This is a difficult argument to sustain, even in relation to nuclear weapons, given their widely varying characteristics and the diverse situations in which they may be used.

Precautions in attack

Article 51 needs to be read in conjunction with the requirements of Article 57. Not content with an abstract definition of what is a disproportionate attack, the Protocol by Article 57 clarifies in practice the obligations imposed by Article 51 and identifies what precautions must

[40] There are those who argue that no conventional weapon is inherently indiscriminate. Such a conclusion would amount to the effective banning of the weapon without any further action by States, a result that has been resisted in the context of weapons causing superfluous injury or unnecessary suffering in the context of combatants. See Doswald-Beck, 'International Humanitarian Law and the Advisory Opinion of the International Court of Justice', pp. 45–6. See also the discussion by Blix, 'Area Bombardment: Rules and Reasons', pp. 49–51 of views on this point at the Diplomatic Conference; and see *Report of the Conference of Government Experts on the Use of Certain Conventional Weapons* (ICRC, Geneva, 1974) (1975), p. 10.

[41] Those judges who address the issue of inherently indiscriminate weapons in the *Legality of the Threat or Use of Nuclear Weapons* Advisory Opinion, ICJ Reports 1996, 226 (General Assembly Opinion) (hereafter *Nuclear Weapons* Advisory Opinion), are divided. See the careful analysis of this aspect of the Opinion in Doswald-Beck, 'International Humanitarian Law and the Advisory Opinion of the International Court of Justice'.

[42] This is the view of Judge Weeramantry in the *Nuclear Weapons* Advisory Opinion, at pp. 514–16.

be taken and by whom before launching an attack. One such obligation placed on those who plan or decide upon an attack is to refrain from launching an attack that may be disproportionate:[43]

With respect to attacks, the following precautions shall be taken:

(a) those who plan or decide upon an attack shall . . .

(iii) refrain from deciding to launch any attack which may be expected to cause incidental loss of civilian life, injury to civilians, damage to civilian objects, or a combination thereof, which would be excessive in relation to the concrete and direct military advantage anticipated . . .

Furthermore, an attack must be cancelled or suspended if it becomes apparent that it may be disproportionate:

an attack shall be cancelled or suspended if it becomes apparent that the objective is not a military one or is subject to special protection or that the attack may be expected to cause incidental loss of civilian life, injury to civilians, damage to civilian objects, or a combination thereof, which would be excessive in relation to the concrete and direct military advantage anticipated.[44]

The other precautions set out in Article 57 are designed to minimise the risk of collateral damage and assist with ensuring that the attack is proportionate:

2. (a) Those who plan or decide upon an attack shall:

(i) do everything feasible to verify that the objectives to be attacked are neither civilians nor civilian objects and are not subject to special protection but are military objectives within the meaning of paragraph 2 of Article 52 and that it is not prohibited by the provisions of this Protocol to attack them;

(ii) take all feasible precautions in the choice of means and methods of attack with a view to avoiding, and in any event to minimizing, incidental loss of civilian life, injury to civilians and damage to civilian objects;

. . .

(c) Effective advance warning shall be given of attacks which may affect the civilian population, unless circumstances do not permit.

3. When a choice is possible between several military objectives for obtaining a similar military advantage, the objective to be selected shall be that the attack on which may be expected to cause the least danger to civilian lives and to civilian objects.

[43] See Art. 57(2)(a)(iii). [44] See Art. 57(2)(b).

Proportionality is frequently equated with the requirements that deal with the minimisation of risks to civilians and civilian objects from attacks. Indeed, some commentators regard this as its only role.[45] There is the view that, given the prevailing narrow definition of military targets and the range of restrictions placed on planners of attacks to minimise the risks thereof to civilians and civilian objects, the additional requirement of proportionality is superfluous. Nevertheless, it is clear from the text of Articles 51 and 57 that proportionality is intended to add another dimension to the protections offered to civilians by measures minimising risk. As some incidental loss of civilian lives and damage to civilian objects is inevitable in armed conflict, the rule of proportionality is designed to ensure that such losses are not excessive. Consequently, the scheme of the Protocol is to require decision-makers to choose means and methods of warfare so as to minimise the risk to civilians, to select, if possible, targets the least likely to result in civilian casualties, to verify the nature of the target and to give prior warning of the attack. Even if all these requirements are complied with, there is the additional obligation not to undertake the attack if it is apparent that the civilian losses and damage to civilian objects are likely to be excessive in light of the anticipated military advantage.

The component parts of the proportionality equation

The prohibition of disproportionate attacks under Additional Protocol I contemplates an assessment of two matters. First, the military advantage to be anticipated from the attack must be considered. Secondly, a judgment must be made as to the likely level of civilian casualties, injury to civilians and damage to civilian objects from the proposed attack and whether these are likely to be excessive in light of the military advantage anticipated. The inherently subjective and imprecise nature of the process is readily apparent, and it is a controversial concept for that very reason.[46] Despite the complexity of assessing proportionality, some guidance for the task can be provided by a more detailed examination of its components, namely, the meaning of 'attack', what is encompassed within the phrase 'military advantage' and the factors that should be taken into account in estimating likely collateral civilian damage, as it

[45] See e.g. W. Hays Parks, 'Air War and the Law of War' (1990) 32 *Air Force Law Review* 1 at 174; and see the further discussion in note 96 and the accompanying text below.

[46] See e.g. Bothe, Partsch and Solf, *New Rules*, p. 310; and Rauch, 'Le Concept de Nécessité Militaire', pp. 225.

is only after these are calculated that the assessment of 'excessive' can be undertaken.

The meaning of 'attack'

The proportionality equation is applied in relation to attacks. The meaning of 'attack', therefore, is pivotal to its operation. It determines in what situations the rule of proportionality applies and brings into operation the obligation in Article 57 on 'those who plan or decide upon an attack'. It also determines the context in which the military advantage is assessed.

'Attacks' are defined in Article 49(1) as 'acts of violence against the adversary, whether in offence or defence'. This can cover a multitude of situations. As one commentator observes, '[c]onsidered in the abstract, this definition is broad enough to designate the act of a single soldier shooting a rifle'.[47] However, if taken in its context in Articles 51(5)(b) and 57(2), 'attack' contemplates a more complex military operation. The difficulty is determining how complex. There is the view that the proportionality test is intended to apply to attacks as individual military operations of a specific unit.[48] This approach has its limitations from a military perspective, in that it does not always reflect the reality of an overall military operation of which such an attack is just a part.[49] In modern-day warfare, the achievement of a single strategic objective may in fact require a number of separate but integrated attacks. Moreover, proportionality is not an easy concept to apply at the low level of command.[50]

It is apparent, therefore, that the assessment of the military advantage will differ considerably depending on what amounts to an attack. One part of an operation may appear disproportionate taken in isolation but not necessarily so when seen in the context of its broader picture.[51] An indication of how States view the meaning of 'attack' is apparent from reservations and interpretative declarations to Article 51(5)(b) of

[47] W. Fenrick, 'The Rule of Proportionality and Protocol I in Conventional Warfare' (1982) 98 *Military LR* 91 at 101–2.

[48] See Sandoz, Swinarski and Zimmerman (eds.), *Commentary on the Additional Protocols*, p. 603.

[49] See Oeter, 'Methods and Means of Combat', p. 162.

[50] See F. Mulinen, 'The Law of War and the Armed Forces' (1978) 202 *IRRC* 20 at 42–3.

[51] See L. Doswald-Beck, 'The Value of the 1977 Geneva Protocols for the Protection of Civilians' in H. Fox and M. Meyer (eds.), *Effecting Compliance: Armed Conflict and the New Law* (British Institute of International and Comparative Law, London, 1993), p. 137 at pp. 156–7.

the Protocol in which a distinction is drawn between attacks 'considered as a whole' on the one hand and 'isolated' or 'particular parts of the attack', on the other.[52] These statements of understanding reflect the view that the meaning of 'attack' for the assessment of the military advantage in the Protocol encompasses an overall operation that may be constituted by several separate targets, such as the components of an electricity generating and distribution system that supports military operations.

The military advantage

Prior to any consideration of proportionality, an assessment of the military advantage of a particular attack will have already been made in the context of determining whether the target is military in nature, as this is a component of the definition of military targets under the Protocol.[53] A military target is one that makes an effective contribution to military action and the 'destruction, capture or neutralization' of which will confer a 'definite military advantage'. Once the military nature of the target is established, the assessment must then be made as to whether the 'concrete and direct military advantage' of attacking this target is proportionate to the anticipated collateral civilian damage from such an attack. The major factor in determining the military advantage of a particular attack in the context of the proportionality equation is the importance of the target for achieving a particular military objective. The more integral the proposed target is to the military strategy, the higher the level of likely civilian casualties and damage to civilian objects that will be acceptable.[54]

The temporal and geographical limits that apply when calculating the military advantage of an attack need to be considered. For example, is it legitimate to include in that assessment the overall advantage that may be experienced over a considerable period of time or one that will manifest itself at a location removed from the attack?[55] It appears that both these scenarios are contemplated by the treaty rule.[56]

[52] See the reservations and interpretative declarations to this effect of e.g. Belgium, Italy, Germany, the Netherlands, New Zealand and the United Kingdom (full list and text of reservations and interpretative declarations available at www.icrc.org).

[53] See Art. 52, and note 31 and the accompanying text above. See also Sandoz, Swinarski and Zimmerman, *Commentary on the Additional Protocols*, p. 636 (for a discussion of the meaning of the phrase 'definite military advantage').

[54] See e.g. Doswald-Beck, 'The Value of the 1977 Geneva Protocols', p. 156.

[55] For an example of such a situation, see Bothe, Partsch and Solf, *New Rules*, p. 325.

[56] See the view expressed to this effect by the ICRC at the Rome Conference that adopted the Statute of the ICC, UN Doc. A/Conf.183/INF/10, 13 July 1998.

The Protocol does, however, attempt to place limits on what can be factored into the military advantage component of the equation by the use of the phrase 'concrete and direct military advantage'. According to the ICRC commentary, the use of this phrase in the Protocol rule of proportionality is intended to indicate that the military advantage to be anticipated from an attack 'should be substantial and relatively close, and that advantages which are hardly perceptible and those which would only appear in the long-term should be disregarded'.[57] In other words, 'concrete' means specific as opposed to general, and 'direct' relates to causation, in that the advantage must not be too remote from the attack itself.[58]

Such an interpretation excludes the assessment of the military advantage on a cumulative basis. The campaign of defoliation undertaken by the United States in the Vietnam conflict illustrates the different results that may ensue depending on whether a case-by-case or cumulative method of assessing the military advantage is adopted. The defoliation of large tracts of forests in South Vietnam during the 1960s was intended to destroy the cover it provided for the Vietcong, the guerrilla forces fighting to overthrow the government of South Vietnam.[59] Each defoliating mission achieved little in itself but resulted in civilian casualties and widespread damage to civilian objects. On this case-by-case analysis, the civilian damage appeared excessive when contrasted with the military advantage. In contrast, if the military advantage of the cumulative effect of these attacks in the long term was the criterion, then the overall civilian losses and damage to civilian objects may not have been excessive.[60]

[57] See Sandoz, Swinarski and Zimmerman, *Commentary on the Additional Protocols*, p. 684; and see also *ibid*., pp. 636–7 (for an explanation of the relationship between the phrases 'definite military advantage' in Art. 52 and 'concrete and direct military advantage' in Arts. 51 and 57).

[58] Bothe, Partsch and Solf, *New Rules*, p. 365.

[59] Today, such attacks may well be regarded as disproportionate under both IHL and *ius ad bellum* due to their effect on the environment. See Chapter 5 below, discussing the environment and proportionality in the context of *ius ad bellum*; and in the context of IHL see e.g. Djamchid Momtaz, 'Le recours à l'arme nucléaire et la protection de l'environnement: l'apport de la cour internationale de justice' in L. Boisson de Chazournes and P. Sands (eds.), *International Law, the International Court of Justice and Nuclear Weapons* (Cambridge University Press, Cambridge, 1999), p. 355.

[60] See Stockholm International Peace Research Institute, *Ecological Consequences of the Second Indochina War* (Humanities Press, Stockholm, 1976), pp. 24–45. See also T. Farer, 'The Laws of War 25 Years after Nuremberg' (May 1971) *International Conciliation* 16–17, discussing the different approaches to proportionality and the result that may ensue depending upon whether a military action is assessed alone or in relation to its contribution to an overall campaign. See also B. Brown, 'The Proportionality Principle

The Protocol rule, therefore, is designed to ensure that the assessment of the military advantage is in the relatively short term rather than to allow for the inclusion of the long-term cumulative impact of attacks. However, this is not to suggest that the military advantage must be assessed on a narrow case-by-case basis in relation to each distinct target. As we have seen in the discussion of the meaning to be ascribed to 'attack', a significant number of State parties to the Protocol have indicated that the military advantage for the purposes of the proportionality rule is to be determined on the basis of 'the advantage anticipated from the attack as a whole and not only from isolated or particular parts of the attack' and this appears a workable interpretation of the rule.[61]

The determination of 'excessive' collateral damage

The Protocol requires a number of steps to be taken to minimise civilian casualties. On completion of this process, the decision-maker responsible for ordering an attack must then make a separate assessment of whether, despite all the precautions taken, the attack may still result in excessive civilian casualties, injury to civilians or damage to civilian objects in light of the anticipated military advantage. This requires a calculation of likely collateral civilian damage and the task is to determine what factors are to be counted in this assessment and those which are to be discounted. The Protocol does not attempt to exhaustively cover all the matters that, depending upon the circumstances, could be relevant in making a decision as to whether an attack could result in a prohibited level of damage under the Protocol. Indeed, any attempt to do so may compromise the ability of the norm to adapt itself to changing means and methods of warfare. The dilemma remains, however, as to whether the Protocol rule as it stands is of sufficient precision, a question returned to later in the discussion.

When calculating the expected level of collateral civilian damage in order to determine whether it is excessive, decision-makers will have to revisit many of the assessments undertaken so as to minimise casualties. The characteristics of various weapons will have been a primary

in the Humanitarian Law of Warfare: Recent Attempts at Codification' (1976) 10 *Cornell ILJ* 134 at 140–2.

[61] See note 52 above; and see Oeter, 'Methods and Means of Combat', p. 162. This interpretation is reflected in the definition of the crime of launching a disproportionate attack in the Statute of the ICC.

consideration in that process. Weapons have widely differing capabilities in terms of targeting accuracy and likelihood of malfunction.[62] Conventional weapons, generally speaking, can be more accurately targeted than non-conventional weapons (to the extent that the latter are lawful at all).[63] Moreover, there are sophisticated guidance systems available today that provide increased precision in the targeting of conventional weapons.[64]

The nature and location of the target must also be considered in determining likely collateral damage. Is the target intermingled with the civilian population and if so to what extent? How dense is the civilian population in the vicinity of the target?

It may be that, even if weapons are chosen that conform to the requirements for the minimisation of casualties, a particular weapon in all the circumstances may nevertheless still pose a risk of excessive collateral civilian damage. For example, the weapon chosen may have the most accurate targeting ability in light of the particular target but, if the target is located in close proximity to residential areas, the level of civilian casualties is likely to be considerable. It then becomes a matter of determining the military advantage provided by the destruction or degradation of the target and balancing this against the anticipated collateral civilian damage.

An issue on which views differ is the extent to which the decision-maker must take into account the likely casualties resulting from the defender locating military objectives close to civilian objects. There may also be evidence that the defenders are deliberately exposing civilians or civilian objects to risk.[65] This was a practice adopted by Iraq in the 1990–1 Persian Gulf conflict and was alleged to be the case in the Kosovo

[62] The use of precision weapons also reduces the risk to aircrew as these weapons theoretically can be accurately targeted from high altitude. For a discussion of developments in weapons technology, see e.g. D. Infeld, 'Precision-Guided Munitions Demonstrated Their Pinpoint Accuracy in Desert Storm: But Is a Country Obligated to Use Precision Technology to Minimize Collateral Civilian Injury and Damage?' (1992) 26 *George Washington Journal of International Law and Economics* 109.

[63] There is a view that unconventional weapons are incapable of being directed at a specific military target and are thus prohibited as indiscriminate under Art. 51(4)(b) of the Protocol.

[64] As to the obligations on States to use the most advanced weaponry possible in order to minimise collateral injury to civilians, see Infeld, 'Precision-Guided Munitions', pp. 126–31. See also House of Commons, Defence Select Committee, Fourteenth Report, 23 October 2000, p. 140 (discussing the limitations of laser-guided technology under poor weather conditions).

[65] See Rogers, *Law on the Battlefield*, p. 19.

conflict.[66] One commentator is of the view that the anticipated casualties in the proportionality equation should not include those that are the result of such a practice by the other side.[67] Perhaps a preferable approach is to identify the factors over which the attacking force has control and to measure their obligations in those terms. Therefore, although this tactic of exposing civilians to risk cannot prevent an attack on a target, it will dictate the manner in which the attack is carried out.[68] This is the approach of the Protocol in this context. Consequently, although the use of civilians to shield military targets is contrary to the rules of the Protocol under Article 51(7), the attacker is not thereby relieved from the obligation to consider whether the likely casualties will be excessive (Article 51(8)).[69]

Another doubtful area in the process of calculating likely civilian casualties is the timeframe for this process. It is not clear to what extent the humanitarian considerations in the determination of what is 'excessive' should be assessed in the short term or in the longer term in the Protocol rule. Indeed, it is not apparent whether long term damage is relevant at all. Greenwood observes that the Protocol was negotiated primarily to minimise casualties during attacks.[70] A short timeframe for the assessment of civilian casualties and damage to civilian objects is more likely to render less effective attempts to limit the level of collateral casualties from the attack.[71]

Target verification may be a factor in the assessment of proportionality. Additional Protocol I deals specifically with this issue. By Article 57(2)(a)(i), 'everything feasible' must be done to verify that the objectives to be attacked are not civilian in nature. However, it may be that, despite the taking of all feasible steps to identify the target, in light of the particular circumstances there may nevertheless remain a wide margin for

[66] See Human Rights Watch, *Needless Deaths in the Gulf War* (Human Rights Watch, New York, 1991), p. 76; and see US Department of Defense News Briefing, 17 May 1999, cited in Amnesty International, *'Collateral Damage'*, p. 8.

[67] See Hays Parks, 'Air War and the Law of War', p. 174.

[68] See F. Hampson, 'Means and Methods of Warfare in the Conflict in the Gulf' in P. Rowe (ed.), *The Gulf War (1990–1991) in International and English Law* (Routledge, London, 1993), pp. 89 and 93.

[69] See also Art. 58 of Additional Protocol I (detailing precautions to be taken against the effects of attacks).

[70] See C. Greenwood, 'Customary International Law and the First Geneva Protocol of 1977 in the Gulf Conflict' in P. Rowe (ed.), *The Gulf War (1990–1991) in International and English Law* (Routledge, London, 1993), p. 63 at p. 79.

[71] See P. Rowe, 'Kosovo 1999: The Air Campaign – Have the Provisions of Additional Protocol I Withstood the Test?' (2000) 837 *IRRC* 147.

error. In such a case, the risk of excessive casualties may be too high. Target verification under the Protocol is an ongoing process. If at any time during the attack it appears that in fact the intended target is not military or that circumstances have changed and there is the likelihood that excessive civilian casualties or damage to civilian objects may occur, the attack must be suspended or cancelled.[72]

Depending on the nature and location of the target, an attack may be likely to lead to incidental release of hazardous substances or result in floods or landslides.[73] The terrain generally, therefore, may be an important factor in the decision-making process. Whether the population had been warned of the impending attack would also be relevant to the level of casualties to be anticipated.[74] The prevailing weather conditions may affect the accuracy of targeting and of the weapons used.[75] The level of altitude at which an aerial attack is conducted, an issue of some controversy in recent conflicts, is also a factor that will require consideration in the determination of the likely level of civilian casualties.

Standard of application

Once decision-makers have determined the concrete and direct military advantage from the proposed attack and the likely level of collateral civilian damage, they must then apply the proportionality equation and determine the likelihood of 'excessive' collateral civilian damage. The rule of proportionality as encapsulated in Articles 51 and 57 prohibits an attack which 'may be expected to cause' excessive civilian losses rather than one that actually produces that result. There is consensus that although the wording of the prohibition implies an objective standard,

[72] See Art. 57(2)(b) of Additional Protocol I.

[73] See Sandoz, Swinarski and Zimmerman, *Commentary on the Additional Protocols*, p. 684 (referring to the importance of the terrain and the possibility of landslides or floods, etc. in determining the likely level of collateral injury to civilians).

[74] Prior to the adoption of the Protocol, the possibility of warning the civilian population before an attack was an element in the proportionality equation, depending upon the particular circumstances. For the history in relation to this requirement, see Rogers, *Law on the Battlefield*, pp. 48–56. The Protocol, however, by Art. 57(2)(c), requires advance warnings of attacks to be given unless circumstances do not permit. See Rogers, *Law on the Battlefield*, p. 61, for a discussion of the meaning of the phrase 'unless circumstances do not permit'.

[75] See e.g. Infeld, 'Precision-Guided Munitions', pp. 132–3 (describing the sensitivity of precision-guided missiles to the weather and the environment); and House of Commons, Defence Select Committee, Fourteenth Report (discussing the impact of poor weather conditions on the accuracy of precision-guided weapons in the 1999 NATO action in Kosovo).

the determination of which attacks will fall within this prohibition is necessarily a subjective one but one that must be made in a diligent and honest manner by a competent commander at the appropriate level of command.[76]

Several States, uneasy about the obligations imposed by the new legal regime protecting civilians against the means and methods of warfare, attempted some clarification. For example, the United Kingdom made the following declaration on signature in relation to Articles 51–58: 'military commanders and others responsible for planning, deciding upon or executing attacks necessarily have to reach decisions on the basis of their assessment of the information from all sources which is available to them at the relevant time.'[77]

Despite the leeway in its application, the treaty norm of proportionality has been very divisive and highlights the differences between those who place the emphasis on the humanitarian side of the equation and those who focus on the demands of military necessity.[78] Obviously, very different conclusions may be reached between the relative value to be ascribed to the military advantage and to the protection of the civilian population, depending on the decision-maker.[79]

An illustration of such contrary approaches can be seen in the context of whether the military significance of the target can justify heavy civilian casualties. One view is that the more important the target, the more civilian casualties that will be acceptable, even if they are considerable.[80] The ICRC commentary on Article 57(2)(a)(iii) disputes this approach:

> The idea has been put forward that even if they are very high, civilian losses and damages may be justified if the military advantage at stake is of great importance. This idea is contrary to the fundamental rules of the Protocol; in particular it conflicts with Article 48 . . . and with paragraphs 1 and 2 of the

[76] See e.g. Oeter, 'Methods and Means of Combat', pp. 178–9 (arguing that, given the predictive nature of the task and the lack of objective standards as to the variables involved in the application of the proportionality equation, there must be a wide margin of appreciation for the decision-maker); and Bothe, Partsch and Solf, *New Rules*, pp. 310–1; and see the further discussion of the grave breach provision of launching a disproportionate attack in note 177 and the accompanying text below.

[77] Available at www.icrc.org/ihl.nsf. See also the statement by Canada, *Official Records*, CDDH/SR.41, vol. 6 Annex, p. 178.

[78] Cf. Hays-Parks, 'Air War and the Law of War'; and J. G. Gardam, 'Proportionality and Force in International Law' (1993) 87 *AJIL* 391 at 406–10. For a more moderate military assessment of the rule, see Fenrick, 'The Rule of Proportionality and Protocol I', pp. 126–7.

[79] See *Final Report to the Prosecutor*, para. 50.

[80] See e.g. Rogers, *Law on the Battlefield*, p. 18.

present Article 51. The Protocol does not provide any justification for attacks which cause extensive civilian losses and damages. Incidental losses and damages should never be extensive.[81]

As Rogers observes, to substitute 'extensive' for 'excessive' destroys the balancing process inherent in the idea of proportionality.[82] Casualties and damage may well be extensive but nevertheless not excessive in light of the military advantage from the attack. Judge Higgins confirms this approach in the *Nuclear Weapons* Advisory Opinion:

One is inevitably led to the question of whether, if a target is legitimate and the use of a nuclear weapon is the only way of destroying that target, any need can ever be so necessary as to occasion massive collateral damage upon civilians. It must be that, in order to meet the legal requirement that a military target may not be attacked if collateral civilian casualties would be excessive in relation to the military advantage, the 'military advantage' must indeed be one related to the very survival of a State or the avoidance of infliction (whether by nuclear or other weapons of mass destruction) of vast and severe suffering on its own population; and that no other method of eliminating this military target be available.[83]

Having considered what was envisaged by the conventional norm of proportionality in Additional Protocol I, it remains to determine how States have interpreted their obligations in practice and the extent to which this practice is also reflected in customary international law. A considerable period of time has elapsed since the adoption of the Protocol and there have been a number of opportunities in the post-Cold War era to test its strengths and weaknesses.

The Protocol rule of proportionality in practice

Generally speaking, it is never a straightforward task to obtain consensus on the status of the treaty rules of armed conflict. States are reluctant to detail on what grounds they make their judgments as to what actions they regard as legitimate. In many situations, the facts speak for themselves and a framework can be constructed for the operation of the legal regime. However, this is not always the case. Moreover, as Greenwood observes, there is often a wide discrepancy between principle and practice in armed conflict.[84] In the view of some commentators, this

[81] See Sandoz, Swinarski and Zimmerman, *Commentary on the Additional Protocols*, pp. 625–6.
[82] Rogers, *Law on the Battlefield*, p. 18.
[83] See *Nuclear Weapons* Advisory Opinion, pp. 587–8.
[84] Greenwood, 'Customary International Law and the First Geneva Protocol', p. 69.

divergence has led to a somewhat different process in relation to the creation or maintenance of norms of IHL, with contrary operational and battlefield practice frequently downplayed or ignored by judges, commentators, governments and NGOs.[85]

In assessing State practice in relation to the Protocol, not only is there secrecy surrounding battlefield decision-making but the phenomenon of States acting in coalition presents difficulties in distinguishing between the practice of State parties and non-State parties. For example, as of 2003, the United States remains outside the Protocol whereas the majority of its traditional allies are parties thereto. In light of the increasing emphasis on the criminal enforcement of IHL, it is an important issue to determine the exact nature of a State's obligations at any given time.

Despite the fact that the customary status of the Protocol, including the rule of proportionality, has always been controversial, arguably it is perhaps less so now than at the time of its adoption.[86] This is due not only to the significant increase in membership of the Protocol but also to the experience of several international conflicts in which the majority of its obligations have proven in the main to be workable.[87] A more cynical view would be that the current state of the law on proportionality is so lacking in clarity that, as long as States, whether parties to the Protocol or not, appear to be acting in good faith and attempting to strike some balance between the military goals and collateral casualties, there will be no adverse repercussions.

Nevertheless, significant differences continue to be expressed as to the operation of the rule of proportionality, in particular as to what should be included or excluded in the calculation.[88] The clarification of these uncertainties remains of considerable importance.

[85] See T. Meron, 'The Humanization of Humanitarian Law' (2000) 94 *AJIL* 239 at 244.

[86] Initially, it was the scope of the Protocol that led to significant divisions amongst States. However, its provisions placing restrictions on the means and methods of combat to protect the civilian population, including the rule of proportionality, also made the Protocol unacceptable to several States including the United States. See e.g. A. Sofaer, 'Agora: The US Decision Not to Ratify Protocol I to the Geneva Conventions on the Protection of War Victims (Cont'd): The Rationale for the United States Decision' (1988) 82 *AJIL* 784.

[87] For the State parties to Protocol I, see note 5 above.

[88] See e.g. *Final Report to the Prosecutor*, para. 49 (identifying the unresolved issue of what to include in the application of the principle of proportionality); and see generally Sandoz, Swinarski and Zimmerman, *Commentary on the Additional Protocols*, p. 684 (for a discussion of the relevant factors in the proportionality equation).

The *travaux préparatoires*

Articles 51 and 57 were put to the vote in the Plenary Session of the Diplomatic Conference and adopted by significant majorities with only France voting against their adoption.[89] The *travaux préparatoires* of the Protocol, although now somewhat overtaken by events, indicate that States are generally prepared to accept proportionality as a customary concept. For example, the United Kingdom delegate at the Diplomatic Conference referred to Article 51(5)(b) as 'a useful codification of a concept that was rapidly becoming accepted by all States as an important principle of international law relating to armed conflict'.[90] The United States delegate in Committee III stated: 'As to the principle of proportionality, the aim was to draft a rule which was in his view already established by custom and in practice . . . [I]t must be explicitly codified in the documents designed to ensure the protection of the civilian population and civilian objects.'[91] One of the commentaries to the Protocol confirms this assessment of Article 51(5)(b), describing it as a codification 'in fairly concrete terms of the principle of proportionality as it applies to the protection of civilians against the collateral effects of attacks directed against military targets'.[92]

The military manuals of States, which are an important source of State practice in this area, were not consistent on this point. For example, proportionality appeared in the United States Air Force pamphlet.[93] In contrast, Chapter VII of the United Kingdom Manual of Military Law, published in 1958, dealt with bombardment by land forces. Its provisions are based on the Hague Rules.[94] It made no reference to proportionality, and paragraph 288 merely declared that bombardment which is directed solely against a non-military objective is unlawful and, moreover, that the infliction of collateral casualties is only lawful 'if incidental to the bombardment of military objectives'.

89 See *Official Records*, CDDH/SR.4, vol. 6, p. 163, paras. 119–48 (explanations of vote).
90 See *ibid.*, CDDH/SR.4, vol. 6, p. 164, para. 120.
91 See *ibid.*, CDDH/III/SR.21, vol. 6, p. 194, para. 91.
92 Bothe, Partsch and Solf, *New Rules*, p. 299.
93 See United States, Department of the Air Force, *International Law – The Conduct of Armed Conflict and Air Operations: Judge Advocate General Activities* (US Department of Air Force, Washington DC, 1976), Chapter 1, para. 1-3a(2), Chapter 5, para. 5-3c(1)(b).
94 War Office, WO Code No. 12333, The Law of War on Land, Part III of the *Manual of Military Law* (1958).

State practice subsequent to the adoption of Additional Protocol I

The differences that emerged at the Diplomatic Conference continued to manifest themselves in various contexts after the adoption of the Protocol. For example, in 1987, a spokesperson for the executive branch of the United States Government declared support for the customary nature of the prohibition of direct attacks against the civilian population and the fundamental principle prohibiting attacks that 'would clearly result in collateral civilian casualties disproportionate to the expected military advantage'.[95] However, it does not appear to have been accepted that the Protocol rule was reflected in customary law. According to one United States military expert, proportionality does not 'establish a separate standard' but is designed to prevent the negligent or deliberate targeting of civilians, and provides a 'means for determining whether a nation or military commander responsible for planning upon, or executing a military operation has engaged in the intentional attack of civilians not engaged in the hostilities'.[96] In other words the level of disparity between the civilian casualties from an attack and the anticipated military advantage may lead to the presumption that civilians had been intentionally targeted.[97]

A more recent document that does reflect the Protocol articulation of proportionality is the *San Remo Manual on International Law Applicable in Armed Conflicts at Sea*.[98] This was an initiative of the Institute of Humanitarian Law at San Remo, which commenced in 1987 and involved the participation of scholars and practitioners from twenty nations. It was intended as the equivalent of the *Oxford Manual on the Laws of Naval War Governing the Relations Between Belligerents* adopted by the Institute of

[95] See M. Matheson and B. Carnahan, 'Sixth Annual American Red Cross-Washington Conference on International Humanitarian Law: A Workshop on Customary International Law and the 1977 Protocols Additional to the 1949 Geneva Conventions' (1987) 2 *American University Journal of International Law and Policy* 419 at 426 and 509.

[96] See Hays Parks, 'Air War and the Law of War', p. 134.

[97] Thus according to that view the formulation of the rule of proportionality is as follows: 'the occurrence of collateral civilian casualties so excessive in nature when compared to the military advantage to be gained as to be tantamount to the intentional attack of individual civilians, or the civilian population, or to a wanton disregard for the safety of the civilian population'. See Hays Parks, *ibid*.

[98] L. Doswald-Beck (ed.), *San Remo Manual on International Law Applicable to Armed Conflicts at Sea* (Cambridge University Press, Cambridge, 1995). Part IV of Additional Protocol I that contains the prohibition on indiscriminate attacks and includes the rule of proportionality is only applicable to naval operations that affect civilians and civilian objects on land: see Art. 49(3) of Additional Protocol I.

International Law in 1913.[99] Several of its provisions adopt the language of the proportionality rule in Additional Protocol I. For example, paragraph 102(b) of the Manual prohibits the establishment or declaration of a blockade if 'damage to the civilian population is, or may be expected to be, excessive in relation to the concrete and direct military advantage anticipated from the blockade'. A somewhat different articulation of proportionality appears in other sections of the Manual. For example, a hospital ship may be attacked if certain criteria are met, including that 'the collateral casualties or damage will not be disproportionate to the military advantage gained or expected'.[100]

The above are helpful indications as to the manner in which the legal requirements of proportionality have been viewed since the adoption of the Protocol. However, the most valuable source of practice as to the customary status and content of the rule of proportionality, and indeed of the Protocol generally, is the subsequent practice in such conflicts as the 1990–1 and 2003 Persian Gulf and 1999 Kosovo conflicts.[101] This practice needs to be seen in its context. The virtually unopposed campaigns of aerial bombardment that characterised these conflicts resulted in considerable public pressure to minimise civilian casualties.[102] On the other hand, underlying battlefield decisions was the perceived 'justness' of the cause leading in some instances to the adoption of strategies to minimise combatant casualties. An added dimension to the Kosovo action was that its aim was avowedly humanitarian in nature. According to one commentator, this should have had an impact on the choice of military targets and the application of proportionality.[103] The aim of

[99] See Doswald-Beck, *San Remo Manual*, p. 5. [100] See *ibid.*, p. 151.

[101] For details of the 1990–1 Persian Gulf conflict, see e.g. Department of Defense, *Final Report to Congress: Conduct of the Persian Gulf War* (USGPO, Washington DC, 1992) (hereafter *US Defense Report*); *Preliminary Lessons of Operation Granby*, Tenth Report. House of Commons, Defence Select Committee, Fourteenth Session 1990–1, reprinted in M. Weller (ed.), *Iraq and Kuwait: The Hostilities and Their Aftermath*, Cambridge International Documents Series, vol. 3 (Grotius, Cambridge, 1993), p. 318; and *Needless Deaths in the Gulf War*. For the details of the military action in Kosovo, see e.g. Human Rights Watch, *Civilian Deaths*, pp. 10–12. For details of the 2003 Persian Gulf conflict, see S. D. Murphy (ed.), 'Contemporary Practice of the United States Relating to International Law' (2003) 97 *AJIL* 419.

[102] See Burrus M. Carnahan, 'The Law of Aerial Bombardment in Its Historical Context' (1975) 17(2) *Air Force LR* 39 at 62, to the effect that 'a belligerent who faces no opposition in his bombing operations has a heavy burden of proof to show that civilian casualties were necessary, unavoidable and proportionate to the military advantage gained'.

[103] See Bothe, 'The Protection of the Civilian Population and NATO Bombing on Yugoslavia', p. 535.

the action, however, is of relevance to the assessment of proportionality in *ius ad bellum* rather than in IHL.

All these conflicts provide clear evidence of both State practice and *opinio iuris* to support the view that some balance between the achievement of the military goal and civilian casualties is a customary principle of international law. During the campaigns, the attacking forces repeatedly confirmed that every effort was being made to minimise civilian casualties and to avoid damage to civilian objects.[104] The Pentagon, for example, claimed that the coalition forces in the 1990–1 Persian Gulf conflict had conducted the 'most discriminate air campaign in history'.[105] Moreover, it was clear that proportionality was regarded as a distinct legal obligation in addition to the duty to minimise civilian casualties: 'An uncodified but similar provision is the principle of proportionality. It prohibits military action in which the negative effects (such as collateral civilian casualties) clearly outweigh the military gain.'[106] The reference to proportionality as uncodified indicates, however, that the Protocol rule was not regarded as determinative of the legal position at the time of the first Persian Gulf conflict. The emphasis on the protection of the civilian population was even more pronounced in the Kosovo campaign,[107] an approach no doubt influenced by the uncertain legal basis of the forceful action and the need to maintain the alliance between NATO members.[108]

[104] See e.g. *US Defense Report*, p. 98; Testimony of Lt General Michael Short before the US Senate Armed Services Committee Hearing on Lessons Learned from Military Operations and Relief Efforts in Kosovo, 21 October 1999, cited in Human Rights Watch, *Civilian Deaths*, note 20; and Murphy, 'Contemporary Practice', p. 430 (detailing denials by US officials of indiscriminate attacks and affirming their concern for collateral casualties during the 2003 Persian Gulf conflict).

[105] *US Defense Report*, p. 612.

[106] See *ibid*., p. 611. Human Rights Watch observes that this enunciation of the rule differs from the Protocol provision that refers to the 'direct and concrete military advantage' rather than the phrase 'military gain': see Human Rights Watch, *Civilian Deaths*, pp. 44–5.

[107] See General W. K. Clark, 'When Force Is Necessary: NATO's Military Response to the Kosovo Crisis' (1999) 47(2) *NATO Review* 14. See also Human Rights Watch, *Civilian Deaths* (citing remarks of General H. H. Shelton, Chairman of the Joint Chiefs of Staff, and Lt General M. R. Esmond, US Deputy Chief of Staff, Air and Space Operations, US Air Force, in relation to the emphasis on avoiding 'collateral damage'). NATO has claimed that its air campaign against Serbia was the 'most precise and lowest-collateral damage air campaign in history': see Joint Statement on the Kosovo After Action Review, Secretary of Defense William S. Cohen and General Shelton, before the United States Senate Armed Services Committee, 14 October 1999.

[108] See statement of Lt General Esmond, 19 October 1999, cited in Human Rights Watch, *Civilian Deaths*, note 21.

Despite this clear affirmation that the principle of proportionality is part of customary law, to what extent does the actual practice in these subsequent conflicts reflect the treaty rule? As previously discussed, Articles 51(5)(b) and 57(2)(a)(iii) and (b) of Additional Protocol I require significantly more than the avoidance of deliberate and negligent attacks on civilians and civilian objectives and the role they assign to proportionality is not merely to determine what attacks should be deemed to constitute the intentional targeting of civilians.[109] On the contrary, what these provisions require is an assessment before the attack as to the anticipated military advantage and whether the civilian damage is likely to be excessive in relation thereto.

To what extent, therefore, does practice in the two Persian Gulf and the Kosovo conflicts indicate that, even if there is no negligence in the assessment of the target or in the conduct of the attack, the likelihood and level of civilian casualties and damage to civilian objects must still be considered? Even if care were taken to ensure the selection of means and methods of attack that minimised the risk to civilians and civilian objects, were attacks avoided or cancelled if the level of civilian casualties and damage to civilian objects appeared unacceptable? In other words, does the practice in these conflicts confirm that proportionality operates in this broad sense in customary law?

The answer to these questions clearly appears to be in the affirmative. However, what requires clarification is exactly what this State practice indicates as to the detailed operation of the rule for both members and non-members of the Protocol and in what respects the requirements of the norm remain obscure. This clarification is not always readily obtained, as although the relevance of proportionality was acknowledged in all these conflicts, there is little detailed information as to exactly how it was applied.

The meaning of attacks and the military advantage

It will be recalled that several States expressed their understanding that the appropriate method of determining the military advantage of an attack under the Protocol is from the attack considered as a whole and not from isolated parts of the attack.[110] Is this approach reflected in State

[109] It will be recalled that this limited role for proportionality has the support of some military commentators: see the discussion in note 96 and the accompanying text above.

[110] See the reservations and interpretative declarations to this effect, in note 52 above.

practice? The air campaign plan of the United States for the 1990–1 Persian Gulf conflict was based on the achievement of five strategic military objectives.[111] A list of sets of targets to achieve these strategic objectives was drawn up and included electricity production facilities and communications networks.[112] It is at this latter level of decision-making, the identification of the means of achieving the strategic objectives, that the IHL rule of proportionality became applicable. The United States Department of Defense report to Congress, *The Conduct of the Persian Gulf War*, states that the military advantage in relation to attacks was assessed in some cases on a target-by-target basis but that the liberty was retained to do so 'in overall terms against campaign objectives'.[113] In relation to many targets, including infrastructure targets, it appears that it was the military advantage of the destruction of the overall target that was included in the proportionality equation and not that of each strike against each component of the target.

Somewhat more information on the method adopted of assessing the military advantage is available from the 1999 Kosovo campaign as there was an investigation by an outside body, the Committee of the Office of the Prosecutor (OTP) of the ICTY, of aspects of this campaign. The extent to which the military advantage is to be assessed in relation to individual attacks or as part of a wider strategic objective arose in the context of the NATO attack on the Serb television and radio station in Belgrade, which resulted in significant civilian casualties.[114] There were a number of controversial aspects to this attack, including whether the target was military in nature,[115] whether there was any 'concrete'

[111] See *US Defense Report*, p. 95 (amongst these objectives were to isolate and incapacitate the Iraqi regime; to gain and maintain air supremacy to permit unhindered air operations; and to eliminate Iraq's offensive military capability).
[112] See *US Defense Report*, p. 95 (the sets of targets included 'crucial aspects of electricity production facilities', 'telecommunications systems', and 'railroads and bridges connecting military forces to means of support').
[113] See *US Defense Report*, p. 611 and further p. 613: '"Military advantage" is not restricted to tactical gains, but is linked to the full context of a war strategy, in this instance, the execution of the Coalition war plan for liberation of Kuwait.'
[114] See Amnesty International, *'Collateral Damage'* (for details of this attack).
[115] There was evidence to suggest that the station had been targeted because of its propaganda role in the conflict: see Amnesty International, *'Collateral Damage'*, pp. 39–41. A similar unease was expressed in relation to the 2003 attack on the main Baghdad television station: see e.g. Human Rights Watch, 'Iraq: Coalition Attack on TV Station May Be Unlawful', available at www.hrw.org/press/2002/03/iraqtv032603.htm.

measurable military advantage to be gained from the attack and the failure to warn of the proposed attack.[116] In considering the assessment of the military advantage, the Committee of the OTP was of the view that '[t]he proportionality . . . of an attack should not necessarily focus exclusively on a specific incident',[117] and accepted the view of NATO that the Serbian command and control network was a complex web that could not be disabled at one strike and consequently the proportionality of this attack was to be assessed on the basis of its contribution to the destruction of the overall Serbian communications network.[118]

The underlying lack of consensus as to the method of calculating the military advantage component of the proportionality equation is reflected in the drafting history and the text of the crime of launching a disproportionate attack in the Statute of the ICC.[119]

A further area of uncertainty in both the Protocol rule and the customary law highlighted in these conflicts (and particularly by the 'zero casualties' campaign of NATO in Kosovo[120]) is the extent to which the minimisation of one's own combatant casualties can be factored into the application of the proportionality equation. The issue of assumption of risk by the attacking forces is nowhere expressly identified as an aspect of the military advantage in the proportionality equation; nevertheless, it is closely associated therewith. Military commanders are under an obligation to limit their casualties, and this factor is a component of many of the decisions in relation to attacks, such as the choice of means, the steps taken to verify the target and warn the civilian population and the timing of the attack. For example, a general zero-casualties approach may mandate certain decisions in relation to individual attacks, such as

[116] See Amnesty International, *'Collateral Damage'*, pp. 39–45 (highlighting the negligible military advantage that could be anticipated from a three-hour disruption of night-time broadcasts from the station); and W. Fenrick, 'Targeting and Proportionality During the NATO Bombing Campaign Against Yugoslavia' (2001) 12 *EJIL* 489 at 495–8. Amnesty International also questioned the proportionality of the attack in light of 'excessive' civilian casualties: see the discussion of this point in note 144 and the accompanying text below. See also Human Rights Watch, *Civilian Deaths* (doubting the proportionality of this attack).

[117] See *Final Report to the Prosecutor*, para. 78.

[118] See *ibid.*, paras. 77–9. This finding of the Committee has not escaped criticism: see e.g. P. Benvenuti, 'The ICTY's Prosecutor and the Review of the NATO Bombing Campaign Against the Federal Republic of Yugoslavia' (2001) 12 *EJIL* 501 at 522–3.

[119] See the discussion in note 201 and the accompanying text below.

[120] See Roberts, 'Nato's "Humanitarian" War over Kosovo', p. 110.

flying at high altitudes for the purpose of both target verification and subsequent attacks on the target.[121]

As Rogers observes, '[t]he rule [of proportionality] is more easily stated than applied in practice, especially in a case where in adopting a method of attack that would reduce incidental damage the risk to the attacking troops is increased. The rule is unclear as to the degree of care required of the soldier and the degree of risk he must take. It is suggested, however, that the risk to the attacking forces is a factor to be taken into consideration when applying the proportionality rule.'[122] Fenrick, on the other hand, is of the view that the policy of minimisation of combatant casualties in itself adds nothing concrete to the proportionality equation. The Committee of the OTP identified such strategies to minimise combatant casualties as relevant in the proportionality equation, but indicated that 'the extent to which a military commander was obliged to expose his own forces to danger in order to limit civilian casualties or damage to civilian objects was as yet unresolved'.[123]

It is widely accepted that the United States Government in the 1990–1 Persian Gulf and 1999 Kosovo conflicts was anxious to minimise its own casualties in light of domestic opinion. This influenced their approach to the requirements of proportionality in both IHL and *ius ad bellum*.[124] The overall policy of the United States in relation to the question of the allocation of risk in the conduct of the 1990–1 Persian Gulf conflict was '[t]o the degree possible and consistent with allowable risks to aircraft and aircrews, aircraft and munitions were selected so that attacks on targets within populated areas would provide the least risk to civilian objects and the civilian population'.[125] The determination of what constitutes 'allowable risks' remains unclear. In the context of IHL, it appears that civilian casualties were not regarded as excessive if they were the result to some extent of tactics chosen to minimise the casualties of the attacking force.[126] The United Kingdom, under no such similar influences from

[121] For example, in the context of the NATO action in Kosovo, Amnesty International reports that initially aircraft 'were restricted to flying above 15,100 feet to protect their aircraft and air crews against FRY air defenses'. NATO, however, although reportedly conceding that this tactic affected the effectiveness of the aerial campaign, denied that it increased civilian casualties: see Amnesty International, '*Collateral Damage*', p. 15.

[122] See Rogers, *Law on the Battlefield*, p. 17.

[123] *Final Report to the Prosecutor*, para. 49.

[124] For a discussion of proportionality in *ius ad bellum*, see the discussion in Chapter 5 below.

[125] See *US Defense Report*, p. 612.

[126] See e.g. J. A. Burger, 'International Humanitarian Law and the Kosovo Crisis: Lessons Learned or to Be Learned' (2000) 837 *IRRC* 129 ('[t]he law of armed conflict establishes

home, reportedly took a different approach on occasions to the question of civilian losses.[127]

At the very least, the willingness to accept casualties is consistent with good faith in the application of proportionality.[128] To put this in the context of the Kosovo action, the insistence of the NATO forces that Operation Allied Force was conducted in accordance with the requirements of proportionality in IHL is brought into question by the statistics. There were 37,465 sorties flown, of which more than 14,006 were strike missions.[129] Although the number is contested, it appears there were at least some 400–500 civilian casualties.[130] NATO forces in comparison incurred no combat casualties.

Determination of likely civilian casualties and damage to civilian objects

There is no doubt that considerable efforts were made by the coalition forces in their conduct of both Persian Gulf conflicts to minimise civilian casualties by adopting means and methods of warfare designed to achieve that end and by taking other precautionary steps, such as target verification.[131] The available information makes this clear. What is not always apparent from the reports of the conflicts is the extent to which, despite all these precautions, attacks were avoided or were cancelled because of the likelihood of disproportionate civilian casualties. This certainly occurred. For example, the United States Department of Defense Report to Congress, on *The Conduct of the Persian Gulf War*, states:

a duty to take reasonable precautions, consistent with mission accomplishment and force protection').

[127] See Hampson, 'Means and Methods of Warfare in the Conflict in the Gulf', p. 109. See, however, Rogers, 'Zero-Casualty Warfare', p. 168 (writing that the British public were prepared to tolerate more casualties where British interests were seen to be at stake, such as in the Falkland Islands conflict, than was the case in the Gulf and Kosovo conflicts).

[128] See Sandoz, Swinarski and Zimmerman, *Commentary on the Additional Protocols*, pp. 683–4. See also Fenrick, 'Attacking the Enemy Civilian', p. 548. See the further discussion of the concept of 'good faith' in the application of proportionality, in note 211 and the accompanying text below.

[129] See Clark, 'When Force Is Necessary: NATO's Military Response to the Kosovo Crisis', p. 158.

[130] See Amnesty International, *'Collateral Damage'* (detailing differing official FRY statistics and those of Human Rights Watch).

[131] See *US Defense Report*, p. 177. See also Infeld, 'Precision-Guided Munitions', pp. 126–31 (for a military analysis of the characteristics of the weapons used in the campaign of aerial bombardment in the 1990–1 Persian Gulf conflict); and J. Fitchett, 'US Air Strikes Get Boost from Use of Smart Bombs', *International Herald Tribune*, 22 March 2003.

'Some targets were specifically avoided because the value of destruction of each target was outweighed by the potential risk to nearby civilians.'[132] This approach was reiterated in the second Persian Gulf conflict.[133] The United Kingdom also avoided attacks in the 1990–1 Persian Gulf conflict that it regarded as potentially disproportionate.[134] Attacks were cancelled on occasion where the location of the military target would have resulted in severe collateral damage if a weapon malfunction had occurred. These incidents, however, confirmed the approach that even if civilian casualties are likely to be extensive an attack may still be undertaken if the military target is perceived as sufficiently essential: '[T]his is the most important issue . . . [T]hey [the targets] were not fundamental to the timely achievement of the victory. Had that been the case then, regrettably, irrespective of what collateral damage might have resulted, one would have been responsible and had a responsibility for accepting those targets and for going against them.'[135]

A controversial aspect of the method of calculating civilian casualties highlighted by the 1990–1 Persian Gulf conflict arose in the context of the broad targeting policy of the coalition allies.[136] There were widespread civilian casualties resulting from the targeting of what were assessed as legitimate military objectives but were also essential for the well-being and, in some cases, the very survival of the civilian population. Among the facilities destroyed by coalition bombing were all the electrical power generation plants, oil refineries, the main oil storage facilities and water-related chemical plants. These facilities were attacked not once but repeatedly, in situations where the military advantage appeared questionable to some observers.[137] This was particularly

[132] *US Defense Report*, pp. 611–12.

[133] See E. Schmitt, 'A Nation at War: Civilians; Rumsfeld Says Dozens of Important Targets Have Been Avoided', *New York Times*, 24 March 2003, p. 12, col. B, line 9 (quoting the US Defense Secretary to the effect that senior US commanders had avoided bombing as many as three dozen high-priority targets for fear of civilian casualties).

[134] See *Preliminary Lessons of Operation Granby*, paras. 17, 318 and 321.

[135] Remarks of Air Vice-Marshal Wratten, British Air Commander in the Middle East, before the House of Commons, Defence Select Committee, Fourteenth Report.

[136] See the discussion in note 111 and the accompanying text above. See also Greenwood, 'Customary International Law and the First Geneva Protocol', pp. 72–3 (for a discussion of the targeting policies of the coalition allies in the 1990–1 Persian Gulf conflict).

[137] See C. Jochnick and R. Normand, 'The Legitimation of Violence: A Critical Analysis of the Gulf War' (1994) 35 *Harvard ILJ* 387 at 405–7; and *Needless Deaths in the Gulf War*, pp. 82–7.

the case in relation to the attacks on Iraq's electrical system. The result was the almost complete destruction of the infrastructure of what was a highly developed post-industrial State, with predictable impact on civilians.[138]

These policies raise complex issues of causation. Assuming that the military advantage is calculated on the basis of the destruction of the overall target, that is, the electricity grid or the communications network, is it legitimate to include in the calculation of likely civilian casualties those that are not directly caused by the attack itself but which occur at a later date as a result thereof? The direct civilian casualties of the attacks may be relatively negligible. However, as was the case in the 1990–1 Persian Gulf conflict, where the Iraqi water treatment and sewerage facilities were dependent on the supply of electricity, the longer-term and more remote damage from such attacks (even on an individual strike basis) may be significant and arguably outweigh the military advantage. State practice in that conflict appears to indicate that this type of damage is discounted.

The combined effects of the attacks on all these infrastructure targets, electricity grids, chemical plants etc., is also not factored into the determination of what is likely to constitute 'excessive' collateral injury to civilians. The destruction of each target is assessed individually rather than as part of the broader picture.[139]

It could be argued that the practice of States in the 2003 Persian Gulf conflict provides some clarification on the issue of infrastructure targets. The allied forces were at pains to stress that they would not attack such targets and apparently did in fact not do so except inadvertently. Arguably, the continuing controversy over the long-term impact on the civilian population of such tactics, that was the legacy of the 1990–1 Persian Gulf conflict, had some influence on policy-makers and may indicate an acceptance that the proportionality equation will henceforth

[138] See International Study Team on the Gulf Crisis, *Health and Welfare in Iraq after the Gulf Crisis*, available at http://www.reliefweb.int/library/documents/ist-irq-oct91.pdf 1991); *Needless Deaths in the Gulf War*; and Jochnick and Norman, 'The Legitimation of Violence', pp. 399–406. Some commentators characterise the attacks on the infrastructure of Iraq as indicating economic and policy aims not in any way related to a military advantage: see Jochnick and Normand, 'The Legitimation of Violence', p. 403; and M. Walzer, *Just and Unjust Wars: A Moral Argument with Historical Illustrations* (2nd edn, Basic Books, New York, 1992). See also Hampson, 'Means and Methods of Warfare in the Conflict in the Gulf', p. 100.

[139] This is a matter for the proportionality equation in *ius ad bellum*: see the discussion in Chapter 5 below.

take account of such likely outcomes. Nevertheless, this conflict cannot be taken as a precedent, as it was the stated intention of the attacking forces not only to overthrow the Iraqi regime but also to assist in the reconstruction of Iraq. The restraint, therefore, seems more likely to have been dictated by economic and political considerations rather than by considerations of proportionality.

The issue of the level of collateral civilian damage was once again an issue in the 1999 NATO campaign in Kosovo. The question of negligence in the conduct of an attack, and the requirements of Article 57(2)(b) of Additional Protocol I that an attack should be cancelled if it becomes apparent that it might result in excessive collateral injury to civilians, arose in the context of the attack on the bridge at Grdelica Gorge in April 1999. Amnesty International, in its report on the incident, concluded that the requirements of proportionality appear to have been violated, as the pilot understood his mission as to destroy the bridge regardless of civilian casualties.[140] There were differing reports of this episode. It was treated as an issue of recklessness rather than one of proportionality by the Committee of the OTP in its investigation, concluding that there was insufficient evidence to warrant further investigation.[141]

The attack on the bridge at Grdelica Gorge also raised the more general issue of what is required in terms of continuing target verification to ensure compliance with the requirements of proportionality. At certain times during the NATO campaign, a 15,000 feet minimum altitude was adopted in order for attacking aircraft to avoid enemy air defences. Amnesty International has claimed that this height restriction only allowed for the confirmation that the target was the one selected in planning. It did not allow for the monitoring of the target to ensure, for example, that civilians had not entered into the vicinity in the meantime.[142] It was alleged that this practice is not consistent with the obligations of Article 57(2)(b) that require an attack to be suspended when it is envisaged that the proportionality rule will be breached.[143]

[140] See Amnesty International, *'Collateral Damage'*, pp. 28–30.

[141] See *Final Report to the Prosecutor*, para. 62.

[142] See Amnesty International, *'Collateral Damage'*, p. 15.

[143] See *Final Report to the Prosecutor*, para. 56 (concluding generally that there was 'nothing inherently unlawful about flying above the height which can be reached by enemy air defences . . . It appears that with the use of modern technology, the obligation to distinguish was effectively carried out in the vast majority of cases during the bombing campaign'). In relation to the obligation for ongoing target verification, the Committee appears to have been influenced in its findings by the very short period of time available in the case in question for the person controlling the bombs to react to the arrival of the civilian train on the target bridge (para. 62).

The attack on the Serb television and radio station, a controversial target in terms of its military nature and the direct and concrete military advantage that could be anticipated from an attack on such a target,[144] also involved considerable civilian casualties.[145] Amnesty International alleged the attack was clearly disproportionate given such casualties and the negligible military gain that was in fact anticipated. The Committee of the OTP, whilst uneasy about the nature of the target and the direct and concrete military advantage conferred by the attack, were only prepared to conclude that the civilian casualties were unfortunately high but did not appear to be clearly disproportionate.[146]

As we have seen, warning the civilian population may in some cases diminish the level of collateral injury to civilians that may be anticipated from an attack. However, it can undermine the element of surprise and pose increased risk to attackers. Amnesty International was informed by NATO officials: 'as a general policy they chose not to issue warnings, for fear that this might endanger the crew of attacking aircraft'.[147]

Having considered the rule of proportionality in the context of international armed conflict, it remains to consider the extent to which proportionality has a role to play in the legal regime regulating non-international armed conflict.

Proportionality and non-international armed conflicts

Although the majority of the rules of IHL, conventional and customary, regulate international armed conflicts, it is non-international conflicts that predominate in the world today.[148] This is not a recent phenomenon, but it has assumed greater proportions since the adoption of the United Nations Charter and the rise of struggles for self-determination. The colonial struggles that were a feature of the 1960s and 1970s have largely given way to nationalist struggles in disintegrating States, such as the former Yugoslavia and Soviet Union. Developments in IHL have been slow to reflect this reality. The inadequacy of the regulation of internal conflicts has been to a large extent the product of

[144] See the discussion in note 114 and the accompanying text above.

[145] *Final Report to the Prosecutor*, para. 71, referred to estimates that between ten and seventeen civilians had been killed in the attack.

[146] See *Final Report to the Prosecutor*, paras. 75–7.

[147] See Amnesty International, *'Collateral Damage'*, p. 43.

[148] See M. Sollenberg (ed.), *States in Armed Conflict 1997* (Department of Peace and Conflict Research, Uppsala University, Uppsala, 1998), p. 7 and Appendix 1, p. 13. For the definition of armed conflicts included in these statistics, see *ibid.*, Appendix 2, p. 19.

the development of international law in the context of, and concerning relations between, nation States. The domestic affairs of a State traditionally have been considered as *prima facie* outside its scope.[149]

It is increasingly recognised, however, that civil wars have ramifications of immense proportions for the international community and pose significant challenges to IHL, not the least of which is the civilian casualties they produce. Despite this changing reality, State sovereignty is still an effective barrier to increased international regulation of non-international armed conflict. Additional Protocol II to the 1949 Geneva Conventions regulating non-international armed conflicts reflects this. Its provisions are quite inadequate. The ICRC had for some years supported the elimination of the distinction between non-international and international conflict for the purposes of the application of IHL. The move to apply all these humanitarian rules to civil conflicts, irrespective of the legal status of the parties to the conflict, commenced as long ago as 1949 in the negotiations of the Fourth Geneva Convention.[150] The original ICRC draft of common Article 2 to the 1949 Geneva Conventions[151] contained a fourth paragraph that read:

> In all cases of armed conflict which are not of an international character, especially cases of civil war, colonial conflicts, or wars of religion, which may occur in the territory of one or more of the High Contracting Parties, the implementing of the principles of the present Convention shall be obligatory on each of the adversaries. The application of the Convention in these circumstances shall in no wise depend on the legal status of the Parties to the conflict and shall have no effect on that status.[152]

[149] The United Nations Charter by Art. 2(7) reinforces this perception of the role of international law: 'Nothing contained in the present Charter shall authorize the United Nations to intervene in matters which are essentially within the domestic jurisdiction of any state or shall require the Members to submit such matters to settlement under the present Charter; but this principle shall not prejudice the application of enforcement measures under Chapter VII.' The organisation, however, has not hesitated, particularly in the post-Cold War era, to involve itself in civil strife in pursuance of its Chapter VII powers: see Promotion and Protection of Human Rights, Fundamental Standards of Humanity, *Report of the Secretary-General Submitted Pursuant to Commission Resolution 2000/69*, Commission on Human Rights, 57th Sess., UN Doc. E/CN.4/2001/91, 12 January 2001.

[150] For a discussion of the very first steps in the movement to protect civilians in internal armed conflicts, see Sandoz, Swinarski and Zimmerman, *Commentary on the Additional Protocols*, pp. 1322–3.

[151] Common Art. 2 of the four Geneva Conventions of 1949 sets out the armed conflicts to which the Conventions apply.

[152] Draft Conventions for the Protection of War Victims, presented to the Seventeenth International Red Cross Conference at Stockholm. Reprinted in J. Pictet (ed.), *Geneva Convention Relative to the Protection of Civilian Persons in Time of War* (ICRC, Geneva, 1958), p. 30.

The draft was not accepted by States, and the outcome was the 'mini-convention' contained in common Article 3.[153] In the meantime, the movement by the ICRC to eliminate the distinction between international and non-international armed conflict[154] received more support from developments in the area of human rights and from several General Assembly resolutions dealing with respect for human rights in all armed conflicts.[155] It is clear from the tenor of these resolutions that it was perceived to be inappropriate to distinguish between international and non-international armed conflict, as principles of human rights in armed conflict know no such artificial boundaries.[156] It was not necessarily intended that the rules relating to traditional armed conflict should apply in their entirety to non-international armed conflict, for instance the complex rules as to prisoners of war, but that the basic principles common to both human rights and humanitarian law should.[157]

This approach did not succeed at the 1974–7 Diplomatic Conference on the Reaffirmation and Development of International Humanitarian Law Applicable in Armed Conflicts, and the view prevailed that there was a need for two separate Protocols. At a very early stage of the negotiations it became clear that the most controversial questions to be resolved by the Diplomatic Conference were in relation to the assimilation of guerrilla warfare and its protagonists into the system of rules regulating international armed conflict. Although several States attempted to ensure an effective Protocol for civil wars, they were frustrated by the political agenda of other States who managed to shift the concentration of efforts to Protocol I.[158] Moreover, such were the divisions amongst

[153] See *ibid.*, pp. 30–4.

[154] The International Committee of the Red Cross 1956 Draft Rules for the Limitation of the Dangers Incurred by the Civilian Population in Time of War, by Art. 2(b) applied the rules to both international and non-international armed conflict. Reprinted in Schindler and Toman, *The Laws of Armed Conflicts*, p. 251.

[155] See GA Res. 2444 (XXIII), 19 December 1968; GA Res. 2675 (XXV), 9 December 1970.

[156] See A. Cassese, 'The Geneva Protocols of 1977 on the Humanitarian Law of Armed Conflict and Customary International Law' (1984) 3 *UCLA PBLJ* 55 at 105–6; and H. Gasser, 'The Sixth Annual American Red Cross Washington Conference on International Humanitarian Law: A Workshop on Customary International Law and the 1977 Protocols Additional to the 1949 Geneva Conventions' (1987) 2 *American University Journal of International Law and Policy* 415 at 481.

[157] This approach is reflected in the attitude of many of the delegations to the Diplomatic Conference. See statement of Finnish delegate, *Official Records*, CDDH/SR.18, vol. 5, para. 15; Swedish delegate *Official Records*, CDDH/SR.14, vol. 5, p. 142, para. 7, and Norwegian delegate *Official Records*, CDDH/SR.10, vol. 5, p. 91, para. 3.

[158] See e.g. the statement by the Norwegian delegate on the adoption of Additional Protocol II in the Plenary Session of the Diplomatic Conference, *Official Records*,

States as to the content of Protocol II that the leader of the Pakistani delegation revised the draft Protocol.[159] The re-draft eliminated half the articles. Included in the deleted provisions were most of the provisions imposing limitations on the means and methods of warfare to protect civilians, including a prohibition on disproportionate attacks.[160] Although Protocol II was adopted by consensus, there remained fundamental differences between States as to the regulation of internal conflicts.[161]

Article 13 of Additional Protocol II sets out the rule for the protection of the civilian population and reads as follows:

> 1. The civilian population and individual civilians shall enjoy general protection against the dangers arising from military operations. To give effect to this protection, the following rules shall be observed in all circumstances.
> 2. The civilian population as such, as well as individual civilians, shall not be the object of attack. Acts or threats of violence the primary purpose of which is to spread terror among the civilian population are prohibited.
> 3. Civilians shall enjoy the protection afforded by this Part, unless and for such time as they take a direct part in hostilities.

CDDH/SR.56, vol. 7, pp. 205–6, paras. 63–6. See also S. Junod, 'Additional Protocol II: History and Scope' (1983) 33 *American University LR* 29, 32–4.

[159] The simplified draft of Additional Protocol II was submitted to the Plenary Session of the Diplomatic Conference in June 1977, with the Pakistani delegate, Mr Hussain, commenting: '[D]uring contacts with many other delegations of both developed and under-privileged countries, however, it had realised that there was considerable dissatisfaction with the length of the text as well as with the fact that it ventured into domains which they considered sacrosanct and inappropriate for inclusion in an international instrument' (*Official Records*, CDDH/SR.49, vol. 7, p. 61, para. 10). See also Junod, 'Additional Protocol II', pp. 33ff; and D. Forsythe, 'Legal Management of Internal War: The 1977 Protocol on Non-International Armed Conflicts' (1978) 72 *AJIL* 272 at 277ff.

[160] See Art. 26 of Draft Protocol Additional to the Geneva Conventions of August 12, 1949 and Relating to the Protection of Victims of Non-International Armed Conflicts, reprinted in *Official Records*, vol. 1, p. 33. The original ICRC draft of what became Additional Protocol II contained a rule of proportionality identical to that in the draft of Additional Protocol I.

[161] *Official Records*, CDDH/SR.56, vol. 7, p. 205, para. 62. Many States declared that, if the Protocol had been put to the vote, they would have abstained. See e.g. Nigeria, *Official Records*, CDDH/SR.56, vol. 7, p. 196, para. 12; Indonesia, *Official Records*, CDDH/SR.56, vol. 7, p. 198, para. 22; Mexico, *Official Records*, CDDH/SR.56, vol. 7, p. 196, para. 28; Sudan, *Official Records*, CDDH/SR.56, vol. 7, p. 199, para. 38; India, *Official Records*, CDDH/SR.56, vol. 7, p. 202, para. 49 and the Philippines, *Official Records*, CDDH/SR.56, vol. 7, para. 61.

Article 13 is thus a restatement of the first three paragraphs of Article 51 of Additional Protocol I.[162] It does not contain the specific limitations on the means and methods of combat contained in the other paragraphs of Article 51. Consequently, Article 13 contains no explicit prohibition against indiscriminate attacks or any requirement as to proportionality. However, the International Court of Justice in the *Nuclear Weapons* Advisory Opinion expressed the view, albeit in the context of international armed conflicts, that the use of weapons that are incapable of distinguishing between civilian and military targets amounts to making civilians the object of attack and is prohibited.[163] Thus, if this analysis is correct, such an indiscriminate attack falls within the treaty rule in Additional Protocol II. This widens the scope of the protection in Article 13 beyond the deliberate targeting of civilians, but only to a limited extent. It does not include disproportionate attacks.

Additional Protocol II, therefore, is of little assistance in protecting civilians against the effects of armed conflict, including attacks that result in disproportionate civilian casualties and damage to civilian objects. The threshold of Additional Protocol II, moreover, is high and only covers 'situations at or near the level of a full-scale civil war or belligerency'.[164]

An important development, however, that reflects the changing perception of the role of international law in non-international armed conflicts is the amended scope of Protocol II to the Conventional Weapons Convention.[165] The amended Protocol includes certain civil conflicts, and contains the requirement that the placement of devices covered by its provisions meet the requirements of proportionality.[166]

Conceding that the treaty regime of IHL governing non-international armed conflicts is inadequate leaves open the possibility that customary norms may compensate to some extent for this deficiency. For many years, it was unclear how far customary law and non-international armed conflicts were compatible. In recent times, however, the

[162] The original ICRC draft of Art. 13 was almost identical to the draft of Art. 51 of Additional Protocol I. The draft rules are reprinted in *Official Records*, vol. 1, Part 3, p. 40. Bothe, Partsch and Solf, *New Rules*, pp. 609ff, contains a comparative table of the provisions of the 1973 ICRC draft Protocol, the draft adopted by Committee II of the Diplomatic Conference and the final text of the Protocol adopted in the Plenary Session of the Diplomatic Conference.

[163] *Nuclear Weapons* Advisory Opinion, para. 78.

[164] See Meron, 'The Humanization of Humanitarian Law', p. 245.

[165] See the further discussion in note 172 and the accompanying text below.

[166] *Ibid.*

development of norms regulating non-international armed conflicts has received new impetus from the activities of the Security Council. Moreover, it is increasingly accepted that breaches of these requirements may attract criminal sanctions. The exception of the Chapter VII powers of the Security Council from the prohibition on the intervention by the organisation in the domestic affairs of States in Article 2(7) of the Charter has proved to be a mechanism for breaking down the rigid distinction between international and non-international armed conflicts. The Security Council, on several occasions, has characterised flagrant breaches of norms of IHL and human rights law as constituting a threat to international peace and security within Article 39 of the Charter. What has activated their concern has been the mistreatment of civilians by warring factions. The response of the Security Council, particularly the legal institutions it has established in response to these events, such as the ICTY and the ICTR, has had a fundamental impact on the development of new norms that are not necessarily dependent on traditional distinctions between non-international and international armed conflicts.[167] The trigger for the applicability of the governing norms has shifted away from a State-centric approach to the impact of the events on individuals. This phenomenon owes much to the influence of human rights. Moreover, States are increasingly accepting the failure of this traditional distinction to reflect the reality of armed conflict and modifying their position in relation to their legal obligations accordingly. For example, the United States has declared that the 'Armed Forces of the United States will comply with the law of war during the conduct of all military operations and activities in armed conflict, however such conflicts are characterised'.[168] It is therefore becoming increasingly realistic to argue that proportionality will soon have a role to play in some non-international armed conflicts.[169]

The Appeals Chamber of the ICTY in the *Tadic* case considered in some detail the question of the applicability of customary norms of IHL to non-international armed conflicts.[170] The Court was considering the issue in

[167] See Meron, 'The Humanization of Humanitarian Law', p. 246.

[168] Chairman, Joint Chief of Staff, Instruction 5810.01, Implementation of the DOD Law of War Program (1996), cited in Meron 'The Humanization of Humanitarian Law', note 122.

[169] Cf. J. Bond, *The Rules of Riot: Internal Conflict and the Law of War* (Princeton University Press, Princeton, 1974), who as early as 1974 was of the view that proportionality was a requirement in internal armed conflicts (*ibid.*, pp. 93, 97 and 110).

[170] *Prosecutor* v. *Tadic*, Case No. IT-94-1, Decision on the Defence Motion for Interlocutory Appeal on Jurisdiction (2 October 1995).

the context of Article 3 of the Statute of the ICTY that punishes violations of the laws and customs of war but draws no distinction between international and non-international armed conflicts. The Court was of the opinion that State practice supported the view that the general rules of international law had developed to regulate certain aspects of internal armed conflicts. These were, however, limited in number, and it is the 'general essence' of the rules and principles applicable to international armed conflicts rather than their detailed form that has become applicable to non-international armed conflicts. Consequently, Article 3 of the Statute of the ICTY fell to be interpreted in light of the customary law position that serious violations of the laws and customs of war are prohibited whether committed in non-international armed conflicts or not. The list of such violations in Article 3 is illustrative rather than exhaustive, and the Court expressed the view that amongst such norms were those that protect the civilian population from hostilities, including the prohibition on indiscriminate attacks.[171] It is apparent from the context that the Court is referring here to indiscriminate attacks in the sense of attacks conducted without due care to distinguish between civilian and military targets and not as the term is used in Additional Protocol I, which, it will be recalled, includes disproportionate attacks. However, should the issue arise directly, there is no reason to suppose that the Court would not find that disproportionate attacks are prohibited under the basic principles applicable in both internal and international armed conflicts. It is, therefore, becoming increasingly realistic to argue that proportionality will soon have a role to play in some internal conflicts.

Protocol II to the Conventional Weapons Convention

Protocol II to the Convention on Prohibitions or Restrictions on the Use of Certain Conventional Weapons Which May Be Deemed to Be Excessively Injurious or to Have Indiscriminate Effects deals with the use of mines, booby-traps and other devices. It was adopted by States on 10 October 1980 and amended on 3 May 1996. Article 3 of the 1980 Protocol prohibits the indiscriminate use of mines, booby-traps and other devices. By Article 3(3)(c), 'indiscriminate use is any placement of such weapons which may be expected to cause incidental loss of civilian life, injury to civilians, damage to civilian objects, or a combination thereof, which would be excessive in relation to the concrete and direct military

[171] *Ibid.*, para. 127.

advantage anticipated'. This provision reflects the definition in Protocol I and is repeated unchanged in the 1996 amended Protocol.[172] The scope of the new instrument, however, encompasses certain types of civil conflicts and is the first treaty expression of proportionality in relation to such conflicts. By Article 1(2) of the Protocol, the scope of the Protocol is extended 'to situations referred to in Article 3 common to the Geneva Conventions of 12 August 1949'.[173]

The suppression of breaches of the requirements of proportionality in IHL[174]

The failure to comply with the requirements of proportionality in relation to civilian losses and damage to civilian objects is a breach of both customary and conventional provisions of IHL.

In Chapter 3 the system of State responsibility and the distinctive regime for the suppression of breaches of IHL was outlined and also the contribution of the United Nations, particularly the Security Council, to this process. It will be recalled that the general principles of State responsibility and the system of individual criminal responsibility in IHL govern this area of the law. The role of reprisals as a method of inducing compliance with IHL was also considered and is equally relevant in the context of proportionality. For example, it is arguable that a State whose civilian population is subjected to grossly disproportionate attacks, given the lack of any other method for inducing compliance with the law, may legitimately resort to the use of prohibited means and methods of combat as a last resort.[175]

In the context of international criminal law, some instances of disproportionate attacks amount to a grave breach of Additional Protocol I. Article 85(3) defines as a grave breach the following acts:

[172] See Art. 3(8).

[173] In 2001, the scope of the Convention as a whole was expanded to cover the same conflicts as provided for in Art. 1(2) of Additional Protocol II. See amended Art. I of the Second Review Conference of the State Parties to the Convention on Prohibitions or Restrictions on the Use of Certain Conventional Weapons Which May Be Deemed to Be Excessively Injurious or to Have Indiscriminate Effects, Final Document, Doc CCW/Conf II/2 (2001), pp. 34–5.

[174] For a discussion of issues of responsibility and enforcement in the context of IHL and peacekeeping forces, see Chapter 6 below.

[175] See G. Aldrich, 'Compliance with International Humanitarian Law' (1991) 282 *IRRC* 294; Judge Cassese, in the *Kupreskic* case, para. 535; and the further discussion in Chapter 3, note 86 and the accompanying text above.

when committed wilfully, in violation of the relevant provisions of this Protocol, and causing death or serious injury to body or health:

. . .

(b) launching an indiscriminate attack affecting the civilian population or civilian objects in the knowledge that such attack will cause excessive loss of life, injury to civilians or damage to civilian objects, as defined in Article 57, paragraph 2(a)(iii).

Moreover, by Article 85(3)(c), the launching of a disproportionate attack against works or installations containing dangerous forces (the subject of a special regime under Article 56 of the Protocol) is a grave breach of the Protocol.[176]

It is not necessary in order to constitute a grave breach under the Protocol that the attack actually results in excessive collateral civilian damage. It is sufficient if the attack causes death or serious injury to body and health.[177] The mental element necessary to establish the offence and whether recklessness is sufficient is in the process of elaboration in the case law of the ICTY.[178] The evidence of the requisite knowledge, however, may be inferred from the surrounding facts and circumstances.[179] Consequently, States have been consistently at pains to ensure that too much is not expected of decision-makers in terms of their obligations to acquire information before making the judgments as to the proportionality of the planned attack.[180]

176 Art. 56(1) prohibits attacks on works and installations containing dangerous forces, even if military in nature, if the attack 'may cause the release of dangerous forces and consequent severe losses among the civilian population'. This special protection for such objects ceases if certain conditions are met (Art. 56(2)). See *Commentary on the Additional Protocols*, pp. 665–75 (for an explanation of the special regime applicable to such objects) and pp. 996–7 (for an explanation of the operation of the related grave breach provision).

177 See the discussion of this issue in the context of the crime of launching a disproportionate attack in the Statute of the ICC, in note 200 and the accompanying text below.

178 See e.g. *Prosecutor* v. *Tihomir Blaskic*, Case No. IT-95-14-T, Judgment, para. 152; but cf. the approach of the ICC Elements of Crimes, discussed in note 206 and the accompanying text below.

179 This was an issue of importance during the negotiations of the ICC Elements of Crimes, and a provision to this effect is included in para. 3 of the General Introduction thereto. See generally K. Dörmann, *Elements of War Crimes under the Rome Statute of the International Criminal Court* (Cambridge University Press, Cambridge, 2003), p. 12.

180 See the reservations and interpretative declarations by States to Arts. 51 and 57 of Additional Protocol I in note 52 and the accompanying text above. See also Art. 8(2)(b)(iv) of the ICC Elements of Crimes to this effect.

The failure to suspend such an attack as mandated by Article 57(2)(b) does not constitute a grave breach of the Protocol but still could constitute a war crime if of a sufficiently serious nature.

As previously discussed, little has been achieved in practical terms from the treaty system of universal jurisdiction for the punishment of war crimes.[181] More significant for the enforcement of individual criminal responsibility has been the establishment on occasion of *ad hoc* tribunals to punish persons alleged to have committed serious breaches of IHL. The Nuremberg War Crimes Tribunal, established by treaty after the Second World War to try offences committed by the Axis powers, made no mention of indiscriminate attacks against the civilian population. This is despite the fact that the Nuremberg Charter recognised 'wanton destruction of cities, towns or villages, or devastation not justified by military necessity' as a war crime.[182] The expected reference by the Nuremberg Tribunal to the wanton destruction of cities in the trial of Hermann Goering, the Commander-in-Chief of the Luftwaffe, was not forthcoming.[183] Furthermore, the United Nations War Crimes Commission received no notice of records of trial concerning the illegal conduct of air warfare.[184] One factor leading to the failure to pursue these crimes was the culpability of the allies themselves for extensive collateral injury to civilians resulting from aerial bombardment.[185]

In contrast, indictments have been issued in relation to attacks upon the civilian population during the conflict in the former Yugoslavia as violations of the laws and customs of war under Article 3 of the Statute of the ICTY.[186] This initiative is a marked development in IHL. There may have been some doubt initially as to whether the launching of an

[181] See the discussion in Chapter 3, note 104, and the accompanying text above.

[182] Art. 6 of the Charter of the International Military Tribunal, annexed to the Agreement for the Prosecution and Punishment of the Major War Criminals of the European Axis, London, 8 August 1945, 82 UNTS 280.

[183] See Fenrick, 'Attacking the Enemy Civilian', p. 550. [184] *Ibid.* [185] *Ibid.*

[186] See e.g. *Prosecutor* v. *Blaskic*, Case No. IT-95-14 Second Amended Indictment, Judgment, 3 March 2000 (the Judgment, issued by the ICTY against Blaskic for crimes committed in the Lasva Valley, included convictions for unlawful attacks on civilians and civilian objects); *Prosecutor* v. *Martic*, Case No. IT-95-11, Indictment (attacks on Zagreb in May 1995); *Prosecutor* v. *Rajic*, Case No. IT-95-12, Indictment (attacks on the village of Stupni Do on 23 October 1993); *Prosecutor* v. *Galic*, Case No. IT-98-29, Indictment; *Prosecutor* v. *Karadzic and Another*, Case No. IT-95-18, Indictment (attacks on civilians in Tuzla, 1995); *Prosecutor* v. *Kordic and Another*, Case No. IT-95-14/2, Indictment (attacks on civilians in the Lasva Valley from January to May 1993); and *Prosecutor* v. *Milosevic and Others*, Case No. IT-99-37, Indictment. See generally Fenrick, 'Attacking the Enemy Civilian'.

indiscriminate or disproportionate attack was within the jurisdiction of the ICTY.[187] The report of the Secretary-General relating to the establishment of the ICTY emphasised the need to ensure that the international tribunal only applied rules of IHL that are 'beyond any doubt part of customary law'.[188] The report did not include Additional Protocol I in that category.[189] However, in the *Tadic* case, the Appeals Chamber of the ICTY interpreted the phrase 'violations of the laws or customs of war' in Article 3 of the Statute so as to encompass any serious violation of IHL under any treaty that was unquestionably binding on the parties at the time of the alleged offence.[190] As this is the case for Additional Protocol I, the ICTY has jurisdiction over disproportionate attacks occurring during that conflict.

The majority of the indictments issued by the ICTY focus on deliberate rather than indiscriminate attacks against the civilian population.[191] One exception was the indictment issued against Djukic[192] that included charges for indiscriminate attacks against civilian targets in Sarajevo. However, the facts giving rise to the charges did not involve allegedly disproportionate attacks. Rather Djukic was charged with crimes against humanity and violations of the laws and customs of war in that he and others 'on a widespread and systematic basis, deliberately or indiscriminately fired on civilian targets that were of no military significance in order to kill, injure, terrorise and demoralise the civilian population of Sarajevo'. The case against Djukic was closed after his death in May 1996.

Although no indictments have been issued for attacks that are alleged to have involved disproportionate civilian casualties, the issue of proportionality was considered by the Trial Chamber of the ICTY in the *Kupreskic* Case.[193] The Court was of the view that proportionality in the sense of

[187] Neither the Statute of the ICTR (established by the UN Security Council pursuant to SC Res. 955, 8 November 1994) nor the Statute of the Special Court for Sierra Leone (see *Report of the Secretary-General on the Establishment of a Special Court for Sierra Leone*, S/2000/915, 4 October 2000, Annex) encompass disproportionate attacks within their subject matter jurisdiction.

[188] *Report of the Secretary-General Pursuant to Paragraph 2 of Security Council Resolution 808 (1993)*, S/25704, 3 May 1993, para. 34.

[189] *Ibid.*, para. 35.

[190] *Prosecutor* v. *Tadic*, Case No. IT-94-1, Decision on the Defence Motion for Interlocutory Appeal on Jurisdiction, 2 October 1995, para. 143.

[191] For a discussion of the issues raised in the context of prosecutions for indiscriminate attacks against the civilian population, see Fenrick, 'Attacking the Enemy Civilian'.

[192] See *Prosecutor* v. *Djukic*, Case No. IT-96-20, Indictment.

[193] *Prosecutor* v. *Kupreskic et al.*, Case No. IT-95-16-T-14, Judgment, January 2000.

Article 57 of Additional Protocol I[194] represents customary international law and, moreover, is a general principle of international law.[195]

Proportionality also was an issue in the investigation by the Prosecutor of the ICTY, under Article 18 of the Statute of the ICTY, of the actions of NATO in Kosovo in 1999.[196] It was alleged by various critics that NATO had, *inter alia*, 'deliberately or recklessly caused excessive civilian casualties in disregard of the rule of proportionality by trying to fight a "zero casualty" war for their own side'.[197] The Committee of the OTP considered a number of incidents in which it was alleged that there had been a failure to abide by the requirements of proportionality. None of these incidents, however, in the view of the Committee, warranted a further investigation by the OTP.

The Statute of the ICC confers jurisdiction on the Court for war crimes. In contrast to the Statute of the ICTY, where disproportionate attacks must be prosecuted as a violation of the laws and customs of war, launching a disproportionate attack is specifically included within the definition of war crimes over which the ICC has jurisdiction. Article 8(2) of the Statute of the ICC defines war crimes so as to include:

> Other serious violations of the laws and customs applicable in international armed conflict, within the established framework of international law, namely, any of the following acts:
>
> . . .
>
> (iv) Intentionally launching an attack in the knowledge that such attack will cause incidental loss of life or injury to civilians or damage to civilian objects or widespread, long-term and severe damage to the natural environment which would be clearly excessive in relation to the direct overall military advantage anticipated.

[194] It will be recalled that Art. 57 of Additional Protocol I imposes requirements on commanders not to undertake or to cancel attacks that may infringe the requirements of proportionality.

[195] Para. 524. Note the criticism of the Trial Chamber's approach to proportionality and cumulative attacks on military targets, in *Final Report to the Prosecutor*, para. 52.

[196] Art. 18 of the Statute of the ICTY requires the Prosecutor to 'initiate investigations ex officio or on the basis of information obtained from any source, particularly from Governments, United Nations organs, intergovernmental and non-governmental organisations. The Prosecutor shall assess the information received or obtained and decide whether there is sufficient basis to proceed.' See S. Boelaert-Suominen, 'The International Criminal Tribunal for the Former Yugoslavia and the Kosovo Conflict' (2000) 837 *IRRC* 217 (for a discussion of the basis of the involvement of the Tribunal in the NATO action in Kosovo).

[197] See *Final Report to the Prosecutor*.

This definition is an advance on the conventional law position as reflected in Additional Protocol I as it includes the environment as a prohibited object of a disproportionate attack. Additional Protocol I prohibits the 'use of methods or means of warfare which are intended or may be expected to cause . . . widespread, long-term and severe damage to the environment'. Such actions, however, are not criminalised, nor does the Protocol proscribe a disproportionate attack on the environment, although arguably this prohibition is reflected in customary international law.[198]

The Elements of Crimes, completed by the Preparatory Commission for the International Criminal Court, for the offence of launching an attack resulting in excessive incidental death, injury, or damage to civilian or civilian objects, reads:[199]

1. The perpetrator launched an attack.
2. The attack was such that it would cause incidental death or injury to civilians or damage to civilian objects or widespread, long-term and severe damage to the natural environment and that such death, injury or damage would be of such an extent as to be clearly excessive in relation to the concrete and direct overall military advantage anticipated.
3. The perpetrator knew the attack would cause incidental death or injury to civilians or damage to civilian objects or widespread, long-term and severe damage to the natural environment and that such death, injury or damage would be of such an extent as to be clearly excessive in relation to the concrete and direct overall military advantage anticipated.

The Elements of Crimes clarifies the issue as to whether, to constitute the crime of launching a disproportionate attack, the attack in question must result in excessive collateral civilian damage. Under the equivalent grave breach provision of Additional Protocol I, it is sufficient if collateral civilian damage ensues from the attack. The extent thereof is irrelevant. The Statute of the ICC adopts the phrase 'such attack will cause', which appears to indicate that not only must the attack result in damage but

[198] See Art. 55(1) of Additional Protocol I.

[199] Part II Addendum Finalized Draft Text of the Elements of Crimes, Report of the Preparatory Commission for the International Criminal Court, PCNICC/2000/I/Add.2. The Elements of Crimes, to be adopted by a two-thirds majority of the members of the future Assembly of State Parties, are provided for by Art. 9 of the Statute of the ICC and are intended to 'assist the Court in the interpretation and application of Arts. 6, 7 and 8' of the Statute. See generally Dörmann, *Elements of War Crimes* (for a commentary on the Elements of Crimes and the background to their adoption).

that it must be excessive. The phrase 'the attack was such that it would cause' adopted in the Elements of Crimes reflects the majority view that a particular result is not a prerequisite to the crime.[200] Of course, the final decision as to this and other contentious matters of interpretation will be for the Court to determine.

The inclusion in the Statute of the ICC of the offence of launching a disproportionate attack increases the likelihood of criminal prosecution in such cases. The enduring controversy over the requirement of proportionality in IHL, and its criminalisation in Additional Protocol I, was reflected in the negotiations of the Statute of the ICC and the draft text of the Elements of Crimes.[201] The result of the unease as to some aspects of the treaty rule led to a departure from the definition of this offence as a grave breach in Additional Protocol I and a number of explanatory notes in the Elements of Crimes, which are not in all respects models of clarity.

There was a perception in some quarters that the Court might require too high a standard of decision-makers when measuring the military advantage in order to determine the 'excessiveness' of an attack. The Statute definition of the offence of launching a disproportionate attack adds the word 'clearly' to the text of the provision as it appears in Additional Protocol I. This addition is intended to indicate to the Court that only obvious cases of disproportionate attacks should be punished.[202] Moreover, it is the 'overall' military advantage of the attack against which the excessiveness of the collateral civilian damage is to be assessed. An explanatory note accompanies the phrase 'concrete and direct overall military advantage anticipated' in the Elements of Crimes, namely:

> The expression 'concrete and direct overall military advantage anticipated' refers to a military advantage that is foreseeable by the perpetrator at the relevant time. Such advantage may or may not be temporally or geographically related to the object of the attack. The fact that this crime admits the possibility of lawful incidental injury and collateral damage does not in any way justify any violation of the law applicable in armed conflict. It does not address justifications or other rules related to *jus ad bellum*. It reflects the proportionality requirement inherent in determining the legality of any military activity undertaken in the context of an armed conflict.

[200] See the discussion of this issue in Dörmann, *Elements of War Crimes*, p. 162.

[201] See H. von Hebel and D. Robinson, 'Crimes Within the Jurisdiction of the Court' in R. S. Lee (ed.), *The International Criminal Court – Issues, Negotiations, Results* (Kluwer Law International, The Hague, 1999), p. 79 at p. 107.

[202] See von Hebel and Robinson, 'Crimes Within the Jurisdiction of the Court', pp. 110–11.

As the ICRC commentary on the Elements of Crimes observes, this paragraph includes clarification on several different issues, including what is envisaged by the word 'overall'.[203] There are differences of view as to the extent to which the interpretation placed by the explanatory note on the phrase 'overall military advantage' changes the scope of the Protocol rule. For some observers, this definition represents an unwarranted lowering of the existing requirements of IHL and negatives the effect of the words 'concrete and direct'. It is argued that it allows for the situation where there is no 'temporal or geographical connection . . . between the foreseeable military advantage and the attack causing civilian loss of life'.[204] Some delegations were of the view that a military advantage that would ensue at a later date or at a different location would be included by the use of the word 'overall'. This approach has been criticised, as inappropriately reducing the standards required of decision-makers under the Protocol and has not achieved the aim of preventing the assessment of the legitimacy of attacks on unreasonable grounds.[205]

A further explanatory note to the Elements of Crimes for the offence of launching a disproportionate attack attempts to clarify differences over the knowledge required of the accused before the mental element of the crime is satisfied. In essence the dispute relates to the extent to which the accused must have appreciated the 'excessiveness' of the collateral civilian damage over the military advantage. The explanatory note, however, does not achieve the goal of clarity and is open to differing interpretations.[206] There appears to be consensus, however, that a reckless perpetrator with the necessary facts at their disposal who does not turn their mind to the assessment of whether the attack will be 'excessive' in its effects will not be thereby exonerated.[207]

Conclusion

Several decades after the adoption of Additional Protocol I, it is now widely accepted that attacks on military targets should not be undertaken or should be cancelled if collateral civilian damage is regarded

[203] See Dörmann, *Elements of War Crimes*, p. 163.
[204] See M. Politi, 'Elements of Crimes' in Lee (ed.), *The International Criminal Court – Issues, Negotiations, Results*, p. 443 at pp. 471–2; and Dörmann, *Elements of War Crimes*, p. 63 (arguing that the interpretation placed on the word 'overall' in this explanatory note may 'invite abusive interpretations of the concept "direct military advantage"').
[205] See Politi, 'Elements of Crimes', pp. 471–2.
[206] See Dörmann, *Elements of War Crimes*, pp. 164–5.
[207] *Ibid.*, p. 165.

as having the potential to outweigh the military advantage, irrespective of the care taken in the selection of the means of warfare and in the conduct of the attack. There remains considerable practice, however, primarily by non-Western States, that disregards any application of proportionality, let alone that of the treaty rule.[208] On the other hand, this practice has been widely condemned. Therefore, the proportionality rule as expressed in Articles 51(5)(b) and 57(2)(a)(iii) and (b), with a degree of confidence, can be viewed as reflected in customary international law.

However, the foregoing discussion has highlighted the significant areas of uncertainty in the detailed operation of proportionality in IHL. There remains considerable debate over the meaning of the phrase 'concrete and direct military advantage' and what is included in the calculation of collateral civilian damage so as to determine whether this will be 'excessive' in relation to the military advantage. These reservations are equally a feature of both the conventional and the customary norm.

Significantly, it was the meaning of 'concrete and direct military advantage' that dominated the deliberations over the crime of launching a disproportionate attack in the Statute of the ICC rather than the method of calculating collateral civilian damage. A number of States were at pains to ensure that the test of the military advantage against which the concept of 'excessive' civilian losses was to be measured provided a considerable leeway for decision-makers.[209]

Given the uncertainties, at the present time the precise demands of the proportionality norm in all circumstances and the scope of the conventional and customary norms respectively, cannot be stated with any degree of confidence.

It is debatable to what extent it is possible or indeed desirable to clarify these issues legislatively. On the one hand, the more detailed the norm the less flexibility it retains to adapt to changing circumstances and be workable in practice. If the norm is perceived as unduly onerous or unrealistic, States will sidestep its requirements, to the detriment of the

[208] For example, in relation to the conflict in Chechnya, see *Situation of Human Rights in the Republic of Chechnya of the Russian Federation*, Commission on Human Rights, Report on the Fifty-Second Session, UN Doc. E/CN.4/1996/177, para. 371 (expressing the concerns of the Commission in relation to the use of disproportionate force by the Russian armed forces in the bombardment of civilian towns and villages); and Meron, 'The Humanization of Humanitarian Law', p. 277 (referring to the indiscriminate bombing of population centres in Chechnya by Russian forces).

[209] See Politi, 'Elements of Crimes', pp. 471–2.

civilian population.[210] On the other hand, the trend reflected in developments in international criminal law is that disproportionate attacks warrant criminal sanctions. The negotiating history of the definition of the crime and its elements during the negotiations of the Statute of the ICC, however, indicate the difficulties inherent in reaching agreement on clarifying the detailed application of proportionality.

Given all the uncertainties that attend the norm, commentators have opted for the concept of 'good faith' as what is required in the application of proportionality.[211] Although the notion of 'good faith' lacks precision, it is becoming increasingly apparent in the practice of States what characteristics of an attack will result in compliance with this standard being seriously questioned. To summarise, depending on the context of the use of force in question, an attack on a dubious military target or one the destruction of which provides a less than transparent military advantage, resulting in the loss of any civilian lives, will almost inevitably attract critical attention even if only from the increasingly powerful NGO quarter. Even attacks on military targets that offer a definite military advantage that is readily apparent to non-expert observers will be problematic if they result in high levels of collateral damage. This is even more so if the means and methods of attack selected do not demonstrate that every effort has been made to spare civilians even at the risk of higher combatant casualties.

Irrespective of the detail of the application of the rule, the mere fact that the obligation nowadays exists, as both a conventional and a customary norm, indicates just how far the law protecting the civilian population from the incidental effects of armed conflict has progressed since its hesitant beginnings in the early part of the twentieth century. The increasingly defensive posture of States on this issue, combined with the fact that the OTP of the ICTY and the Tribunal itself have considered allegations of disproportionate attacks, is an indication of things to come.

[210] See Hampson, 'Means and Methods of Warfare in the Conflict in the Gulf', pp. 94–5 (arguing that any enforcement of an objective standard across the armed forces of all States as to the minimisation of military casualties could result in the acceptance of the lowest common denominator).

[211] See e.g. Sandoz, Swinarski and Zimmerman, *Commentary on the Additional Protocols*, pp. 683–4 ('the interpretation [of proportionality] must above all be a question of common sense and good faith for military commanders'). See also Fenrick, 'Attacking the Enemy Civilian', p. 548; and Dörmann, *Elements of War Crimes*, p. 165.

5 Necessity, proportionality and the unilateral use of force in the era of the United Nations Charter

Introduction

Chapter 2 considered the early development of necessity and proportionality as components of the law on the use of force by States during the period prior to the Second World War (1939–45). This chapter analyses the content of these principles under the United Nations Charter regime, and encompasses a consideration of their operation in the context of self-defence, both individual and collective, the so-called right of humanitarian intervention and reprisals involving the use of force. As will become apparent, although the demands of necessity are readily identifiable in the practice of States, the detailed operation of proportionality in modern *ius ad bellum* is somewhat clouded in obscurity and awaits further clarification. Nevertheless, it is possible to distil from State practice a legal framework for the proportionality principle and to identify, albeit tentatively, concrete obligations derived from its constraints.

The United Nations Charter fundamentally changes the pre-existing law on the use of force. Despite considerable contrary State practice, there remains an uneasy consensus that States must limit their unilateral forceful actions to individual and collective self-defence in response to an armed attack.[1] Under the Charter system, therefore, it is the scope of self-defence itself that is the first criterion a State will need to consider when deciding whether or not to take forceful action. What constitutes an armed attack? If a State is subjected to actions that meet the description of an armed attack, it must then assess whether a forceful

[1] See Art. 2(4) of the United Nations Charter (requiring States to settle their disputes by peaceful means) and Art. 51 (retaining the right to individual and collective self-defence in the face of an armed attack) and see the further discussion in note 12 and the accompanying text below.

response is necessary. If so, the next step is to determine what measures in response will be consistent with the requirements of proportionality. This in turn requires an assessment of the aims of self-defence against which to measure the response. In assessing the legitimacy of means, for example, the extent to which the territory of the aggressor State can be invaded or the degree to which its military capability can be destroyed, depends on what view one takes of the aims of self-defence. The same considerations apply to States that intervene forcefully by way of collective self-defence on behalf of a State subjected to an armed attack.

The practical relevance of necessity and proportionality under the United Nations Charter regime is in fact considerably broader than outlined so far. Prior to the adoption of the Charter, the right of self-defence was not restricted to a response to an armed attack, and over the years States have not always been prepared to accept the loss to their freedom of action imposed by the terms of the Charter.[2] In particular, there have been considerable differences as to the legality of preventative action to remove or deter a threat of an armed attack.[3] From time to time, States have asserted even more extensive rights to use force.[4]

An important development in the 1990s was that of forceful intervention to prevent widespread human rights violations. Forceful action by States in such circumstances received some support in State practice in the years following the adoption of the Charter.[5] The 1999 NATO action in Kosovo has led to renewed debate as to the role of force in the legal framework protecting human rights.[6] Sometimes humanitarian

[2] See I. Brownlie, *International Law and the Use of Force by States* (Clarendon Press, Oxford, 1963), pp. 231–47 (for a discussion of the situations in which States regarded themselves as at liberty to resort to force during the pre-Charter era).

[3] See e.g. Brownlie, *Use of Force by States*, pp. 275–7; and O. Schachter, *International Law in Theory and Practice* (Martinus Nijhoff, Dordrecht, 1991), pp. 150–2; and see the further discussion in note 33 and the accompanying text below. See also C. Gray, *International Law and the Use of Force* (Oxford University Press, Oxford, 2000), pp. 111–15 (observing the tension between the actual practice of States of using preventative force and their reluctance to justify it on such a ground).

[4] See e.g. A. Cassese, *International Law* (Oxford University Press, Oxford, 2001), pp. 305–24 (for a discussion of the State practice in this area).

[5] See F. Tesón, *Humanitarian Intervention: An Inquiry into Law and Morality* (2nd edn, Transnational, Irvington-on-Hudson, NY, 1996); and S. D. Murphy, *Humanitarian Intervention: The United Nations in an Evolving World Order* (University of Pennsylvania Press, Philadelphia, 1996).

[6] See generally S. Chesterman, *Just War or Just Peace? Humanitarian Intervention and International Law* (Oxford University Press, Oxford, 2001); and Gray, *Use of Force*, pp. 26–42. For a consideration of the doctrine prior to the events in Kosovo, see Tesón, *Humanitarian Intervention*.

intervention is treated as synonymous with the right to protect nationals abroad, an aspect of self-defence asserted by States from time to time but not receiving widespread support.[7] The more traditional view of humanitarian intervention is that it is an independent doctrine unrelated to self-defence that allows States to intervene forcefully in situations of gross human rights violations. In addition to unilateral humanitarian intervention by States, support for the practice of intervening on humanitarian grounds experienced resurgence in the 1990s under the auspices of the Security Council.[8]

Irrespective of the theoretical basis legitimating the use of force, necessity and proportionality are regarded as being essential components thereof, although their articulation and application will vary depending on the context.[9] Indeed, this is the one common theme that runs throughout all arguments legitimating the resort to force in international relations. Moreover, proportionality in particular has assumed a pivotal role in delimiting the legitimate use of force in the context of State-sponsored terrorism and the relationship between self-defence and reprisals in such circumstances.[10] With the adoption of the United Nations Charter, the resort to reprisals involving the use of force became illegal.[11] However, the distinction between reprisals and

[7] See M. Akehurst, 'The Use of Force to Protect Nationals Abroad' (1977) 5 *International Relations* 3.

[8] This development is considered in Chapter 6 below. For a discussion of so-called collective humanitarian intervention, see e.g. P. Alston, 'The Security Council and Human Rights: Lessons to Be Learned from the Iraq–Kuwait Crisis and Its Aftermath' (1992) 13 *AYIL* 107; and F. Tesón, 'Collective Humanitarian Intervention' (1996) 17 *Michigan JIL* 323.

[9] See e.g. the statement of the representative of Israel to the Security Council in the debates over the 1976 military operation undertaken by that State to rescue its nationals in Uganda, UN Doc. S/PV 1939, 9 July 1976, pp. 51–3.

[10] States also regard such actions as legitimate only if peaceful means have failed to achieve the required result. See the discussion in note 73 and the accompanying text below.

[11] This is the view of most commentators: see e.g. Brownlie, *Use of Force by States*, p. 223, and the references discussed at p. 281; but see D. Bowett, 'Reprisals Involving Recourse to Armed Force' (1972) 66 *AJIL* 1. Reprisals involving non-forceful acts remain legitimate and are more commonly known nowadays as countermeasures to distinguish them from the pre-Charter system of reprisals that encompassed forceful actions. Necessity and proportionality are requirements of legitimate countermeasures and their operation has been considered at some length by the International Law Commission in its work on State responsibility. See e.g. Report of the International Law Commission on the Work of Its 52nd Session, 1 May–9 June and 10 July–18 August 2000, GAOR, 55th Sess. Supp. No. 10 (A/55/10), paras. 306–10 (in relation to proportionality) and paras. 298–305 (in relation to necessity).

self-defence under the Charter has proved difficult to maintain, and a wide discrepancy exists between the theory and the actual practice of States in their response to State-sponsored terrorism. Proportionality has featured in the debates over the distinction between reprisals and self-defence. The Security Council from time to time in its consideration of counter-insurgent activities has used the test of proportionality to distinguish between forceful actions that qualify as self-defence and those that constitute illegal reprisals. This practice has not assisted in maintaining the distinction between what are two separate questions, namely, the legal basis of the response on the one hand and its proportionality on the other.

Despite the inconsistency in the practice of States in relation to the situations in which they claim the right to use force, the prevailing view of the Charter system is that, with the possible exception of forceful intervention on humanitarian grounds, a response to an armed attack is the only situation that warrants the unilateral use of force by States. The discussion in this chapter consequently is primarily focused on the operation of necessity and proportionality in the situations in which there is consensus that the resort to force is legitimate under the Charter. However, the part played by these two doctrines in the context of preventative self-defence and the relationship between self-defence, reprisals and State-sponsored terrorism warrants a careful appraisal in light of its significance in the practice of States, and is included in the analysis that follows.

The resort to unilateral force under the United Nations Charter

The scope of self-defence under the UN Charter: Article 51

The United Nations Charter adopted by States in 1945 represents the culmination of the attempts last century to limit the situations in which States can legitimately resort to force to resolve their disputes. Articles 2(4) and 51 of the Charter are the foundation of modern *ius ad bellum*. Article 2(4) requires that '[a]ll Members shall refrain in their international relations from the threat or use of force against the territorial integrity or political independence of any state, or in any other manner inconsistent with the Purposes of the United Nations'.[12] Article 51

[12] For a history of the drafting of the United Nations Charter, including Art. 2(4), see L. Goodrich, E. Hambro and A. Simons, *The Charter of the United Nations: Commentary and Documents* (3rd edn, Columbia University Press, New York, 1969).

retains the inherent right of States to use force in individual or collective self-defence in response to an armed attack. Under the Charter scheme, therefore, in the case of unilateral State action, the proportionality equation involves an assessment of the forceful actions against the legitimate goals of the use of force, namely, self-defence. Self-defence, however, has no fixed meaning. Its scope has differed from time to time. What does it consist of under the Charter? Accepting that it is only an armed attack that gives rise to the right to use force, what constitutes such an event and where does preventative action against a threat of such an event fit within this scheme?

There are wide differences of opinion as to the ambit of Article 51.[13] In Brownlie's view, all the controversial aspects of the Charter regime on the use of force, with one exception (that of humanitarian intervention), centre around the concept of self-defence.[14] During the 1990s, attempts to broaden the scope of Article 51 largely gave way to debates as to the collective powers of States acting under the auspices of the Security Council. The international response to the 11 September 2001 terrorist attacks against the United States, however, has brought the scope of Article 51 once again to the forefront of discussions.[15]

Self-defence against an armed attack

There is nothing in the *travaux préparatoires* of the Charter to indicate the meaning to be ascribed to the phrase 'armed attack'. It may have been regarded as self-evident.[16] It is accepted that what is primarily contemplated is an attack by one State against another of some gravity and

[13] There is a vast literature on this topic. See e.g. Brownlie, *Use of Force by States*, pp. 351–8; D. Bowett, *Self-Defence in International Law* (Manchester University Press, Manchester, 1958), pp. 182–99; and Gray, *Use of Force*. For an indication of the differing views amongst North American commentators, see L. Henkin *et al.*, *Right* v. *Might: International Law and the Use of Force* (Council on Foreign Affairs, New York, 1989).

[14] I. Brownlie, 'The United Nations Charter and the Use of Force, 1945–1958' in A. Cassese (ed.), *The Current Legal Regulation of the Use of Force* (Martinus Nijhoff, Dordrecht, 1986), p. 497.

[15] See e.g. S. Murphy (ed.), 'Contemporary Practice of the United States Relating to International Law' (2002) 96 *AJIL* 237 (detailing the events surrounding the 11 September events and the legal position taken in relation thereto by States). See also M. Glennon, 'The Fog of Law: Self-Defence, Inherence, and the Incoherence in Article 51 of the United Nations Charter' (2002) 25 *Harvard Journal of Law and Public Policy* 539; M. Byers, 'Terrorism, the Use of Force and International Law after September 11' (2002) 51 *ICLQ* 401.

[16] See Brownlie, *Use of Force by States*, p. 278.

magnitude.[17] The most obvious examples of such actions are the large-scale invasion of or bombardment of one State by the traditional armed forces of another. However, this somewhat narrow meaning excludes activities that many States regard as warranting an armed response. Particular problems have been caused in this context by the phenomenon of sporadic border incursions by irregular armed bands and the practice of States of providing support for the forceful activities of insurgent groups. States generally analyse these activities in the framework of Article 51 of the Charter and attempt either to expand the meaning of armed attack to include such activities,[18] or to argue that Article 51 does not exclude the right of self-defence in all circumstances other than that of an armed attack.[19]

The International Court of Justice in the *Nicaragua Case* considered the meaning of the phrase 'armed attack' and its relationship to the cross-border activities of irregular forces.[20] The assessment of the law by the Court was limited to the situation where an armed attack had already occurred. The issue of the lawfulness of a response to the imminent threat of armed attack was not addressed. Despite considerable evidence to the contrary, the Court expressed the view that there was general agreement as to what acts amount to an armed attack. No definition, however, was provided as to what constitutes this accord. The Court confined itself to the finding that the term encompasses not only action across borders by regular armed forces but the description contained in Article 3(g) of the 1975 General Assembly Definition of Aggression:[21] 'the sending by or on behalf of a State of armed bands, groups, irregulars or mercenaries, which carry out acts of armed force against another State of such gravity as to amount to [*inter alia*, an actual armed attack conducted by regular forces] or its substantial involvement therein'.[22]

[17] See generally Y. Dinstein, *War, Aggression and Self-Defence* (2nd edn, Grotius, Cambridge, 1994), pp. 187–202.

[18] See e.g. J. Stone, *Legal Controls of International Conflict* (Maitland, Sydney, 1954), p. 244; and Letter from the Permanent UN Representative of the United States to the President of the UN Security Council, 7 October 2001, UN Doc. S/2001/946; and see S. Murphy, 'Terrorism and the Concept of "Armed Attack" in Article 51 of the UN Charter' (2002) 43 *Harvard ILJ* 41 at 45–51.

[19] See Bowett, 'Reprisals Involving Recourse to Armed Force', pp. 17–23.

[20] *Case Concerning Military and Paramilitary Activities in and against Nicaragua* (*Nicaragua* v. *United States*), Merits, ICJ Reports 1986, 14 (hereafter *Nicaragua Case*); and see the dissenting view on proportionality of Judge Schwebel, *ibid.*, pp. 367–9.

[21] UN GA Res. 3314 (XXIX) 1974.

[22] *Nicaragua Case*, note 20 above, p. 103.

A prohibited armed attack could, thus, be constituted by an operation that 'because of its scale and effects, would have been classified as an armed attack rather than as a mere frontier incident had it been carried out by regular armed forces'.[23] This definition envisages a certain level of violence before the right to self-defence comes into play, whether in relation to attacks by paramilitary or regular forces. State practice is not consistent on this point, and commentators differ, with some regarding any armed action as amounting to an armed attack.[24] On the issue of military assistance to rebels by the provision of weapons or logistical or other support, the Court considered this to be outside the concept of armed attack.[25]

In relation to the activities of irregular forces, it is not only whether these activities amount to an armed attack within the meaning of Article 51 that has been the subject of intense debate but also the degree of State involvement necessary to establish responsibility and give rise to the right of self-defence. The Court in the *Nicaragua Case* was clear that liability for the actions of irregulars that reached a certain degree of violence would involve State responsibility if it could be established that these forces were sent by or on behalf of the State or were under the effective control of that State.[26] The Court was silent on the issue of State responsibility in situations of lesser involvement where the State, for example, acquiesces in or is unable to control such activities on its territory.

There are numerous illustrations of States relying on the right of self-defence to justify their forceful actions against other States on the basis of the latter's responsibility for the activities of non-State actors.[27] The

[23] *Ibid.*

[24] See C. Greenwood, 'Command and the Laws of Armed Conflict' (1993) 4 *The Occasional* 1 at 4–5 (for a discussion of the meaning of armed attack under Art. 51 of the UN Charter); and cf. B. Simma (ed.), *The Charter of the United Nations: A Commentary* (Oxford University Press, Oxford, 1994), p. 669. The response of the United States to the events of 11 September 2001 has provided another layer of complexity in the search for the ambit of the phrase 'armed attack' in terms of the level of violence necessary before an armed attack occurs. See Murphy, 'Terrorism and the Concept of "Armed Attack" in Article 51 of the UN Charter'.

[25] *Nicaragua Case*, note 20 above, p. 103.

[26] See Art. 8 of the Draft Articles on the Responsibility of States for Internationally Wrongful Acts, Report of the International Law Commission, 53rd Session, 23 April–1 June and 2 July–10 August 2001, GAOR, 56th Sess. Supp. No. 10 (A/56/10) (confirming that a State is responsible for the activities of those under its control).

[27] See the comprehensive discussion of the relevant State practice in Gray, *Use of Force*, pp. 99–105.

11 September 2001 terrorist attacks on targets in the United States has generated considerable State practice in this area of State responsibility. The passive harbouring of members of the Al-Qaeda network by the Taliban regime in Afghanistan was treated as sufficient to justify a military operation against that State of unprecedented magnitude that led to the deposing of the government.[28] Although commentators have expressed disquiet, the reaction of the international community to these events was generally positive, which provides evidence of a shift that appears likely to continue in the governing legal principles in relation to State-sponsored terrorist activities.[29]

Apart from the examples discussed above, what other situations are contemplated by the phrase 'armed attack'? As Simma observes, Article 3 of the Definition of Aggression provides some guidance as to its meaning.[30] The *travaux préparatoires* of the Definition indicate that the terms 'aggression' and 'armed attack' were not regarded as synonymous by the negotiating States. Nor was it intended that the Definition of Aggression, either directly or by analogy, provide an interpretation of armed attack for the purposes of Article 51. Nevertheless, several of the specific cases of the use of armed force listed in Article 3 as amounting to aggression within the meaning of the Definition may, in the right circumstances, amount to an armed attack.[31] It is also uncontroversial that forceful action involving, for example, the forces of a State on the high seas can constitute an armed attack within the meaning of Article 51. Attacks on non-military targets situated outside the territory of the State are not generally regarded as coming within the definition.[32]

[28] See Letter from the Permanent UN Representative of the United States to the President of the UN Security Council, 7 October 2001, UN Doc. S/2001/946 ('the attacks on 11 September and the ongoing threat to the United States posed by the Al-Qaeda organization have been made possible by the decision of the Taliban regime to allow parts of Afghanistan that it controls to be used by this organization as a base of operation'). For the details of the actions against Afghanistan, see Murphy, 'Contemporary Practice'.

[29] See F. Mégret, '"War"? Legal Semantics and the Move to Violence' (2002) 13 *EJIL* 361 at 383–4 (arguing that State responsibility does not arise for the mere tolerance of the presence of terrorists on a State's territory); and see also A. Cassese, 'Terrorism is Also Disrupting Some Crucial Legal Categories of International Law' (2002) 12 *EJIL* 993.

[30] See Simma, *The Charter of the United Nations*, p. 669.

[31] See *ibid.*, p. 670.

[32] See Simma, *The Charter of the United Nations*, pp. 670–1. See also the *United States Diplomatic and Consular Staff in Tehran (Hostages Case)*, Provisional Measures, ICJ Reports 1979, 7, where the International Court of Justice referred to the takeover of the US embassy as an armed attack.

Anticipatory self-defence

One of the most controversial questions in relation to self-defence is the extent to which a State can take preventative action in individual or collective self-defence. Although the International Court of Justice left this issue open in the *Nicaragua Case*, the text of Article 51 seems to rule out this interpretation.[33] A textual approach, however, to interpreting the terms of the Charter, particularly those dealing with the use of force, has not found universal favour.[34] Article 51, moreover, refers to the inherent right of self-defence, and anticipatory self-defence was a customary right prior to the Charter.[35]

Undoubtedly, the right of self-defence relied on by States to justify their forceful actions frequently has a preventative element. This right, however, is most commonly asserted in the face of a prior attack or series of armed attacks. States have generally preferred if possible to rely overtly on self-defence in response to an armed attack in such circumstances, rather than on any right to use pre-emptive force.[36] This practice of States is often referred to as the 'culmination of events' theory of self-defence. That is, a series of terrorist acts or armed incursions should be viewed as a whole, and action taken to prevent future attacks in the series is legitimate self-defence.

In the context of the long-standing Arab-Israeli conflict, Israel has relied on this argument on numerous occasions over the years, and the bombing of Libya in 1986 by the United States was justified on this ground.[37] A similar scenario was presented by the response of the United States to the 11 September 2001 terrorist attacks. Although expressing its

[33] The majority of commentators, moreover, support this view. See Brownlie, *Use of Force by States*, pp. 257–61. But cf. Bowett, *Self-Defence in International Law*, pp. 187–93; and see also *Oppenheim's International Law*, vol. I, *Peace, Introduction and Part I* (ed. by R. Jennings and A. Watts, 9th edn, Longman, Harlow, 1992), p. 421, note 18 (for a collection of the relevant authorities).

[34] See in particular Myres S. McDougal and Florentino P. Feliciano, *Law and Minimum World Public Order: The Legal Regulation of International Coercion* (Yale University Press, New Haven, 1961), pp. 232–8 (querying the very concept of textual interpretation in the context of the United Nations Charter).

[35] See Brownlie, *Use of Force by States*, p. 257; and C. H. M. Waldock, 'The Regulation of the Use of Force by Individual States in International Law' (1952-II) 81 *Recueil des Cours* 455 at 497–9.

[36] See Gray, *Use of Force*, p. 111; and see *Oppenheim's International Law*, vol. I, *Peace* (ed. by R. Jennings and A. Watts), pp. 421–2.

[37] See *ibid.*, pp. 423–4 (detailing incidents involving attacks by Israel on Palestine Liberation Organization bases in Arab States that were justified on this basis); and see C. Greenwood, 'International Law and the United States Air Operation Against Libya' (1987) 89 *WVLR* 933.

reliance on the inherent right of individual and collective self-defence in response to an armed attack, the United States administration, after referring to the 'ongoing threat to the United States and its nationals posed by the Al-Qaeda organization', announced its intention to use force to 'prevent and deter further attacks on the United States'.[38]

The 2002 National Security Strategy of the United States, however, explicitly claims that international law recognises the right to use pre-emptive force against an 'imminent threat' although accepting that such a right is often conditioned, for example, by 'a visible mobilization of armies, navies and air forces preparing to attack'.[39] The Strategy, moreover, urges that the concept of 'imminent threat' be adapted to the reality of the threat posed not only by terrorists but also by so-called 'rogue States', the latter characterisation being based on the desire to develop or acquire weapons of mass destruction.[40] The identification of States with such aspirations as posing a threat warranting pre-emptive force is a considerable expansion of the existing boundaries of international law.

The difficulty of drawing a distinction between self-defence, anticipatory self-defence and forceful reprisals is readily apparent in many of the situations that have confronted States since the adoption of the Charter. Moreover, there are obvious difficulties posed by a literal application of the requirements of Article 51 in these days of sophisticated weapons with enormous destructive capabilities.[41] Nevertheless, to date, the fiction is generally maintained in practice that a right of anticipatory self-defence is not available to States.

Humanitarian intervention

The so-called right of humanitarian intervention, although strongly advocated by some commentators, was not one that received a great deal of support in State practice until the NATO action in Kosovo in 1999. The new, albeit fragile, harmony on the Security Council following the end of the Cold War enabled States acting under the authority

[38] See Letter from the Permanent United Nations Representative of the United States of America to the President of the United Nations Security Council, 7 October 2001, UN Doc. S/2001/946.

[39] National Security Strategy of the United States of America, 17 September 2002, available at www.whitehouse.gov/nsc/print/nssall.html.

[40] *Ibid.*, Part V.

[41] See Gray, *Use of Force*, p. 96, note 41 (for a discussion of when an armed attack arises in the case of certain weapons); and D. P. O'Connell, *The Influence of Law on Sea Power* (Manchester University Press, Manchester, 1975), pp. 70–84 (discussing the difficulties of applying the constraints of Art. 51 of the Charter in the context of naval weaponry).

of the Security Council to undertake forceful actions on humanitarian grounds.[42] Such Security Council authorisation, however, was not forthcoming in response to the widespread human rights atrocities perpetrated against the Kosovars by Serbian forces in 1999.[43] Despite this lack of explicit authorisation, NATO forces conducted a campaign of high-altitude aerial bombardment in an attempt to halt these criminal activities.[44] Although many commentators had serious misgivings as to the legality of this action, the attitude of States generally was positive.[45] It remains to be seen to what extent this is a precedent for further action of a similar kind.[46]

Having considered the ambit of the legitimate unilateral resort to force by States under the United Nations Charter, the discussion now turns to consider the content of necessity and proportionality as part of that regime.

The content of necessity in self-defence under the United Nations Charter[47]

Self-defence against an armed attack

The formulation of necessity in the 1837 *Caroline Incident* is accepted as encapsulating the requirement of the right of self-defence under the

[42] For a discussion of the legal basis for such actions, see e.g. C. Chinkin, 'Kosovo: A "Good" or "Bad" War?' (1999) 93 *AJIL* 84; J. Charney, 'Anticipatory Humanitarian Intervention in Kosovo' (1999) 93 *AJIL* 834; A. Cassese, '*Ex Iniuria Ius Oritur*: Are We Moving Towards International Legitimation of Forcible Humanitarian Countermeasures in the World Community?' (1999) 10 *EJIL* 23; N. Blokker, 'Is the Authorization Authorized? Powers and Practice of the UN Security Council to Authorize the Use of Force by "Coalitions of the Able and Willing"' (2000) 11 *EJIL* 541.

[43] See Chesterman, *Just War or Just Peace?*, pp. 207–10 (for a full discussion of the role of the Security Council in the events leading up to the NATO strikes against Kosovo); and see generally C. Tomuschat (ed.), *Kosovo and the International Community: A Legal Assessment* (Kluwer Law International, The Hague, 2002).

[44] NATO's stated aims were to stop all military action, violence and repression against the Kosovars; the withdrawal from Kosovo of the military, police and paramilitary; the stationing in Kosovo of an international military presence; the unconditional and safe return of all refugees and displaced persons; and a political settlement for Kosovo. See the statement by the Secretary-General of NATO, Lord Robertson of Port Ellen, 'Kosovo One Year On: Achievement and Challenge', available at www.nato.int/kosovo/repo2000/report-en.pdf.

[45] See Chesterman, *Just War or Just Peace?*, pp. 210–15 (for a discussion of the views of commentators and the response of States to the NATO action).

[46] *Ibid.*, pp. 215–17 (outlining the concerns of States that the Kosovo action was not to be regarded as setting a precedent for future intervention).

[47] See generally B. Cheng, *General Principles of Law as Applied by International Courts and Tribunals* (Stevens and Sons, London, 1953), pp. 94–6.

United Nations Charter: '[n]ecessity of self-defence, instant, overwhelming, leaving no choice of means, and no moment of deliberation'.[48] Necessity is consistently referred to (almost as an incantation) but rarely, if ever, analysed in relation to the Charter scheme on self-defence.[49] The formulation of the requirement of necessity in the *Caroline Incident* must be viewed against the background of the then unsettled situations in which States were regarded as having the right to use force. At that time, there was considerable uncertainty as to the extent of the right of self-preservation and the doctrines of necessity and necessity of defence. The requirement that a forceful action be necessary could be viewed as performing the function of controlling to some extent the wide range of situations in which States could arguably resort to force. Consequently, necessity was a limiting factor at a time when there were no other limits, and took the place of restraints on the resort to force. Nowadays, the situations in which States may resort to force are already limited, and this factor should be borne in mind in determining the requirements of necessity under the Charter system. The other distinctive feature of the *Caroline Incident* was that the action taken by the British was preventative in nature.[50] This factor may also have affected the content of the formulation so as to make it less relevant where self-defence is limited to a response to an armed attack that has already occurred.

The *Caroline* requirement of 'overwhelming', according to Schwarzenberger, limits self-defence under the Charter to situations where important rights and interests are involved.[51] If one accepts a narrow definition of the circumstances that constitute an armed attack under Article 51 of the Charter, it seems not unreasonable to regard such an event as usually satisfying that description. This may not, however, always be the case, and McDougal and Feliciano argue that a certain level of 'consequentiality' of the values in question is required.[52]

It is arguable that the only aspect of the *Caroline* 'necessity' formulation that needs to be satisfied if an armed attack has occurred within the meaning of Article 51 is that of 'instancy': '[t]hat is, when the act is accomplished, damage suffered, and the danger passed, then the

[48] See the discussion of the *Caroline Incident* in Chapter 2, note 62 and the accompanying text above.

[49] See Brownlie, *Use of Force by States*, p. 429.

[50] See McDougal and Feliciano, *Law and Minimum World Public Order*, p. 231; and E. Jimenez de Aréchaga, 'International Law in the Past Third of a Century' (1978) 159 *Recueil des Cours* 9 at 97.

[51] G. Schwarzenberger, 'The Fundamental Principles of International Law' (1955-I) 87 *Recueil des Cours* 195 at 333.

[52] McDougal and Feliciano, *Law and Minimum World Public Order*, pp. 224–8.

incidents of self-defence cease'.[53] The requirement of immediacy is in fact inherent in the text of Article 51. What is contemplated by the Charter is that States have the right to respond to an armed attack only for the period that it takes for the Security Council to be notified and for the necessary action to be taken to restore international peace and security. With the failure of this scheme, States have been reluctant to accept this 'instancy' or 'immediacy' requirement of self-defence under the Charter, and support has developed for the legitimacy of 'defensive reprisals' and anticipatory self-defence, particularly in the context of sustained insurgent activities.[54] Nevertheless, State practice and the views of commentators confirm the relevance of instancy to a legitimate exercise of self-defence.[55]

However, exactly what the requirement of immediacy consists of under the Charter is by no means clear. A strict view would be that once the armed attack is over the right of self-defence comes to an end and States must then rely on the Security Council for assistance.[56] State practice is generally not consistent with this narrow view of immediacy, and States are traditionally allowed a leeway of time in which to initiate their defensive action.[57] During this period, however, it appears that it is anticipated that States will attempt to resolve the dispute by peaceful means.[58] Moreover, the longer the period between the armed attack and

[53] *The Ralph*, 1904 US Court of Claims, 204 at 207, cited in Cheng, *General Principles of Law*, p. 94. See also Schachter, *Theory and Practice*, p. 153 (considering the argument by Argentina to use force to recover the Falkland Islands).

[54] See e.g. Dinstein, *War, Aggression and Self-Defence*, pp. 215–26; and McDougal and Feliciano, *Law and Minimum World Public Order*, pp. 231–40.

[55] For Schachter, the resort to peaceful methods of settling a dispute becomes relevant when a significant period of time has elapsed since the armed attack: O. Schachter, 'The Lawful Resort to Unilateral Use of Force' (1985) 10 *Yale JIL* 291 at 292.

[56] See e.g. Cassese, 'Terrorism is Also Disrupting Some Crucial Legal Categories of International Law', pp. 995 and 997–8 (arguing this view of the requirement of immediacy in the context of the 11 September 2001 terrorist attacks on the US, but cf. the actual practice of States in that context).

[57] The 1982 Falkland Islands conflict is an illustration of State practice in this area. See Schachter, *Theory and Practice*, p. 153 (considering the argument by Argentina to use force to recover the Falkland Islands). See also Murphy, 'Contemporary Practice' (discussing the response of the US and its allies to the 11 September 2001 terrorist attacks on the US).

[58] Whether or not this is a legal obligation is not entirely clear. For example, the UK did not regard itself as under any legal obligation to search for a peaceful settlement of the 1982 Falkland Islands dispute in the face of the occurrence of an armed attack. See British Government Document, 'Falkland Islands: Negotiations for a Peaceful Settlement' (HMSO, London, 21 May 1982), para. 3.

the response, the more pressure there will be on the State concerned to resolve the matter by peaceful means.[59]

The 1982 conflict between Argentina and the United Kingdom over the Falkland Islands illustrates this phenomenon. It was relatively uncontroversial that in the circumstances of that conflict the United Kingdom retained the right to self-defence for some time after the initial attack and the ensuing occupation of the targeted territory.[60] However, international support for the British position waned thereafter, particularly when a large-scale conflict ensued.[61]

The 1990–1 Persian Gulf conflict was another situation of an armed attack resulting in the ongoing forceful occupation of a State. The issue of immediacy in that conflict in relation to the action of the coalition allies is complicated by the uncertainty as to its legal basis – collective self-defence or Security Council authorised action.[62] Nevertheless, the practice of States in that conflict is consistent with the view that, when an initial armed attack is over, alternative means of settling the dispute must be considered before forceful action is taken to liberate the occupied territory.

The relevance of the temporal or immediacy aspect of necessity is also confirmed in the judgment of the International Court of Justice in the *Nicaragua Case*.[63] That case, moreover, provides a practical illustration of the application of the Charter regime of self-defence. The Court was considering the plea of collective self-defence by the United States in

[59] See *Oppenheim's International Law*, vol. I, *Peace* (ed. by R. Jennings and A. Watts), p. 418, note 5; and Schachter, *Theory and Practice*, p. 153.

[60] The British Cabinet met on the same day as the attack by Argentina against the Islands and agreed to send a task force to the area. See *Falkland Islands Review: Report of a Committee of Privy Councillors* (Cmnd 8787, HMSO, London, 1983), p. 72. The matter was reported to the Security Council, which passed SC Res. 502 on 3 April 1982 (calling on Argentina to withdraw from the Islands).

[61] See I. Claude Jr, 'UN Efforts at Settlement of the Falkland Islands Crisis' in Alberto R. Coll and Anthony C. Arend (eds.), *The Falklands War: Lessons for Strategy, Diplomacy, and International Law* (Allen & Unwin, Boston, MA, 1985), p. 118 at pp. 129–30. For a discussion of the various diplomatic efforts that were made to settle the dispute, see D. Kinney, 'Anglo-Argentine Diplomacy and the Falkland Crisis' in Coll and Arend (eds.), *The Falklands War: Lessons for Strategy, Diplomacy, and International Law*, p. 81 at p. 87; D. C. Gompert, 'American Diplomacy and the Haig Mission: An Insider's Perspective' in Coll and Arend (eds.), *The Falklands War: Lessons for Strategy, Diplomacy, and International Law*, p. 106.

[62] For a discussion of the legal basis of the resort to force by the coalition allies in the 1990–1 Persian Gulf conflict, see C. Greenwood, 'New World Order or Old? The Invasion of Kuwait and the Rule of Law' (1992) 55 *MLR* 153.

[63] *Nicaragua Case*, note 20 above.

response to an alleged armed attack by Nicaragua against El Salvador. The armed attack, it was argued, consisted of the provision of aid by Nicaragua to insurgents in El Salvador. In the view of the Court, the first issue to be resolved where there is reliance by a State on the right of self-defence, or, as they put it, the condition *sine qua non*,[64] is whether an armed attack has occurred.[65] The criteria of necessity and proportionality then become relevant. The Court concluded that no armed attack had occurred.[66] Not even strict compliance by the United States with the elements of necessity and proportionality in their actions could overcome this unlawfulness.[67] Moreover, any failure to meet these conditions would result in additional breaches of the law, an eventuality that the Court found in fact had occurred.

In relation to necessity, it was the lapse of time between the events on which the necessity was based and the change in circumstances that the Court regarded as inconsistent with a plea of necessity. On the question of necessity, the Court observed that the United States measures taken in December 1981:

> cannot be said to correspond to a 'necessity' justifying the United States action against Nicaragua on the basis of assistance given by Nicaragua to the armed opposition in El Salvador. First, these measures were only taken, and began to produce their effects, several months after the major offensive of the armed opposition against the Government of El Salvador had been completely repulsed . . . and the actions of the opposition considerably reduced in consequence. Thus it was possible to eliminate the main danger to the Salvadorian government without the United States embarking on activities in and against Nicaragua. Accordingly, it cannot be held that these activities were undertaken in the light of necessity.[68]

State practice, therefore, supports the need for a temporal link between an armed attack and a defensive response. The *Caroline* formulation of legitimate self-defence, however, also stipulates that the attacked State has 'no choice of means' available other than force to defend itself. Is this a component of the Charter regime? Jennings and Watts regard action involving armed force, including the invasion of another State's territory, as legitimate by way of self-defence only if there is no practicable alternative to such an action, such as appeal to the authorities or an international organisation.[69] In many cases, the occurrence of an

[64] *Ibid.*, p. 122. [65] *Ibid.*, p. 119. [66] *Ibid.*, p. 119. [67] *Ibid.*, p. 122.
[68] *Ibid.* Cf. Dissenting Opinion of Judge Schwebel, pp. 362–7.
[69] See *Oppenheim's International Law*, vol. I, *Peace* (ed. by R. Jennings and A. Watts), p. 422.

armed attack will meet this broader test of necessity, such as where a State subjected to an ongoing armed attack can demonstrate that there is no reasonable prospect of the efficacy of peaceful measures of settlement. This was the situation initially experienced by Kuwait in the 1990–91 Persian Gulf conflict. This, however, may not always be the case and States may need to consider whether an armed response is indeed the only alternative to repulsing the attack. As Ago, the then Special Rapporteur on State Responsibility, observes:

> [t]he reason for stressing that action taken in self-defence must be necessary is that the State attacked . . . must not, in the particular circumstances, have had any means of halting the attack other than recourse to armed force. In other words, had it been able to achieve the same result by measures not involving the use of armed force, it would have no justification for adopting conduct which contravened the general prohibition against the use of force.[70]

Other commentators take a slightly different approach, regarding self-defence as nullified if a State that is the victim of an ongoing armed invasion must seek peaceful means of resolving the dispute first. Schachter, for example, is of the view that a State subjected to an armed attack is 'under a necessity of armed defence irrespective of probabilities as to the effectiveness of peaceful settlement'.[71]

To summarise, it appears that State practice is generally consistent with the desirability of pursuing peaceful means of resolving a dispute once an armed attack is over. There is reluctance, however, to accept that the continued existence of the right to self-defence is dependent as a matter of law on so doing.

Anticipatory self-defence

The *Caroline* formulation of necessity itself articulated in the context of pre-emptive action, has particular significance when considering the legitimacy of anticipatory self-defence under the Charter regime. Whatever the differences as to the continued existence of this right, there is consensus amongst commentators that forceful action by a State in response to an imminent threat cannot be justified if there were any practicable alternatives to removing the threat.[72] Indeed, it appears that

[70] Addendum to the Eighth Report on State Responsibility, by Mr Roberto Ago, Agenda Item 2, A/CN.4/Ser.A/1980/Add.1 (Part 1), A/CN.4/318/Add.5–7 (1980) II (1) *YBILC* 69.

[71] Schachter, *Theory and Practice*, p. 152.

[72] See *Oppenheim's International Law*, vol. I, *Peace* (ed. by R. Jennings and A. Watts), pp. 421–2. See also M. Reisman, 'Assessing Claims to Revise the Laws of War' (2003) 97 *AJIL* 82 at 87.

the need to establish that a forceful response is necessary is more onerous in the case of preventative action than in the case of a response to an armed attack. Not only would the futility of peaceful means to remove the threat need to be demonstrated but also that the threat is real.[73] One instance where there is general accord that a forceful action will be legitimate is where there is overwhelming evidence of the intention 'to launch a devastating attack almost immediately'.[74]

An illustration of this broad operation of necessity is provided by the reaction of States to Israel's 1981 pre-emptive strike against the Iraqi nuclear reactor at Osirac.[75] Among the grounds of objections by States to this action were those based on necessity, namely, that not only had there been a failure to exhaust peaceful means of avoiding the threat but that the threat had not been established. The critical role of necessity in the context of preventative action is also apparent from the reaction of States such as France and Russia to the declared intention of the United States in 2002–3 to use force against Iraq in light of its perceived intransigence over the issue of weapons of mass destruction.[76] Part of the concern evident in certain sections of the international community over such a course of action was based on the fact that the threat had not been sufficiently well established and that, even assuming such a threat, all peaceful means of removing it had not been exhausted.[77] Finally, necessity has also found its place in the context of reactions to State-sponsored terrorism.[78]

[73] See e.g. *Oppenheim's International Law*, vol. I, *Peace* (ed. by R. Jennings and A. Watts), pp. 421–2 (stressing that the requirements of necessity (and proportionality) are of even more significance in cases of preventative action).

[74] See Brownlie, *Use of Force by States*, p. 259; and see further *ibid*., pp. 367–8. See also National Security Strategy of the United States of America, note 39 above.

[75] For a description of this incident, see A. D'Amato, 'Israel's Air Strike upon the Iraqi Nuclear Reactor' (1983) 77 *AJIL* 584.

[76] The legal basis of such an action is by no means clear. States such as the US and the UK were of the view that such a forceful response was warranted by the terms of the cease-fire resolution that ended the 1990–1 Persian Gulf conflict. See SC Res. 687, 3 April 1991. There is, however, no consensus on this point.

[77] See e.g. SC Res. 1441, 8 November 2002 (allowing Iraq a 'final opportunity to comply' with its obligations under previous SC resolutions); and 'Iraq: Blix Says US, UK Should Provide More Information to Back Claims', UNWIRE, 20 December 2002, available at www.unwire.org; and see S. D. Murphy (ed.), 'Contemporary Practice of the United States Relating to International Law' (2003) 97 *AJIL* 419.

[78] See the deference to necessity in the US response to the events of 11 September 2001 (although characterised as an exercise of self-defence against an armed attack and not as pre-emptive in nature). See Letter from the Permanent UN Representative of the

In summary, therefore, under existing international law, States can legitimately use force in response to an armed attack if the requirements of immediacy and necessity, in the sense that there are no alternative means available to repel the attack, are satisfied. The continuing validity of the forceful response now depends on its proportionality to the legitimate aims of self-defence. This is not to suggest, however, that necessity becomes entirely redundant during any ensuing hostilities. On the contrary, States regard themselves as under a continuing obligation to endeavour to settle their differences by peaceful means. Depending on the circumstances, the failure to acknowledge peaceful overtures could transform a legitimate response in self-defence into an aggressive use of force.

The content of proportionality in self-defence under the United Nations Charter

In such a highly politicised and sensitive area as the resort to and the scale of force, it is to be expected that there would be considerable differences of opinion on how to measure proportionality. A significant factor contributing to the uncertainty surrounding the application of proportionality is that the issue is rarely carefully analysed.[79] Proportionality is consistently referred to as a concept whose application and operation is self-evident. Such an assumption, however, is misplaced. Very different conclusions may be reached as to what is proportionate action depending on how the equation is defined and applied. Moreover, commentators do not always maintain the distinction between proportionality in relation to an armed attack, an anticipated armed attack or a reprisal action. It is possible, however, to extract from State practice and *opinio iuris*, assisted by the jurisprudence of the International Court of Justice and the views of commentators, some guiding principles as to how proportionality functions as an aspect of self-defence.

United States to the President of the UN Security Council, 7 October 2001, UN Doc. S/2001/946; and 'Address to the Nation Announcing Strikes Against Al Qaida Training Camps and Taliban Military Installations', 37 *Weekly Comp Pres Doc* 1432 at 1432 (7 October 2001).

[79] The lack of analysis of proportionality in *ius ad bellum* can be contrasted with the considerable detailed analysis of its requirements in *ius in bello*. See the discussion in Chapters 3 and 4 above.

Self-defence against an armed attack

The aims of self-defence

The first step in applying the proportionality equation is to determine the legitimate aim of self-defence under the Charter. As McDougal and Feliciano observe, 'proportionality in coercion constitutes a requirement that responding coercion be limited in intensity and magnitude to what is reasonably necessary to promptly secure the permissible objectives of self-defence'.[80] Proportionality, moreover, remains relevant throughout a conflict. A State cannot assess proportionality at the time of making the decision as to the appropriate response to an armed attack and then dispense with it.[81] The majority of decisions required to ensure the proportionality of a forceful response will be taken at the planning stage and at a senior level of command. Nevertheless, any ensuing forceful action will need to be monitored continuously to ensure that the strategic objectives and the methods chosen to achieve them remain proportionate to the aim of the response.[82]

In the case of self-defence against an armed attack that has already occurred, it is the repulsing of the attack giving rise to the right that is the criterion against which the response is measured.[83] Repulsion of the attack in this context encompasses not only resistance to an ongoing armed attack but the expulsion of an invader and the restoration of the territorial *status quo ante bellum*.[84] In the former situation, the measurement of proportionality will differ depending upon whether the assessment is made in relation to an isolated armed attack or whether there is an ongoing state of armed conflict. In the latter situation, it

[80] McDougal and Feliciano, *Law and Minimum World Public Order*, p. 242; and see Jimenez de Aréchaga, 'International Law', p. 97.

[81] Cf. the view expressed by some experts in the course of the preparation of the *San Remo Manual on International Law Applicable to Armed Conflicts at Sea* (ed. by L. Doswald-Beck, Cambridge University Press, Cambridge, 1995), pp. 76–7 (arguing that proportionality (and necessity) in *ius ad bellum* cannot affect decisions as to such matters as the selection of means and methods of warfare and targets once a response in self-defence has commenced).

[82] For an explanation of the relationship between proportionality in *ius ad bellum* and IHL, see Chapter 1 above.

[83] In the words of McDougal and Feliciano, *Law and Minimum World Public Order*, pp. 222–4, the legitimate objective of self-defence is the conservation of the defender's values rather than the extension thereof.

[84] R. Higgins, *Problems and Process: International Law and How We Use It* (Oxford University Press, Oxford, 1994), p. 232; and Greenwood, 'New World Order or Old?', p. 164 (arguing that an armed attack continues as long as an invader uses its armed forces to retain control of the targeted State).

is a relatively straightforward task to state the theoretical obligation of the defending force – it is to ensure that only those actions are taken that are proportionate to achieving the expulsion of the invader. However, the practical implementation of the obligation in such a case is far from straightforward. The Falkland Islands and the 1990–1 Persian Gulf conflicts illustrate this point. In both these conflicts, despite the fact that compliance with legal norms was regarded by the defending States and their allies as an integral aspect of the campaigns, questions were raised as to the proportionality of the actions taken to dislodge the invading force.[85]

Ago cautions against any suggestion that self-defence has a punitive character.[86] To regard it as such distorts the proportionality equation. He confirms the need to distinguish between the measurement of proportionality in reprisals and its assessment in the context of self-defence. In his view, because the aim of reprisals is to punish, there should be some equivalence between the response and the offending conduct. With self-defence, '[i]ts lawfulness [the action in self-defence] cannot be measured except by its capacity for achieving the desired result'.[87] Ago's view as to the purpose of reprisals is not one that is universally shared.[88] However, his identification of a distinction between the assessment of proportionality in the law on self-defence on the one hand and reprisals on the other is uncontroversial.

There is support for the view that the legitimate aims of self-defence include the right to restore the security of the State after an armed attack.[89] This issue is not strictly speaking one of proportionality but a question of whether preventative measures are legitimate in self-defence, and is considered in the later discussion.[90]

[85] The doubts about the proportionality of the response in the Falkland Islands conflict related primarily to the effect on neutral shipping of the maritime exclusion zone established by the UK. In the case of the 1990–1 Persian Gulf conflict, concerns were expressed in some quarters as to the extent of destruction of the infrastructure of Iraq and the subsequent impact on the civilian population. See the further discussion in note 160 and the accompanying text below.

[86] Brownlie agrees with this approach: see Brownlie, *Use of Force by States*, p. 368 (distinguishing between acts by way of 'interception and defence on the one hand and retaliation on the other').

[87] See *Addendum to the Eighth Report on State Responsibility*, p. 69.

[88] See the further discussion of the purpose of reprisals in Chapter 2 above.

[89] Such an interpretation of the purpose of self-defence received support from the international response to the 11 September 2001 terrorist attacks.

[90] See note 130 and the accompanying text below.

The International Court of Justice considered the question of proportionality in the *Nicaragua Case*, in the context of collective self-defence. The judgment of the majority on that question is not, however, particularly illuminating on the issue. As the Court found that no armed attack had in fact occurred to justify the forceful response, the issue of proportionality was moot. It will be recalled that in that case the United States had alleged a right of collective self-defence in support of El Salvador, based on the provision of aid by Nicaragua to the armed opposition in that State. The activities of the United States that came under scrutiny were the laying of mines in Nicaraguan ports and some ten attacks involving the use of force on such targets as oil installations.[91] The Court balanced these activities with the wrong provoking them, the aid to Salvadorian guerrillas, and concluded that 'whatever uncertainty may exist as to the exact scale of the aid received by the Salvadorian armed opposition from Nicaragua, it is clear that these latter United States activities in question could not have been proportionate to that aid'.[92] The Court thus confirmed that what is proportionate in self-defence is what is needed to respond to an attack and such reactions to the provision of aid did not meet that requirement.[93] By inference, it was the targets selected, the scale of the attacks and the effect on third States' rights that led to the response failing to meet the requirement of proportionality.

Judge Higgins, in her dissenting opinion in the *Nuclear Weapons* Advisory Opinion, supports the view expressed by Ago and adopted by the Court in the *Nicaragua Case* that the approach is not to focus on the nature of the attack itself and ask what is a proportionate response but rather to determine what is proportionate to achieving the legitimate goal under the Charter, the repulsion of the attack.[94] On such an analysis, if nuclear weapons are not unlawful *per se*, their first use, depending on the circumstances, could be a proportionate response to an attack confined to conventional weapons. This is a point of view shared by several commentators.[95]

[91] See *Nicaragua Case*, note 20 above, pp. 48 and 50–1 (for a full list of the activities that the Court found were established by the evidence and which it took into account in its assessment of proportionality).

[92] *Ibid.*, pp. 122–3.

[93] Cf. the Dissenting Opinion of Judge Schwebel, *Nicaragua Case*, note 20 above, pp. 367–9.

[94] See the Dissenting Opinion of Judge Higgins, *Legality of the Threat or Use of Nuclear Weapons* Advisory Opinion, ICJ Reports 1996, 226 (General Assembly Opinion) (hereafter *Nuclear Weapons* Advisory Opinion), pp. 583–4.

[95] Whether nuclear weapons can be a legitimate response to the use of conventional weapons has been widely debated. See Brownlie, *Use of Force by States*, pp. 262–3;

State practice, as evidenced for example by the Falkland Islands and 1990–1 Persian Gulf conflicts, is generally consistent with the aim of self-defence being the halting or repulsion of the attack. In the former conflict, the British demand was for compliance with Security Council Resolution 501, calling on Argentina to withdraw from the Islands.[96] In the case of the Persian Gulf conflict, the involvement of the Security Council under its Chapter VII powers arguably broadened the legitimate aims of the forceful action.[97] However, the initial Security Council Resolution 660 called upon Iraq to withdraw its forces from Kuwait.[98] Resolution 661 reiterated this demand and at the same time affirmed the inherent right of individual or collective self-defence in response to the armed attack by Iraq against Kuwait.[99] The later forceful response by the coalition allies was to achieve compliance with these resolutions.

The response in self-defence

Despite the seeming general accord as to the aims of self-defence, there are considerable inconsistencies in the relevant practice as to what amounts to action that is proportionate to halting or repulsing the attack. Much of this uncertainty is attributable to the fact that each case depends on the individual circumstances.[100] As O'Connell observes, 'so much resides in the contingencies of a situation'.[101] The 1990–1 Persian Gulf conflict illustrates how complex the assessment of this aspect of the proportionality equation can be. Of considerable importance to the determination of the response in that conflict were the scale and effect of the attack. In this case, the situation was a full-scale armed invasion resulting in the occupation of the victim State. Other significant issues were the likely level of casualties (combatant and civilian) on both

McDougal and Feliciano, *Law and Minimum World Public Order*, p. 244; and M. Singh, 'The Right of Self-Defence in Relation to the Use of Nuclear Weapons' (1956) 5 *Indian Yearbook of International Affairs* 3. The Court in the *Nuclear Weapons* Advisory Opinion appears to answer this query in the affirmative: see note 150 and the accompanying text below.

[96] See SC Res. 502, 3 April 1982, in which the Security Council determined the existence of a breach of the peace, called for an immediate cessation of hostilities, an immediate withdrawal of Argentine forces from the Falkland Islands and for the parties to seek a diplomatic resolution of the dispute.

[97] See the further discussion of the legal basis of the resort to force in this conflict in Chapter 6, note 90, and the accompanying text below.

[98] See SC Res. 660, 2 August 1990. [99] See SC Res. 661, 6 August 1990.

[100] See e.g. McDougal and Feliciano, *Law and Minimum World Public Order*, p. 243 (observing that proportionality in *ius ad bellum* involves a consideration of all aspects of the alleged aggressor's use of force and the victim's response).

[101] See O'Connell, *The Influence of Law on Sea Power*, p. 64.

sides, the potential impact of the forceful action on third States and the military capability of Iraq (which appears to have been somewhat overestimated, although perhaps this is only in hindsight) and its anticipated military response.

The remarks of David Hannay, the United Kingdom representative at the relevant time on the Security Council, illustrate the significance attached to this latter factor in the assessment of what was a proportionate response:[102]

> Some have suggested that military action being taken by the allies is in some way excessive or disproportionate and thus exceeds the 'all necessary means' authorized in resolution 678 (1990) to bring about the liberation of Kuwait. But the nature and scope of the military action is dictated not by some abstract set of criteria but by the military capacity of the aggressor, who has refused all attempts to remove him from Kuwait.[103]

Having described the extent of Iraq's military capability, he continued: '[I]t is that military machine which now has to be removed from Kuwait by force. It is to that aim and in those specific circumstances that the force used must correspond.'[104]

Other relevant factors in the decision-making process as to the appropriate response (although not necessarily of a legal nature) were the volatility of the region, with the attendant need for a quick end to the conflict and the intransigence of the then Head of State, Saddam Hussein, in the face of peaceful efforts to solve the situation. Moreover, the States involved in making the assessment of proportionality in that conflict would have been aware that a lot less in the way of civilian casualties would be tolerated by the international community than would have been the case prior to the Charter. This awareness is confirmed by the many public statements that were issued throughout the conflict in relation to civilians and civilian targets.[105]

A common assumption in discussions of proportionality is that there should be equivalence between the force used and the response in self-defence. However, an assessment of what will achieve the end result of self-defence, 'that of halting and repelling the attack', consists neither merely of a comparison of weapons or the scale of force used nor, as

[102] UN Doc. S/PV.2977, Part II, para. 72, 14 February 1991.

[103] *Ibid.* [104] *Ibid.*

[105] See e.g. *ibid.*: 'The allied forces have been given the strictest instructions to strive to keep such casualties [civilian] to a minimum and to avoid damaging sites of religious or cultural significance.'

Ago puts it, 'the forms, substance and strength of the action itself'.[106] Indeed, the action needed to halt and repulse an attack may well have to assume dimensions that would be disproportionate using such a comparison. 'A limited use of armed force may sometimes be sufficient for the victim State to resist a likewise limited use of armed force by the attacking State, but this is not always certain.'[107] Moreover, when dealing with a series of attacks, the scale of the action taken to repulse such a series of attacks may differ from that which would be appropriate in response to an isolated armed attack. Ago writes: 'If . . . a State suffers a series of successive and different acts of armed attack from another State, the requirement of proportionality will certainly not mean that the victim State is not free to undertake a single armed action on a much larger scale in order to put an end to this escalating succession of attacks.'[108]

In Ago's view, the doubts that have been expressed from time to time as to the applicability of proportionality in self-defence relate to this idea that there should be some equivalence between the strength and scale of the attack and the response.[109] Such an approach would make the principle unacceptable as lacking the necessary flexibility: 'A State which is the victim of an attack cannot really be expected to adopt measures that in no way exceed the limits of what might just suffice to prevent the attack from succeeding and bring it to an end.'[110] The reverse is also the case. It may be that a State can adopt measures that are of less intensity than the attack that provoked them to achieve the aims of self-defence. Everything depends on the individual circumstances. O'Connell, in his study of the operation of proportionality as a requirement of self-defence in naval hostilities, confirms this approach. After observing that the pattern of the forceful use of sea power by Western States is one of graduated escalation, he concludes that consequently proportionality cannot be 'equated in naval thinking with equilibrium of action and reaction'.[111] Nevertheless, he discerns a practice, since the adoption of the Charter, of matching the response with the mode of attack. Thus, for

[106] See *Addendum to the Eighth Report on State Responsibility*, p. 69; and see McDougal and Feliciano, *Law and Minimum World Public Order*, p. 244; and O'Connell, *The Influence of Law on Sea Power*, p. 69.

[107] *Addendum to the Eighth Report on State Responsibility*, p. 69.

[108] See *ibid.*, pp. 69–70.

[109] See also the criticisms of D. Greig, *International Law* (2nd edn, Butterworths, London, 1976), pp. 886–7.

[110] See *Addendum to the Eighth Report on State Responsibility*, p. 69.

[111] See O'Connell, *The Influence of Law on Sea Power*, p. 64.

example, surface force is not generally met by submarine or air attack but by counter-surface force.[112]

Despite the initial contextualised nature of the assessment of proportionality, it is possible to advance beyond generalities and identify loose categories of factors that are relevant to assessing whether responses to an armed attack are proportionate, all of which to varying degrees are reflected in the practice of States. There appears to be general accord that proportionality in *ius ad bellum* requires a consideration of such matters as the geographical and destructive scope of the response, the duration of the response, the selection of means and methods of warfare and targets and the effect on third States.[113]

All these elements obviously overlap to a certain extent. For example, the choice of weapons will in some circumstances be dictated by their potential effect on third States. Similarly, the geographical scope of the response may also require an assessment of its impact not only on the aggressor State but also on third States.

The level of collateral civilian damage is generally not specifically articulated as a factor of relevance to proportionality in *ius ad bellum*. However, underlying such matters as the destructive scope of the response and the choice of weaponry and targets in *ius ad bellum* are considerations of civilian casualties and damage to the infrastructure of the State that supports the civilian population.[114] It appears, however, that to some extent the existence of the IHL rule of proportionality, with its focus on collateral civilian damage, may deflect attention from this factor under *ius ad bellum*.

Factors relevant to assessing the proportionality of the response in self-defence

The geographical and destructive scope of the response

According to Oppenheim, the region of war during the period when war was not outlawed extended to the high seas, 'all such territories

[112] *Ibid.*

[113] O'Connell, in the context of naval warfare, identifies (a) the theatre of operations, (b) the scale of operations and the level of weaponry, and (c) the graduation of force and the scale of response, as relevant to the assessment of proportionality: see D. P. O'Connell, *The International Law of the Sea* (ed. by I. Shearer, Clarendon Press, Oxford, 1984), vol. II, p. 1096. C. Greenwood, 'Self-Defence and the Conduct of International Armed Conflict' in Y. Dinstein (ed.), *International Law at a Time of Perplexity: Essays in Honour of Shabtai Rosenne* (Martinus Nijhoff, Dordrecht, 1989), p. 273 at p. 275, adds the element of the degree of coercion that may be applied against neutrals.

[114] See e.g. Schachter, *Theory and Practice*, p. 154.

as are as yet not occupied by any State . . . and the whole of the territories and territorial waters of the belligerents'.[115] This freedom was considerably diminished upon the adoption of the Charter, limiting forceful actions to self-defence that is both necessary and proportionate. As some writers describe it, armed conflict became limited as opposed to total.

Under the Charter system, it is the accepted view that, generally speaking, proportionality requires that forceful actions in self-defence must be confined to the area of the attack that they are designed to repel.[116] In the context of naval hostilities, the majority of State practice since 1945 is consistent with the proportionality requirement of self-defence as imposing significant geographical limits on hostile actions at sea.[117] Thus, for example, attacks on naval forces of an aggressor State in waters distant from the conflict would generally not be seen as proportionate measures in self-defence. O'Connell, after a survey of State practice since the adoption of the Charter, affirms this limit on hostile actions at sea to territorial waters or waters adjacent to the territories of the belligerents. However, he expresses doubt as to whether this restraint is dictated by legal rather than political considerations. Moreover, the level of compliance therewith depends very much on the geographical location and the political circumstances.[118]

The exception to such geographically limited actions are disputes concerning rights over the high seas itself, such as fishing disputes and those involving the extent of the high seas and national jurisdiction.[119] Moreover, the declaration of exclusion zones in the high seas for self-defensive purposes may be proportionate actions in self-defence.[120]

[115] See *Oppenheim's International Law*, vol. II, *Disputes, War and Neutrality* (ed. by H. Lauterpacht, 7th edn, Longmans, Green and Co. Ltd, London, 1952), pp. 237–8 and see generally *ibid.*, pp. 236–47. Oppenheim distinguishes between the region of war, namely, 'that part of the surface of the earth in which belligerents may pursue and execute hostilities against each other', and the theatre of operations where hostilities are actually taking place.

[116] See O'Connell, *The Influence of Law on Sea Power*, p. 65 (citing the localised reaction of the US to the seizure of the USS *Pueblo* by North Korea in 1968 and of the Portuguese against Indian shipping in response to the 1961 annexation of Goa); and O'Connell, *The International Law of the Sea*, vol. II, pp. 1096–7. See also Greenwood, 'Self-Defence and the Conduct of International Armed Conflict', p. 277.

[117] See O'Connell, *The Influence of Law on Sea Power*, p. 65.

[118] O'Connell, *The International Law of the Sea*, vol. II, p. 1097.

[119] O'Connell, *The Influence of Law on Sea Power*, p. 115.

[120] See the discussion of this issue below in the context of the impact of hostile actions on third States.

The *San Remo Manual* provides a broad definition of the maritime area where hostile actions of naval forces may take place.[121] The *Manual*, however, is primarily an IHL document and its provisions must be read against the background of the additional restrictions derived from *ius ad bellum*.[122] Consequently, although the *Manual* contemplates hostile actions by armed forces on the high seas and in the exclusive economic zones and continental shelves of neutral States, such actions would have to be necessary and proportionate measures to repel an armed attack.[123]

The extent to which interference with the territorial rights of an aggressor State is consistent with limitations inherent in proportionate self-defence will differ from case to case. The repulsion of an attack, particularly in the sense of expelling the invader, will sometimes warrant the invasion of the territory of the aggressor State. A contrast between the practice in the Falkland Islands and 1990–1 Persian Gulf conflicts is illustrative of what States regard as legitimate in this context. In the case of the Falkland Islands conflict, it was generally accepted that to remove Argentina from the Islands did not require attacks on targets in Argentina itself and the campaign was in fact so limited.[124] No attacks were made on the territory of Argentina and the sea battle was restricted (with the exception of the sinking of the Argentine cruiser *General Belgrano*)[125] to the exclusion zone around the Islands.[126]

During the 1990–1 Persian Gulf conflict, the question arose as to whether the use of force by the coalition allies to expel Iraq from Kuwait should be restricted to the territory of Kuwait. It was argued in some quarters that to attack targets in Iraq was disproportionate to this aim. The coalition allies, whilst confirming that their objective was limited to forcing the withdrawal of Iraq from Kuwait, took the view that tactically, in light of Iraq's military capability, the response could not be restricted to Kuwaiti territory.

Much of the other State practice in the context of the extent of the invasion of territory is perhaps best seen as a breach of the requirements

[121] See Doswald-Beck, *San Remo Manual*, pp. 80–2.

[122] See *ibid.*, pp. 75–8 and 80–2 (describing the application of the law on self-defence to armed conflicts at sea).

[123] See *ibid.*, pp. 80–2.

[124] See Higgins, *Problems and Process: International Law and How We Use It*, p. 232.

[125] See the further discussion of this incident in note 156 and the accompanying text below.

[126] See *Hansard*, 7 April 1982, col. 1045 and *Hansard*, 29 April 1982, cols. 980–1; and see the further discussion of the practice of exclusion zones in the Falkland Islands conflict in note 180 and the accompanying text below.

of proportionality rather than the establishment of a different rule. So, for example, the United States' invasions of Grenada,[127] and Panama,[128] to the extent that they were justified as self-defence, were widely regarded as disproportionate.

When considering the scope of the defensive response, State practice and the views of commentators differ as to the extent to which the destruction of the enemy is justified in order to repulse the attack. In this context, the line between the aims of self-defence and how to accomplish them becomes somewhat blurred. So, for example, do the requirements of proportionality in self-defence under the Charter proscribe action taken to remove a continuing threat? If it is accepted that legitimate self-defence is restricted to repelling or halting the attack, is it proportionate to take action that is designed to prevent such an attack occurring again and restore the security of the State? In extreme cases, it has been argued that the total defeat of the armed forces of the aggressor State would be necessary to achieve this end.[129]

The line between anticipatory self-defence and proportional self-defence in response to an armed attack is difficult to draw in this context. Anticipatory self-defence consists of the use of force by a State in the face of a threatened attack. Many commentators would argue that, when an armed attack has occurred and there is the possibility of more such actions, anticipatory self-defence is not the issue.[130] What requires assessment in their view is the legitimate scope of defensive action in the face of an armed attack that has already occurred. These questions were raised by the Falkland Islands and 1990–1 Persian Gulf conflicts. The United Kingdom action in the former conflict, as we have seen, did not involve the territory of Argentina itself. Greenwood, however, argues that the United Kingdom had the right to use force not only to retake the Islands but also to guarantee their future security against further attack.[131] A similar view was expressed in the context of the 1990–1 Persian Gulf conflict by writers who regarded this as an action

[127] For the legal arguments supporting the invasion of Grenada, see 'Letter from the Legal Adviser, United States Department of State' (1984) 18 *International Lawyer* 381 at 385; and statement of Deputy Secretary of State Kenneth E. Dam before the House Committee on Foreign Affairs, 2 November 1983, cited in 'Contemporary Practice of the United States Relating to International Law' (1984) 78 *AJIL* 200.

[128] See the discussion in note 134 and the accompanying text below.

[129] See Doswald-Beck, *San Remo Manual*, p. 77.

[130] See Schachter, *Theory and Practice*, pp. 150–1; and see Dissenting Opinion of Justice Schwebel in the *Nicaragua Case*, note 20 above, pp. 269–70.

[131] Greenwood, 'Command and the Laws of Armed Conflict', pp. 7–8.

in collective self-defence. Some went as far as to argue that Operation Desert Storm could legitimately continue into Iraq and destroy the military capability of Iraq and, moreover, overthrow the regime of Saddam Hussein.[132]

However, the 1990–1 Persian Gulf conflict is not a particularly satisfactory precedent for the view that self-defence involves forceful measures to restore the security of the State, as there is a compelling argument that the coalition allies were acting under the authority of the Security Council. For the purposes of that analysis, what was at stake was not so much the restoration of the security of the State that had been subjected to an armed attack but the restoration of stability to the region under the Security Council's mandate to restore international peace and security.

A similar situation involving the intersection between proportionate self-defence in the face of an armed attack and preventative action is presented by the forceful response to the 11 September 2001 terrorist attacks against the United States that culminated in the overthrow of the Taliban regime in Afghanistan. The issue of proportionality in that context is considered under the later discussion of self-defence, reprisals and State-sponsored terrorism.[133]

A relatively clear-cut example of a disproportionate response, taking into account all the relevant factors, is the United States' invasion of Panama in 1989. The official basis of the action was 'an exercise of the right of self-defence . . . and was necessary to protect American lives in imminent danger'.[134] Leaving aside the difficulties of establishing that the right of self-defence extends to the protection of nationals abroad, the response thereto was clearly disproportionate. The acts allegedly giving rise to the right of self-defence were the death of one United States soldier and the threatening of two others by Panamanian Defence Force personnel. The United States' response was to launch a full-scale invasion, resulting in significant civilian casualties, destruction of property

[132] See E. V. Rostow, 'Until What? Enforcement Action or Collective Self-Defence?' (1991) 85 *AJIL* 506 at 514; and Dinstein, *War, Aggression and Self-Defence*, pp. 234–5. In 2002, this debate revived. However, with the lapse in time since the original invasion of Kuwait by Iraq, the issue of a proportionate response to a prior armed attack is not part of the discussion. The legitimacy of a forceful response depends on the scope of SC Res. 668 or the availability of a right of pre-emptive self-defence.

[133] See note 201 and the accompanying text below.

[134] President Bush, Letter to Congress, HR Doc. No. 127, 101st Cong. 2nd Sess. (1990).

and the overthrow of the government of General Noriega. This action was widely criticised by States and commentators.[135] It was the scale of the territorial invasion of Panama with the attendant civilian casualties that attracted the most criticism. The deposing of a notorious head of State attracted little comment.

At the turn of the twenty-first century, a shift is discernible towards the acceptance of a more comprehensive solution to ongoing regimes that are perceived to threaten the stability and security of the international community. Depending as always on the context, in traditional terms it is difficult, however, to regard such widespread actions as the wholesale destruction of the military forces of an aggressor State and the overthrow of a perceived hostile regime other than as more appropriately the province of the Security Council and as a disproportionate response in self-defence.

Temporal scope

A response that may initially satisfy the requirements of proportionality may lose that character if it continues past the point in time that is necessary to deal effectively with the armed attack (although sometimes such a situation is dealt with under the rubric of necessity). This point was made by the Court in the *Nicaragua Case*: 'the reaction of the United States in the context of what is regarded as self-defence was continued long after the period in which any presumed armed attack by Nicaragua could reasonably be contemplated.'[136] In the case of Grenada, even assuming that the United States' action could meet the other criteria for legitimacy under the Charter system as an exercise to protect its nationals, the fact that the forces remained in place some period after the initial invasion was regarded as disproportionate.[137] What were required were measures of protection strictly confined to the object of protecting the nationals involved against injury.[138] The same condemnation was forthcoming in relation to the Israeli occupation of parts

[135] See e.g. L. Henkin, 'The Invasion of Panama under International Law: A Gross Violation' (1991) 29 *Columbia JTL* 293 at 306 and 308–9.

[136] *Nicaragua Case*, note 20 above, pp. 122–3; and see the Dissenting Opinion of Judge Schwebel, *ibid.*, p. 369.

[137] See M. J. Levitin, 'The Law of Force and the Force of Law: Grenada, the Falklands, and Humanitarian Intervention' (1986) *27 Harvard ILJ* 621.

[138] See Waldock, 'The Regulation of the Use of Force by Individual States in International Law', p. 467.

of Lebanon from 1978 to 2000 and the buffer zone occupied by South Africa in Angola from 1981 to 1988.[139]

The Charter has affected certain rights that were available to States after the cessation of hostilities. Prior to the adoption of the Charter, the IHL doctrine known as belligerent rights determined what actions a State could take after the cessation of hostilities.[140] Until the state of war was formally at an end, certain such rights remained available to States. Nowadays, it appears that necessity and proportionality in *ius ad bellum* determine the legality of belligerent acts after hostilities have ceased rather than the doctrine of belligerent rights. For example, in the context of Egypt's claim to exercise belligerent rights against shipping bound to and from Israel in the Suez Canal, despite the 1949 armistice with Israel, the Security Council determined: 'neither party can reasonably assert that it . . . requires to exercise the right of visit, search and seizure for any legitimate purpose of self-defence.'[141]

The choice of means and methods of warfare

The requirements of proportionality in the exercise of self-defence also regulate the choice of means and methods of warfare and targets that are available to States in the exercise of this right. Integral to decisions relating to the choice of means and methods of warfare and targets must be a consideration of the anticipated overall scale of civilian casualties, the level of destruction of the enemy forces, and finally damage to territory, the infrastructure of the target State and the environment generally. For example, the impact of a campaign that combines air and land forces will differ from one in which high-altitude aerial bombardment is the major component.

From time to time, there have been suggestions that issues such as the means and methods of warfare adopted by a State in the exercise of its right of self-defence are purely in the province of IHL.[142] Certainly,

[139] See e.g. SC Res. 425, 19 March 1978 (in relation to Israel) and SC Res. 545, 20 December 1983 (in relation to South Africa).

[140] See generally *Oppenheim's International Law*, vol. II, *Disputes, War and Neutrality* (ed. by A. D. McNair, 4th edn, Longmans, Green & Co. Ltd, London, 1926), Part III. See the further discussion of the IHL doctrine of belligerent rights and self-defence in *ius ad bellum* under the Charter, in note 174 and the accompanying text below.

[141] SC Res. 95, 1 September 1951; and see C. Greenwood, 'The Concept of War in Modern International Law' (1987) 36 *ICLQ* 283 at 287.

[142] This was the view put forward by some participants in the drafting of the *San Remo Manual*, p. 77.

the provisions of IHL that define military targets,[143] prohibit indiscriminate attacks[144] and weapons causing superfluous injury and unnecessary suffering,[145] are of great significance in the context of weapons and targets. However, the requirements of proportionality in its *ius ad bellum* sense must also be met, a view confirmed by the International Court of Justice in the *Nuclear Weapons* Advisory Opinion and one that enjoys the majority support of commentators.[146] State practice, moreover, is generally consistent with the relevance of proportionality to these questions.

Therefore, in relation to means and methods of warfare and targets, the different proportionality equations in both IHL and *ius ad bellum* must be satisfied. For example, the possibility exists that an attack with a particular weapon may be legitimate under IHL but fail to meet the proportionality requirements of self-defence. A similar situation may arise in relation to the choice of targets. A target such as an electricity grid may meet the definition of a legitimate military target in IHL but its destruction in the particular circumstances pertaining at the time may be excessive in terms of achieving the aims of self-defence.

In the context of weapons there is a distinction between whether a particular weapon is inherently disproportionate and the manner in which it is used. Generally speaking, the outlawing of specific weapons is primarily a matter for IHL. A weapon prohibited under IHL can never be used legitimately irrespective of the position under *ius ad bellum*. However, can it be argued that some weapons by their very nature can never constitute a proportionate measure in self-defence? It is non-conventional weapons that raise this issue most directly. The majority of conventional weapons *per se* do not raise questions as to whether they are capable of meeting the proportionality requirement of self-defence. In that context, it is how and when they are used and in what quantity and against what targets that will involve an assessment of proportionality.[147] These questions are also relevant to weapons of mass destruction, but additionally it is arguable that the latter are inherently

[143] See the discussion of military targets in Chapter 4 above.

[144] See the discussion of indiscriminate attacks in Chapter 4 above.

[145] See the discussion of weapons causing unnecessary suffering in Chapter 3 above.

[146] See e.g. C. Greenwood, '*Jus ad Bellum* and *Jus in Bello* in the Nuclear Weapons Advisory Opinion' in L. Boisson de Chazournes and P. Sands (eds.), *International Law, the International Court of Justice and Nuclear Weapons* (Cambridge University Press, Cambridge, 1999), p. 247 at p. 258.

[147] See O'Connell, *The Influence of Law on Sea Power*, pp. 86–90 and 92–6 (discussing the issue of proportionality in relation to the use of missiles and mines in naval hostilities).

disproportionate. Moreover, weapons of mass destruction not only have the potential to inflict unique levels of damage on the territory and population of the target State, but also are environmentally catastrophic in terms of States at large. Thus, the proportionality of their effects on third States must be considered.[148]

Whether the requirements of *ius ad bellum* could outlaw a particular weapon, irrespective of the position under IHL, was one of the arguments presented to the Court in the *Nuclear Weapons* Advisory Opinion. The Court was unable to 'reach a definitive conclusion as to the legality or illegality of the use of nuclear weapons by a State, in extreme circumstances of self-defence, in which its very survival would be at stake'.[149] Apart from confirming that necessity and proportionality are part of international law (citing its own judgment in the *Nicaragua Case*) and, by inference, that weapons are a matter for the self-defence aspect of proportionality, the majority opinion adds little to the existing jurisprudence on the demands of these criteria. In relation to proportionality, the Court was of the view that this principle '[might] not in itself exclude the use of nuclear weapons in self-defence in all circumstances'.[150] In response to the arguments presented to the Court that the very nature of nuclear weapons was inconsistent with compliance with proportionality, the somewhat unhelpful response was to the effect that 'it suffices for the Court to note that the very nature of all nuclear weapons and the profound risks associated therewith are further considerations to be borne in mind by States believing they can exercise a nuclear response in self-defence in accordance with the requirements of proportionality'.[151]

Several other members of the Court do not share the hesitant views of the majority either regarding the use of nuclear weapons as lawful *per se* under both *ius ad bellum* and IHL or according primacy to the right of self-defence over IHL.[152] Several members of the Court, on the other hand, find the use of nuclear weapons unlawful under current international law.[153] They do not, however, derive this illegality from *ius ad bellum*.

[148] See the further discussion in note 166 and the accompanying text below.
[149] See *Nuclear Weapons* Advisory Opinion, p. 263.
[150] *Ibid.*, p. 245. [151] *Ibid.*
[152] See e.g. Dissenting Opinion of Vice-President Schwebel, *ibid.*, p. 311, Dissenting Opinion of Judges Fleischauer, *ibid.*, p. 305 and Higgins, *ibid.*, p. 583 and Separate Opinion of Judge Guillaume, *ibid.*, p. 287.
[153] See Dissenting Opinion of Judges Shahabuddeen, *ibid.*, p. 380 and Weeramantry, *ibid.*, p. 429.

As things stand currently, therefore, it appears difficult to argue that nuclear weapons, or indeed any other weapon, will be deemed illegal as disproportionate *per se* under *ius ad bellum*. Nevertheless, although not as such outlawing any particular weapon, proportionality in *ius ad bellum* imposes significant limitations on the weapons available to States in the exercise of their right to self-defence. The weaponry chosen in any particular case must remain defensive in character. In other words, if the resort to a particular weapon represents a considerable escalation of the hostilities, it may fail the test of proportionality.[154] This is not to say, however, that a State must match its mode of response to that of the attack. Indeed, as we have seen, there is support for the view that the use of nuclear weapons may, in appropriate circumstances, constitute a proportionate response to an attack with conventional weapons.[155]

In the case of the choice of targets, the incident of the sinking of the Argentine cruiser *General Belgrano* during the Falkland Islands conflict illustrates how the proportionality requirement in self-defence may limit attacks on military targets.[156] At the time of the attack, the *General Belgrano* was outside the total exclusion zone declared by the United Kingdom and appeared to pose no immediate threat. The strike was thus pre-emptive in nature and a considerable escalation of the conflict. These factors led to the misgivings as to the attack constituting a proportionate measure of self-defence.[157] Targeting a military vessel outside a declared exclusion zone, however, is not an act excessive in itself. The delimitation of the exclusion zone was designed to ensure conformity with the limited scope of the right of self-defence under the Charter. The United Kingdom judged that control over the area encompassed by the zone was necessary in order to achieve the expulsion of the Argentine forces from the Islands. However, the declaration of the zone did not necessarily prevent the United Kingdom legally from extending the scope of its hostile actions to targets in the high seas. Indeed, the United Kingdom had reserved the right to take 'whatever additional measures may be needed in the exercise of its right of self-defence under Article 51 of the United

[154] See e.g. O'Connell, *The Influence of Law on Sea Power*, pp. 64–5.

[155] See the sources cited in note 95 above.

[156] See M. Hastings and S. Jenkins, *The Battle for the Falklands* (Michael Joseph, London, 1983), pp. 147–50 (for a description of the facts surrounding the sinking of the *General Belgrano*); and see generally H. Levie, 'The Falkland Crisis and the Laws of War' in Coll and Arend (eds.), *The Falklands War: Lessons for Strategy, Diplomacy, and International Law*, p. 66.

[157] See e.g. the statement by L. Freedman, in *Foreign Affairs*, Autumn 1982.

Nations Charter'.[158] The question then became whether the attack on the *General Belgrano* qualified as such a measure given the requirements of proportionality. Ultimately, however, the outrage expressed in some quarters over the sinking of the *General Belgrano* was not so much based on legal criteria but on the perception that the attack was in some way dishonourable in light of the inference that vessels outside the exclusion zone would not be attacked.

The practice of States in the 1990–1 Persian Gulf conflict is also indicative of what States regard as proportionate in the context of targets. If there are any sustainable misgivings as to the proportionality of the actions of the coalition allies in that conflict under *ius ad bellum*, they are probably based on the massive destruction of the infrastructure of Iraq and the impact thereof on the civilian population.[159] No doubt these actions contributed to the early capitulation of Iraq. Moreover, the installations targeted satisfied the definition of military targets under IHL. Some commentators argue, however, that more was done than was proportionate to the expulsion of Iraq from Kuwait.[160]

The application of proportionality in *ius ad bellum* is by no means clear in the case of the targeting of such infrastructure targets as electricity grids that may qualify as legitimate military targets but are also indispensable for the survival and well-being of the civilian population.[161] It is uncontroversial that direct or immediate civilian casualties resulting from attacks are a particularly relevant factor in the assessment of proportionality in self-defence. There appears to be, however, insufficient State practice to indicate the relevance of such factors as the possible long-term effects on the civilian population, including the creation of a large refugee outflow, in delimiting overall targeting policies.[162] This is not to suggest that these are not relevant considerations, but more clarity is required as to exactly how States interpret their obligations in this context. The same is true for overall combatant casualties. Indeed, there seems little evidence of any real restraint in this context.

158 See statement in the House of Commons, 7 April 1982–23 April 1982.

159 See e.g. Human Rights Watch, *Needless Deaths in the Gulf War* (Human Rights Watch, New York, 1991).

160 See e.g. M. Walzer, *Just and Unjust Wars: A Moral Argument with Historical Illustrations* (2nd edn, Basic Books, New York, 1991), p. xx.

161 See the discussion of the issue of the targeting of such objects under IHL in Chapter 4 above.

162 See e.g. R. Falk, 'Kosovo, World Order and the Future of International Law' (1999) 93 *AJIL* 847 at 851–2 (detailing the refugee outflow following the NATO action in Kosovo).

The 1990–1 Persian Gulf conflict also illustrates an area in which the proportionality equation in the context of methods of warfare would benefit from clarification. For example, the law is not clear on the extent to which the choice of means and methods of combat can legitimately be dictated by the aim of minimising a State's own combatant losses. The adoption of means and methods of warfare that prioritise the protection of a State's own combatants may increase the dangers to the civilian population of targeted States. For example, aerial bombardment at high altitude may minimise combatant casualties but leads to increased risk of civilian casualties and widespread damage to civilian objects.[163] The prioritising of combatants' lives in 'morally' (if not always legally) justifiable resorts to force can be seen not only in the conduct of the 1990–1 Persian Gulf conflict but also in the 'zero casualties' policy adopted by NATO forces in the 1999 Kosovo conflict.[164]

As we have seen, the proportionality equation in current IHL is not designed to deal with the extent to which a military commander must assume a higher level of risk for his or her own combatants in order to protect the civilian population of the opposing side.[165] It is the proportionality equation in *ius ad bellum* that is perhaps better suited to performing this function. *Ius ad bellum* determines what is proportionate to achieving the overall aim of the use of force. For example, it controls the choice of campaign and, in this broad sense, the means and methods of warfare. It appears, however, that under the current state of the law a State has a considerable degree of liberty to plan its campaign, including its preferred method of warfare, in order to reduce its own combatant casualties, without infringing the requirements of *ius ad bellum*.

Effect on third States

There are many situations where third States are detrimentally affected by the use of force in individual or collective self-defence by other States.

[163] See the discussion of this issue in Chapter 4 above.

[164] See A. P. V. Rogers, 'Zero-Casualty Warfare' (2000) 837 *IRRC* 165. For the results of this policy on civilians and civilian objects, see Report on the Human Rights Situation Involving Kosovo, submitted by Mary Robinson, UN High Commissioner for Human Rights, Geneva, 30 April 1999; and Human Rights Watch, *Civilian Deaths in the NATO Air Campaign*, vol. 12, No. 1(D), February 2000, available at www.hrw.org/hrw/reports/2000/nato/.

[165] See W. Fenrick, 'Attacking the Enemy Civilian as a Punishable Offense' (1997) 7 *Duke Journal of Comparative and International Law* 539 at 548–9 (highlighting the difficulty in determining the obligations on a commander to expose his or her forces to risk).

There may be a violation of third States' sovereignty from the over-flying of aircraft and missiles, or actual damage to its territory or population from the use of certain types of weapons such as nuclear weapons. Weapons may also be faulty or negligently targeted and damage may ensue to third States. A State may decide that its effective defence requires the intrusion by its armed forces into the territory of a third State. The mining of ports and waters may detrimentally affect third States, as was the case in the *Corfu Channel*[166] and *Nicaragua Cases*. Neutral shipping may be damaged or interfered with by naval hostilities[167] or blockades,[168] and on many occasions the rights of third States are interfered with by the establishment of various types of maritime zones. To what extent are such actions legitimate under the Charter system and how much damage to or interference with the rights of third States is acceptable?

The resolution of the relationship between the exercise of self-defence and the rights of third States under the Charter regime awaits full elaboration. The 2001 commentary to the International Law Commission Draft Articles on the Responsibility of States for Internationally Wrongful Acts, whilst confirming that neutral States 'are not unaffected by the existence of a state of war', 'leaves open all the issues of the effect of action in self-defence vis-à-vis third States'.[169]

Prior to the Charter, the law of neutrality governed the impact of hostilities on third States.[170] Views differ as to the continued relevance of the institution of neutrality under the Charter.[171] Neutrality assumes

[166] *Corfu Channel Case* (*UK* v. *Albania*), Merits, ICJ Reports 1949, 24.

[167] See O'Connell, *The Influence of Law on Sea Power*, pp. 86–90 (in relation to missiles) and pp. 92–6 (in relation to mines).

[168] See *ibid*., pp. 101–3 (in relation to belligerent blockades of straits) and pp. 114–31 (in relation to belligerent rights, including the right of blockade over the high seas).

[169] See Commentary to Article 21, Commentaries to the Draft Articles on the Responsibility of States for Internationally Wrongful Acts, adopted by the International Law Commission at its 53rd Session Report of the International Law Commission, 53rd Session, 23 April–1 June and 2 July–10 August 2001, GAOR, 56th Sess. Supp. No. 10 (A/56/10).

[170] See *Oppenheim's International Law*, vol. I, *Peace* (ed. by R. Jennings and A. Watts), pp. 535–625 (for a description of the institution of neutrality). See also Hague Convention V Respecting the Rights and Duties of Neutral Powers and Persons in Case of War on Land, 18 October 1907; and Hague Convention XIII Concerning the Rights and Duties of Neutral Powers in Naval War, 18 October 1907.

[171] See generally C. Chinkin, *Third Parties in International Law* (Clarendon Press, Oxford, 1993), pp. 299–314; and see also Greenwood, 'Self-Defence and the Conduct of International Armed Conflict', pp. 283–6.

that States have the right to remain impartial in a dispute and this is no longer the case under certain provisions of the Charter.[172] However, the International Court of Justice in the *Nuclear Weapons* Advisory Opinion accepted that the law of neutrality applied as part of customary international law to all weapons used in international armed conflict. Exactly what was required of States to avoid contravening the requirements of neutrality was not elaborated.[173]

One area in which there has been considerable disagreement as to the relationship between the Charter regime and the institution of neutrality is in the context of belligerent rights over neutral shipping. Belligerent rights are an important part of the institution of neutrality and 'permit the seizure of enemy ships or property at sea or on land under the law of naval warfare, and trading with the enemy legislation, as well as the rights of visit, search, and seizure exercised with respect to neutral merchant shipping'.[174] The effect of the proportionality requirement of self-defence under the Charter on the exercise of belligerent rights, particularly the conduct of naval operations, has been part of the controversy. Some experts argue that as long as naval operations comply with the requirements of IHL and the law of neutrality then the proportionality requirement of self-defence is irrelevant.[175] Other commentators disagree, maintaining the relevance of proportionality to such activities.[176] State practice is inconsistent.[177] For example, the United Kingdom relied on the law of self-defence rather than the institution of neutrality to determine the limits of belligerent rights in relation to third State shipping in the 1980–8 Iran/Iraq conflict.[178] The United States in contrast

172 See Arts. 2(5), 25 and Chapter VII of the United Nations Charter.

173 *Nuclear Weapons* Advisory Opinion, pp. 260–1 and 262.

174 R. Baxter, 'The Legal Consequences of the Unlawful Use of Force under the Charter' (1968) *Proc. ASIL* 68 at 68–9.

175 See e.g. Doswald-Beck, *San Remo Manual*, p. 76.

176 See O'Connell, *The Influence of Law on Sea Power*, p. 160; C. Greenwood, 'Comment' in I. Dekker and H. Post (eds.), *The Gulf War of 1980–1988: The Iran–Iraq War in International Legal Perspective* (Martinus Nijhoff, Dordrecht and Boston, 1992), p. 212 at p. 215; and R. Lagoni, 'Neutrality, the Rights of Shipping and the Use of Force in the Persian Gulf War (Part I)' (1988) 82 *Proc. ASIL* 161 at 162.

177 See P. Norton, 'Between the Ideology and the Reality: The Shadow of the Law of Neutrality' (1976) 17 *Harvard ILJ* 249 at 254–78; and C. Gray, 'The British Position in Regard to the Gulf Conflict, Part I' (1988) 37 *ICLQ* 420.

178 See C. Greenwood, 'Neutrality, the Rights of Shipping and the Use of Force in the Persian Gulf War (Part I)' (1988) 82 *Proc ASIL* 158 at 158–9; and Gray, 'The British Position', pp. 422–3.

used the language of belligerent rights.[179] Overall, it appears the position is that, although these former belligerent rights are not necessarily inconsistent with self-defence, their legality depends on whether they are proportionate.

Another practice of States that raises issues of proportionality in the context of third States is the establishment of maritime exclusion zones. From time to time since the adoption of the Charter, States have established 'zones' over areas of the high seas in which they have excluded the passage of neutral ships or aircraft without permission. This occurred, for example, in the Vietnam, Falkland Islands, Iran/Iraq and 1990–1 Persian Gulf conflicts.[180] O'Connell regards these as legitimate measures of self-defence as long as States are notified of their existence and that neutral shipping is not put 'unduly at risk'.[181] The *San Remo Manual* states that, 'in determining the extent, location and duration' of such zones, there must be a 'proportional and demonstrable nexus between the zone and the measures imposed, including both restrictive and enforcement measures' and the requirements of self-defence.[182]

With respect to State practice, in the Falkland Islands conflict the United Kingdom first declared a maritime exclusion zone 200 miles around the Islands and stated that any Argentine warship and naval auxiliaries within that zone would be treated as hostile and liable to be attacked.[183] It converted this to a total exclusion zone some days later,[184] and ultimately extended its area to within 12 miles of the Argentine coast. The then Soviet Union complained that this zone was excessive and unlawful.[185] Argentina extended its initial exclusion area of 200 miles around the Islands to a declaration that the whole South Atlantic was a war zone. The latter would appear to be disproportionate to its needs of self-defence and impacted unnecessarily on neutral shipping.[186]

The establishment of such zones in the Persian Gulf raises very complex issues of proportionality, as the potential interference with third States is so much greater.[187] The Persian Gulf is bordered by eight States

[179] See Gray, 'The British Position', p. 423, citing Secretary of Defense (Weinberger), 'Report to the Congress on Security Arrangements in the Persian Gulf', 15 June 1987, (1987) 26 ILM 1433 at 1458.

[180] For State practice in relation to naval zones, see O'Connell, *The International Law of the Sea*, vol. II, pp. 1096–7.

[181] *Ibid*., pp. 1110–11.

[182] Doswald-Beck, *San Remo Manual*, p. 182.

[183] See *Hansard*, 7 April 1982, col. 1045.

[184] See *Hansard*, 29 April 1982, cols. 980–1.

[185] See H. Levie, 'The Falkland Crisis', p. 66.

[186] Doswald-Beck, *San Remo Manual*, p. 182.

[187] *Ibid*., p. 182; and see D. Peace, 'Neutrality, the Rights of Shipping and the Use of Force in the Persian Gulf War Part I' (1988) 82 *Proc. ASIL* 146–51.

and is the source of a large percentage of the world's trade in oil at any given time. During the so-called 'tanker war' in the 1980s, in addition to declaring exclusion or war zones, Iran and, to a much lesser extent, Iraq indiscriminately attacked shipping in the Persian Gulf. Iran, moreover, exercised extensive belligerent rights of search and visit over ships of many third States. It is evident that many of the forceful actions of both the belligerents in the Iran/Iraq conflict went well beyond what could legitimately be regarded as proportionate to the needs of self-defence.[188]

In the context of the effect of armed conflict on third States, a developing area of the law is the effect of warfare on the environment. Armed conflict has always been environmentally destructive. One can point to many examples, such as the defoliation of large tracts of Vietnam during the Vietnam War[189] and the actions of Iraq in the 1990–1 Persian Gulf conflict, in which some 732 oil wells in Kuwait were deliberately set on fire and an estimated 4–6 million barrels of oil were spilled into the Gulf.[190] The impact on the environment of depleted uranium in ammunition has also become controversial as its use can lead to contamination of the environment.[191] Weapons containing this substance were used in the 1990–1 and 2003 Persian Gulf conflicts, in Bosnia-Herzegovina (1995) and in Kosovo (1999).[192] Sometimes the environment is deliberately targeted, such as was apparently the case in relation to the release of oil into the Persian Gulf by Iraq during the 1990–1 Persian Gulf conflict. Usually, however, the effect on the environment is incidental to military operations.

188 See R. Lekow, 'The Iran–Iraq Conflict in the Gulf: The Law of War Zones' (1988) 37 *ICLQ* 629 at 636–7 (legality of the Iraqi exclusion zone), 638–40 (the tanker war) and 640–3 (the international reaction to the tanker war). The Iran/Iraq conflict (1981–8) generally was conducted without any restraints: see *The Iran–Iraq War (1981–88)* (Federation of American Scientists, Military Analysis Network), available at www.fas.org (for details of this conflict).

189 See Stockholm International Peace Research Institute, *Ecological Consequences of the Second Indochina War* (Humanities Press, Stockholm, 1976), pp. 24–40.

190 See e.g. A. Roberts, 'Environmental Destruction in the 1991 Gulf War' (1992) 291 *IRRC* 538.

191 See S. A. Egorov, 'The Kosovo Crisis and the Law of Armed Conflicts' (2000) 837 *IRRC* 183; and UNEP, 'Depleted Uranium in Kosovo – Post-Conflict Environmental Assessment', Appendices I (Risk Assessment), IV.2 (Potential Health and Environmental Effects) and V (Possible Effects of DU on Groundwater) at www.balkans.unep.ch/du/reports/reports.html.

192 See e.g. Press Release Hab/163 Unep/67, 'NATO Confirms to United Nations Use of Depleted Uranium During Kosovo Conflict', 22 March 2000, available at www.un.org/News/Press/Docs/2000/20000322.hab163.doc.html.

Until recent times, the environmental degradation caused by armed conflict and the attendant consequences for third States was unregulated by principles of international law, although arguably the law of neutrality regulates transboundary damage caused to third States by the means and methods of warfare of a belligerent State. Developing concern for the environment and the consequent emergence of legal norms in response, however, gradually extended into the area of armed conflict and is now reflected in the conventional and customary regime of IHL.[193]

The International Court of Justice in the *Nuclear Weapons* Advisory Opinion considered the obligations imposed on States in relation to the environment during times of armed conflict. The majority was unable to conclude that there were any obligations derived from general international law that operated as a total restraint on the use of nuclear weapons in self-defence as a result of States' obligations to protect the environment.[194] However, the Court was of the view that 'States must take environmental considerations into account when assessing what is necessary and proportionate in the pursuit of legitimate military objectives. Respect for the environment is one of the elements that go to assessing whether an action is in conformity with the principles of necessity and proportionality.'[195] Little indication is provided, however, in the judgment as to how this balance will operate in practice. The developing law on the protection of the environment nevertheless will influence perceptions of what is proportionate in self-defence in such circumstances.

This leaves open the question as to the relationship between concern for the environment and other factors in the proportionality equation. For example, if the use of a particular weapon is a proportionate measure in self-defence in all other respects, could it nevertheless be illegitimate because of its impact on the environment of third States? It seems that logically the answer must be in the affirmative, although it seems unlikely that such a result would readily ensue. It is far more likely that it will be what the Court refers to as 'obligations of total restraint' that will perform this role in the future rather than the proportionality

[193] For a discussion of the responsibility of States for environmental damage to neutral States in times of armed conflict, see L. Low and D. Hodgkinson, 'Compensation for Wartime Environmental Damage: Challenges to International Law after the Gulf War' (1995) 35 *Virginia JIL* 405 at 419–23. See also B. Baker, 'Legal Protections for the Environment in Times of Armed Conflict' (1993) 33 *Virginia JIL* 51 at 54–8; and see Report of the Secretary-General on the Protection of the Environment in Times of Armed Conflict, UN Doc. A/48/269 (29 July 1993).

[194] See *Nuclear Weapons* Advisory Opinion, p. 242. [195] *Ibid.*

requirement of self-defence.[196] The same phenomenon can be observed in the context of weapons control. It will be specific treaty prohibitions of weapons that will control their use rather than the dictates of proportionality.

Finally, in the context of the impact of armed conflict on third States, the question of the relationship between the law of neutrality and the proportionality equation of self-defence awaits further elaboration.

Anticipatory self-defence and proportionality

The legality of anticipatory self-defence remains controversial.[197] Irrespective of the validity of forceful preventative action as such, there is accord that proportionality is of even more significance in such circumstances.[198] The reluctance of some observers to accept the legitimacy of such action is the alleged difficulty in tailoring the reaction where all that is present is a threat.[199] However, necessity provides the initial limitation on undertaking a forceful action in the face of a threat of force, and it is submitted that that requirement will not be satisfied until there is a distinct quantifiable threat.[200] Nevertheless, on completion of this process, there may still remain a great deal of uncertainty regarding the exact nature of the threat. In such circumstances, the application of proportionality becomes somewhat of a haphazard process. Much depends on the past relationship of the States concerned. If there has been a previous attack or series of attacks or a threat of specific action, then the assessment of what is required to repel the threat is more straightforward.

Assuming the legitimacy of preventative force, the application of the proportionality equation will first require identifying the aim of the use of force. As with the response to a prior armed attack, the response must be limited to countering the threatened attack and no more. Secondly,

[196] See e.g. the Convention on the Prohibition of Military or Any Other Hostile Use of Environmental Modification Techniques, 18 May 1977, (1978) 1108 UNTS 151. For a discussion of the general topic of constraints on the conduct of self-defence, see Report of the International Law Commission on the Work of Its 54th Session, Chapter V, State Responsibility (April 1999), GAOR, 54th Sess. Supp. No. 10 (A/54/10), paras. 329–31 and Commentary on Article 21 of the Draft Articles, pp. 178–9.

[197] See the discussion of this issue in note 33 and the accompanying text above.

[198] See e.g. *Oppenheim's International Law*, vol. I, *Peace*, Introduction and Part I (ed. by R. Jennings and A. Watts), pp. 421–2.

[199] See e.g. Brownlie, *Use of Force by States*, p. 259. Brownlie's objection, however, appears to be based on the difficulty of establishing the necessity of the action rather than one that relates to proportionality.

[200] See the discussion of this issue in note 74 and the accompanying text above.

the scale and mode of the response will be dictated by the nature and magnitude of the anticipated armed attack. Limitations on the temporal and geographical scope of the response, the means and methods of warfare and the likely impact of the actions on third States must all be respected so as to retain the proportionate and thus defensive nature of the undertaking.

States, however, have rarely relied as such on any doctrine of preventative self-defence to justify their forceful actions, so the above discussion owes more to theory than to practice. Admittedly, there are signs of change with the avowed intention of States such as the United States to act pre-emptively in the face of terrorist threats. The target of pre-emptive action, moreover, has expanded to include the threat from so-called 'rogue States' with their aspirations to acquire weapons of mass destruction. Most of the debate, however, to date over what in reality appears to be preventative action has taken place in the context of the phenomenon of State-sponsored terrorism and the respective boundaries of legitimate self-defence and reprisals in State responses thereto.

State-sponsored terrorism and proportionality

The legal framework of the response of States to State-sponsored terrorist attacks and counter-insurgent activities is extremely complex, and there is a great deal of conflicting State practice.[201] There is, however, accord on the one aspect of the debate, the need for such actions to be proportionate whatever their legal basis.[202] Indeed, proportionality has played a major role over the years in determining the international response to the forceful counter-insurgent activities of States. The frequent failure of States to ensure a proportionate response in such circumstances has provided the Security Council with a convenient way of dealing with the issue without addressing the underlying framework of the relationship between self-defence and reprisal action under the Charter. The Security Council has been able to adopt the tactic of labelling such actions as unlawful reprisals in light of their disproportionate nature

[201] See G. Haffner, 'Certain Issues of the Work of the Sixth Committee at the Fifty-Sixth General Assembly' (2003) 97 *AJIL* 147 at 156–9 (for a discussion of the progress towards achieving an acceptable definition of terrorism).

[202] For example, the US was at pains to assert that its 1998 attacks on a missile training camp in Afghanistan and a pharmaceuticals camp in Sudan were both necessary and proportionate: see Letter dated 20 August 1998 from the Permanent Representative of the United States to the United Nations Addressed to the President of the Security Council, UN Doc. S/1998/780 (1998).

without addressing squarely the limits of legitimate self-defence in such contexts.[203] Part of the explanation for the frequent condemnation of counter-insurgent activities as excessive is the method adopted by States of assessing what is a proportionate response in such situations. States such as the United States and Israel have argued that the proportionality of their actions should be measured on the 'accumulation of events basis' and not in relation to each individual action.[204] These arguments have never found acceptance on the Security Council and frequently proportionality has been relied on in characterising these actions as unlawful reprisals. Thus, for example, the Argentine representative to the Security Council, in the context of the events of 27–28 February 1972, involving Israeli armed incursions into the territory of Lebanon, stated as follows:

> Proportion has not been respected, either in terms of the scale of the action, or even in terms of the duration. Faced with this situation, we must conclude that the events described in the complaint are in the nature of a punitive expedition, and these acts, as well as preventative war, are completely incompatible with the purposes, principles and tenets of the Charter.[205]

In a similar vein, other States over the years have condemned such actions as excessive.[206]

This practice of the Security Council has not been helpful in maintaining the distinction between the legitimacy of the grounds for the resort to force and the issue of whether, irrespective of the grounds asserted, the use of force to achieve them is proportionate. The same phenomenon can be seen amongst commentators in their analyses of

[203] For a comprehensive review of Security Council practice in this regard up to 1970, see Bowett, 'Reprisals Involving Recourse to Armed Force', pp. 4–17; and for a discussion of the post-1970 practice of the Security Council in the context of reprisals, see W. O'Brien, 'Reprisals, Deterrence and Self-Defence in Counter Terror Operations' (1990) 30 *Virginia JIL* 421 at 426–69. See also the debate between R. A. Falk, 'The Beirut Raid and the International Law of Retaliation' (1969) 63 *AJIL* 415; and Y. Blum, 'The Beirut Raid and the International Double Standard: A Reply to Professor R. A. Falk' (1970) 64 *AJIL* 73; and see also R. W. Tucker, 'Reprisals in Self-Defence: The Customary Law' (1972) 66 *AJIL* 587.

[204] See e.g. UN SCOR, p. 5 (1643rd Meeting, 1972); UN SCOR, p. 5 (1648th Meeting, 1972); UN SCOR (2674th Meeting, 1988).

[205] UN SCOR, p. 3 (1644th Meeting, 1972); and see the statement of the representatives of France and the Sudan at pp. 2 and 19 respectively (1650th Meeting, 1972).

[206] See e.g. the statement of the representative of the United States to the Security Council at UN SCOR, p. 2 (1407th Meeting, 1968); UN SCOR, p. 2 (1440th Meeting, 1968) (regarding excessive nature of retaliatory attacks by Israel on Jordanian territory).

the response to the 11 September 2001 terrorist attacks on the United States.[207] The law governing the relationship between reprisals and self-defence appears to have undergone considerable development in light of the ongoing response to these events. What in previous times may have been regarded as reprisal action by the United States and its allies has received significant State support as constituting legitimate self-defence in response to a prior armed attack and, moreover, not as pre-emptive in nature.[208] As is so often the case in this area, the tension between what States do and what they say does not make the task of identifying the customary law an easy one.

The test of the proportionality of the ensuing forceful action by the United States against Afghanistan was articulated in the joint resolution of the United States Congress authorising the President to use force: '[t]he President is authorized to use all necessary and appropriate force against those nations, organizations or persons he determines planned, authorized, committed, or aided the terrorist attacks . . . or harbored such organizations or persons, in order to prevent any future acts of international terrorism against the United States'.[209] Thus empowered, the United States, assisted by the United Kingdom, adopted a campaign of aerial attacks followed by the deployment of ground forces to destroy a range of military targets primarily in the Afghan capital, Kabul, and in Kandahar, the centre of the Taliban movement.[210] These actions also resulted in a number of civilian deaths and damage to civilian objects.[211] Simultaneous military support for the armed insurgent group, the Northern Alliance, rapidly resulted in the overthrow of the ruling Taliban regime and the installation of an interim

[207] See e.g. the analysis of proportionality by Glennon, 'The Fog of Law: Self-Defence, Inherence', pp. 550–3.

[208] See Cassese, 'Terrorism Is Also Disrupting Some Crucial Legal Categories of International Law', pp. 997–8 (expressing misgivings as to the impact of State practice surrounding the 11 September 2001 events on the existing legal framework of self-defence). Although the forceful response to these events did not receive the direct imprimatur of the Security Council, the inherent right of individual and collective self-defence was confirmed by the Council, along with the need to 'combat by all means' the 'threats to international peace and security caused by terrorist acts' (SC Res. 1368, 12 September 2001).

[209] See 'Authorization for Use of Military Force' (2001) Pub. L. No. 107-40, 115 Stat. 224.

[210] See Murphy, 'Contemporary Practice', p. 248 (for a description of these events).

[211] See e.g. Human Rights Watch, *United States/Afghanistan, Fatally Flawed: Cluster Bombs and Their Use by the United States in Afghanistan*, December 2002, vol. 14, No. 7 (G) available at www.hrw.org/reports/2002/us-afghanistan/.

government.[212] The reaction of the international community was generally positive as to the extent of the campaign, although the Organization of the Islamic Conference called upon the United States to restrict its military action to Afghanistan.[213] This muted response is in contrast to previous occasions where States have resorted to pre-emptive action in such circumstances.

The difficulty with applying proportionality is apparent when the aim against which to measure the response is so open-ended, as was the case in relation to the Afghan campaign. In traditional terms, the most that can be justified as a legitimate objective in such circumstances is the removal of an identifiable terrorist threat. Assuming, therefore, that it is valid to hold States directly responsible for lower levels of support for terrorist activities than has traditionally been the case, such as the mere tolerance of their presence, armed action on their territory appears legitimate as long as it is solely aimed at the destruction of the group concerned. Any level of collateral damage to civilians and civilian objects, however, will be questionable. To go further and target the military forces of the State and overthrow the government in such circumstances seems unlikely to constitute a proportionate response. There is growing support, however, for the position that it is a proportionate response to the threat of terrorism to remove a regime that is either incapable of the action necessary to deal with terrorist activity on its territory or lacks the motivation to do so. The acceptance of such a view extends the established boundaries of permissible means to an unprecedented and illegitimate extent. At the very least, some level of complicity would need to be demonstrated against the State to justify such a reaction.

Where the parameters of the threat are so uncertain as is the case with an ongoing terrorist threat of global dimensions, discussions of proportionality take on a somewhat unreal air. Where the aim against which to measure the response has no identifiable boundaries, the norm cannot realistically restrain the impact of a forceful response. More attention, therefore, should be focused on, first, ensuring the necessity of counter-terrorist action and, secondly, on detailing its aims more carefully. In a more general sense, there is no reason to suppose that the

[212] See Murphy, 'Contemporary Practice', p. 250.

[213] *Ibid.*, p. 248 (for a description of the reaction of States to the US-led actions against Afghanistan).

growing intolerance of civilian casualties evident in certain sections of the international community will not impact on the latitude of States in determining their ongoing responses to the worldwide terrorist threat. There is frequently a lapse of time between States' forceful reaction to a new type of threat and the emergence of pressure for moderation in the response. Proportionality has a pivotal role to play in the context of the global nature of the current terrorist threat and the stated determination of States like the United States to take pre-emptive action anywhere in the world where they perceive a threat.[214]

Humanitarian intervention

Irrespective of the validity of humanitarian intervention under the Charter scheme, States and commentators accept that the necessity and proportionality criteria apply to such actions.[215] Indeed, of all the conditions advanced as hallmarks of any emerging right of humanitarian intervention, these would be the least controversial.[216] It must be kept in mind, however, that humanitarian intervention owes its development more to the work of commentators than to any claim by States to such a right. Nevertheless, whatever the basis of such actions, State practice is consistent with the view that forceful intervention in such situations is only justified as a last resort in the face of intransigence on the part of the perpetrator State. When that point has been reached is the subject of much disagreement. How complex this issue can be is apparent from the background to the 1999 forceful action by NATO in Kosovo. The Independent Commission for Kosovo investigated the question of whether the goal of protecting the Kosovars could have been achieved by peaceful means and the use of force avoided.[217] After considering the complex and confusing diplomatic background to the situation, the

[214] See National Security Strategy of the United States of America, note 39 above.

[215] See e.g. Chinkin, 'Kosovo: A "Good" or "Bad" War?', pp. 844–5; Charney, 'Anticipatory Humanitarian Intervention in Kosovo', p. 839; Cassese, '*Ex Iniuria Ius Oritur*: Are We Moving Towards International Legitimation of Forcible Humanitarian Countermeasures in the World Community?', p. 27.

[216] See Chesterman, *Just War or Just Peace?*, pp. 228–9 (outlining the common factors (including proportionality) identified by commentators for determining the legitimacy of humanitarian intervention).

[217] The Independent International Commission on Kosovo, *Kosovo Report: Conflict, International Response, Lessons Learned* (Oxford University Press, Oxford, 2000), pp. 131–61; and see Falk, 'Kosovo, World Order and the Future of International Law', pp. 850–1 (assessing the opposing arguments as to whether all non-forceful means had been exhausted prior to the use of force by NATO).

Commission was unable to reach any firm conclusions on this point.[218] Other observers have not been so reticent in their assessment.[219]

States, moreover, have not asserted that any means are warranted in forceful intervention to address human rights abuses and accept that any such action must be measured against the aim of bringing the infringements to an end.[220] However, as is often the case with proportionality in other contexts, the actual practice of States in such situations almost always transcends the limits of a proportionate response whatever the justification advanced for the forceful intervention.[221] In the case of the 1999 NATO action in Kosovo, there were several aspects of this campaign that attracted criticism based on a perception of a lack of proportion between the ends and the methods used to achieve them.[222] In particular, the choice of a campaign of aerial bombardment rather than one involving ground forces was seen as particularly problematic.[223] When an action purports to be legitimate on the basis of the need to bring an end to human rights violations, any level of civilian deaths or damage to civilian objects appears incongruous and will be difficult to justify. This dilemma is exemplified in the assessment by one observer that the action in Kosovo was necessary but 'impossible'.[224]

[218] The Independent International Commission on Kosovo, *Kosovo Report: Conflict, International Response, Lessons Learned*, pp. 158–9. The Commission, however, did query the compatibility of the use of unlawful strategies such as the threat to use force with ensuring the settlement of the dispute by peaceful means.

[219] Cf. e.g. Falk, 'Kosovo, World Order and the Future of International Law', p. 855; and M. Reisman, 'Kosovo's Antinomies' (1999) 93 *AJIL* 860.

[220] See L. Henkin, 'The Use of Force: Law and US Policy' in L. Henkin *et al.*, *Right v Might: International Law and the Use of Force* (Council on Foreign Affairs, New York, 1989), p. 37 at pp. 41–2.

[221] See Chesterman, *Just War or Just Peace?*, pp. 65–84 (for a comprehensive analysis of the forceful actions that are variously cited by commentators as examples of humanitarian intervention (although not necessarily claimed as such by States)). Almost all appear disproportionate. E.g., Tanzania's intervention in Uganda in 1978–9 was problematic given the length of time that Tanzanian troops remained in Uganda. The same difficulty was posed by Vietnam's invasion of Kampuchea (Cambodia) in 1978–9. The invasion of the State, the overthrow of the regime and the installation of a communist government, supported by the continued presence of Vietnamese troops, was widely condemned as going beyond what was justified to bring an end to the human rights abuses.

[222] See the discussion of the legitimacy of the Kosovo campaign in terms of the requirements of IHL, Chapter 4 above.

[223] See Chinkin, 'Kosovo: A "Good" or "Bad" War?', p. 844.

[224] See Falk, 'Kosovo, World Order and the Future of International Law', pp. 852; and see further *ibid.*, pp. 855–6.

There is an underlying theme to the debate over humanitarian intervention that is reminiscent of that conducted in the context of pre-emptive self-defence. That is, that in light of the dubious legality of such actions, their necessity and proportionality must be established beyond doubt by demonstrating that every possible alternative has been exhaustively pursued and that the forceful response was in no manner excessive.[225]

Conclusion

At the beginning of the twenty-first century, necessity and proportionality are firmly established as integral components of the law in relation to the unilateral resort to force by States. Despite the equivocal legal basis of many of the conflicts that have characterised the international community since the adoption of the United Nations Charter, State practice and *opinio juris* is consistent with the view that the use of force in international relations, irrespective of its alleged legal basis, must be both necessary and proportionate. As for the former requirement, the idea of force as an absolute last resort when all other peaceful means are of no avail theoretically poses few problems. The differences in its application primarily relate to when all peaceful means have been in fact exhausted. The norm, however, in the main does operate within that degree of uncertainty so as to constitute a real restraint on the resort to force by States. Proportionality, in contrast, to date lacks the precision required in a legal norm. This lack of clarity undermines its ability to function as a mechanism for limiting the impact of armed force. Much of the confusion that surrounds its application would be eliminated by a more considered approach by States to articulating carefully the aim of their proposed forceful actions. The process of focusing attention on the aim of any use of force may also have the side effect of narrowing the scope of any subsequent use of force.

Once the aim of a forceful action is clearly identified, to some extent the limits on the means become apparent. For example, if the aim is to bring an end to human rights contraventions, then the means and methods selected to achieve this end should not involve shifting the

[225] This phenomenon is illustrated by the conditions precedent to the use of force on humanitarian grounds developed by commentators: see e.g. Falk, 'Kosovo, World Order and the Future of International Law', p. 856; and Cassese, '*Ex Iniuria Ius Oritur*: Are We Moving Towards International Legitimation of Forcible Humanitarian Countermeasures in the World Community?', p. 27.

burden of suffering to the civilian population of the perpetrator State. States must recognise that there is a price to be paid in terms of their own combatants' lives for such undertakings. What that price consists of can be determined by a good faith application of proportionality in *ius ad bellum* (as well as in IHL). If this approach is taken, States contemplating unilateral intervention on such grounds may be more inclined to actively pursue alternative means of solving the situation.

The potential of necessity and proportionality to restrain unnecessary and excessive force should not be underestimated, particularly during times when the legal regime regulating the situations in which States can resort to force is under strain. The more dubious the arguments validating the use of force in the first place, arguably the more stringent the requirements of necessity and proportionality become. This phenomenon is increasingly evident in the writings of commentators. However, to a considerable degree, proportionality remains a rhetorical tool in the hands of States that they rely on either to justify their forceful actions or to condemn those of other States. Consequently, although there is belated acknowledgment in some quarters of the potential of proportionality in *ius ad bellum* to contribute significantly to limiting the destructive impact of armed conflict for all victims, its detailed application in the practice of States awaits further development.

6 Necessity, proportionality and the United Nations system: collective actions involving the use of force

Introduction

The dispute settlement powers of the Security Council are located in Chapters VI and VII of the United Nations Charter. Chapter VII deals with non-pacific means of resolving international disputes. Article 39 sets out the jurisdiction of the Council in such matters. If the Council determines that a threat to the peace, breach of the peace, or act of aggression exists, it must take measures to restore international peace and security. To achieve this aim, the Council has available to it non-forceful measures under Article 41 and forceful measures under Article 42. These provisions are frequently referred to collectively as the enforcement powers of the Security Council.[1] This chapter addresses the relevance of the principles of necessity and proportionality to collective actions involving the use of force. This issue is considered in the context of both *ius ad bellum* and IHL.

In relation to *ius ad bellum*, the previous chapter concluded that necessity and proportionality are well-established components of the regime governing the legitimate unilateral resort to force by States under the Charter, although allowance has to be made for considerable differences of view as to their correct application. What is unclear is to what extent necessity and proportionality can be regarded also as applicable to collective military enforcement actions and, if so, how they are to be assessed.

The requirement that the Council consider whether the use of military force is warranted is specifically articulated in the Charter. If the Council determines, pursuant to Article 39, the existence of a threat to the peace, breach of the peace or act of aggression, it may adopt forceful measures under Article 42 to maintain and restore international peace

[1] See Art. 2(7) of the United Nations Charter 1945.

and security but not before it has satisfied itself that any non-forceful measures have been or would be ineffective.[2] In relation to necessity, therefore, the question becomes not so much whether Chapter VII forceful actions must be necessary – the Charter determines that question in the affirmative – but rather whether the terms of the Charter are seen as acting as a limit on the powers of the Council in the sense that a failure to comply with this requirement has a legal dimension.[3] Moreover, apart from the specific requirement in Article 42, it can be argued that necessity is a principle of general international law that all force shall be by way of last resort. Can the requirement of necessity in this latter sense be superimposed on the Charter regime and the decisions of the Council in the exercise of its Chapter VII powers?

The constraints of proportionality are also recognised in the words of Article 42 of the United Nations Charter in that 'the Council may only take such [forceful] action . . . as may be necessary to maintain or restore international peace and security'. The reference to 'necessary' in this context carries with it an understanding that the measures adopted will be proportionate to that aim.[4] Once again, whether this phrase can be seen as imposing a constraint other than of a political nature on the Council depends on the broader inquiry as to the relationship between the Council and, as one observer puts it, the rule of law.[5]

What was once a largely theoretical issue, that is, constraints on the exercise of the military enforcement powers of the Security Council, is nowadays of considerable practical importance with the practice that developed in the 1990s of the Council authorising States to use force under Chapter VII of the Charter.[6] The legal regime governing the use

[2] Such an analysis assumes that military enforcement actions are seen as sourced in Art. 42. It is, however, difficult to imagine that the situations in which the Security Council can 'authorise' States to use force are wider than its powers to take action itself under Art. 42. See the further discussion in note 27 and the accompanying text below.

[3] The issue of necessity in this sense attracted considerable comment in the Persian Gulf conflict (1990–1). See e.g. J. Quigley, 'The United States and the United Nations in the Persian Gulf War: New Order or Disorder' (1992) 25 *Cornell ILJ* 1 (arguing that the Council's failure to comply with the procedural requirements of Art. 42 in passing SC Res. 678, 29 November 1990, was unlawful).

[4] See B. Simma (ed.), *The Charter of the United Nations: A Commentary* (Oxford University Press, Oxford, 1994), p. 631.

[5] I. Brownlie, *The Rule of Law in International Affairs* (Martinus Nijhoff, Dordrecht, 1998), pp. 211–28 (discussing the role of the Security Council and the rule of law).

[6] For a description of these initiatives, see D. Sarooshi, *The United Nations and the Development of Collective Security: The Delegation by the UN Security Council of Its Chapter VII Powers* (Clarendon Press, Oxford, 1999), pp. 168–246; see also SC Res. 1244, 10 June 1999

of force by States in such circumstances remains in the process of evolution.[7] The compatibility of the practice of authorisation with the Charter system, although originally controversial, is now widely accepted.[8] However, the details of the legal framework remain elusive. Considerable work remains to be undertaken. In particular, the clarification of the applicable primary rules, including the extent to which actions of these forces are governed by the requirements of necessity and proportionality, is critical for the determination of questions of responsibility. This chapter undertakes the task of determining the relevance of these traditional restraints, previously manifested in the context of the unilateral use of force, to the collective security system.[9]

In discussing the question of limitations on military enforcement actions under Chapter VII of the Charter, it is necessary to bear in mind the distinction between restraints derived from the terms of the particular mandate conferred on the force concerned and those derived from the Charter system itself that restrain the Security Council in terms of the mandate it may confer. An example of a mandate that sets specific

(establishing KFOR, an international security force under NATO command to work in conjunction with UNMIK, the 'international civil presence' in Kosovo. KFOR is authorised under Chapter VII to use the necessary means to carry out its mandate); SC Res. 1264, 15 September 1999 (establishing INTERFET, a multinational force under a unified command structure to restore international peace and security in East Timor; the force is authorised under Chapter VII to take all necessary measures to fulfil its mandate); and SC Res. 1386, 20 December 2001 (establishing the International Security Assistance Force for East Timor, authorised under Chapter VII to take all necessary measures to fulfil its mandate).

[7] Increasingly, commentators are focusing on the unresolved legal questions that are raised by these activities. See e.g. Sarooshi, *Development of Collective Security*; N. Blokker, 'Is the Authorization Authorized? Powers and Practice of the UN Security Council to Authorize the Use of Force by "Coalitions of the Able and Willing"' (2000) 11 *EJIL* 541; and T. D. Gill, 'Legal and Some Political Limitations on the Power of the UN Security Council to Exercise Its Enforcement Powers Under Chapter VII of the Charter' (1995) 26 *NYIL* 33 at 72–90.

[8] See the further discussion of this issue in note 27 and the accompanying text below.

[9] Other constraints that are the most widely regarded as applicable to the exercise of Chapter VII enforcement powers are those derived from norms of *jus cogens* and those that protect fundamental humanitarian values. See e.g. Gill, 'Enforcement Powers Under Chapter VII', pp. 72–90 (identifying the duty to respect human rights, IHL, the right of self-determination and the territorial integrity of States as limitations on the military enforcement powers of the Council); and W. M. Reisman and D. Stevick, 'The Applicability of International Law Standards to United Nations Economic Sanctions Programmes' (1998) 9 *EJIL* 86 at 129. Cf. B. Martenczuk, 'The Security Council, the International Court and Judicial Review: What Lessons from Lockerbie?' (1999) 10 *EJIL* 517 (arguing that the only justiciable restraints on the Council are those derived from Art. 39 of the Charter).

limits as to proportionality on the States concerned is Resolution 816 of 31 March 1993, authorising '[m]ember States . . . to take all necessary measures in the airspace of Bosnia and Herzegovina . . . to ensure compliance with the ban on flights' that are 'proportionate to the specific circumstances and nature of the flights'.[10] It is, however, the second, more general query, the inherent limits of the powers of the Council, that is addressed in this chapter. The terms of the mandate are merely one method by which the Council can implement any obligations of restraint to which it may itself be subject.

With respect to IHL, the issue of what rules are applicable to forces exercising the military enforcement powers of the Security Council is in one respect more straightforward. There is a body of existing customary rules independent of the Charter system that is readily applicable to such Chapter VII operations. Moreover, it is arguable that the United Nations could become bound by the relevant conventional instruments.[11] Nevertheless, the relationship between IHL and the organs of the United Nations has already given rise to some difficult legal problems in the context of traditional peacekeeping operations of the United Nations.[12] The provisions of the Charter do not specifically provide for these forces. Their compatibility with its provisions, however, was confirmed by the International Court of Justice in the *Certain Expenses*

[10] See I. Brownlie, *International Law and the Use of Force by States* (Clarendon Press, Oxford, 1963), pp. 334–5, note 1 (referring to the 1960s action in the Congo, where forces were alleged to have acted *ultra vires* a valid Security Council resolution); and Quigley, 'New Order or Disorder' (arguing that the coalition allies in the Persian Gulf conflict exceeded the mandate conferred by SC Res. 678). See also J. Lobel and M. Ratner, 'Bypassing the Security Council: Ambiguous Authorizations to Use Force, Cease Fires and the Iraqi Inspection Regime' (1999) 93 *AJIL* 124 (critically analysing the practice of the Council in recent years of providing States with open-ended authorisations to use force).

[11] See the further discussion of this issue in note 111 and the accompanying text below.

[12] See R. Higgins, *United Nations Peacekeeping 1946–1967: Commentary and Documents*, vol. I, *The Middle East* (Oxford University Press, Oxford, 1969), p. ix (for the various meanings in which the term 'peacekeeping' is used); and see also M. Goulding, 'The Evolution of United Nations Peacekeeping' (1993) 69 *International Affairs* 451 at 452–5 (for a description of the distinguishing characteristics of peacekeeping operations prior to the end of the Cold War). For a comprehensive discussion of the situation in relation to IHL and United Nations forces up to the 1960s, see F. Seyersted, *United Nations Forces in the Law of Peace and War* (Sijthoff, Leiden, 1966); and for a modern account, see Shraga and Zacklin, 'The Applicability of International Humanitarian Law to United Nations Peace-keeping Operations: Conceptual, Legal and Practical Issues' in U. Palwankar (ed.), *International Committee of the Red Cross Symposium on Peace-Keeping Operations* (1994), p. 40.

Case.[13] The Court was of the view that the organisation was constitutionally empowered to establish peacekeeping operations under the control and command of the United Nations. However, the extent to which the relevant parties in peacekeeping operations are subject to the requirements of IHL is an area of legal uncertainty that has never been satisfactorily resolved. Despite this uncertainty, traditional peacekeeping activities posed limited problems for IHL, as the use of force in such operations has been restricted to a very limited concept of self-defence: 'The force will be provided with weapons of a defensive character . . . Self-defence would include resistance to attempts by forceful means to prevent it from discharging its duties under the mandate of the Security Council.'[14] Therefore, as Bowett observes, although a peacekeeping force may be armed and may become involved in fighting, its main function is not the use of military force to maintain or restore international peace and security.[15] Moreover, generally speaking, there is no situation amounting to a state of armed conflict between the United Nations peacekeeping forces and the other parties involved, so the application of IHL for many years did not constitute a major issue.[16]

The need to resolve the issue of IHL and United Nations forces, however, became more pressing with the development of 'peace

[13] *Certain Expenses of the United Nations (Art. 17, Para. 2 of the Charter)*, ICJ Reports 1962, 151 at 167. See D. Bowett, *United Nations Forces: A Legal Study* (Stevens and Sons, London, 1964), pp. 266–311 (for a comprehensive coverage of the constitutionality of forces exercising peacekeeping and enforcement roles) and pp. 484–92 (for discussion of the legal position in relation to IHL and peacekeeping forces); and see Seyersted, *Law of Peace and War.*

[14] Report of the Secretary-General on the Setting Up of (UNIFIL) United Nations Interim Force in Lebanon, UN Doc. S/12611 (1978), p. 2. For a full statement of the meaning of self-defence in the context of peacekeeping forces, see Aide Mémoire dated 10 April 1964 Concerning Some Questions Relating to the Function and Operation of the United Nations Peace-Keeping Force in Cyprus, reprinted in R. Higgins, *United Nations Peacekeeping: Documents and Commentary*, vol. IV, *Europe 1946–1979* (Oxford University Press, Oxford, 1981), pp. 151–2.

[15] Bowett, *United Nations Forces*, p. 268.

[16] Consequently, until the 1990s there were no legal rules protecting peacekeepers from activities of the warring factions, a problem that became more acute in peacekeeping operations such as Somalia. For this reason, the General Assembly adopted the Convention on the Safety of United Nations and Associated Personnel, UNGA Res. 49/59, UNGAOR, 49th Sess., Agenda Item 141, UN Doc. A/Res/49/59 (1994), reprinted in (1995) 34 ILM 482. The Convention imposes obligations on individuals in relation to the protection of persons coming within its scope, the breach of which entails criminal responsibility. See C. Greenwood, 'Protection of Peacekeepers: The Legal Regime' (1995) 7 *Duke Journal of Comparative and International Law* 185 (for a discussion of the current legal regime for the protection of peacekeepers).

enforcement' operations that involve the exercise of the military enforcement powers of the Security Council.[17] These operations are not necessarily based on consent and pre-suppose the use of some degree of force, and a situation amounting to armed conflict would be envisaged in these actions. In contrast to peacekeeping, therefore, the use of force plays a much more comprehensive role in peace enforcement operations increasing the relevance of such rules of IHL as proportionality and the restrictions on legitimate weapons.

The fact that IHL is an independent body of rules outside the Charter, therefore, has facilitated a resolution in favour of its applicability to the use of the military enforcement powers of the Security Council. It is evident that, apart from some initial doubts, the restraints of IHL are perceived as compatible with the Council's role in facilitating the restoration of international peace and security, whereas the requirements of conformity with other general legal restraints derived from pre-existing *ius ad bellum* have not been so readily accepted as appropriate to the Council's activities.

With this background it will become apparent why the structure of this chapter differs somewhat from the previous chapter dealing with the unilateral resort to force by States. Moreover, much of the discussion tends to be of a theoretical nature. In dealing with unilateral forceful action by States there was never any real question that the legal limits of necessity and proportionality in both *ius ad bellum* and IHL were applicable to such actions. The primary task was to ascertain their content and detailed operation. There is also a considerable amount of State practice that can be assessed in order to arrive at a detailed picture of these norms. This, however, is not the case with the relatively recent phenomenon of collective military enforcement action. Consequently, the focus of the following discussion is the general scheme of the Charter in order to determine the extent to which the Council operates within a legal setting and, if so, whether an argument can be sustained that the requirements of necessity and proportionality in the exercise of the Chapter VII military enforcement powers are a component of this framework. The same process is undertaken in the context of IHL.

The discussion also includes a consideration of how these requirements might operate in practice. As far as the *ius ad bellum*

[17] Peace enforcement operations have been defined by the then Secretary-General of the United Nations as 'peace-keeping activities that do not necessarily involve the consent of the parties concerned': Boutros Boutros-Ghali, *An Agenda for Peace* (2nd edn, United Nations, New York, 1995), p. 12.

proportionality equation is concerned, this requires an assessment of the legitimate aim of collective enforcement actions. Once having identified the aim of such an undertaking, the analysis of what means are proportionate to achieving the aims can be largely extrapolated from the discussion in Chapter 3.

Before discussing these issues in detail, in light of the complexity of the topic of the legal regime governing military operations of the United Nations, the situations contemplated by this term are considered. The chapter concludes with a brief examination of the issues of responsibility that are part of the legal framework of the exercise of Chapter VII military enforcement powers.

Collective actions involving the use of force

From the Charter scheme it would appear to be readily apparent whether a particular use of force constitutes a Security Council military enforcement action under Chapter VII. This, however, has not proved to be the case. It was contemplated by the drafters of the Charter that the Security Council would take enforcement action under Article 42 using forces supplied under the agreements provided for by Article 43. The extent to which the Security Council is subject to the requirements of necessity and proportionality would be directly raised if a permanent military force were established under Article 43 of the Charter. This system, however, never eventuated due to the failure of States to implement Article 43 and provide the Security Council with a permanent standing force to carry out its mandate to maintain international peace and security.[18] In fact, for many years after the adoption of the Charter, it was the meaning of peacekeeping and its constitutionality that was of more significance than the Chapter VII military enforcement powers of the Council.

The absence of Article 43 forces has led to a number of developments in relation to the collective use of force under the Charter that are difficult to reconcile with its express terms. In 1968, Bowett argued that 'the only unequivocal United Nations enforcement action' was the 1950–3 Korean conflict, although he refers to the doubts as to whether this could be correctly designated as an action by a 'United Nations Force'.[19] Many

[18] For the background to this failure, see T. Franck, *Fairness in International Law and Institutions* (Oxford University Press, Oxford, 1995), p. 298.

[19] Bowett, *United Nations Forces*, p. 267. For a description of the events surrounding the Korean War, see H. Kelsen, *Recent Trends in the Law of the United Nations* (Stevens and

commentators share Bowett's view that the use of force in the Korean conflict was a United Nations enforcement action in pursuance of a recommendation by the Security Council under Article 39.[20] Writers such as Kelsen and Stone in contrast regard it as an action in collective self-defence, as in their view the only United Nations military enforcement action contemplated by the Charter is by way of decision under Article 42. Consequently, for them, recommendations under Article 39 are restricted to measures for the peaceful settlement of disputes.[21] Moreover, military enforcement action by the United Nations was dependent on the implementation of Article 43 agreements.[22]

For many years after the Korean conflict, the military enforcement powers of the Security Council were in abeyance. The practice of peacekeeping continued to develop and to some extent the Article 41 powers of the Council contributed to the maintenance of international peace and security through the imposition of sanctions on recalcitrant States.[23] The question of proportionality, nevertheless, was of some relevance during this period. It was accepted that United Nations forces established under Chapter VI of the Charter were entitled to use force in self-defence and in order to carry out their mandate.[24] It became the practice that such force be exercised in a proportionate manner.[25] Otherwise, the focus of attention in relation to the use of force during these years was on

Sons, London, 1951), pp. 927–49; Bowett, *United Nations Forces*, pp. 29–60; R. Higgins, *United Nations Peacekeeping 1946–1967: Documents and Commentary*, vol. II, *Asia* (Oxford University Press, Oxford, 1970), pp. 153–312.

[20] See e.g. Bowett, *United Nations Forces*, p. 32; Seyersted, *Law of Peace and War*, p. 33; and O. Schachter, 'Authorized Uses of Force by the United Nations and Regional Organizations' in L. Damrosch and D. Scheffer (eds.), *Law and Force in the New International Order* (Westview, Boulder, 1991), p. 65.

[21] See Kelsen, *Recent Trends*, pp. 936–7; and J. Stone, *Legal Controls of International Conflict* (Maitland, Sydney, 1954), p. 232.

[22] Stone, *Legal Controls*, p. 233; and see Bowett, *United Nations Forces*, pp. 276–7. The *Certain Expenses* Advisory Opinion is of little assistance on this point as it deals with the constitutionality of peacekeeping as opposed to enforcement action. The Court did not, however, include in its definition of enforcement action the requirement that it be by way of decision, thus leaving open the question of the ability of the Security Council to recommend enforcement action under Art. 39.

[23] See generally V. Gowlland-Debbas, *Collective Responses to Illegal Acts in International Law: United Nations Action in the Question of Southern Rhodesia* (Martinus Nijhoff, Dordrecht, 1990).

[24] See the sources cited in note 14 above.

[25] See e.g. Aide-Mémoire of the Secretary-General Relating to the Function and Operation of the United Nations Peacekeeping Force in Cyprus, UN Doc. S/5653, 11 April 1964, paras. 16–18; and see G. J. F. van Hegelsom, 'The Law of Armed Conflict and UN Peacekeeping and Peace-Enforcing Operations' (1993) 6 *Hague YIL* 44 at 54 (for a

unilateral rather than collective action, the right of States to use force in self-defence. Complex legal arguments were developed by States to bring their forceful actions within the ambit of this concept.[26]

All this changed with the end of the Cold War era. The dormant Chapter VII powers were revived by a reinvigorated Security Council. The Council, however, has not followed the precedent of the Korean conflict of 'recommending action' by States. Instead, the language of 'authorisation' has been used. The relevant resolutions, moreover, although not specifying the Article under which they are adopted, all state that the Security Council is acting under Chapter VII of the Charter.[27] Originally, States and commentators expressed considerable misgivings about this practice.[28] Nowadays, however, it is relatively undisputed that the Charter supports the exercise of Chapter VII military enforcement powers without reliance on Article 43 forces, and that various arrangements using national forces are consistent with Article 42.[29] The legal analyses supporting these activities vary. These range from theories that rely specifically on the terms of the Charter, particularly Article 42,[30] to those that base the validity of such undertakings on the exercise of implied powers.[31] There is agreement, however, that the Security Council

discussion of the application of proportionality in the case of self-defence by peacekeepers).

[26] See the discussion in Chapter 5 above.

[27] See the sources cited in note 6 above for the relevant resolutions.

[28] See the discussion of the views of States on the practice of authorisation in Blokker, 'Is the Authorization Authorized?', pp. 555–60; and see Sarooshi, *Development of Collective Security*, pp. 167–246 (for a comprehensive discussion of the practice of authorisation up to 1996).

[29] Indeed, this had been the view expressed by some commentators early on in the history of the Charter: see e.g. L. Goodrich and A. Simons, *The Charter of the United Nations: Commentary and Documents* (2nd edn, World Peace Foundation, Boston, MA, 1949), p. 281. See also R. Higgins, *Problems and Process: International Law and How We Use It* (Oxford University Press, Oxford, 1994), p. 265; and O. Schachter, 'United Nations Law in the Gulf Conflict' (1991) 85 *AJIL* 452 at 463–4. Note, however, the concerns expressed as to the wide-ranging nature of the authorisations and the lack of Council control of these undertakings: see e.g. Lobel and Ratner, 'Bypassing the Security Council'; and F. L. Kirgis Jr, 'The Security Council's First Fifty Years' (1995) 89 *AJIL* 506 at 522 (arguing that the Council should demonstrate that the requirements of necessity in Art. 42 have been met).

[30] See e.g. Higgins, *United Nations Peacekeeping*, vol. II, p. 176; and C. Greenwood, 'New World Order or Old? The Invasion of Kuwait and the Rule of Law' (1992) 55 *MLR* 153 at 168.

[31] The approach to implied powers also varies between commentators. See e.g. Kirgis, 'First Fifty Years', p. 52 (arguing on the basis of the *Reparations* and *Certain Expenses* Advisory Opinions that the practice of authorisation is consistent with the view that

can only require (as opposed to authorise) States to take forceful action through the permanent military forces contemplated by this Article.[32] Moreover, whatever the legal framework of the practice of authorisation, it is relatively uncontroversial that the Council cannot confer on States (or for that matter on any permanent military force) more power than it possesses itself.[33]

To add to the difficulties in determining the legal regime applicable to all these activities, the distinction between peacekeeping and so-called 'peace enforcement' has been almost impossible to maintain. Although the peacekeeping operation in the Congo in the 1960s involved a considerable degree of force to end the secession of Katanga, generally speaking the use of force has not been an issue in relation to these activities.[34] However, this is no longer the situation, and forces acting under the control and command of the United Nations are increasingly being authorised to use significantly more force than previously was the case.[35]

an organisation can exercise the powers necessary for it to carry out its responsibilities); Sarooshi, *Development of Collective Security* (developing a theory of legitimate delegation implied from the terms of the Charter to supply the legal framework for the practice of the Council of conferring its Chapter VII military enforcement powers on UN subsidiary organs and States and through regional arrangements). See also Blokker, 'Is the Authorization Authorized?'. All these commentators, however, place considerable restrictions on the exercise of implied powers: see e.g. Sarooshi, *Development of Collective Security*, pp. 32–46.

[32] See L. Goodrich and A. Simons, *The United Nations and the Maintenance of International Peace and Security* (Greenwood, Westport, CT, 1974); and Higgins, *United Nations Peacekeeping*, vol. II, pp. 175–7. This is also true of peacekeeping forces: see R. Higgins, 'A General Assessment of UN Peacekeeping' in A. Cassese (ed.), *United Nations Peacekeeping: Legal Essays* (Sijthoff & Noordhoof, Alphen aan den Rijn, 1978), p. 1 at pp. 3–4.

[33] E.g., if the approach of delegated powers is relied on as justifying the practice of authorisation, this limitation derives from the general principle that a delegator cannot delegate powers that it does not itself possess: see Sarooshi, *Development of Collective Security*, pp. 42–4.

[34] See E. M. Miller, 'Legal Aspects of the United Nations Action in the Congo' (1961) 55 *AJIL* 1 (for an account of the UN action in the Congo).

[35] For example, the mandate of UNOSOM II in Somalia and UNPROFOR in Bosnia-Herzegovina included the specific authorisation to use force. See SC Res. 794, 3 December 1992, authorising the 'Secretary-General and Member States cooperating . . . to conduct the operation using all necessary means to establish as soon as possible a secure environment for humanitarian relief operations in Somalia'; and SC Res. 770, 13 August 1992, and SC Res. 776, 14 September 1992, in relation to Bosnia-Herzegovina. See also generally R. Higgins, 'The New United Nations and Former Yugoslavia' (1993) 69 *International Affairs* 465; and W. M. Reisman, 'Preparing to Wage Peace: Toward the Creation of an International Peacemaking Command and Staff College' (1994) 88 *AJIL* 76. For a description of the categories of peacekeeping current as of 2000, some of which involve the use of significant amounts of force, see C. Gray, *International Law and the Use of Force* (Oxford University Press, Oxford, 2000), pp. 158–83.

The post-Cold War innovations in the context of the Chapter VII powers of the Council commenced with Resolution 678 of 29 November 1990 authorising 'Member States cooperating with the Government of Kuwait . . . to use all necessary means to . . . restore international peace and security in the area'. This resolution is not, however, a particularly useful precedent as there is real doubt as to the legal basis of the forceful actions in that conflict.[36] On the one hand, it is arguable that the coalition allies were exercising the right of collective self-defence and that Resolution 678 merely confirmed its continued existence.[37] On the other hand, there is support for the view that the actions of the coalition allies were a collective enforcement action.[38] The specific reference in several of the Council resolutions to the right of collective self-defence, on this view, is not necessarily determinative.[39]

None of the subsequent 'authorisations' by the Council for States to resort to the use of 'all necessary means' (assumed to encompass the use of force) have raised questions as to the possibility of the forceful action being by way of self-defence. They have ranged from the attempts to ensure the provision of humanitarian assistance in Somalia[40] and Rwanda[41] to the restoration of democracy in Haiti.[42] Moreover, the Council has in some cases conferred Chapter VII powers on forces operating under United Nations command and control, as for example to enable UNPROFOR to protect the safe areas in the former Yugoslavia.[43]

[36] Greenwood writes that SC Res. 678 appears to have been deliberately ambiguous perhaps to make it more acceptable to China or to resist any suggestion that the forces should be under United Nations command. See Greenwood, 'Invasion of Kuwait', p. 169.

[37] See e.g. Schachter, 'Gulf Conflict'; and E. V. Rostow, 'Until What? Enforcement Action or Collective Self-Defense?' (1991) 85 *AJIL* 506.

[38] See e.g. Greenwood, 'Invasion of Kuwait', pp. 167–9; and see Higgins, *Problems and Process*, pp. 260–2.

[39] For the full text of the twelve resolutions passed by the Security Council in relation to the Gulf crisis prior to the commencement of hostilities, see E. Lauterpacht *et al.* (eds.), *The Kuwait Crisis: Basic Documents* Cambridge International Documents Series, vol. I (Grotius, Cambridge, 1991), pp. 88–98.

[40] See note 35 above.

[41] See SC Res. 929, 2 June 1994, authorising the member States cooperating with the Secretary General to 'use all necessary means to achieve the humanitarian objectives' set out in the resolution.

[42] See SC Res. 940, 31 July 1994, authorising 'Member States to form a multinational force under unified command and control . . . and to use all necessary means to facilitate the departure from Haiti of the military leadership . . . and the restoration of the legitimate authorities of the Government of Haiti, and to establish and maintain a secure and stable environment'.

[43] See, *inter alia*, SC Res. 836, 4 June 1993, authorising 'UNPROFOR . . . acting in self-defence, to take the necessary measures, including the use of force, in reply to

The appropriate categorisation of United Nations military operations involving the use of force is thus a far from straightforward task and one which may well depend on the purpose of such classification.[44] The terminology adopted by commentators in this area, moreover, can be confusing to the general reader. The phrase 'United Nations forces' usually refers to forces acting under the control and command of the United Nations, whereas 'military operations of the United Nations' and 'United Nations enforcement action' are broader terms that would, generally speaking, encompass not only forces under United Nations control and command but also forces that remain under national command although exercising the Chapter VII enforcement powers of the Security Council.

It is not necessary for this work to exhaustively distinguish between the types of responses adopted by the Security Council to fulfil its mandate of maintaining international peace and security, or to assess the increasingly blurred distinction between traditional peacekeeping and the activities based on the enforcement powers of the Security Council. The emphasis in the present context is not so much on what these forces are called but what they do. If their mandate relies on the military enforcement powers of the Security Council under Chapter VII of the Charter, the questions arise, first, of whether their actions must be both necessary and proportionate to their aim and, secondly, of whether the prohibition on disproportionate casualties and prohibited means and methods of warfare in IHL must be respected. These are the issues considered below.

Ius ad bellum of enforcement actions

In contrast to *ius in bello*, the only current source of *ius ad bellum* is the Charter itself. Under its provisions, the use of force is restricted to self-defence under Article 51 and collective enforcement action under Chapter VII.[45] The Charter does incorporate to a limited extent pre-existing

bombardments against the safe areas by any of the parties or to armed incursion into them'.

[44] See C. Greenwood, 'International Humanitarian Law and United Nations Military Operations' (1998) 1 *Yearbook of International Humanitarian Law* 3 at 12 (distinguishing between the various types of United Nations operations according to (i) the extent to which they are envisaged as being involved in hostilities and (ii) whether they operate under United Nations or national command and control).

[45] There is State practice supporting the view that the use of force to prevent widespread violations of human rights is consistent with the Charter scheme; see the discussion in Chapter 5 above.

ius ad bellum.[46] The reference to the 'inherent' right of self-defence in Article 51 is regarded as incorporating the customary principles relevant to its exercise, such as proportionality and necessity.[47] Aside from the case of self-defence, however, the Charter represents the totality of the law on the use of force. What, therefore, conditions the use of force to restore international peace and security including that of States acting under Security Council authorisation?[48]

The Security Council is empowered under the Charter to make decisions involving the use of force only when there has been a 'threat to the peace, breach of the peace, or act of aggression' within the meaning of Article 39. In all other situations, the use of force, irrespective of its benefits, is outside the province of the Security Council.[49] The drafters of the Charter, therefore, determined the parameters of legitimate Security Council military enforcement action as a response to a threat to the peace, breach of the peace or act of aggression. As is the case with self-defence in the case of an armed attack, a forceful response does not follow automatically upon the finding of such an event.[50] The Charter deals specifically with the question of when resort to the collective use of force can be regarded as necessary. There is, therefore, no suggestion of superimposing on its terms the requirements of general international law based on the *Caroline Incident*.[51] In the words of Article 42, the Council can resort to military force if it considers that 'the measures provided for in Article 41 would be inadequate or have proved to be inadequate'.

[46] See *Case Concerning Military and Paramilitary Activities in and against Nicaragua (Nicaragua v. United States)*, Merits, ICJ Reports 1986, 14 (hereafter *Nicaragua Case*), paras. 176 and 193, but note the view of the Court that the present content of the customary right of self-defence was as 'confirmed and influenced by the Charter'. See the further discussion of necessity and proportionality as components of a legitimate exercise of self-defence in Chapter 5 above.

[47] See *ibid.*, paras. 176 and 194.

[48] Whether States acting under the authority of the Council must take into account considerations of necessity and proportionality in carrying out their mandate depends on whether the Council itself is subject to such restraints, as these will apply to States acting under its authorisation. E.g., if the legal basis of the practice of 'authorisation' of the use of force by member States is a delegation of its Chapter VII powers by the Security Council, certain consequences follow. One of these is that the general rule that a delegator cannot delegate a power that it does not itself possess applies equally to the actions of international organisations such as the United Nations.

[49] For a discussion of the interpretation of the ambit of this phrase by the Council, see Franck, *Fairness in International Law*, pp. 222–42.

[50] See the discussion in Chapter 5 above.

[51] For a discussion of the *Caroline Incident*, see Chapter 2, note 62, and the accompanying text above.

Standing alone, Article 42 does not require the consideration of all peaceful alternatives as a prerequisite to the resort to non-pacific means by the Council. It is only the efficacy of the measures under Article 41 that fall into this category. However, it is not appropriate to regard Article 42 in isolation from the remainder of the Charter. The concept of necessity in the use of military force under Article 42 operates within a distinctive broader framework. It is a basic tenet of the Charter scheme that the use of force is a last resort after all peaceful means have failed. A number of provisions of the Charter establish procedures designed to forestall the use of force, and it is anticipated that proper resort to such procedures will precede Chapter VII action.[52] The question remains, however, whether such limitations on the Council's military enforcement powers should be perceived as either primarily within the unfettered discretion of the Council or, alternatively, as having a legal dimension.

In the context of proportionality, as we have seen, the only collective actions involving the use of force contemplated under Chapter VII of the Charter are those taken to maintain or restore international peace and security under Article 42 in the face of a threat to the peace, breach of the peace or act of aggression. Article 42 requires that the Council only resort to measures necessary to maintain or restore international peace and security. Articles 39 and 42 read together, therefore, constitute the yardstick for determining the application of proportionality. These two provisions identify the legitimate ends against which forceful actions are to be assessed, namely, to maintain or restore international peace and security in the face of a threat to the peace, breach of the peace or act of aggression. The aim of proportionality in collective security action thus differs from that in self-defence. The latter, it will be recalled, has as its objective the repulsion of an armed attack.[53] Moreover, the phrase 'to maintain or restore international peace and security' is far less precise than the language of Article 51 with its reference to an armed attack. In the context of collective actions, it is, therefore, difficult to establish a relatively clear aim against which to measure the means employed. Nevertheless, the reference in Articles 39 and 42 to the maintenance and 'restoration of international peace and security'

[52] See e.g. Arts. 32, 33(2), 34 and 36. See e.g. the concerns expressed by States that all peaceful means had not been exhausted prior to the adoption under Chapter VII of SC Res. 748, 31 March 1992, in relation to the Lockerbie incident, SC PV 3063, 31 March 1992, pp. 24–5 (Jordan); p. 31 (Mauritania); p. 46 (Cape Verde); p. 52 (Zimbabwe); p. 56 (India); p. 59 (China); and p. 64 (Morocco).

[53] See the discussion of this issue in Chapter 5 above.

appears to justify a much broader range of measures than is legitimate in actions in self-defence. For example, depending on the circumstances, it could be argued that the destruction of a State's aggressive capabilities would be legitimate as a measure to maintain international peace and security.[54]

The application of the second aspect of the proportionality equation, the consideration of the means employed to achieve the legitimate ends, appears to be more straightforward. The same factors that apply in the assessment of the means in the case of self-defence are also applicable in the context of Security Council enforcement action.[55] Therefore, the Council and States acting under its authority must assess, amongst other things, the type of campaign to be undertaken, the means and methods of warfare, and the potential interference of the proposed action with the rights of third States generally, including the impact on the environment.

Despite the ability to discern within the terms of Chapter VII of the Charter the aim against which to measure the proportionality of any forceful response, the Charter is silent on its relevance to the collective security system. The question, therefore, is whether this norm of general international law can be imported into the Charter system. The general question of legal limits on the powers of the Security Council is by no means new. In the early decades of the Charter, the question of whether there are constraints on the measures the Security Council can adopt to achieve its primary role of restoring international peace and security, and the related question as to whether the criteria for the assumption of jurisdiction by the Security Council under Article 39 must be objectively satisfied, attracted some attention from commentators.[56] Security Council action in the post-Cold War era, however, has led to increased interest in these topics. The broad question as to the appropriate role of international law in relation to the activities of the Security Council has

[54] See Greenwood, 'Invasion of Kuwait', pp. 169–71 (for a discussion of this view in the context of Iraq in the 1990–1 Persian Gulf conflict); and Rostow, 'Enforcement Action'.

[55] See the discussion of these factors in Chapter 5, note 116, and the accompanying text above.

[56] The actions of the Security Council in relation to Southern Rhodesia in the 1960s gave rise to some debate over these issues: see R. Higgins, 'International Law, Rhodesia and the UN' (1967) 23 *World Today* 94. See also O. Schachter, 'The Quasi-Judicial Role of the Security Council and the General Assembly' (1964) 58 *AJIL* 960; and R. Higgins, 'The Place of International Law in the Settlement of Disputes by the Security Council' (1970) 64 *AJIL* 1.

gripped the imagination of scholars since Resolution 687, the 'cease-fire' resolution that terminated the Persian Gulf hostilities[57] and has been fuelled by the allegations of *ultra vires* in the *Lockerbie*[58] and *Genocide*[59] cases.[60] There is an increasing perception that there must be some limits not only to the Council's assumption of jurisdiction[61] but also to the methods it uses to carry out its Chapter VII mandate.[62] After all, the Security Council is a treaty body and dependent on treaty provisions. The debate about methods, however, has occurred almost exclusively in the context of Article 41 enforcement powers. There is seldom any acknowledgment that non-forceful and forceful measures, in theory, raise different legal questions. The exercise of the power under Article 41 has considerable potential to interfere with States' rights under general international law. The military enforcement powers of the Security Council in contrast are to a large extent a self-contained code.

[57] See SC Res. 687, 3 April 1991 (imposing comprehensive measures against Iraq as a condition of the cease-fire).

[58] *Question of Interpretation and Application of the 1971 Montreal Convention Arising from the Aerial Incident at Lockerbie (Libya* v. *US; Libya* v. *UK)*, Request for Provisional Measures, ICJ Reports 1992, 3 (hereafter *Lockerbie Case*).

[59] *Application of the Convention on the Prevention and Punishment of the Crime of Genocide (Bosnia and Herzegovina* v. *Yugoslavia (Serbia and Montenegro))*, Requests for Provisional Measures, ICJ Reports 1993, 3 at 114 (hereafter *Genocide Case*).

[60] See the further discussion of these issues at note 158 and the accompanying text below.

[61] See B. Graefrath, 'Leave to the Court What Belongs to the Court – The Libyan Case' (1993) 4 *EJIL* 184 at 195–7 and 199, citing (at 197) a passage from the opinion of Judge Fitzmaurice in *Legal Consequences for States of the Continued Presence of South Africa in Namibia (South West Africa) Notwithstanding Security Council Resolution 276 (1970)*, Advisory Opinion, ICJ Reports 1971, 16 (hereafter *Namibia* Advisory Opinion). See also T. Franck, 'The Security Council and "Threats to the Peace": Some Remarks on Remarkable Recent Developments' in R. Dupuy (ed.), *The Development of the Role of the Security Council: Workshop, The Hague, 21–23 July 1992* (Martinus Nijhoff, Dordrecht, 1993), p. 83; and the argument based on limits derived from Art. 24(1) in B. Conforti, 'Le Pouvoir Discrétionnaire du Conseil de Sécurité en Matière de Constatation d'une Menace Contre la Paix, d'une Rupture de La Paix ou d'un Acte d'Agression' in R. Dupuy (ed.), *The Development of the Role of the Security Council Peace-Keeping and Peace-Building: Workshop, The Hague, 21–23 July 1992* (Martinus Nijhoff, Dordrecht, 1993), p. 51 at p. 56. See also M. Bothe, 'Les Limites des Pouvoirs du Conseil de Sécurité' in R. Dupuy (ed.), *The Development of the Role of the Security Council Peace-Keeping and Peace-Building: Workshop, The Hague, 21–23 July 1992* (Martinus Nijhoff, Dordrecht, 1993), p. 67 at p. 69.

[62] See e.g. I. Brownlie, 'The Decisions of Political Organs of the United Nations and the Rule of Law' in R. St J. Macdonald (ed.), *Essays in Honour of Wang Tieya* (Martinus Nijhoff, Dordrecht, 1994), p. 91 at pp. 96–7.

There is nowadays a daunting array of literature on the topic of the Security Council in recent years, particularly the judicial role in scrutinising any limits on the powers of the Council.[63] Some common strands can be identified. North American commentators are inclined to approach the question from a constitutional perspective of 'checks and balances'[64] and the 'proper' relationship between the International Court of Justice and the Security Council.[65] The debate they conduct is frequently characterised in terms of 'legitimacy'.[66] Other writers adopt a more positivist approach that relies on an analysis of the terms of the Charter itself, particularly its Purposes and Principles, to conclude that the Council operates within the rule of law and, moreover, that the International Court of Justice has a role to play in ensuring this result.[67] Those of a more 'realist' persuasion see the issue primarily in political terms with any control mechanism based in the veto or States' refusal to comply with Council decisions.[68] The Security Council and its powers have also attracted the attention of scholars of a more critical persuasion.[69]

The differing opinions that are expressed on the question of legal restraints on Security Council enforcement action reveal a certain vision as to the role of the Security Council in the post-Cold War era and indeed, at a more fundamental level, the relationship between politics and law.[70] There is considerable support for the view that the primary goal of the

63 See the sources cited by D. Akande, 'The International Court of Justice and the Security Council: Is There Room for Judicial Control of Decisions of the Political Organs of the United Nations?' (1997) 46 *ICLQ* 309, note 2. See also B. Graefrath, 'Iraqi Reparations and the Security Council' (1995) 55 *Heidelberg Journal of International Law* 1.

64 See e.g. M. W. Reisman, 'The Constitutional Crisis in the United Nations' (1993) 87 *AJIL* 83 at 92 (although not subscribing to the view that the Court can review Security Council decisions).

65 See e.g. T. Franck, 'The Powers of Appreciation: Who Is the Ultimate Guardian of UN Legality?' (1992) 86 *AJIL* 519 at 522.

66 See e.g. Franck, *Fairness in International Law*, pp. 219–44.

67 See e.g. D. Bowett, 'The Impact of Security Council Decisions on Dispute Settlement Procedures' (1994) 5 *EJIL* 89 at 95–6 ('[m]ember States have every right to insist that the Council keeps within the powers they have accorded to it under the Charter').

68 See e.g. Reisman, 'Constitutional Crisis in the United Nations'.

69 See e.g. A. Orford, 'The Politics of Collective Security' (1996) 17 *Michigan JIL* 373 (addressing the new role of the Security Council from a feminist perspective and arguing that no consideration has been given to the different effects of these activities on women).

70 See e.g. S. Scott, 'International Law as Ideology: Theorizing the Relationship Between International Law and International Politics' (1994) 5 *EJIL* 313; and see also M. Koskenniemi, 'The Place of Law in Collective Security' (1996) 17 *Michigan JIL* 455.

Council is the effective or efficient restoration of peace and security.[71] Some writers, perhaps uneasy about the untrammelled operation of the Council, but equally uneasy with a simplistic application to it of the rule of law, see the need for the Council to demonstrate by various means the legitimacy of its actions.[72] A common view amongst those who regard the Council as operating within some constraints is that these relate to fundamental humanitarian values.[73] This is to be expected, as human rights are nowadays a powerful factor in moulding the operation of so many diverse areas of international law.

Another consistent theme, sometimes articulated as a component of legitimacy, other times as a legal rule, is that the Council's actions should be in some ways proportionate to its aims.[74] A significant emphasis on efficiency or effectiveness in the context of the Council's forceful actions will of course yield a very different assessment of what is proportionate than if the emphasis is placed on other factors, such as inalienable rights and freedoms of individuals.[75]

Conceding this developing mood that there should be some restraints of a legal nature on the Chapter VII powers of the Council, the consistent view since the adoption of the Charter has been that the determination by the Security Council under Article 39 is a matter within its own discretion and, moreover, is non-justiciable.[76] Which is not to say that such

[71] Effectiveness of Council action is a strong refrain that runs throughout much of the published work in this area. See the review of European scholarship on this question in O. Korhonen, 'Current Trends in European International Law Publications' (1998) 9 *EJIL* 553.

[72] See J. Alvarez, 'Judging the Security Council' (1996) 90 *AJIL* 1 at 19; and Kirgis, 'First Fifty Years'.

[73] See Graefrath, 'Iraqi Reparations'. See also Brownlie, 'Decisions of Political Organs', pp. 100–1. Cf. Bowett, 'Dispute Settlement Procedures', p. 90, whose concern is that the Council is under a general duty to States to uphold international law and protect the legal rights of States.

[74] See e.g. Kirgis, 'First Fifty Years', p. 517; and Alvarez, 'Judging the Security Council', p. 17 (discussing the acceptance by otherwise opposed schools of thought of the applicability of proportionality to the Council's actions).

[75] See Graefrath, 'Iraqi Reparations'. A similar tension between humanitarian values and military efficiency is evident in the application of proportionality in IHL: see the discussion of this issue in Chapter 4 above.

[76] See R. Higgins, *The Development of International Law Through the Political Organs of the United Nations* (Oxford University Press, Oxford, 1963), p. 66; Higgins, 'The Place of International Law', p. 16; H. Kelsen, *The Law of the United Nations: A Critical Analysis of Its Fundamental Problems* (Praeger, New York, 1950), p. 735; and the sources cited by V. Gowlland-Debbas, 'The Relationship Between the International Court of Justice and the Security Council in the Light of the Lockerbie Case' (1994) 88 *AJIL* 643 at 662, note 103. See also the Dissenting Opinion of Judge Weeramantry in the *Lockerbie Case*, note 58

an assessment should not be more transparent.[77] However, Article 39 is widely regarded as incorporating a political rather than a legal judgment.[78] Some observers would extend this immunity to the assessments involving the exercise of the military enforcement powers of the Council under Article 42, particularly those relating to whether non-forceful means would be or have been to no avail.

There is a range of arguments that support the need for the Council to be the final word on whether the resort to force is warranted. As long as the Council appears to be addressing the issue of necessity in Article 42 and is not flagrantly disregarding the terms of the Charter, it is hard to envisage any scrutiny of this process that would give rise to legal consequences. It is not so much that it is impossible to apply sufficiently precise legal criteria to such assessments. After all, necessity is a legal concept in the law on self-defence. It is more that any legal scrutiny would be perceived as unnecessarily hampering the flexibility of the Council to address effectively the task entrusted to it by States to ensure the maintenance of international peace and security.

With respect to the claim that proportionality exerts a restraining influence on the forceful actions of the Council, some guidance as to resolving this issue may be available from a consideration of the Purposes and Principles of the Charter. Many commentators who seek some measure of control over the activities of the Council rely on these fundamental guiding tenets of the Charter as performing this role. Article 24(2) of the Charter requires the Council to 'act in accordance with the Purposes and Principles of the United Nations'. Indeed, the decision of the International Court of Justice in the *Namibia Case*[79] supports the view that the fundamental Purposes and Principles of the Charter are in fact the only limitations on the powers of the Council.

According to Article 1(1), one of the Purposes of the Charter with which the Security Council must comply is:

above and the Separate Opinion of Ad Hoc Judge Lauterpacht in the *Genocide Case*, note 59 above, p. 439. Cf., however, the sources cited in note 61 above; Brownlie, 'Decisions of Political Organs', p. 96; and B. Martenczuk, 'What Lessons from Lockerbie?' (arguing that Art. 39 in fact contains the only justiciable limits on the Council's powers).

[77] See e.g. Kirgis, 'First Fifty Years', p. 517 (arguing that the Council should make 'principled Art. 39 determinations, publicly explicated, that do not set unlimited or unintended precedents'). Kirgis also extends this requirement to the assessment of whether any forceful action is necessary under Art. 42 (*ibid.*, p. 522).

[78] See Kelsen, *Law of the United Nations*, p. 735.

[79] See *Namibia* Advisory Opinion, note 61 above.

to take effective collective measures for the prevention and removal of threats to the peace, and for the suppression of acts of aggression or other breaches of the peace, and to bring about by peaceful means, and in conformity with the principles of justice and international law, adjustment or settlement of international disputes or situations which might lead to a breach of the peace.

The reference to international law in Article 1(1) can be viewed as encompassing proportionality as a principle of general international law that is applicable to all uses of force. There is, however, the view that the requirement that the Council act in conformity with 'the principles of justice and international law' is limited to when the Council is attempting to settle the dispute by peaceful means under Chapter VI. Hans Kelsen was a strong proponent of such an approach, arguing that '[t]he purpose of the enforcement action under Article 39 is not to maintain or restore the law, but to maintain or restore the peace, which is not necessarily identical with the law'.[80] The *travaux préparatoires* of the Charter, however, do not support this narrow interpretation of the reference to international law in Article 1(1).[81] The difficulty remains, nevertheless, of determining just how far the reference to acting in conformity with the principles of justice and international law imposes a restraint on the Council to ensure that its actions are in conformity with those similar considerations applicable to States.

There is little doubt that the Council when acting under Chapter VII of the Charter can derogate from the existing rules of international law in its response to threats to the peace, breaches of the peace and acts of aggression within the meaning of Article 39 of the Charter in order to maintain or restore international peace and security. As a general proposition, this conclusion has never been seriously in doubt, and Article 103 of the Charter confirms it.[82] But are there no limits? It may indeed be

[80] Kelsen, *Law of the United Nations*, p. 208. Cf. the Dissenting Opinion of Judge Fitzmaurice in the *Namibia* Advisory Opinion, note 61 above, p. 294, to the effect that even when acting under Chapter VII of the Charter the Security Council is subject to general principles of international law, in that case the inability to abrogate or alter territorial rights other than through the process of peace settlement. Other commentators support this approach: see e.g. Higgins, 'The Place of International Law in the Settlement of Disputes by the Security Council', p. 9; and Brownlie, 'Decisions of Political Organs', pp. 96–9.

[81] See Akande, 'Judicial Control of Decisions', pp. 319–20 (for details of the debates on this point in the Committee on the Structure and Procedure of the Security Council at the San Francisco Conference).

[82] Art. 103 of the Charter provides that, when there is a conflict between a Charter obligation and a treaty obligation, the former shall prevail. By virtue of Art. 25 of the Charter, obedience to Security Council decisions is such an obligation.

necessary and appropriate in particular cases for the Council to derogate from existing norms of international law in order to maintain or restore international peace and security. However, the need is less apparent for the Council to disregard the requirement that any such forceful action it may authorise must be proportionate. This limitation seems integral to achieving a lasting and just settlement of disputes. Disproportionate and excessive actions serve no purpose and are hardly likely to contribute to the maintenance of international peace and security.

There is another paragraph of the Purposes and Principles of the Charter that may provide some further guidance in this context, namely, Article 1(3). By virtue of Article 1(3), one of the Purposes of the Charter is to promote and encourage respect for human rights. This reference to human rights could be interpreted as indicating that the activities of all the organs of the Charter, including the Security Council, must be consistent with the standards of international law that have been developed in this area and regulate all actors in the international arena. To that extent, the Security Council operates within the general system of international law and is subject to appropriate principles thereof. In this way, the mention of human rights in Article 1(3) can provide the link between the activities of the Security Council and the general international legal system.

The construction of a more complete picture of the relationship between the Council and the fundamental Purposes of the Charter depends upon whether proportionality can be seen to have a role to play in their promotion. A narrow interpretation of the function of proportionality is inimical to importing broader based humanitarian principles into the legal framework of the Security Council when it is undertaking military enforcement actions. This norm has not traditionally been perceived as protecting humanitarian values in *ius ad bellum*, other than incidentally.[83] Proportionality in that regime is more commonly perceived as designed to limit the impact of any forceful action on the sovereign rights of a delinquent State and helping to ensure a more lasting peace at the end of hostilities. Traditionally, in times of armed conflicts, when human rights to a large extent are in abeyance, it is IHL that is designed to provide a measure of protection for individuals from its effects. Arguably, therefore, if an expanded scope is accorded to Article 1(3), it should be restricted to requiring the Council to ensure

[83] See the discussion of the operation of necessity and proportionality in *ius ad bellum* in Chapter 5 above.

that States acting under its authority comply with relevant principles of IHL.

Nevertheless even if it is the case that proportionality in *ius ad bellum* is not primarily designed with a humanitarian focus in mind, it performs this function at a secondary level. For example, the need to assess overall anticipated civilian casualties has always been a major component of the proportionality equation in *ius ad bellum*. To ensure compliance with its requirements, States must carefully analyse whether their overall forceful strategy will result in an unacceptable level of civilian losses in order to achieve the legitimate aims. Moreover, increasingly there is the view that considerations of humanity play a part in the proportionality equation in *ius ad bellum*. It is becoming apparent that to rely solely on IHL to regulate the humanitarian consequences of armed conflict fails to acknowledge the often greater potential of *ius ad bellum* to achieve this goal. The United Nations was established to advance and protect human rights. In theory, therefore, the Council should set an example for States to emulate.

The view that there are limits on the powers of the United Nations when taking military enforcement action is supported by the practice in the 1950–3 Korean conflict[84] and to a lesser extent by that of the 1990–1 Persian Gulf conflict. A question raised early in the Korean campaign was the legitimate aims of the action. The Security Council in Resolution 82 of 25 June 1950 found that the armed attack by North Korea on South Korea constituted a breach of the peace within the meaning of Article 39 of the Charter. The resolution called upon the North Korean authorities to withdraw their armed forces to the 38th parallel and further called upon member States to render every assistance to the United Nations to give effect to the resolution.[85] Resolution 83 of 27 June 1950 recommended 'that the Members of the United Nations furnish such assistance to the Republic of Korea as may be necessary to repel the armed attack and to restore international peace and security in the area'.[86] In neither resolution was there any reference to a particular Article of the Charter. At one stage, the forces established pursuant to this resolution pursued the North Korean forces beyond the 38th parallel. General MacArthur, appointed by the Security Council as overall commander of the forces, advocated the destruction of the North Korean forces rather than limiting the campaign to their expulsion from South Korean territory and the

[84] See the discussion of this issue by Bowett, *United Nations Forces*, pp. 43–5.
[85] SC Res. 82, 25 June 1950. [86] SC Res. 83, 27 June 1950.

restoration of the *status quo*. To achieve this goal, he wanted to advance to the border of China. Although the United Nations forces were rapidly driven back when China entered the conflict and the question became moot, it was one that led to much debate and disagreement amongst various members of the United Nations.[87]

The perception in some quarters that there were legal limits on the Security Council in the Korean situation is evidenced in the following passage from Bowett:

> Whereas, traditionally, a State waging war was entitled to do so to the stage of complete annihilation and subjugation of the other side, it can scarcely be maintained that United Nations action can be pursued so far. Such 'collective' or 'enforcement' action, as distinct from war, is limited to the measures necessary to resist aggression and to maintain and restore international peace and security. To this extent the United Nations can only wage a limited 'war', and it is evident that it is this precise question of the constitutional limits on United Nations action which weighed heavily in the doubts of some United Nations Members over the propriety of crossing the 38th parallel – quite apart from the political desirability of that course. The ends of war and of United Nations action thus differ.[88]

Bowett concludes that although this action was constitutionally valid he could envisage examples of United Nations action that could have gone 'beyond the necessity and purposes of United Nations action' such as the wholesale destruction by aerial attack of all the major towns in North Korea.[89]

A not dissimilar situation arose in the 1990–1 Persian Gulf conflict. For political reasons the Council left the assessment of what was proportionate to achieve the aims of the forceful response to the coalition allies. The phrase 'all necessary means' in Resolution 661 placed the decision as to the appropriate means to achieve the aim of the resolution on the States concerned. Towards the end of the campaign there was some disquiet expressed by several members of the Security Council as to the direction of the allied actions and their advance into Iraqi territory.[90] Some commentators shared this concern on the basis that there are limits to the measures the Security Council can take to maintain and

[87] L. Goodrich, *Korea: A Study on US Policy in the United Nations* (1st edn, Council on Foreign Relations, New York, 1956), pp. 133–4 and 142–3.

[88] Bowett, *United Nations Forces*, pp. 54–5.

[89] *Ibid.*, p. 55. See also Reisman, 'Preparing to Wage Peace', p. 76 (expressing the view that peacemaking will tolerate much less collateral destruction than war-making – an argument based on proportionality).

[90] See Greenwood, 'Invasion of Kuwait', p. 171.

restore international peace and security.[91] The analysis of State practice in this conflict, however, is complicated by the fact that the use of force was arguably by way of collective self-defence.

In conclusion, as Brownlie has argued in the context of Article 41 measures, although the Council has a wide discretion when acting under Chapter VII, its selection of methods to achieve the end result of maintaining or restoring international peace and security have a legal dimension.[92] Consequently, it has been argued in the context of decisions of the Council in the 1990s that the Council cannot arbitrarily impose new boundaries on States nor compel a State to extradite its citizens in the absence of an extradition treaty.[93] Moreover, procedural safeguards must be respected.[94] It is, therefore, one thing to allow the Security Council to determine its own jurisdiction and, moreover, to make an assessment as to the effectiveness or otherwise of measures under Article 41. It is another thing to conclude that in the consequential exercise of its powers it is similarly unrestrained. A distinction exists between the determination of threshold decisions that for any number of reasons may be viewed as controlled by political means, and subsequent actions taken by a treaty organ of enumerated powers that have always been regarded as having a legal dimension. The use of force in both municipal and international law traditionally has always constituted a primary area for legal regulation.[95] This is merely another way of saying that the Council operates to some extent within the general system of law in which all international legal persons operate.

It seems that the preferred interpretation nowadays of the Charter is one that places the Council to some extent within the system of general international law. Moreover, it is likely that any restraints on the powers of the Council will be derived from the increasing emphasis on human rights and humanitarian values that increasingly constitute the fundamental aim of the entire international legal system.[96] Whatever

[91] See e.g. Schachter, 'Authorized Uses of Force', pp. 74–5.

[92] See Brownlie, 'Decisions of Political Organs', p. 102 (arguing in relation to the Lockerbie suspects that the requirements of procedural fairness should be complied with by the Council).

[93] See Graefrath, 'The Libyan Case', pp. 187–91; and Koskenniemi, 'Collective Security', p. 485.

[94] See Brownlie, 'Decisions of Political Organs', p. 100.

[95] So fundamental in fact that the failure of international law to regulate the resort to force, prior to the developments last century, was one of the grounds for alleging that the system could not be legal. See the discussion of this issue by Hans Kelsen, *General Theory of Law and State* (Russell, New York, 1961), p. 332.

[96] See e.g. Brownlie, 'Decisions of Political Organs', p. 102: 'when the rights of individuals are involved, the application of human rights standards is a legal necessity'.

the situation in relation to other principles of international law that might be perceived as unduly fettering the Security Council in its role of maintaining international peace and security, the requirements of proportionality are distinguishable. The development of the law on the use of force indicates that the requirement of proportionality has long been a determinant of the legitimacy of the use of force. Although the development of this principle as a legal rule has previously occurred primarily in the context of self-defence, there is no reason to suppose that its scope is so limited. It is a principle of general international law that governs all use of force, whether individual or through collective security systems.[97] The recognition that the Charter has changed the legitimate ends for the use of force is sufficient to allow the Security Council the scope to fulfil its mandate. The achievement of these aims does not require the use of any means.

Enforcement actions and IHL

Having considered the extent to which forces exercising the Chapter VII enforcement powers of the Security Council are constrained by considerations of necessity and proportionality derived from *ius ad bellum*, it remains to address the same question in the context of IHL.

The regime of IHL, unlike that of *ius ad bellum*, operates independently of the United Nations Charter.[98] It is a separate body of rules that is theoretically unaffected by the provisions of the Charter. States continue to be bound in their hostile relations according to their treaty commitments and the relevant rules of customary international law. The involvement of the United Nations and the different forms that military operations under its auspices can take, however, complicates the issue. The legal obligations of the participants under IHL may differ

[97] See e.g. Bothe, 'Les Limites des Pouvoirs du Conseil de Sécurité', pp. 78–9; G. R. Watson, 'Constitutionalism, Judicial Review and the World Court' (1993) 34 *Harvard ILJ* 1; cf. D. Greig, 'Reciprocity, Proportionality and the Law of Treaties' (1994) 34 *Virginia JIL* 295. F. Krüger-Sprengel, 'Le Concept de Proportionnalité dans le Droit de la Guerre', Rapport présenté au Comité pour la protection de la vie humaine dans les conflits armés, VIIIe Congrès de la Société internationale de droit pénal militaire et de droit de la guerre, Ankara, October 1979, Brussels (Société international de droit pénal militaire et de droit de la guerre, 1981), is of the view that proportionality 'est un principe général dont il faut tenir compte dans l'interprétation des règles pertinentes du droit international'.

[98] This view was confirmed by the International Court of Justice in *Legality of the Threat or Use of Nuclear Weapons* Advisory Opinion, ICJ Reports 1996, 26 (General Assembly Opinion).

depending on the nature of the force.[99] As we have seen, military operations may be undertaken by forces acting under the authority and control of the United Nations, such as UNOSOM II in Somalia[100] and UNPROFOR in Bosnia-Herzegovina.[101] In both these cases, the mandate of traditional peacekeeping forces was expanded under Chapter VII of the United Nations Charter. Alternatively, States themselves may be authorised to use force by the Security Council under Chapter VII of the Charter to support existing or contemplated United Nations peacekeeping operations, such as Operation Restore Hope by UNITAF in Somalia,[102] Operation Turquoise in Rwanda,[103] and the United States force in Haiti.[104]

Shortly after the adoption of the Charter, it was suggested that United Nations forces should only be required to comply with the laws of war as were fit for their purposes.[105] There were basically two justifications provided for this view. One was that as the use of force was prohibited under the Charter any forcible action by the United Nations would necessarily be in response to unlawful aggression.[106] The other approach doubted the extent to which it could be said that the purpose of United Nations enforcement action was compatible with the concept of warfare and the rules developed to regulate its conduct.[107]

For some time after the adoption of the Charter, this topic received a degree of attention. The consensus, however, was against drawing such a distinction between United Nations forces and an aggressor State in relation to the application of the principles of IHL, the same position

[99] See the discussion in note 18 and the accompanying text above of the various ways in which the Chapter VII military enforcement powers of the Security Council may be exercised.

[100] See SC Res. 814, 26 March 1993 (acting under Chapter VII of the Charter and replacing UNITAF with UNISOM II and expanding its mandate in accordance with the recommendations of the Report of the Secretary General of 2 March 1993).

[101] See SC Res. 836, 4 June 1993 (acting under Chapter VII of the Charter and extending the mandate of UNPROFOR, 'acting in self-defence, to take the necessary measures, including use of force, in reply to bombardments against the safe areas').

[102] See SC Res. 794, 2 December 1992 (acting under Chapter VII of the Charter and authorising member States to 'use all necessary means to secure a safe environment' for humanitarian relief operations).

[103] See note 41 above. [104] See note 42 above.

[105] See e.g. 'Should the Laws of War Apply to UN Enforcement Action?', Report of the American Society of International Law Committee on Legal Problems of the UN, reprinted in (1952) *Proc. ASIL* 216–20; and see the sources cited in G. Weissberg, *The International Status of the UN* (Oceana, Dobbs Ferry, NY, 1961), p. 105, note 101.

[106] Bowett, *United Nations Forces*, pp. 493–6 (referring to this as the 'reprisal theory' and critically assessing the arguments of its adherents).

[107] See *ibid.*, pp. 496–9.

that had been reached in relation to inter-State conflicts.[108] The growing emphasis on the humanitarian basis of these rules and the increasing acceptance that their primary objective basis was to provide protection for individuals in armed conflict reinforced this approach. Thus, it seemed to be accepted that an unlawful aggressor was entitled to the benefits of IHL irrespective of whether the forceful response was an exercise of the right of self-defence or a collective enforcement action.[109] Although the legal issues were never formally resolved, the policy adopted in relation to United Nations peacekeeping forces, where the issue has been of some practical importance, was consistent with the view that the United Nations should be bound to the extent necessary by the same principles of IHL as States. The United Nations fulfilled its obligations in this respect through entering into agreements requiring the observance of IHL with States supplying peacekeeping forces and the host State.[110] Peacekeeping activities until recently have been predicated on there being no active hostilities taking place and no situation of armed conflict between the United Nations forces and other parties. The applicability of the provisions of IHL to these forces was thus, generally speaking, of relatively minor concern.

In discussing the extent to which the United Nations is bound by IHL it is necessary to draw a distinction between the conventional and customary rules of IHL. Although the United Nations has sufficient international personality to undertake rights and duties under international law, including treaty obligations, there are particular difficulties in the context of the application of humanitarian law treaties to the United Nations.[111] Although the four 1949 Geneva Conventions were adopted

[108] See e.g. the resolution adopted in 1971 by the Institut de Droit International, reproduced in (1971) 54 *Annuaire de l'Institut de Droit International* 465–70. For the situation in relation to inter-State conflicts, see the Preamble to Protocol Additional to the Geneva Conventions of 12 August 1949, and Relating to the Protection of Victims of International Armed Conflicts, adopted in 1977 (Additional Protocol I), 12 December 1977, (1979) 1125 UNTS 3; and see the discussion of this issue in Greenwood, 'United Nations Military Operations', pp. 7–8.

[109] This position remains largely unchallenged: see e.g. H. Meyrowitz, 'La Guerre du Golfe des Conflits Armés', (1992) 96 *Revue Générale de Droit International Publique* 551 at 553–4.

[110] For details of some of these agreements in relation to peacekeeping operations, see R. Higgins, *United Nations Peacekeeping: Commentary and Documents 1946–1967*, vol. I, *The Middle East*, vol. II, *Asia*, vol. III, *Africa*, vol. IV, *Europe 1946–1979* (Oxford University Press, Oxford, 1969–70).

[111] On the status of the United Nations generally, see Weissberg, *International Status*; and see the work of the International Law Commission on the general topic of international organisations and treaties (1981) *YBILC* Part II. See also H. Schermers,

after the Charter, efforts by the ICRC to allow for accession thereto by international organisations was unsuccessful.[112] However, otherwise it was 'uncontested that the United Nations is bound by the customary rules of IHL when engaged in hostilities'.[113] The legal basis underlying this assertion has always been somewhat unclear. Presumably, it is on the basis that, in common with States, the United Nations is bound by principles of general international law. It is an easier task to reconcile this view of IHL with the terms of the Charter than it is in the case of constraints derived from *ius ad bellum*. It will be recalled that the Charter requires the Security Council to act in conformity with the Purposes and Principles of the Charter.[114] One of the Purposes of the Charter, as elaborated in Article 1(3), is to promote and encourage respect for human rights. Nowadays, the meaning of human rights in this context is sufficiently broad so as to encompass IHL, a view confirmed in the practice of the organization itself.[115]

The issue of IHL and enforcement action appears settled in one context. Despite some lingering juridical problems, it seems established that operations authorised under the authority of the Security Council but remaining under national command and control are governed solely by their respective IHL obligations.[116] The fact that these forces

International Institutional Law (Martinus Nijhoff, The Hague, 1972), vol. II, pp. 696–725; and F. Morgenstern, *Legal Problems of International Organizations* (Grotius, Cambridge, 1986), pp. 13–19. In relation to conventional IHL and the UN, see Bowett, *United Nations Forces*, pp. 506–16 (for a comprehensive description of the legal and practical obstacles to the UN becoming a party to IHL treaties); and see Greenwood, 'Protection of Peacekeepers'. There is a contrary view: see Greenwood, 'Protection of Peacekeepers', p. 16, note 42, for details.

112 See Commentary submitted by the ICRC to the Second Session of the Conference of Government Experts on the Reaffirmation and Development of International Humanitarian Law Applicable in Armed Conflicts, Part I (ICRC, Geneva, 1972), p. 159; and Report on the Work of the Conference of Government Experts on the Reaffirmation and Development of International Humanitarian Law Applicable in Armed Conflicts, Second Session, 3 May–3 June 1972 (ICRC, Geneva, 1972), vol. I, pp. 193–5.

113 D. Schindler, 'United Nations Forces and International Humanitarian Law' in C. Swinarski (ed.), *Studies and Essays on International Humanitarian Law and Red Cross Principles in Honour of Jean Pictet* (Martinus Nijhoff, The Hague, 1984), p. 521 at p. 526, citing Seyersted, *Law of Peace and War*; and see the more cautious assessment by Bowett, *United Nations Forces*, p. 506.

114 See the discussion of this point in note 79 and the accompanying text above.

115 See e.g. UNGA Res. 2444 (XXIII), Respect for Human Rights in Armed Conflicts, adopted on 19 December 1969; UNGA Res. 2627 (XXV), Basic Principles for the Protection of Civilian Populations in Armed Conflict, adopted 9 December 1970.

116 This was the practice adopted in the 1990–1 Persian Gulf conflict: see e.g. Department of Defense, *Final Report to Congress: Conduct of the Persian Gulf War* (USGPO, Washington,

are exercising the enforcement powers of the Council does not affect their position.[117] In all their forceful actions, therefore, State contingents must comply with the requirements of proportionality and avoid the use of weapons of a nature to cause superfluous injury or unnecessary suffering.[118]

This leaves unresolved the situation of forces acting under United Nations command and control. The ICRC has consistently argued for the applicability of the whole body of IHL whenever United Nations forces resort to force. In this view, it has received the support of the Institute of International Law, who declared in 1975 that the entire body of IHL was applicable to hostilities conducted by United Nations forces.[119] Moreover, the practice of the United Nations during the Korean conflict was consistent with this approach. Despite some initial resistance, the United Command in Korea agreed to be bound by the law of armed

DC, 1992), Appendix O. See also A. Ryniker, 'Respect du Droit International Humanitaire par les Forces des Nations' (1999) 836 *IRRC* 795; and Greenwood, 'Protection of Peacekeepers', p. 17.

[117] See e.g. ICRC Bulletin, 'Outline of the Legal Aspects of the Conflict in the Middle East', 21 January 1991, reproduced in M. Weller (ed.), *Iraq and Kuwait: The Hostilities and Their Aftermath*, Cambridge International Documents Series, vol. 3 (Grotius, Cambridge, 1993), p. 332 ('[t]he fact that military action has been authorized by Security Council resolution 678 does not affect . . . the application of the laws of armed conflict').

[118] It is also assumed by the 1999 Secretary-General's Bulletin on the Observance by United Nations Forces of International Humanitarian Law, ST/SGB/1999/13, 6 August 1999, that States acting under the authority of the Security Council are to be distinguished in terms of their legal obligations from United Nations forces. The Secretary-General's Bulletin does not cover forces other than those under the command and control of the United Nations. Thus, the preamble reads: 'The Secretary-General, for the purpose of setting out fundamental principles and rules of international humanitarian law applicable to United Nations forces conducting operations under United Nations command and control . . .'. See the further discussion of the Secretary-General's Bulletin in note 135 and the accompanying text below.

[119] See Institute of International Law, Resolutions and Voteux Adopted by the Institute at its Zagreb Session (26 August–3 September 1971), No. I, 'Conditions of Application of Humanitarian Rules of Armed Conflict in Hostilities in Which United Nations Forces May Be Engaged', (1971) 54-II *Annuaire de l'Institut de Droit International* 465–6; stating: '[t]he humanitarian rules of the law of armed conflict apply to the United Nations as of right and they must be complied with in all circumstances by United Nations Forces which are engaged in hostilities'. The Institute later extended the scope of this resolution to provisions of IHL that were not specifically humanitarian in character. See Resolutions Adopted and Recommendations Made by the Institute at its Wiesbaden Session (6–15 August 1975), No. II, 'Conditions of Application of Rules Other than Humanitarian Rules of Armed Conflict to Hostilities in Which United Nations Forces May Be Engaged', (1975) 56-II *Annuaire de l'Institut de Droit International* 540.

conflict, including the four 1949 Geneva Conventions, despite the fact that the Conventions had not entered into force for any of the major contributing States to the operation.[120]

Subsequently, however, the United Nations opposed such an interpretation, adopting the position that the forces it deploys should observe the 'principles and spirit' of the general international conventions applicable to the conduct of military personnel.[121] There are clearly difficulties with determining what exactly constitute the 'principles and spirit' of IHL and it was not until 1999 that the organisation has been prepared to spell out what these encompass.[122]

Nevertheless, a conclusion that IHL is either inapplicable or limited in its application to United Nations military operations is tempered by the fact that most commentators assume that national contingents remain bound by customary principles of IHL and their individual treaty obligations in cases of enforcement action.[123] From the commencement of peacekeeping operations, as a matter of practice, national contingents have regarded themselves as bound by their respective States' treaty obligations.[124] Bowett observes that 'it is difficult [apart from the unlawful aggressor theory which he finds unsustainable] to posit any persuasive theories that would release a State's military forces from the binding force of the laws of war, as a matter of law, simply because they are engaged in fulfilling a United Nations mandate'.[125] Thus, he concludes that national contingents remain bound by the treaty and customary obligations that would apply if they were engaged in an international armed conflict against another State. There are unsatisfactory aspects to

[120] See S. Bailey, *How Wars End: The United Nations and Termination of Armed Conflicts, 1946–64* (Clarendon Press, Oxford, 1982), p. 444.

[121] This approach was adopted by the model agreement drawn up to regulate the relations between the United Nations and States contributing forces to the UN force: see UN Doc. A/46/185 (23 May 1991).

[122] See the discussion in note 132 and the accompanying text below.

[123] See e.g. Bowett, *United Nations Forces*, pp. 503–6; and Schachter, 'Authorized Uses of Force', p. 76. Cf. F. Seyersted, *Law of Peace and War*, pp. 197–209 (distinguishing between forces under UN command and forces under national command); and P. Benvenuti, 'The Implementation of International Humanitarian Law in the Framework of United Nations Peace-Keeping Operations' in European Commission, *Law in Humanitarian Crises* (Office for Official Publications of the European Communities, Luxembourg, 1995), vol. 1, *How Can International Humanitarian Law Be Made Effective in Armed Conflicts?*, p. 83 at p. 94.

[124] See Bowett, *United Nations Forces*, p. 503 (for details of State practice in this context).

[125] *Ibid.*, pp. 503–4.

this approach. In practical terms, it means that different national contingents, although engaged in the same operation, have differing obligations in relation to the other party, a most confusing and unsatisfactory situation. As Greenwood observes, the major problem in this context is likely to be with Additional Protocol I.[126] Although the four 1949 Geneva Conventions have some 188 State parties and are regarded as representing customary international law, the same is not true for Additional Protocol I.[127] Moreover, as Bowett observes, it is conceivable that the State against whom the United Nations forces are engaged will have difficulty in determining its obligations in relation to humanitarian law, with foreseeable consequences for United Nations forces.[128] This latter situation has been ameliorated to a limited extent by the adoption in 1994 of the Convention on the Safety of United Nations and Associated Personnel.[129]

There are, moreover, theoretical shortcomings in the analysis that State contingents remain bound by their respective treaty obligations in United Nations operations. It is not beyond debate that national contingents are bound in Security Council sanctioned enforcement actions by their legal obligations derived from the rules regulating inter-State conflicts, even less so if Article 43 forces were established. Moreover, given the existence of such a force, the view that the contingents involved retain their independent status when acting in accordance with a Security Council decision, in so far as the requirements of IHL are concerned,

[126] See Greenwood, 'United Nations Military Operations', pp. 18–19.

[127] As at 20 January 2003, there were 161 State parties to Additional Protocol I. Not all the provisions of the Protocol (including the rules on indiscriminate attacks) are indisputably customary in nature: see L. Doswald-Beck and J.-M. Henckaerts (eds.), *Customary International Humanitarian Law*, vol. I, *Rules*, vol. 2, *Practice* (Cambridge University Press, Cambridge, 2003).

[128] Bowett, *United Nations Forces*, p. 505. Moreover, most of the conventional rules are only binding if all participants are parties to them. The legal effect of the participation of UN forces who cannot accede to these instruments is arguably to release the other parties from their obligations thereunder: see H. J. Taubenfeld, 'International Armed Forces and the Rules of War' (1951) 45 *AJIL* 674.

[129] Convention on the Safety of United Nations and Associated Personnel. However, the Convention is not intended to cover forces likely to undertake high-level hostilities: see Greenwood, 'Protection of Peacekeepers'. The scope of the Convention is widely regarded as inadequate: see the Report to the Sixth Committee of the General Assembly by the Secretary-General on the Convention, Scope of Legal Protection Under the Convention on the Safety of UN and Associated Personnel, UN Doc. A/55/637 (2000); and see also G. Hafner, 'Certain Issues of the Work of the Sixth Committee at the Fifty-Sixth General Assembly' (2003) 97 *AJIL* 147 at 150–6 (discussing the report of the Secretary-General on the Convention and the discussion thereof in the Sixth Committee of the General Assembly).

activates Articles 25 and 103 of the Charter. The Council, therefore, could theoretically override the treaty obligations of States.[130]

Nowadays, there seems little likelihood that arguments privileging United Nation forces in relation to the requirements of IHL would succeed. Nevertheless, the question of whether national contingents remain bound by their respective obligations under IHL is not the same question as whether the United Nations itself is bound by some obligations of IHL. If the organisation is subject to rules of IHL it becomes bound to ensure that the forces under its command obey such constraints, irrespective of their differing national obligations. It thus remains important to determine the position of the United Nations itself and, most importantly, exactly what constitute the IHL obligations of the organisation.

Despite the unresolved legal issues, the practice adopted by the United Nations that forces under its control and command would abide by the principles and spirit of IHL appeared to work relatively well in practice during the Cold War era. The advent of a broader range of United Nations military operations, however, raises new problems. The solutions adopted in relation to peacekeeping forces are not satisfactory nor are they necessarily analogous to forces that are intended to use force not just as a last resort in self-defence but as part of the mandate of the Security Council to restore international peace and security by more forceful measures. In contrast to traditional peacekeeping activities, enforcement functions envisage the possibility of a situation of armed conflict coming into existence between the United Nations forces and the other parties involved. All the complex issues of IHL, such as the determination of what sort of attacks are legitimate in terms of the likelihood of civilian casualties, the lawfulness of the use of certain weapons in light of their potential to cause unnecessary suffering and what constitutes a military target, never arose in peacekeeping actions.[131]

[130] Cf. D. Bowett, 'Judicial and Political Functions of the Security Council and the International Court of Justice' in R. St J. Macdonald (ed.), *Essays in Honour of Wang Tieya* (Martinus Nijhoff, Dordrecht, 1993) (expressing the view that a decision by the Security Council is not the equivalent of a Charter obligation under Art. 103; consequently, although members are obliged to obey such a decision by Art. 25, the decision does not operate as a Charter obligation so as to nullify an inconsistent treaty obligation by virtue of Art. 103).

[131] Cf., however, the United Nations Operation in the Congo (ONUC) (July 1960–June 1964) (involving the use of considerable amounts of force). For a description of the factual background and the attitude of the United Nations and member States to the question of the application of IHL in that conflict, see Bowett, *United Nations Forces*, p. 222. See also Seyersted, *Law of Peace and War*, pp. 192–7.

The current solution to the dilemma of the applicable rules of IHL to forces acting under the command and control of the United Nations has been to develop a mechanism by which the United Nations can undertake to comply with specified 'fundamental principles and rules' of IHL.[132] In 1995, the Fourth Committee of the United Nations General Assembly called for a comprehensive review of the whole question of peacekeeping operations in all their aspects.[133] The Special Committee on Peacekeeping Operations then requested the Secretary-General to 'complete the elaboration of a code of conduct for United Nations peacekeeping personnel, consistent with applicable humanitarian law'.[134] In response to this request, in August 1999 the Secretary-General issued a Bulletin on the Observance by United Nations Forces of International Humanitarian Law.[135]

The scope of application of the Bulletin is not based on whether the United Nations force concerned is exercising the enforcement powers of the Security Council but rather on whether the contingent in question is likely to find itself in a situation of exercising armed force.[136] In such circumstances, the issue of IHL can assume considerable significance. Thus, the Bulletin applies not only to 'United Nations forces conducting operations under United Nations command and control when in situations of armed conflict in which they are actively engaged as combatants to the extent and for the duration of their engagement', but also to 'peacekeeping operations when the use of force is permitted in self-defence'.[137]

The juridical position of forces under United Nations command and control remains potentially confusing, as there are now three regimes applicable to such operations. First, there are the provisions of the Bulletin itself. Secondly, the Bulletin does not purport to be an 'exhaustive list of principles and rules of international humanitarian law binding upon military personnel'.[138] Therefore, military personnel remain bound by their respective national laws. Finally, the provisions of the

[132] See C. Caratsch, 'Humanitarian Design and Political Interference: Red Cross Work in the Post-Cold War Period' (1993) 11 *International Relations* 301 at 312. There are various possibilities that have been canvassed by other writers: see e.g. Bowett, *United Nations Forces*, pp. 515–16.

[133] UNGA 51 Sess., Fourth Committee, Agenda item 86.

[134] UN Doc. A/50/230, para. 73.

[135] Secretary-General's Bulletin on the Observance by United Nations Forces of International Humanitarian Law, ST/SGB/1999/13, 6 August 1999.

[136] This is the approach advocated by Greenwood, 'Protection of Peacekeepers'.

[137] See Secretary-General's Bulletin, Section 1, para. 1.1.

[138] *Ibid.*, Section 2.

Convention on the Safety of United Nations and Associated Personnel remain applicable.[139]

The rule of proportionality is included in the Bulletin as one of the fundamental principles of IHL. Section 5, paragraph 5.5, prohibits a United Nations force 'from launching operations of a nature likely to strike military objectives and civilians in an indiscriminate manner, as well as operations that may be expected to cause incidental loss of life among the civilian population or damage to civilian objects that would be excessive in relation to the concrete and direct military advantage anticipated'.[140]

The only distinction of significance between this provision and the treaty rule in Additional Protocol I is the reference to 'operations' rather than 'attack'. No doubt this is intended to take account of the nature of United Nations enforcement actions, to which the concept of attacks is somewhat inappropriate.

What are lacking in the Bulletin are the other provisions of the Protocol that clarify and facilitate the operation of the rule of proportionality. It will be recalled that the Protocol deals specifically with such matters as the parties' obligations in relation to the choice of means and methods of warfare, target verification and the duties on commanders in relation to disproportionate attacks. A general statement of the binding nature of the proportionality rule on the United Nations is a significant step forward, but it leaves unclear the exact scope of the obligation, which will have to be supplemented by an assessment of the customary law requirements.

Section 6 of the Bulletin deals with the means and methods of combat. Both methods of warfare 'which may cause superfluous injury or unnecessary suffering' as well as 'weapons and methods of combat of a nature to cause unnecessary suffering' are prohibited.

To summarise, it appears the current legal position is that national contingents involved in United Nations operations in theory are never released from their respective obligations to abide by the requirements of proportionality and the prohibition on the use of weapons that may cause superfluous injury or unnecessary suffering. For forces not under United Nations command and control this can lead to differences of

[139] However, this Convention is designed to protect peacekeepers who are not involved in enforcement actions, and who are therefore the equivalent of and entitled to similar protections as civilians under IHL. See the sources cited in note 129 above (for details of the scope of the Convention and the shortcomings thereof).

[140] See Secretary-General's Bulletin, Section 1, para. 1.1.

opinion in relation to particular attacks between the contributing States but the legal position is relatively straightforward. With forces under United Nations command and control, obligations in relation to IHL are imposed on respective State contingents and on the United Nations itself. In previous times, the organisation considered that it had fulfilled its obligations by accepting the application of the principle and spirit of IHL and requiring States through its various agreements to respect these obligations. Nowadays, the United Nations has specifically adopted the Additional Protocol I rule of proportionality and the customary prohibition on the use of weapons of a nature to cause superfluous suffering or unnecessary injury as applicable in all its operations involving the use of force whether by peacekeeping or peace-enforcement contingents. There is some potential for differences in relation to the exact requirements of proportionality as some of the participating contingents may be bound by the potentially more onerous provisions of the Protocol at the national level. It may become significant in future United Nations operations to determine the relationship between the treaty and the customary rule of proportionality to overcome potential conflicts.

Responsibility for the acts of Chapter VII forces[141]

As previously observed, the determination of whether the constraints of necessity and proportionality (in both *ius ad bellum* and *ius in bello*) are a component of the Chapter VII military enforcement powers of the Security Council lays the groundwork for the resolution of questions of responsibility for such forceful actions.

Although it has been evident since the era of the peacekeeping operations in the Congo in the 1960s[142] that the question of responsibility of the organisation for forces acting under its authority was of some practical import, the regime of accountability in such circumstances still awaits further elaboration. The issue has become more pressing in the

[141] Issues of responsibility may arise also in the case of peacekeeping forces set up under Chapter VI of the UN Charter.

[142] It was alleged that States had acted *ultra vires* the relevant Security Council resolutions in the case of the Congo operation. The United Nations accepted responsibility for the actions of the peacekeepers in that conflict and entered into a number of compensation agreements with various States; see 'Report of the ILC on the Work of its Twenty-Seventh Session, 5 May–25 July 1975' (1975) II *YBILC* 87–8 (detailing the agreements made by the UN with various States); and see the sources cited in Brownlie, *Use of Force by States*, p. 335.

post-Cold War era with the expanded use of the organisation's military enforcement powers.

Theoretically, Chapter VII military enforcement action can result in a range of unlawful acts with differing consequences in terms of responsibility. Forces engaged in Chapter VII military operations, whether they are United Nations forces or State contingents whose actions are authorised by the Security Council, might fail to abide by relevant principles of IHL. Moreover, collective enforcement action may exceed what is proportionate to achieving the mandate of the Council to restore and maintain international peace and security.

There is also the further question of the division of responsibility between the organisation itself and its member States. For example, if the Security Council is found to have exceeded its mandate under the Charter, can State members be responsible secondarily or concurrently in such cases?[143] It may be that a State acts *ultra vires* the Security Council resolution. To add to the complexities, it is by no means apparent in what forum issues of determination and enforcement of any legal restraints on the Council belong.[144]

Generally speaking, if States are acting as subsidiary organs of the United Nations (as is the case with peacekeeping forces) the responsibility for these forces lies with the organisation. It is established that in appropriate circumstances international organisations may be held responsible for their actions that are in breach of international law.[145] Consequently, the organisation may be liable on general principles of responsibility for such actions. Moreover, the regime of the criminal responsibility of individuals for breaches of IHL is equally applicable to

[143] This issue arose in the *Tin Council* cases (*Maclaine Watson & Co. Ltd* v. *Department of Trade and Industry* [1988] 3 All ER 257; and *J. H. Rayner Ltd* v. *Department of Trade and Industry* [1989] 3 WLR 969). See C. Amerasinghe, 'Liability to Third Parties of Member States of International Organizations: Practice, Principle and Judicial Precedent' (1991) 85 *AJIL* 259.

[144] The *Lockerbie Case*, note 58 above, and the *Genocide Case*, note 59 above, provide illustrations of how the question of *ultra vires* actions of the Security Council can arise in contentious cases.

[145] 'If an organisation has a legal personality distinct from that of its member States and has functions conferred on it that in the hands of States may create responsibility, then it is in principle reasonable to impute responsibility to the organisation': I. Brownlie, *Principles of Public International Law* (5th edn, Oxford University Press, Oxford, 1998), p. 686; and see *Reparations for Injuries Suffered in the Service of the United Nations* Advisory Opinion, ICJ Reports 1949, 174 at 178–9. See generally E. Lauterpacht, 'The Legal Effects of Illegal Acts of International Organisations' in *Cambridge Essays in International Law in Honour of Lord McNair* (Stevens, London, 1965), p. 88.

United Nations forces.[146] Clearly, however, there are some circumstances in which the corporate veil of the organisation will be lifted and States themselves will incur individual responsibility for the actions of their forces. For example, this may occur if State contingents exceed their mandate in circumstances where it is unreasonable to attribute responsibility to the organisation.

The situation is somewhat different for coalitions of State forces acting under the authorisation of the Security Council. These are not subsidiary organs of the United Nations and there are differences amongst commentators as to issues of responsibility in such cases.[147] The potential for difficulties in this area is exacerbated by the practice of the Council of delegating to individual States the determination of what amounts to 'all necessary means' in order to carry out their mandate.[148] This lack of Council control was a cause for concern for some States during the 1990–1 Persian Gulf conflict[149] with some commentators of the view that the coalition allies may have exceeded the Security Council mandate.[150]

The issue of control has continued to be controversial in the context of the delegation of Chapter VII powers to States or coalitions of States. For example, several States expressed concern over the question of United Nations control in the debates leading up to Resolution 794 establishing UNITAF, a United States led coalition established under Chapter VII of the Charter to establish a secure environment for the delivery of humanitarian aid in Somalia.[151] The argument favoured by many observers, that the Security Council retains ultimate control over States acting under

[146] There are, however, difficulties for the organisation in fulfilling its obligations in relation to the criminal enforcement of IHL: see C. Greenwood, 'IHL and UN Military Operations' (1998) 1 *YBIHL* 3 at 15.

[147] See e.g. Sarooshi, *Development of Collective Security*, pp. 163–6 (arguing that responsibility is determined solely by the issue of the overall control of the authorised operation; in his view, this lies with the Council). Cf. J. Peck, 'The UN and the Laws of War: How Can the World's Peacekeepers Be Held Accountable?' (1995) 21 *Syracuse Journal of International Law and Commerce* 283 at 292–3 (arguing that it is the operational command of peacekeeping and peace enforcement forces that determines responsibility).

[148] See Blokker, 'Is the Authorization Authorized?' (for a discussion of the issue of responsibility in relation to forces acting under the Chapter VII powers of the Security Council). This tendency has been exacerbated on occasions by a failure to carefully delimit the aim of the authorised undertaking.

[149] See e.g. UN Docs. S/PV.2976, S/PV.2977 (Part I) and S/PV.2977 (Part II).

[150] See Quigley, 'New Order or Disorder', pp. 25ff.

[151] See note 100 above. In the case of UNITAF, however, the Security Council specifically conferred a command and control role on the Secretary-General. UNOSOM II, which

its authorisation, belies the reality that the Council does not have established mechanisms for overseeing such operations nor are States, the United States in particular, always willing to relinquish control over their forces. In fact, no effort has been made in the post-Cold War era to follow the practice of the Korean conflict where the fiction was maintained that this was a United Nations operation.

All these issues of responsibility await further development. One question that has attracted a great deal of discussion in recent years, albeit of a somewhat inconclusive nature, is whether there is a role for judicial scrutiny, in particular by the International Court of Justice, of any limits on the activities of the Security Council. The United Nations is not a party to the Statute of the Court, so the issue can only arise tangentially in a contentious case if, for example, a State were to allege disproportionate damage inflicted by another State in an action authorised by the Security Council under Chapter VII. The question of limits on the powers of the Council, however, could arise directly in a request for an Advisory Opinion.

The terms of the Charter provide limited guidance on this issue of the relationship between the respective roles of the Security Council and the International Court of Justice under the Charter.[152] Moreover, the negotiating history of the Charter is unclear as to the place of judicial review in relation to the Security Council.[153] The jurisprudence of the Court itself, however, throws some light on how the Court perceives its role *vis-à-vis* the other organs of the United Nations.

Two advisory opinions, the *Certain Expenses* Advisory Opinion[154] and the *Namibia* Advisory Opinion,[155] have considered the relationship between the Council and the Court. In both these cases, the Court adopted the approach of a presumption of validity in relation to resolutions of the organs of the United Nations and that 'each organ must, in the first place at least, determine its own jurisdiction'.[156] If an action

largely replaced UNITAF, was solely under the command and control of the Secretary-General.

[152] See Watson, 'Constitutionalism, Judicial Review and the World Court', pp. 4–8 (for a comprehensive discussion of the terms of the United Nations Charter and the Statute of the ICJ on this point).

[153] See *ibid.*, pp. 8–14 (for a discussion of the *travaux préparatoires* on this point).

[154] *Certain Expenses* Advisory Opinion, note 13 above.

[155] *Namibia* Advisory Opinion, note 61 above.

[156] *Certain Expenses* Advisory Opinion, note 13 above, p. 168; and see the full discussion of the issue of judicial review in the context of these cases by Watson, 'Constitutionalism, Judicial Review and the World Court', pp. 14–22.

warranted 'the assertion that it was appropriate for the fulfilment of one of the stated purposes of the United Nations, the presumption is that such action is not *ultra vires* the Organization'.[157] Nevertheless, these statements do not appear to be inconsistent with judicial scrutiny of resolutions of the organs of the organisation. In the *Namibia* Advisory Opinion, the Court explicitly addressed the question of the validity of the relevant General Assembly and Security Council resolutions. However, both these cases involved Advisory Opinions at the request of the organs of the United Nations itself. One of the purposes of the Advisory Opinion process is to assist the organisation in determining the limits of its powers under the Charter. The situation is somewhat different if the issue of validity is brought up in a contentious case.

The most significant contentious case to date involving the division of powers between these two Charter bodies is the *Lockerbie Case*, which has spawned numerous scholarly analyses[158] and is widely regarded as of pivotal jurisprudential importance.[159] Although not the first occasion that the Court has had the question before it in a contentious case, on all previous occasions[160] what the Court was dealing with was not judicial review of Security Council action by the Court but the question of whether the Court could play any role at all if the Security Council had assumed jurisdiction in the matter, quite a different question.[161] Moreover, as Justice Weeramantry observes in his Dissenting Opinion

[157] *Certain Expenses* Advisory Opinion, note 13 above.

[158] See e.g. T. Franck, 'The Powers of Appreciation: Who Is the Ultimate Guardian of UN Legality?' (1992) 86 *AJIL* 519 at 521; Brownlie, 'Decisions of Political Organs', pp. 96–7; V. Gowlland-Debbas, 'The Relationship Between the International Court of Justice and the Security Council in the Light of the *Lockerbie* Case' (1994) 88 *AJIL* 643; J. Alvarez, 'Judging the Security Council', p. 19; and Akande, 'Judicial Control of Decisions' p. 309, note 2.

[159] Franck, 'Powers of Appreciation', p. 519, observes that it 'may be the most important and jurisprudentially rich of any handed down since the end of the Cold War'; and see Graefrath, 'Iraqi Reparations', p. 203.

[160] See *Aegean Sea Continental Shelf*, Interim Protection, ICJ Reports 1976, 3; *United States Diplomatic and Consular Staff in Tehran*, Provisional Measures, ICJ Reports 1979, 7; and *Military and Paramilitary Activities in and against Nicaragua*, Provisional Measures, ICJ Reports 1984, 169.

[161] It is not in dispute that the Court has a part to play in the peaceful settlement of disputes. This role is supported by the terms of the Charter itself. As the Court observed in the *United States Diplomatic and Consular Staff in Tehran Case*, note 160 above, p. 21, para. 40, 'it does not seem to have occurred to any member of the Council that there was or could be anything irregular in the simultaneous exercise of their respective functions by the Court and the Security Council. Nor is there in this any cause for surprise.'

in the *Lockerbie Case*, in all those cases the Court and the Council were approached by the same party seeking to use the powers of each organ in a complementary way.[162] In the *Lockerbie Case*, however, the Court and the Council were placed in potentially adversarial roles.[163]

The majority Opinion on the Request for Provisional Measures somewhat frustratingly throws no real light on the question of whether the Court regards itself as having the power to find Council action *ultra vires*.[164] With the exception of Judge Weeramantry, no member of the Court indicated that Security Council decisions under Chapter VII were beyond the scrutiny of the Court. In fact, several judges indicated that the Court had a definite role to play, but not in the particular fact situation before the Court.

The issue of the respective roles of the Court and the Security Council in the Charter was also before the Court in the *Genocide Case*. One of the arguments of Bosnia-Herzegovina in its second request for provisional measures was that the arms embargo imposed by the Security Council in respect of the whole of the territory of the former Yugoslavia was *ultra vires* as it deprived Bosnia-Herzegovina of its Charter right of self-defence. Ad Hoc Judge Lauterpacht, after rejecting the view that the Security Council acts free of all legal restraint, observed 'there can be no less doubt that it [the Charter] does not embrace any right of the Court to substitute its discretion for that of the Security Council in determining the existence of a threat to the peace, a breach of the peace or an act of aggression, or the political steps to be taken following such a determination'.[165]

Even if it transpires that the actions of the Security Council are subject to some measure of judicial scrutiny, the determination of proportionality in the context of collective enforcement actions would be viewed by many as a concept too imprecise to apply in any objective fashion to

[162] *Lockerbie Case*, note 58 above, p. 542; and see Reisman, 'Constitutional Crisis in the United Nations', p. 84.

[163] Or, as one commentator puts it, the case raises the question of whether the Security Council can 'interfere with Court procedures so as to render them meaningless'. See Graefrath, 'Iraqi Reparations', p. 199.

[164] See Gowlland-Debbas, 'Lockerbie Case', for a full discussion of the judgments in the *Lockerbie Case*.

[165] Separate Opinion of Ad Hoc Judge Lauterpacht, *Application of the Convention on the Prevention and Punishment of the Crime of Genocide (Bosnia and Herzegovina* v. *Yugoslavia (Serbia and Montenegro))*, Further Requests for Indications of Provisional Measures, Order of 13 September 1993, ICJ Reports 1993, 325 at 439.

the complex situations that can confront the Security Council in exercising its responsibility for the maintenance of international peace and security. This is, however, a problem inherent in the very nature of the task this principle must perform, irrespective of the particular circumstances. The assessment of proportionality, however, is undoubtedly a much more straightforward process in the law of self-defence. The prevailing view is that a State can only legitimately use force in response to an armed attack to the degree necessary to defend itself.[166] The determination of the existence of an armed attack and measures that qualify as defensive, although not beyond dispute, are capable of being determined with some precision.[167] In the only judicial precedent that considers the application of the requirements of necessity and proportionality in the context of self-defence under the Charter, the *Nicaragua Case*, the International Court of Justice had little difficulty with applying these concepts to the facts before it.[168] Admittedly, the facts before the Court in that case could be regarded as presenting relatively clear-cut examples of disproportionate and unnecessary actions in the context of self-defence.

In contrast to self-defence, the restoration of international peace and security is a much more nebulous concept. There would be vast differences of opinion as to what actions, for example, would be proportionate to achieve this goal. It is in the context of 'threats to the peace', rather than breaches of the peace or acts of aggression, that the assessment of proportionality becomes extremely difficult, particularly in light of the recent practice of the Security Council of interpreting the phrase so widely. If the activity against which the response must be judged is inherently vague, as is the case with a 'threat to the peace', the comparison with the means required by proportionality becomes very complex. This is somewhat reminiscent of the difficulties of assessing proportionality in the context of anticipatory self-defence, which is also predicated on a 'threat' rather than an actuality.[169] At the very least, the characterisation of the dispute as a threat to the peace would, generally speaking,

[166] See the discussion in Chapter 5 above.

[167] See the discussion in Chapter 5 above.

[168] See also the *Nuclear Weapons* Advisory Opinion, note 98 above, where the Court considered in the abstract the proportionality of the threat or use of nuclear weapons in self-defence. See the discussion on this point in Chapter 5, note 169, and the accompanying text above.

[169] See the discussion of this point in Chapter 5, note 171, and the accompanying text above.

warrant a more restrained response in terms of the use of force than a breach of the peace or an act of aggression. Similarly, where there is a situation that merely constitutes a threat to the peace, to establish the requisite state of necessity to use military force would be a more significant task than where there is a situation involving an act of aggression.

Bibliography

Accioly, Hildebrando, *Traité de Droit International Public* (Recueil Sirey, Paris, 1940)
African Rights, *Somalia, Human Rights Abuses by United Nations Peace-keeping Forces* (African Rights, London, 1993)
Akande, Dapo, 'The International Court of Justice and the Security Council: Is There Room for Judicial Control of Decisions of the Political Organs of the United Nations?' (1997) 46 *ICLQ* 309
Alexander, D. C. (ed.), *Contemporary International Law Issues: Sharing Pan-European and American Perspectives, Proceedings of the Joint Conference Held in The Hague, The Netherlands, July 4–6 1991* (Martinus Nijhoff, Dordrecht, 1992)
Alston, Philip, 'The Security Council and Human Rights: Lessons to Be Learned from the Iraq–Kuwait Crisis and Its Aftermath' (1992) 13 *Australian YIL* 107
Alvarez, Jose E., 'Judging the Security Council' (1996) 90 *AJIL* 1
Amerasinghe, Chittharanjan F., *Principles of the Institutional Law of International Organizations* (Cambridge University Press, Cambridge, 1996)
'Liability to Third Parties of Member States of International Organisations: Practice, Principle and Judicial Precedent' (1991) 85 *AJIL* 259
American Society of International Law, 'Should the Laws of War Apply to UN Enforcement Action?', Report of the American Society of International Law Committee on Legal Problems of the UN, reprinted in (1952) *Proc. ASIL* 216
Amnesty International, *Peace-Keeping and Human Rights* (Amnesty International, London, 1994)
Report on the Gulf War (Amnesty International, London, 1991)
Arangio-Ruiz, Gaëtano, 'Third Report on State Responsibility' (1991) II *YBILC* 63
Baarda, Th. A. van, 'The Involvement of the Security Council in Maintaining International Humanitarian Law' (1994) 12 *Netherlands Quarterly of Human Rights* 137
Bainton, Roland H., *Christian Attitudes Toward War and Peace: A Historical Survey and Critical Re-evaluation* (Abingdon, Nashville, TN, 1960)
Baker, Betsy, 'Legal Protection for the Environment in Times of Armed Conflict' (1993) 33 *Virginia JIL* 51

Barboza, J., 'Necessity (Revisited) in International Law' in J. Makarczyk (ed.), *Essays in International Law in Honour of Judge Manfred Lachs* (Martinus Nijhoff, The Hague, 1984)
Bassett Moore, J., *International Law and Some Current Illusions and Other Essays* (Macmillan, New York, 1924)
Baxter, Robert, 'Humanitarian Law or Humanitarian Politics? The 1974 Diplomatic Conference on Humanitarian Law' (1975) 16 *Harvard ILJ* 1
'The Legal Consequences of the Unlawful Use of Force under the Charter' (1968) *Proc. ASIL* 68
'Weary Word on the Law of War' (1965) 59 *AJIL* 920
Bayne, P., 'Reasonableness, Proportionality and Delegated Legislation' (1993) 67 *Australian LJ* 448
Best, Geoffrey F. A., *War and Law Since 1945* (Oxford University Press, 1994)
'The Place of Grotius in the Development of International Humanitarian Law' in Alfred Dufour, Peter Haggenmacher and Jirí Toman (eds.), *Grotius et l'Ordre Juridique International: Travaux du Colloque Hugo Grotius, Geneva, 10–11 November 1983* (Payot, Lausanne, 1985), p. 101
Humanity in Warfare: The Modern History of the International Law of Armed Conflict (Weidenfeld & Nicolson, London, 1980)
'Restraints on War by Land Before 1945' in M. Howard (ed.), *Restraints on War: Studies in the Limitation of Armed Conflicts* (Oxford University Press, Oxford, 1979), p. 17
Blix, H., 'Area Bombardment: Rules and Reasons' (1978) 49 *BYIL* 31
Blokker, N., 'Is the Authorization Authorized? Powers and Practice of the UN Security Council to Authorize the Use of Force by "Coalitions of the Able and Willing"' (2000) 11 *EJIL* 541
Boisson de Chazournes, Laurence, 'The Collective Responsibility of States to Ensure Respect for Humanitarian Principles' in Arie Bloed *et al.* (eds.), *Monitoring Human Rights in Europe: Comparing International Procedures and Mechanisms* (Martinus Nijhoff, Dordrecht, 1993), p. 247
Boisson de Chazournes, Laurence and L. Condorelli, 'Common Article 1 of the Geneva Conventions Revisited: Protecting Collective Interests' (2000) 837 *IRRC* 67
Boisson de Chazournes, Laurence and Philippe Sands (eds.), *International Law, the International Court of Justice and Nuclear Weapons* (Cambridge University Press, Cambridge, 1999)
Bond, James E., *The Rules of Riot: Internal Conflict and the Law of War* (Princeton University Press, Princeton, 1974)
Bothe, Michael, 'The Protection of the Civilian Population and NATO Bombing on Yugoslavia: Comments on a Report to the Prosecutor of the ICTY' (2001) 12 *EJIL* 531
'Peacekeeping and the Use of Force – Back to the Charter or Political Accident?' (1994) 1 *International Peacekeeping* 2
'Les Limites des Pouvoirs du Conseil de Sécurité' in René J. Dupuy (ed.), *The Development of the Role of the Security Council Peace-Keeping and Peace-Building:*

Workshop, The Hague, 21–23 July 1992 (Martinus Nijhoff, Dordrecht, 1993), p. 67
Bothe, Michael, Karl J. Partsch and Waldemar A. Solf, *New Rules for Victims of Armed Conflict* (Martinus Nijhoff, The Hague, 1982)
Bourloyannis, Christiane, 'The Security Council of the United Nations and the Implementation of International Humanitarian Law' (1992) 20 *Denver Journal of International Law and Policy* 335
Boutros-Ghali, Boutros, *An Agenda for Peace* (2nd edn, United Nations, New York, 1995)
Bowett, Derek W., 'The Impact of Security Council Decisions on Dispute Settlement Procedures' (1994) 5 *EJIL* 89
'Reprisals Involving Recourse to Armed Force' (1972) 66 *AJIL* 1
United Nations Forces: A Legal Study (Stevens and Sons, London, 1964)
Self-Defence in International Law (Manchester University Press, Manchester, 1958)
Boyron, S., 'Proportionality in English Administrative Law: A Faulty Translation?' (1992) *Oxford Journal of Legal Studies* 237
Brierly, James L., *The Law of Nations* (6th edn, Clarendon Press, Oxford, 1963)
'Règles Générales du Droit de la Paix' (1936-IV) 58 *Recueil des Cours*
The Law of Nations (Clarendon Press, Oxford, 1928)
Brown, B., 'The Proportionality Principle in the Humanitarian Law of Warfare: Recent Efforts at Codification' (1976) 10 *Cornell ILJ* 134
Brownlie, Ian, *Principles of Public International Law* (5th edn, Clarendon Press, Oxford, 1998)
The Rule of Law in International Affairs (Martinus Nijhoff, Dordrecht, 1998)
'The Decisions of Political Organs of the United Nations and the Rule of Law' in Ronald St J. Macdonald (ed.), *Essays in Honour of Wang Tieya* (Martinus Nijhoff, Dordrecht, 1993)
'The United Nations Charter and the Use of Force, 1945–1958' in Antonio Cassese (ed.), *The Current Legal Regulation of the Use of Force* (Martinus Nijhoff, Dordrecht, 1986), p. 497
International Law and the Use of Force by States (Clarendon Press, Oxford, 1963)
Bull, Hedley, 'The Importance of Grotius in the Study of International Relations' in Hedley Bull, Benedict Kingsbury and Adam Roberts (eds.), *Hugo Grotius and International Relations* (Clarendon Press, Oxford, 1990), p. 85
Bull, Hedley, Benedict Kingsbury and Adam Roberts (eds.), *Hugo Grotius and International Relations* (Clarendon Press, Oxford, 1990)
Bynkershoek, Cornelius van, *Quaestionum Juris Publici Libri Duo* (1737), trans. by T. Frank in James B. Scott (ed.), *The Classics of International Law* (Carnegie Endowment for International Peace, Washington, DC, 1930)
Caratsch, Claudio, 'Humanitarian Design and Political Interference: Red Cross Work in the Post-Cold War Period' (1993) 11 *International Relations* 301
Carnahan, Burrus M., 'Lincoln, Lieber and the Laws of War: The Origins and Limits of the Principle of Military Necesity' (1998) 92 *AJIL* 213
'The Law of Aerial Bombardment in its Historical Context' (1975) 17(2) *Air Force LR* 39

Carnahan, Burrus M. and M. Robertson, 'The Protocol on "Blinding Laser Weapons": A New Direction for International Humanitarian Law' (1996) 90 *AJIL* 484
Caron, David D., 'Legitimacy of the Collective Authority of the Security Council' (1993) 87 *AJIL* 552
Cassese, Antonio, '*Ex Iniuria Ius Oritur*: Are We Moving Towards International Legitimation of Forcible Humanitarian Countermeasures in the World Community?' (1999) 10 *EJIL* 23
'The Geneva Protocols of 1977 on the Humanitarian Law of Armed Conflict and Customary International Law' (1984) 3 *UCLA PBLJ* 55
'Weapons Causing Unnecessary Suffering: Are They Prohibited?' (1975) 48 *Riv. DI* 12
Charney, J., 'Anticipatory Humanitarian Intervention in Kosovo' (1999) 93 *AJIL* 834
Cheng, Bin, *General Principles of Law as Applied in International Courts and Tribunals* (Stevens and Sons, London, 1953)
Chinkin, Christine, 'Kosovo: A Good or Bad War?' (1999) 93 *AJIL* 84
Third Parties in International Law (Oxford, Clarendon Press, 1993)
Ciobanu, Dan, 'The Power of the Security Council to Organise Peace-Keeping Operations' in Antonio Cassese (ed.), *United Nations Peace-keeping: Legal Essays* (Sijthoff & Noordhoff, Alphen aan den Rijn, 1978), p. 15
Claude, Iris Jr, 'UN Efforts at Settlement of the Falklands Islands Crisis' in Alberto R. Coll and Anthony C. Arend (eds.), *The Falklands War: Lessons for Strategy, Diplomacy, and International Law* (Allen and Unwin, Boston, MA, 1985), p. 118
Clausewitz, Carl von, *On War*, trans. by A. Rapoport (Penguin, Baltimore, MD, 1968)
Colbert, Evelyn S., *Retaliation in International Law* (King's Crown, New York, 1948)
Conforti, Benedetto, 'Le Pouvoir Discrétionnaire du Conseil de Sécurité en Matière de Constatation d'une Menace Contre la Paix, d'une Rupture de la Paix ou d'un Acte d'Agression' in René J. Dupuy (ed.), *The Development of the Role of the Security Council Peace-Keeping and Peace-Building: Workshop, The Hague, 21–23 July 1992* (Martinus Nijhoff, Dordrecht, 1993), p. 51
Cooper, M., *The Birth of Independent Air Power* (Allen and Unwin, London, 1986)
Coupland, R. (ed.), *The SirUS Project: Towards a Determination of Which Weapons Cause Superfluous Injury or Unnecessary Suffering* (ICRC, Geneva, 1997)
de Brouckère, L., 'La Prévention de la Guerre' (1934-IV) 50 *Recueil des Cours* 33
de Guttry, Andrea de and Natalino Ronzitti (eds.), *The Iran–Iraq War (1980–1988) and the Law of Naval Warfare* (Grotius, Cambridge, 1993)
de Vattel, Emer, 'Le Droit de Gens, ou Principes de la Loi Naturelle, Appliqués à la Conduite et aux Affaires des Nations et des Souverains', trans. by Charles G. Fenwick in James B. Scott (ed.), *The Classics of International Law* (Carnegie Endowment for International Peace, Washington, DC, 1916), vol. 3
Dekker, I. F. and H. H. G. Post (eds.), *The Gulf War of 1980–1988: The Iran–Iraq War in International Legal Perspective* (Martinus Nijhoff, Dordrecht, 1992)

Delbruck, J., 'Proportionality' in R. Bernhardt (ed.), *The Encyclopedia of Public International Law* (New Holland Publishing, New York, 1981–91), vol. 3, p. 1144

DeSaussure, H., 'The Laws of Air Warfare: Are There Any?' (1971) 5 *International Lawyer* 527

DeSaussure, H. and R. Glasser, *Law and Responsibility in Warfare: The Vietnam Experience* (ed. by P. Trooboff, University of North Carolina Press, Chapel Hill, NC, 1975)

Dinstein, Yoram, *War, Aggression and Self-Defence* (2nd edn, Grotius, Cambridge, 1994)

'Implementing Limitations on the Use of Force: The Doctrine of Proportionality and Necessity' (1992) *Proc. ASIL* 39

Dinstein, Yoram and M. Tabory (eds.), *War Crimes in International Law* (Martinus Nijhoff, Boston, 1996)

Doswald-Beck, Louise, 'International Humanitarian Law and the Advisory Opinion of the International Court of Justice on the Legality of the Threat or Use of Nuclear Weapons' (1997) 316 *IRRC* 35

(ed.), *San Remo Manual on International Law Applicable to Armed Conflicts at Sea* (Cambridge University Press, Cambridge, 1995)

'Vessels, Aircraft and Persons Entitled to Protection During Armed Conflict at Sea' (1994) 65 *BYIL* 211

'Obstacles to Regulating New Weaponry: Battlefield Laser Weapons' in Hazel Fox and Michael H. Meyer (eds.), *Effecting Compliance, Armed Conflict and the New Law* (British Institute of International and Comparative Law, London, 1993), p. 107

'The Value of the 1977 Geneva Protocols for the Protection of Civilians' in Hazel Fox and Michael H. Meyer (eds.), *Effecting Compliance: Armed Conflict and the New Law* (British Institute of International and Comparative Law, London, 1993), p. 137

Draper, Gerald, 'The Modern Pattern of War Criminality' in Y. Dinstein and M. Tabory (eds.), *War Crimes in International Law* (Martinus Nijhoff, Boston, 1996)

'The Development of International Humanitarian Law' (1988) 67 *International Dimensions of Humanitarian Law* 179

'Human Rights and the Law of War' (1972) 12 *Virginia JIL* 326

Dunbar, N. C. H., 'Military Necessity in War Crimes Trials' (1952) 29 *BYIL* 442

Farer, T., 'The Laws of War 25 Years After Nuremberg' (1971) *International Conciliation* No. 583, p. 16

Fenrick, W., 'The Rule of Proportionality and Protocol I in Conventional Warfare' (1982) 98 *Military LR* 91

'New Developments in the Law Concerning the Use of Conventional Weapons in Armed Conflict' (1981) 19 *Canadian YIL* 229

Fenwick, C., *International Law* (4th edn, Appleton Century Crofts, New York, 1965)

Fonteyne, J. P., 'Forcible Self-Help by States to Protect Human Rights: Recent Views from the United Nations' in Richard B. Lillich (ed.), *Humanitarian Intervention and the United Nations* (University of Virginia Press, Charlottesville, VA, 1973), p. 197

Ford, John C., 'The Morality of Obliteration Bombing' (1955) 5 *Theological Studies* 261

Forsythe, David P., 'Legal Management of Internal War: The 1977 Protocol on Non-International Armed Conflicts' (1978) 72 *AJIL* 272

Fox, Richard G., 'The Meaning of Proportionality in Sentencing' (1994) 19 *MULR* 489

Franck, Thomas M., *Fairness in International Law and Institutions* (Oxford University Press, Oxford, 1995)

'The Security Council and "Threats to the Peace": Some Remarks on Remarkable Recent Developments' in René J. Dupuy (ed.), *The Development of the Role of the Security Council Peace-Keeping and Peace-Building: Workshop, The Hague, 21–23 July 1992* (Martinus Nijhoff, Dordrecht, 1993)

'The Emerging Right to Democratic Governance' (1992) 86 *AJIL* 46

'The Powers of Appreciation: Who Is the Ultimate Guardian of UN Legality?' (1992) 86 *AJIL* 519

Freedman, L. and E. Karsch, *The Gulf Conflict 1990–1991: Diplomacy and War in the New World Order* (Princeton University Press, Princeton, 1993)

Gardam, Judith G., 'The Contribution of the International Court of Justice to the Development of International Humanitarian Law' (2001) 14 *Leiden JIL* 349

(ed.), *Humanitarian Law* (Dartmouth Publishing Co. Ltd, Aldershot (UK), 1999)

Non-Combatant Immunity as a Norm of International Humanitarian Law (Martinus Nijhoff, Dordrecht, 1993)

'Proportionality and Force in International Law' (1993) 87 *AJIL* 391

'Noncombatant Immunity and the Gulf Conflict' (1992) 33 *Virginia JIL* 813

Gasser, H., 'The Sixth Annual American Red Cross Washington Conference on International Humanitarian Law: A Workshop on Customary International Law and the 1977 Protocols Additional to the 1949 Geneva Conventions' (1987) 2 *American Journal of International Law and Policy* 415

Gentili, Alberico, *De Iure Belli Libri Tres* (1612), trans. by John C. Rolfe in James B. Scott (ed.), *The Classics of International Law* (Carnegie Endowment for International Peace, Washington, DC, 1933), vol. II, Book II, Chapter I

Gill, T. D., 'Legal and Some Political Limitations on the Power of the UN Security Council to Exercise its Enforcement Powers Under Chapter VII of the Charter' (1995) 26 *NYIL* 33

Giraud, Emile, 'La Théorie de la Légitime Défence' (1934-III) 49 *Recueil des Cours* 691

Goodrich, Leland M., *Korea: A Study on US Policy in the United Nations* (1st edn, Council on Foreign Relations, New York, 1956)

Goodrich, Leland M. and Anne P. Simons, *The United Nations and the Maintenance of International Peace and Security* (Greenwood, Westport, CT, 1974)
The Charter of the United Nations: Commentary and Documents (2nd edn, World Peace Foundation, Boston, MA, 1949)
Goodrich, Leland M., Edvard Hambro and Anne P. Simons, *The Charter of the United Nations: Commentary and Documents* (3rd edn, Columbia University Press, New York, 1969)
Goulding, Marrack, 'The Evolution of United Nations Peacekeeping' (1993) 69 *International Affairs*. 451
Gowlland-Debbas, Vera, 'Security Council Enforcement Action and Issues of State Responsibility' (1994) 43 *ICLQ* 55
'The Relationship Between the International Court of Justice and the Security Council in the Light of the Lockerbie Case' (1994) 88 *AJIL* 643
Graefrath, Bernhard, 'Iraqi Reparations and the Security Council' (1995) 55 *Heidelberg Journal of International Law* 1
'Leave to the Court What Belongs to the Court – The Libyan Case' (1993) 4 *EJIL* 184
Gray, Christine, *International Law and the Use of Force* (Oxford University Press, Oxford, 2000)
'The British Position in Regard to the Conflict' (1988) 37 *ICLQ* 420
Green, Leslie C., *The Contemporary Law of Armed Conflict* (Manchester University Press, Manchester, 1993)
'The Geneva Humanitarian Law Conference, 1975' (1975) 13 *Canadian YIL* 295
Greenwood, Christopher, '*Jus ad Bellum* and *Jus in Bello* in the *Nuclear Weapons Advisory Opinion*' in L. Boisson de Chazournes and P. Sands (eds.), *International Law, the International Court of Justice and Nuclear Weapons* (Cambridge University Press, Cambridge, 1999)
'International Humanitarian Law and United Nations Military Operations' (1998) 1 *Yearbook of International Humanitarian Law* 3
'Protection of Peacekeepers: The Legal Regime' (1995) 7 *Duke Journal of Comparative and International Law* 185
'Command and the Laws of Armed Conflict' (1993) 4 *The Occasional* 1
'The International Tribunal for Former Yugoslavia' (1993) 69(4) *International Affairs*. 641
'Comment' in Ige F. Dekker and Harry H. G. Post (eds.), *The Gulf War of 1980–1988: The Iran–Iraq War in International Legal Perspective* (Martinus Nijhoff, Dordrecht, 1992), p. 212
'Customary International Law and the First Geneva Protocol of 1977 in the Gulf Conflict' in Peter Rowe (ed.), *The Gulf War (1990–91) in International and English Law* (Routledge, London, 1992), p. 63
'New World Order or Old? The Invasion of Kuwait and the Rule of Law' (1992) 55 *MLR* 153

'Self-Defence and the Conduct of International Armed Conflict' in Yoram Dinstein (ed.), *International Law at a Time of Perplexity: Essays in Honour of Shabtai Rosenne* (Martinus Nijhoff, Dordrecht, 1989), p. 273

'International Law and the United States Air Operation Against Libya' (1987) 89 *WVLR* 933

'The Concept of War in Modern International Law' (1987) 36 *ICLQ* 283

'The Relationship Between *Ius ad Bellum* and *Ius in Bello*' (1983) 9 *Review of International Studies* 221

Greig, D. W., 'Reciprocity, Proportionality and the Law of Treaties' (1994) 34 *Virginia JIL* 295

International Law (2nd edn, Butterworths, London, 1976)

Grotius, H., 'De Jure Belli ac Pacis Libri Tres', trans. by Francis W. Kelsey in James B. Scott (ed.), *The Classics of International Law* (Carnegie Endowment for International Peace, Washington, DC, 1925), vol. 2, Book III

Haggemacher, Peter, *Grotius et la Doctrine de la Guerre Juste* (Presses Universitaires de France, Paris, 1983)

Hall, William E., *A Treatise on International Law*, (ed. by P. Higgins, 8th edn, Clarendon Press, Oxford, 1924)

A Treatise on International Law (4th edn, Clarendon Press, Oxford, 1895)

International Law (Clarendon Press, Oxford, 1880)

Hampson, Françoise, 'Means and Methods of Warfare in the Conflict in the Gulf' in Peter Rowe (ed.), *The Gulf War (1990–91) in International and English Law* (Routledge, London, 1993), p. 89

'Belligerent Reprisals and the 1977 Protocols to the Geneva Conventions of 1949' (1988) 37 *ICLQ* 818

Hargrove, J., 'The Nicaragua Judgement and the Future of the Law of Force and Self-Defence' (1987) 81 *AJIL* 135

Hartigan, S., *The Forgotten Victim: A History of the Civilian* (Precedent, Chicago, 1982)

'Noncombatant Immunity: Reflections on Its Origins and Present Status' (1966) *Review of Politics* 204

Hartley, T., *Foundations of European Community Law: An Introduction to the Constitutional and Administrative Law of the European Community* (4th edn, Oxford University Press, New York, 1998)

Harvard International Study Team on the Gulf Crisis, *Health and Welfare in Iraq After the Gulf Crisis: An In Depth Assessment* (Harvard International Study Team on the Gulf Crisis, 1991)

Hays Parks, W., 'Air War and the Law of War' (1990) 32 *Air Force LR* 1

Hebel, H. von and D. Robinson, 'Crimes Within the Jurisdiction of the Court' in R. S. Lee (ed.), *The International Criminal Court – Issues, Negotiations, Results* (Kluwer Law International, The Hague, 1999), p. 79

Hegelson, G. J. F. van, 'The Law of Armed Conflict and UN Peacekeeping and Peace-Enforcing Operations' (1993) 6 *Hague YIL* 44

Henkin, Louis, 'Law and War After the Cold War' (1991) 15 *Maryland Journal of International Law and Trade* 147

'The Invasion of Panama under International Law: A Gross Violation' (1991) 29 *Columbia JTL* 293

'The Use of Force: Law and US Policy' in Louis Henkin *et al.*, *Right v. Might: International Law and the Use of Force* (Council on Foreign Affairs, New York, 1989), p. 37

Henkin, Louis *et al.*, *Right v. Might: International Law and the Use of Force* (Council on Foreign Affairs, New York, 1989)

Herby, Peter, 'Third Session of the Review Conference of States Parties to the 1980 United Nations Convention on Certain Conventional Weapons (CCW)' (1996) 312 *IRRC* 361

Higgins, Alexander P., *Non-Combatants and the War* (Oxford University Press, Oxford, 1914)

Higgins, Rosalyn, *Problems and Process: International Law and How We Use It* (Oxford University Press, Oxford, 1994)

'The New United Nations and Former Yugoslavia' (1993) 69 *International Affairs* 465

'A General Assessment of UN Peacekeeping' in Antonio Cassese (ed.), *United Nations Peacekeeping: Legal Essays* (Sijthoff & Noordhoff, Alphen aan den Rijn, 1978)

'The Place of International Law in the Settlement of Disputes by the Security Council' (1970) 64 *AJIL* 1

United Nations Peacekeeping 1946–1967: Commentary and Documents, vol. I, *The Middle East* (Oxford University Press, Oxford, 1969)

United Nations Peacekeeping 1946–1967: Commentary and Documents, vol. II, *Asia* (Oxford University Press, Oxford, 1969)

United Nations Peacekeeping 1946–1967: Commentary and Documents, vol. III, *Africa* (Oxford University Press, Oxford, 1969)

United Nations Peacekeeping: Commentary and Documents, vol. IV, *Europe 1946–1979* (Oxford University Press, Oxford, 1981)

'International Law, Rhodesia and the UN' (1967) 23 *World Today* 94

The Development of International Law Through the Political Organs of the United Nations (Oxford University Press, Oxford, 1963)

Holland, Sir Thomas E., *The Laws of War on Land (Written and Unwritten)* (Clarendon Press, Oxford, 1928)

Human Rights Watch, *Civilian Deaths in the NATO Air Campaign, 2000* (No. 1(D), 2000), vol. 12

The Lost Agenda: Human Rights and UN Field Operations (Human Rights Watch, New York, 1993)

Needless Deaths in the Gulf War (Human Rights Watch, New York, 1991)

Hyde, C. C., *International Law Chiefly as Interpreted and Applied by the United States* (3 vols., 2nd edn, Little, Brown & Co., Boston, MA, 1951)

ICRC, *Banning Anti-Personnel Mines: The Ottawa Treaty Explained* (ICRC, Geneva, 1998)

Working Paper Prepared by the ICRC for the Preparatory Committee for the Establishment of an International Criminal Court (ICRC, Geneva, 1997)

Anti-Personnel Landmines: Friend or Foe? (ICRC, Geneva, 1996)

Report of the ICRC for the Review Conference of the 1980 United Nations Convention on Prohibitions or Restrictions on the Use of Certain Conventional Weapons Which May Be Deemed to Be Excessively Injurious or to Have Indiscriminate Effects (ICRC, Geneva, 1994)

'Blinding Weapons' in *Reports of the Meetings of Experts Convened by the International Committee of the Red Cross on Battlefield Laser Weapons* (1989–91) (ICRC, Geneva, 1993), p. 71

Report of the Conference of Government Experts on the Use of Certain Conventional Weapons, Lugano, 1976 (ICRC, Geneva, 1976)

Report of the Conference of Government Experts on the Use of Certain Conventional Weapons, Lucerne, 1974 (ICRC, Geneva, 1975)

Conference of Government Experts on the Reaffirmation and Development of International Humanitarian Law Applicable in Armed Conflicts, Geneva, 3 May–3 June 1972, Second Session, Report on the Work of the Conference (2 vols., ICRC, Geneva, 1972), annexes

Conference of Government Experts on the Reaffirmation and Development of International Humanitarian Law Applicable in Armed Conflicts, Geneva, 24 May–12 June 1971, Report on the Work of the Conference (ICRC, Geneva, 1971)

Infeld, D., 'Precision-Guided Munitions Demonstrated Their Pinpoint Accuracy in Desert Storm: But Is a Country Obligated to Use Precision Technology to Minimize Collateral Civilian Injury and Damage?' (1992) 26 *George Washington Journal of International Law and Economics* 109

Jennings, R. Y., 'The Caroline and McLeod Cases' (1938) 32 *AJIL* 82

Jiménez de Aréchaga, Eduardo, 'International Law in the Past Third of a Century' (1978-I) 159 *Recueil des Cours 1*

Jochnick, Chris af and Roger Normand, 'The Legitimation of Violence: A Critical History of the Laws of War' (1994) 35 *Harvard ILJ* 49

Johnson, D., *Rights in Air Space* (Manchester University Press, Manchester, 1965)

Johnson, James Turner, *Can Modern War Be Just?* (Yale University Press, New Haven CT, 1984)

Just War Tradition and the Restraint of War: A Moral and Historical Inquiry (Princeton University Press, Princeton, 1981)

Ideology, Reason and the Limitation of War: Religious and Secular Concepts (Princeton University Press, Princeton, 1975)

Kalshoven, Frits, 'State Responsibility for Warlike Acts of the Armed Forces' (1991) 40 *ICLQ* 827

'Arms, Armaments and International Law' (1985-II) 191 *Recueil des Cours* 183

'Grotius' *Jus in Bello* with Special Reference to Ruses of War and Perfidy' in Alfred Dufour, Peter Haggenmacher and Jirí Toman (eds.), *Grotius et l'Ordre Juridique International: Travaux du Colloque Hugo Grotius, Geneva, 10–11 November 1983* (Payot, Lausanne, 1985), p. 89

'The Soldier and His Golf Clubs' in C. Swinarski (ed.), *Studies and Essays on International Humanitarian Law and Red Cross Principles* (Martinus Nijhoff, Geneva, 1984), p. 369

'Reaffirmation and Development of International Humanitarian Law Applicable in Armed Conflicts: The Diplomatic Conference, Geneva, 1974–1977, Part I' (1977) 8 *NYIL* 107

'The Conference of Government Experts on the Use of Certain Conventional Weapons, Lucerne, 24 September–18 October 1974' (1975) 6 *NYIL* 77

The Law of Warfare (Sijthoff, Leiden, 1973)

Belligerent Reprisals (Sijthoff, Leiden, 1971)

Keen, Maurice H., *The Laws of War in the Late Middle Ages* (Routledge, London, 1965)

Kelsen, Hans, *General Theory of Law and State* (Russell, New York, 1961)

Recent Trends in the Law of the United Nations (Stevens & Sons, London, 1951)

Law of the United Nations: A Critical Analysis of Its Fundamental Problems (Praeger, New York, 1950)

Kenny, Douglas, 'Anglo-Argentine Diplomacy and the Falklands Crisis' in Alberto R. Coll and Anthony C. Arend (eds.), *The Falklands War: Lessons for Strategy, Diplomacy, and International Law* (Allen & Unwin, Boston, MA, 1985), p. 81

Kirgis, Frederic L. Jr, 'The Security Council's First Fifty Years' (1995) 89 *AJIL* 506

Kirk, J., 'Constitutional Guarantees, Characterisation and the Concept of Proportionality' (1997) 21 *MULR* 1

Knopp, Karen, 'Re/Statements: Feminism and State Sovereignty in International Law' (1993) 3 *Transnational Law and Contemporary Problems* 293

Kolb, R., 'Origin of the Twin Terms *Jus ad Bellum* and *Jus in Bello*' (1997) 320 *IRRC* 553

Komenov, Tihomir, 'The Origin of State and Entity Responsibility for Violations of International Humanitarian Law in Armed Conflicts' in Frits Kalshoven and Yves Sandoz (eds.), *Implementation of International Humanitarian Law in Armed Conflicts: Research Papers by Participants in the 1986 Session of the Centre for Studies and Research in International Law and International Relations of the Hague Academy of International Law* (Martinus Nijhoff, Dordrecht, 1989), p. 169

Korhonen, Outi, 'Current Trends in European International Law Publications' (1998) 9 *EJIL* 553

Koskenniemi, M., 'The Place of Law in Collective Security' (1996) 17 *Michigan JIL* 455

Kotzsch, Lothar, *The Concept of War in Contemporary History and International Law* (E. Dioz, Geneva, 1956)

Krüger-Sprengel, Friedhelm, 'Le Concept de Proportionnalité dans le Droit de la Guerre', *Rapport présenté au Comité pour la protection de la vie humaine dans les conflits armés, VIIIe Congrès de la Société internationale de droit pénal militaire et de droit de la guerre, Ankara, October 1979* (Société international de droit pénal militaire et de droit de la guerre, Brussels, 1981), p. 194

Kunz, Josef L., 'Bellum Just and Bellum Legal' (1951) 45 *AJIL* 528

Lagoni, R. 'Neutrality, the Rights of Shipping and the Use of Force in the Persian Gulf War Part I' in Ige F. Dekker and Harry H. G. Post (eds.), *The Gulf War of 1980–1988: The Iran–Iraq War in International Legal Perspective* (Martinus Nijhoff, Dordrecht, 1992), p. 162

Lammers, Johan G., 'General Principles of Law Recognised by Civilised Nations' in Frits Kalshoven, Pieter J. Kuyper and Johann G. Lammers (eds.), *Essays on the Development of the International Legal Order: In Memory of Haro F. van Panhuys* (Sijthoff & Noordhoff, Alphen aan den Rijn, 1980), p. 53

Lauterpacht, Sir Hersch, 'The Legal Effects of Illegal Acts of International Organisations' in *Cambridge Essays in International Law in Honour of Lord McNair* (Stevens, London, 1965), p. 88

'The Problem of the Revision of the Law of War' (1959) 29 *BYIL* 360

The Function of Law in the International Community (Clarendon Press, Oxford, 1933)

Levie, Howard S., 'The Falklands Crisis and the Laws of War' in Alberto R. Coll and Anthony C. Arend (eds.), *The Falklands War: Lessons for Strategy, Diplomacy, and International Law* (Allen & Unwin, Boston, MA, 1985), p. 64

Protection of War Victims: Protocol I to the 1949 Geneva Conventions (4 vols., Oceana, Dobbs Ferry, NY, 1979–85)

When Battle Rages How Can Law Protect? (Oceana, Dobbs Ferry, NY, 1971)

Levitin, M. J., 'The Law of Force and the Force of Law: Grenada, the Falklands, and Humanitarian Intervention' (1986) 27 *Harvard ILJ* 621

Lillich, Richard B. (ed.), *Humanitarian Intervention and the United Nations* (University of Virginia Press, Charlottesville, VA, 1986)

Lobel, J. and M. Ratner, 'Bypassing the Security Council: Ambiguous Authorizations to Use Force, Cease Fires and the Iraqi Inspection Regime' (1999) 93 *AJIL* 124

Low, Luan and David Hodgkinson, 'Compensation for Wartime Environmental Damage: Challenges to International Law after the Gulf War' (1995) 35 *Virginia JIL* 405

Lysaght, Charles, 'The Scope of Protocol II and Its Relation to Common Article 3 of the Geneva Conventions of 1949 and Other Human Rights Instruments' (1983) 33 *American University Law Review* 9

Maccoby, S., 'Reprisals as a Measure of Redress Short of War' (1924) 2 *Cambridge LJ* 60

Malanczuk, Peter, *Humanitarian Intervention and the Legitimacy of the Use of Force* (Het Spinhuis, Amsterdam, 1993)

Matheson, Michael J., 'The Opinion of the International Court of Justice on the Threat or Use of Nuclear Weapons' (1997) 91 *AJIL* 417

Matheson, Michael J. and Burrus M. Carnahan, 'The Sixth Annual American Red Cross-Washington Conference on International Humanitarian Law: A Workshop on Customary International Law and the 1977 Protocols Additional to the 1949 Geneva Conventions' (1987) 2 *American University Journal of International Law and Policy* 415

Mathews, R. J. and T. L. H. McCormack, 'The Influence of Humanitarian Principles in the Negotiation of Arms Control Treaties' (1999) 834 *IRRC* 331
McDougal, Myres M. and Florentino P. Feliciano, *The International Law of War: Transnational Coercion and World Public Order* (Martinus Nijhoff, Dordrecht, 1994)
Law and Minimum World Public Order: The Legal Regulation of International Coercion (Yale University Press, New Haven, CT, 1961)
Mégret, F., '"War"? Legal Semantics and the Move to Violence' (2002) 13 *EJIL* 361
Meron, Theodor, 'The Humanization of Humanitarian Law' (2000) 94 *AJIL* 239
'International Criminalization of Internal Atrocities' (1995) 89 *AJIL* 554
'The Time Has Come for the United States to Ratify Geneva Protocol I' (1994) 88 *AJIL* 678
Human Rights and Humanitarian Norms as Customary Law (Oxford University Press, Oxford, 1989)
Human Rights in Internal Strife: Their International Protection (Grotius, Cambridge, 1987)
Meyrowitz, Henri, 'The Principle of Superfluous Injury or Unnecessary Suffering' (1994) 299 *IRRC* 98
'La Guerre du Golfe des Conflits Armés' (1992) 96 *Revue Générale de Droit International Publique* 551
Morgenstern, Felice, *Legal Problems of International Organizations* (Grotius, Cambridge, 1986)
Murphy, Sean D. (ed.), 'Contemporary Practice of the United States Relating to International Law' (2003) 97 *AJIL* 419
(ed.), 'Contemporary Practice of the United States Relating to International Law' (2002) 96 *AJIL* 237
'Terrorism and the Concept of "Armed Attack" in Article 51 of the UN Charter' (2002) 43 *Harvard ILJ* 41
Humanitarian Intervention: The United Nations in an Evolving World Order (University of Pennsylvania Press, Philadelphia, 1996)
Nahlik, S. E., 'Belligerent Reprisals as Seen in the Light of the Diplomatic Conference on Humanitarian Law, Geneva, 1974–1977' (1978) 42 *Law and Contemporary Problems* 36
Nanda, Ved P., 'The Validity of United States Intervention in Panama under International Law' (1990) 84 *AJIL* 494
Normand, Roger and Chris af Jochnick, 'A Critical Look at the Gulf War' (1994) 35 *Harvard ILJ* 387
Norton, Patrick M., 'Between the Ideology and the Reality: The Shadow of the Law of Neutrality' (1976) 17 *Harvard ILJ* 249
Nurick, L., 'The Distinction Between Combatant and Non-Combatant in the Law of War' (1945) 39 *AJIL* 680
Nussbaum, Arthur, *A Concise History of the Law of Nations* (Macmillan, New York, 1947)
O'Brien, James, 'The International Tribunal for Violations of International Humanitarian Law in the Former Yugoslavia' (1993) 87 *AJIL* 639

O'Brien, William V., 'Reprisals, Deterrence and Self-Defence in Counter Terrorist Operations' (1990) 30 *Virginia JIL* 421

The Conduct of Just and Limited War (Praeger, New York, 1981)

O'Connell, Daniel P. *The International Law of the Sea,* vol. I (ed. by I. A. Shearer, Clarendon Press, Oxford, 1984)

The Influence of Law on Sea Power (Manchester University Press, Manchester, 1975)

'International Law and Contemporary Naval Operations' (1970) 44 *BYIL* 19

Oeter, Stefan, 'Methods and Means of Combat' in Dieter Fleck (ed.), *The Handbook of Humanitarian Law in Armed Conflicts* (Oxford University Press, Oxford, 1995), p. 105

Oppenheim, Lassa, *International Law: A Treatise*, vol. II, *Disputes, War and Neutrality* (1st edn, Longmans, Green and Co. Ltd, London, 1906)

Oppenheim's International Law: A Treatise, vol. II, *Disputes, War and Neutrality* (ed. by Arnold D. McNair, 4th edn, Longmans, Green and Co. Ltd, London, 1926)

Oppenheim's International Law, vol. II, *Disputes, War and Neutrality* (ed. by Sir Hersch Lauterpacht, 7th edn, Longmans, Green and Co. Ltd, London, 1952)

Oppenheim's International Law, vol. I, *Peace* (ed. by R. Jennings and A. Watts, 9th edn, Longmans, Harlow (UK), 1992)

Orford, Ann, 'The Politics of Collective Security' (1996) 17 *Michigan JIL* 373

Osgood, Robert and Robert W. Tucker, *Force, Order and Justice* (Johns Hopkins University Press, Baltimore, MD, 1967)

Palwankar, Umesh, 'Applicability of International Humanitarian Law to United Nations Peace-Keeping Forces' (1993) 294 *IRRC* 227

Peace, David L., 'Neutrality, the Rights of Shipping and the Use of Force in the Persian Gulf War Part I' in Ige F. Dekker and Harry H. G. Post (eds.), *The Gulf War of 1980–1988: The Iran–Iraq War in International Legal Perspective* (Martinus Nijhoff, Dordrecht, 1992)

Peck, J., 'The UN and the Laws of War: How Can the World's Peacekeepers Be Held Accountable?' (1995) 21 *Syracuse Journal of International Law and Commerce* 283

Pictet, Jean S. (ed.), *Geneva Convention Relative to the Protection of Civilian Persons in Time of War* (ICRC, Geneva, 1958)

Pilloud, C. *et al.* (eds.), *Commentary on the Additional Protocols of 8 June 1977 to the Geneva Conventions of 12 August 1949* (ICRC, Geneva, 1987)

Politi, M. 'Elements of Crimes' in R. S. Lee (ed.), *The International Criminal Court – Issues, Negotiations, Results* (Kluwer Law International, The Hague, 1999), p. 443

Quigley, John, 'The United States and the United Nations in the Persian Gulf War: New Order or Disorder?' (1992) 25 *Cornell ILJ* 1

Ramsey, Paul, *The Just War: Force and Political Responsibility* (University of America Press, Lanham, MD, 1983)

War and the Christian Conscience: How Shall Modern War Be Conducted Justly? (Duke University Press, Durham, NC, 1961)

Rauch, E., 'Le Concept de Nécessité Militaire dans le Droit de la Guerre', *Rapport présenté au Comité pour la protection de la vie humaine dans les conflits*

armés, VIIIe Congrès de la Société internationale de droit pénal militaire et de droit de la guerre, Ankara, October 1979 (Société international de droit pénal et de droit de la guerre, Brussels, 1981), p. 209
Reisman, W. Michael, 'Assessing Claims to Revise the Laws of War' (2003) 97 *AJIL* 82
'Kosovo's Antinomies' (1999) 93 *AJIL* 861
'The Constitutional Crisis in the United Nations' (1998) 87 *AJIL* 83
'Preparing to Wage Peace: Towards the Creation of an International Peacemaking Command and Staff College' (1994) 88 *AJIL* 76
'Sovereignty and Human Rights in Contemporary International Law' (1990) 84 *AJIL* 866
Reisman, W. Michael and Douglas L. Stevick, 'The Applicability of International Law Standards to United Nations Economic Sanctions Programmes' (1998) 9 *EJIL* 86
Roberts, Adam and Richard Guelff, *Documents on the Law of War* (2nd edn, Clarendon Press, Oxford, 1989)
Rodick, Burleigh C., *The Doctrine of Necessity in International Law* (Columbia University Press, New York, 1928)
Rogers, A. P. V., 'Zero-Casualty Warfare' (2000) 837 *IRRC* 165
Law on the Battlefield (Manchester University Press, Manchester, 1996)
'Conduct of Combat and Risks Run by the Civilian Population' (1982) *Military Law and Law of War Review* 295
Rosas, Allan, *The Legal Status of Prisoners of War: A Study in International Humanitarian Law Applicable in Armed Conflicts* (Suomalainen tiedeakatemia, Helsinki, 1976)
Rostow, Eugene V., 'Until What? Enforcement Action or Collective Self-Defense?' (1991) 85 *AJIL* 506
Rousseau, Jean J., *The Social Contract and Discourses*, trans. by George D. H. Cole (Dent, London, 1973)
Russell, Frederick H., *The Just War in the Middle Ages* (Cambridge University Press, Cambridge, 1975)
Russell, Jeffrey B., *A History of Medieval Christianity: Prophecy and Order* (T. Y. Crowell, New York, 1968)
Ryan, John K., *Modern War and Basic Ethics* (Bruce Publishing Co., Milwaukee, WI, 1941)
Ryniker, A., 'Respect du Droit International Humanitaire par les Forces des Nations' (1999) 835 *IRRC* 795
Sandoz, Yves, 'The Application of Humanitarian Law by the Armed Forces of the United Nations Organisation' (1978) 206 *IRRC* 283
Sarooshi, Danesh, *The United Nations and the Development of Collective Security: The Delegation by the UN Security Council of Its Chapter VII Powers* (Clarendon Press, Oxford, 1999)
Schachter, Oscar, 'United Nations Law' (1994) 88 *AJIL* 1
'Implementing Limitations on the Use of Force: The Doctrine of Proportionality and Necessity' (1992) 85 *Proc. ASIL* 39

'Authorized Uses of Force by the United Nations and Regional Organizations' in Lori F. Damrosch and David J. Scheffer (eds.), *Law and Force in the New International Order* (Westview, Boulder, 1991)

International Law in Theory and Practice (Martinus Nijhoff, Dordrecht, 1991)

'United Nations Law in the Gulf Conflict' (1991) 85 *AJIL* 452

'The Lawful Resort to Unilateral Use of Force' (1985) 10 *Yale JIL* 292

'The Quasi-Judicial Role of the Security Council and the General Assembly' (1964) 58 *AJIL* 960

Schermers, Henry G., *International Institutional Law*, vol. 2 (Martinus Nijhoff, The Hague, 1972)

Schindler, D., 'The Different Types of Armed Conflicts According to the Geneva Conventions and Protocols' (1979-II) 163 *Recueil des Cours* 117

Schindler, D. and J. Toman (eds.), *The Laws of Armed Conflicts: A Collection of Conventions, Resolutions and Other Documents* (2nd edn, Sijthoff & Noordhoff, Alphen aan den Rijn, 1981)

Schwarzenberger, Georg, 'The Fundamental Principles of International Law' (1959-I) 96 *Recueil des Cours* 195

'Principles of International Law' (1955-I) 87 *Recueil des Cours* 343

Scott, Shirley V., 'International Law as Ideology: Theorizing the Relationship Between International Law and International Politics' (1994) 5 *EJIL* 313

Séfériadès, M. S., 'La Question des Represailles Armées en Temps de Paix, en l'Etat Actuel du Droit des Gens' (1934) 17 *Revue de Droit International et de Législation Comparée* 138

Seyersted, Finn, *United Nations Forces in the Law of Peace and War* (Sijthoff, Leiden, 1966)

Shaw, Martin, *International Law* (4th edn, Cambridge University Press, Cambridge, 1997)

Simma, Bruno (ed.), *The Charter of the United Nations: A Commentary* (Oxford University Press, Oxford, 1994)

Singh, M. N., 'The Right of Self-Defence in Relation to the Use of Nuclear Weapons' (1956) 5 *Indian Yearbook of International Affairs* 3

Sofaer, A., 'Agora: The US Decision Not to Ratify Protocol I to the Geneva Conventions on the Protection of War Victims (cont'd): The Rationale for the United States Decision' (1988) 82 *AJIL* 784

Sornarajah, M., 'An Overview of the Asian Approaches to International Humanitarian Law' (1985) 9 *Australian YIL* 238

Spaight, James M., *Air Power and War Rights* (3rd edn, Longmans, Green, London, 1947)

Stockholm International Peace Research Institute, *Ecological Consequences of the Second Indochina War* (Humanities Press, Stockholm, 1976)

Stone, Julius, *Legal Controls of International Conflict* (Maitland, Sydney, 1959)

Taubenfeld, 'International Armed Forces and the Rules of War' (1951) 45 *AJIL* 674

Taylor, Telford, *Nuremberg and Vietnam: An American Tragedy* (Quadrangle, Chicago, 1970)

Tesón, Fernando R., 'Collective Humanitarian Intervention' (1996) 17 *Michigan JIL* 323

Humanitarian Intervention: An Inquiry into Law and Morality (2nd edn, Transnational, Irvington-on-Hudson, NY, 1996)

Tomuschat, Christian, 'Obligations Arising for States Without or Against Their Will' (1993-IV) 241 *Recueil des Cours* 311

Tucker, Robert W., *The Just War: A Study in Contemporary American Doctrine* (Johns Hopkins University Press, Baltimore, MD, 1960)

United States, Department of Defense, *Conduct of the Gulf War: Final Report to Congress* (US Department of Defense, Washington, DC, 1992)

United States Army Field Manual (US Department of Defense, Washington, DC, 1956)

United States, Department of the Air Force, *International Law – The Conduct of Armed Conflict and Air Operations: Judge Advocate General Activities* (US Department of the Air Force, Washington, DC, 1976)

Waldock, C. H. M., 'General Course on Public International Law' (1963-II) 106 *Recueil des Cours* 1

'The Regulation of the Use of Force by Individual States in International Law' (1952-II) 81 *Recueil des Cours* 455

Walzer, Michael, *Just and Unjust Wars: A Moral Argument with Historical Illustrations* (2nd edn, Basic Books, New York, 1991)

War Office, WO Code No. 12333, 'The Law of War on Land', Part III of the *Manual of Military Law* (War Office, London, 1958)

Watson, G. R., 'Constitutionalism, Judicial Review and the World Court' (1993) 34 *Harvard ILJ* 1

Weissberg, Guenter, *The International Status of the UN* (Oceana, Dobbs Ferry, NY, 1961)

Weston, Burns H., 'Security Council Resolution 678 and Persian Gulf Decision Making: Precarious Legitimacy' (1991) 85 *AJIL* 516

Wheaton, Henry, 'Elements of International Law' (1866) in James B. Scott (ed.), *Classics of International Law* (Carnegie Endowment for International Peace, Washington, DC, 1936)

Wigmore, J. H., 'The Case of Italy v. Greece under International Law and the Pact of Nations' (1923) 18 *Illinois LR* 131

Wilson, Heather A., *International Law and the Use of Force by National Liberation Movements* (Oxford University Press, Oxford, 1988)

Wolff, Christian, Freiherr von, *Jus Gentium Methodo Scientifica Pertractatum* (1764), trans. by H. Drake in James B. Scott (ed.), *The Classics of International Law* (Carnegie Endowment for International Peace, Washington, DC, 1934)

Wright, Quincy, 'The Meaning of the Pact of Paris' (1933) 27 *AJIL* 39

Wynen-Thomas, A. van and A. Thomas Jr, *Legal Limits on the Use of Chemical and Biological Weapons* (Southern Methodist University Press, Dallas, 1970)

Index

Cambridge Studies in International and Comparative Law

Books in the series

Compensation for Personal Injury in English, German and Italian Law
A Comparative Outline
Basil Markesinis, Michael Coester, Guido Alpa, Augustus Ullstein

Dispute Settlement in the UN Convention on the Law of the Sea
Natalie Klein

The International Protection of Internally Displaced Persons
Catherine Phuong

Colonialism, Sovereignty and the Making of International Law
Antony Anghie

Local Remedies in International Law, Second Edition
C. F. Amerasinghe

Necessity, Proportionality and the Use of Force by States
Judith Gardam

International Legal Argument in the Permanent Court of International Justice
The Rise of the International Judiciary
Ole Spiermann

Reading Humanitarian Intervention
Human Rights and the Use of Force in International Law
Anne Orford

Conflict of Norms in Public International Law
How WTO Law Relates to Other Rules of Law
Joost Pauwelyn

The Search for Good Governance in Africa
Making Constitutions in the States of the Commonwealth
Peter Slinn and John Hatchard

Transboundary Damage in International Law
Hanqin Xue

European Criminal Procedures
Edited by Mireille Delmas-Marty and John Spencer

The Accountability of Armed Opposition Groups in International Law
Liesbeth Zegveld

Sharing Transboundary Resources
International Law and Optimal Resource Use
Eyal Benvenisti

International Human Rights and Humanitarian Law
René Provost

Remedies Against International Organisations
Basic Issues
Karel Wellens

Diversity and Self-Determination in International Law
Karen Knop

The Law of Internal Armed Conflict
Lindsay Moir

International Commercial Arbitration and African States
Amazu A. Asouzu

The Enforceability of Promises in European Contract Law
James Gordley

International Law in Antiquity
David J. Bederman

Money-Laundering
Guy Stessens

Good Faith in European Contract Law
Reinhard Zimmerman and Simon Whittaker

On Civil Procedure
J. A. Jolowicz

Trusts
A Comparative Study
Maurizio Lupoi

The Right to Property in Commonwealth Constitutions
Tom Allen

International Organizations Before National Courts
August Reinisch

The Changing International Law of High Seas Fisheries
Francisco Orrego Vicuña

Trade and the Environment
Damien Geradin

Unjust Enrichment
Hanoch Dagan

Religious Liberty and International Law in Europe
Malcolm D. Evans

Ethics and Authority in International Law
Alfred P. Rubin

Sovereignty Over Natural Resources
Nico Schrijver

The Polar Regions and the Development of International Law
Donald R. Rothwell

Fragmentation and the International Relations of Micro-States
Jorri Duursma

Principles of the Institutional Law of International Organisations
C. F. Amerasinghe

Printed in Great Britain
by Amazon